Restorative JUSTICE Critical Issues

CRIME, ORDER AND SOCIAL CONTROL • **COURSE TEAM**

The Open University

Mandy Anton *Graphic Designer*
Sally Baker *Subject Information Specialist, Library*
Hilary Canneaux *Course Manager*
John Clarke *Professor of Social Policy*
Donna Collins *Secretary*
Lene Connolly *Print Buying Controller*
Dianne Cook *Secretary*
Jonathan Davies *Graphic Design Co-ordinator*
Nigel Draper *Editor, Social Sciences*
Clive Emsley *Professor of History, Arts*
Ross Fergusson *Senior Lecturer in Social Policy*
Liz Freeman *Copublishing Advisor*
Anne-Marie Gallen *Producer, BBC/OUPC*
Richard Golden *Production and Presentation Administrator*
Peggotty Graham *Sub-Dean (Curriculum), Social Sciences*
Fiona Harris *Editor, Social Sciences*
Celia Hart *Picture Researcher, Rights*
Pauline Hetherington *Social Policy Discipline Secretary*
Gordon Hughes *Senior Lecturer in Social Policy*
Mary Langan *Sub-Dean (Quality), Social Sciences*
Eugene McLaughlin *Senior Lecturer in Criminology and Social Policy (Course Team Chair)*
John Muncie *Professor of Criminology (Course Team Chair)*
Winifred Power *Editor, Social Sciences*
Esther Saraga *Staff Tutor, Social Sciences*
Louise Westmarland *Lecturer in Criminology*
Rebecca White *Course Secretary*
Marilyn Woolfson *Open University Associate Lecturer and Lecturer in Criminology, University of Luton*

Consultant Authors

Chris Cunneen *Professor of Criminology, University of Sydney*
Loraine Gelsthorpe *Senior Lecturer in Criminology, University of Cambridge*
Jim Sharpe *Professor of History, University of York*
Richard Sparks *Professor of Criminology, University of Keele*
Sandra Walklate *Professor of Criminology, Manchester Metropolitan University*

External Assessors

Tony Jefferson *Professor of Criminology, University of Keele*

Restorative JUSTICE
Critical Issues

edited by

Eugene McLaughlin, Ross Fergusson, Gordon Hughes and Louise Westmarland

SAGE Publications
London • Thousand Oaks • New Delhi

in association with

This book is the third in a series published by Sage Publications in association with The Open University.

The Problem of Crime
edited by John Muncie and Eugene McLaughlin

Controlling Crime
edited by Eugene McLaughlin and John Muncie

Restorative Justice: Critical Issues
edited by Eugene McLaughlin, Ross Fergusson, Gordon Hughes and Louise Westmarland

The books are part of The Open University course D315 *Crime, Order and Social Control.* Details of this and other Open University courses can be obtained from the Course Information and Advice Centre, PO Box 724, The Open University, Milton Keynes MK7 6ZS, United Kingdom: tel. +44 (0)1908 653231, e-mail general-enquiries@open.ac.uk

Alternatively, you may visit the Open University website at http://www.open.ac.uk where you can learn more about the wide range of courses and packs offered at all levels by The Open University.

To purchase a selection of Open University course materials visit the webshop at www.ouw.co.uk, or contact Open University Worldwide, Michael Young Building, Walton Hall, Milton Keynes MK7 6AA, United Kingdom for a brochure: tel. +44 (0)1908 858785; fax +44 (0)1908 858787; e-mail ouwenq@open.ac.uk

The Open University
Walton Hall, Milton Keynes
MK7 6AA

© The Open University 2003

First published in 2003

The opinions expressed are not necessarily those of the Course Team or of The Open University.

All rights reserved. No part of this publication may be reproduced, stored in a retrieval system, transmitted or utilized in any form or by any means, electronic, mechanical, photocopying, recording or otherwise, without permission in writing from the Publishers.

SAGE Publications Ltd
6 Bonhill Street
London EC2A 4PU

SAGE Publications Inc
2455 Teller Road
Thousand Oaks
California 91320

SAGE Publications India Pvt Ltd
32, M-Block Market
Greater Kailash – I
New Delhi 110 048

British Library Cataloguing in Publication data
A catalogue record for this book is available from The British Library.
ISBN 0-7619-4208-4
ISBN 0-7619-4209-2 (pbk)

Library of Congress Cataloging-in-Publication data
A catalogue record for this book has been requested.

Edited, designed and typeset by The Open University.

Printed and bound in the United Kingdom by The Bath Press, Bath.

Contents

Preface

Restorative Justice: Critical Issues is one of four volumes published by Sage in association with The Open University. The series, entitled *Crime, Order and Social Control*, explores key issues in the study of crime and criminal justice by examining the diverse and contested nature of crime, the different formal and informal means designed to effect its control, and the multiplicity of approaches and interpretations that criminologists have brought to bear on this field of study.

Each volume introduces readers to different aspects of the complex bodies of knowledge and knowing that make up contemporary criminology. By emphasizing diversity – both in the nature of criminological knowledge and in its objects of study – the series engages with stereotypical representations of the extent and causes of crime and the rationales and practices of criminal justice. Above all, we maintain that the study of crime cannot be divorced from the study of how the social is ordered and reproduced. Definitions of crime, and the ways that it is understood and responded to, are contingent on the interplay of social, political and economic circumstances.

This volume, *Restorative Justice: Critical Issues*, brings together key international writings that trace the development of restorative justice from its diverse beginnings to today's global policies and practices. Restorative justice is rapidly becoming the focal point for debates about the future of criminal justice among academics, practitioners and politicians. Its central demand that the harms and disputes covered by the concept of 'crime' be removed from the criminal justice system and restored to the community is also contributing to political debates beyond the immediate concern of criminology. We have constructed the volume around four main themes:

1 The theoretical and ideological origins of restorative justice.

2 Key principles and substantive practices associated with restorative justice.

3 Controversial issues and debates.

4 Future directions and possibilities.

The editorial introduction has been written to provide readers with an authoritative overview of the critical issues facing restorative justice at the beginning of the twenty-first century.

The production of this volume – and the series – has been made possible not simply through the work of its editors, but through the collective endeavours of an Open University course team. We are also indebted to assessors who gave us invaluable feedback on what we might include; a course manager who – against all the odds – ensured that all our efforts have been co-ordinated and that deadlines were met; course secretaries who have suffered more than most from being asked to do the impossible; and a supportive production team of editors and designers who have made sure that, in putting together this volume, we have maintained the quality of the other volumes in the series.

We also have to thank Miranda Nunhofer at Sage and Professor Tony Jefferson (external assessor) and Professor Sandra Walklate (external examiner) for being persuaded that restorative justice could make an important contribution to The Open University project of rethinking criminology. We thank them all.

Eugene McLaughlin
(on behalf of The Open University Course Team)

Introduction: Justice in the Round – Contextualizing Restorative Justice

by Eugene McLaughlin, Ross Fergusson, Gordon Hughes and Louise Westmarland

The emergence of restorative justice has resurrected a number of the most profoundly contested debates in criminal justice since the 1960s: it gives new meaning and force to potentially radical imaginaries that seemed consigned to the dustbin of criminological history. Indeed, what is remarkable is the relatively short period of time it has taken a politically astute and well-connected network of restorative justice enthusiasts from assorted jurisdictions to exert a significant institutional influence on developing modes of governance in the twenty-first century. Global and regional policy exchange in the field of criminal justice knowledge, information and expertise is not new but its current proliferation and intensification is unprecedented and restorative justice is located at the centre of many of these contemporary exchanges.

It is no coincidence that restorative justice has come to the fore globally at a time when – across a variety of jurisdictions – acknowledgement of the systemic shortcomings and failures of the dominant model of crime control is extensive and a sense of injustice widespread. State-centred criminal justice systems stand accused of investing ever greater public funds in cumbersome bureaucracies that have little verifiable impact on conviction, reconviction or recidivism rates. These bureaucracies are also indicted for not requiring offenders to acknowledge and attend to the consequences of their anti-social actions and their indifference to the needs of crime victims. As a consequence, many proponents of restorative justice argue that they have little to contribute to tackling the *underlying* causes of criminality, building safe communities and cultivating pro-social communal values and responsibilities. The limitations of a prison-centred response to crime stand cruelly exposed: despite wave after wave of reform, not only are prisons (both public and private) extremely expensive, they also fail to rehabilitate offenders. In fact, they make repeat criminality more, rather than less, likely by bonding similarly minded individuals who may be in no position to make peace with society. The prison system also stands accused of punishing and stigmatizing the innocent bystander who gets caught up in its tentacles. What is significant is that this accusation of systemic failure is now not only accepted by but also increasingly emanates from within the criminal justice system itself.

Restorative justice's quite distinctive contribution to this commonplace critique of formal criminal justice is to articulate an alternative philosophy and set of practices that are premised on an acknowledgement of the emotional, subjective and shared 'lived experience' of crime and justice. Formal criminal justice processes are seen as inimical to the resolution of conflicts and harms generating and/or resulting from 'crime' because they work through legal-bureaucratic discourses and ritualistic procedures that neutralize the emotional and social dynamics of crime, criminality and victimization. Moreover, the criminal justice system's construction of 'victims', 'offenders', 'witnesses' and 'criminal events' into a legal test case of culpability sharpens the participants' sense of separateness. Restorative justice practitioners view this as contributing to the likelihood of failed deterrents, ineffective sentences, victim dissatisfaction, public fear of crime and in the end social discord.

In addition, restorative justice concerns itself – directly or otherwise – not merely with proposing alternatives to the malfunctioning criminal justice system, but also much more fundamentally and significantly with how 'the social' itself is ordered. According to restorative justice proponents, the established social system embodies and seeks to promote a dominant, traditional, hierarchical, and ostensibly mechanistic mode of governance. Restorative justice envisages radical transformation in favour of a 'Third Way' that is partially decentralized, informal, participatory and communitarian. Its detractors are inclined, however, to either point to the hegemonic if circumscribed powers of the state (in which the institutions of law and the judiciary are one arm of government) or put forward much more diffuse, dispersed and provisional understandings of governance that move beyond the dominant model and view restorative justice as simply a manifestation of a new mode of governance.

Here, we look broadly at the origins of restorative justice, its founding definitions and principles; the process of institutionalization as policy and practice; its claims to efficacy and relevance; and its significance as a mode of governance.

Part One: Conceptualizing restorative justice

Restorative justice has many roots that cannot be easily separated. It emerged as a 'movement' espoused by a relatively small but energetic group of activists, academics, non-governmental organizations and policy entrepreneurs, many of who have campaigned for many years to highlight the shortcomings of dominant western systems of criminal justice (Braithwaite, 2002). Interestingly, writers in this area come from a diverse set of political and ideological allegiances, affiliations and backgrounds, including neo-traditional dispute resolution; faith-based approaches; communitarianism and peace-making criminology and abolitionism.

Many restorative justice advocates refer to a history that provides credibility and a weight of 'ancient tradition' to informal methods of social control and dispute resolution. These claims variously refer to anthropological, religious, indigenous aboriginal or pre-modern origins. Drawing on extensive anthropological sources, much of the restorative justice literature argues that essentially restorative methods of conflict resolution were dominant in non-state, pre-state and early state societies. These societies bound individuals very strongly to the social group, and dealt with conflict primarily through mediation and restitution (see Weitekamp and Kerner, 2002). Some restorative justice advocates, such as Braithwaite in Chapter 5, cite such origins, and their restorative approaches as 'anthropological universals'. Perhaps the most striking feature of the many 'origin stories' of restorative justice is this inextricable association of modern restorative method with strongly identifiable indigenous cultures in European colonized regimes. The short history of the 'revival' of restorative methods consistently begins with New Zealand's Maori, and Australia's Aboriginals, closely followed by First Nation peoples of Canada and the USA. In very different ways, the indigenous peoples of all these countries have highly preserved and partially protected cultures and identities, often associated with special separation on successfully claimed land, and carefully circumscribed degrees of self-determination.

Some of the founding policy innovations that inspired the current wave of interest in conferencing, for instance, took place in Auckland, New Zealand, in Wagga Wagga, Australia and among the Metis people of Alberta, Canada. It is here that the 'origin stories' become complex: certainly, commentators on all these initiatives point to the long history of restorative elements in the cultural and political traditions of indigenous peoples (see Jaun Tauri and Allison Morris in Chapter 4). But it is worth pointing out that the initiatives also arose because of the combination of a heavy over-representation of indigenous people in formal criminal justice systems and prisons and an emerging recognition – often in response to vehement demands – of the legitimate claims of indigenous groups to an acknowledgement of their own culture and tradition, and to sovereign self-determination. At first sight, this may appear as an overdue rediscovery of restorative traditions in distinctive cultural groups that have against all the odds survived within modern western colonial cultures – 'living evidence' of the arguments made by Weitekampf and Kerner. However, this is open to other analyses, to which we will return in Part Three.

The prominence of faith-based ideas is also very evident in much of the promotion of restorative justice: the claim that it holds a powerful spiritual provenance in all the major world religions is a notable feature of many studies. Hadley's (2001) collection traces restorative elements in philosophy, doctrine, tradition and contemporary practice in Buddhism, Hinduism, Islam, Judaism, Sikhism and Chinese religions, as well as in Christianity. Faith-based principles of reconciliation, restoration and healing are evident in all, but it is Christianity whose strong presence is expressed or used to underpin much Western and Anglophone work. Christian injunctions to confession, repentance, forgiveness, 'hating the sin and not the sinner', reciprocity, 'doing unto others', neighbourliness, civility, honour and generosity, alongside duty, obedience, respect for authority, allegiance to community and proportionality are all present in much of the more evangelical 'faith community' advocacy of restorative justice.

The influence of Christianity can be found particularly amongst those who adopt a proselytizing approach to restorative justice. In Belgium, for instance, the Catholic University of Leuven is a major source of research and outreach in pursuit of restorative justice, particularly regarding juvenile justice (see for example Walgrave, 1998). In the US the protestant Mennonite sect is highly influential and active in advancing the cause of restorative justice, particularly amongst those based at the Eastern Mennonite University in Virginia, including Howard Zehr (Chapter 3 in this volume). A leading and long-standing English proponent of restorative justice, Martin Wright (1996) chose the Bishop of Manchester to write the preface to the first edition of his influential book, in which he identifies restorative justice with New Testament virtues. Howard Zehr (1985) also links it with the Old Testament, and with the concept of shalom, writing wrongs and living in harmony.

It is not surprising to find that North American communitarians have also been enthusiastic champions of restorative justice. During the 1990s, communitarian political thought developed as a major intellectual response to what were seen as the limits of contemporary liberal theory and practice in the US. Centred on concepts of civic virtue, moral order and bounded autonomy, communitarians such as Amatai Etzioni (1998) attribute the central failings of modern liberal market societies to a weakening of traditional associational ties of community. A key feature of communitarian writing has been the critiquing of what has been defined as liberalism's one-sided emphasis on individual rights, unregulated free choice and a sense of entitlement. This emphasis on universal rights has undermined social responsibilities and obligations. A rights culture has exacerbated claims-making, polarized public discourse and is employed without a corresponding sense of responsibilities. The 'rights culture' also ruptures the self because it uproots it from cultural meanings, community attachments and the life stories that constitute the full identities of real human beings.

Communitarian theorists argue that civil society can be revitalized by rebuilding community associations and attachments to bolster a highly localized democratic culture. The re-establishment of community is conceptualized not just as a social but also as a normative and moral project requiring: the strengthening of institutional relationships; the enhancement of processes of public participation; the development of the capacity for self-help, mutual responsibility and self-regulation; and the promotion of structures of empowerment, connectedness and cohesion. Excessively individualistic societies have lost their equilibrium and suffer from high levels of crime, anti-social behaviour, incivility and disrespect. Instead of 'defining deviance down' strategies, communitarians support the re-establishment of social bonds, values, norms and a moral infrastructure that identifies what is right and what is wrong. What is significant is how crime is viewed as a 'communitarian incident' which provides the opportunity to activate communal processes, shore up the personal and social bonds that have frayed, and assist both the victim and the offender to find ways of dealing with their trauma by re-establishing their community ties and reconnecting them to community values. This is why informal social controls such as 'reintegrative shaming' have an important role to play.

Finally, there is the connection between restorative justice and critical and peace-making criminology, upon which Nils Christie in Chapter 1 touches in citing Ivan Illich and Paul Freire. Illich's (1977) central thesis contains powerful elements of radical communitarianism, ranging from the critique of the commodification of collective goods and values, through their professional appropriation and state-licensing, to the post-industrial collapse of spirituality, mutuality and community in fractured urbanized localities. Christie envisages a community locally controlled and policed. He developed a critique of adversarial, institutionalized and professionally dominated legal processes on grounds of delay, cost, exclusivity and limited access and advocates instead community-based pre-judicial systems and greater lay participation in mediation and 'conflict resolution' following criminal indictment.

Proponents of peacemaking criminology foreground compassion, reconciliation, healing reintegration, co-operation and caring. Peacemaking criminology can be traced to the version of radical and critical criminology that emerged in North America in the 1970s. During the 1980s and 1990s key proponents such as Quinney and Pepinsky (1991) reworked their originally highly structuralist Marxist perspective as a result of their contact with a variety of traditions, including pacifism, humanism, New Age spiritualism and feminism. Peacemaking criminologists, such as Kay Harris in Chapter 2, insist that official stigmatizing/labelling in the shape of a criminal conviction is likely to *increase* rather than diminish delinquent behaviour. Harris also insists that we can construct affirmative ways of responding to crime and violence if we establish and nurture democratic, non-violent and non-oppressive forms of human interaction.

The European 'abolitionist' tradition (of which Christie is a leading light) must also be acknowledged. Mathiesen (1990) argues that challenging the primacy of criminalization and penalization discourses requires the development of a culture of 'compensatory solidarity' where victims of crime are offered not just material and status but also symbolic compensation that involve new rituals of sorrow, grief and forgiveness. De Haan (1990) developed notions of 'redress' and 'participatory justice' which also foreground an ethics of care and solidarity for offenders and victims. He argues that it is only by 'refusing' to respond to or be contained within a criminal justice framework that progressive transformative agendas can take root.

As we shall see in the next section, despite differences of emphasis, the core overlapping concerns of these traditions explain why the restorative justice movement is able to offer a much broader critique than just pointing to the limitations of the criminal justice system.

Foundational propositions

Each reading in Part One has a substantial claim to being pivotal in the constitution of the foundational propositions of restorative justice. We describe them as 'founding propositions' because they are neither necessarily constituted as origins, nor can they yet be said to have the consistency, the ubiquity and the theoretical rationale that characterize principles. From significantly different starting-points, each chapter proposes a critique of dominant western models of criminal justice, and, in doing so, each offers alternatives that can claim to make good a shortcoming through introducing a strong restorative element.

Hence, in Chapter 1, Christie's essay is a philosophical critique of a core principle of criminal justice procedures: he argues that the state 'steals' conflicts by taking possession of them and by taking control of their 'resolution'. In Chapter 2, Kay Harris calls for the abandonment of conventional frames of thought and practice in criminal justice when considering its future – to be replaced by modes of conflict resolution and personal interaction that draw on feminism. In Chapter 3, Zehr and Mika sharply delineate restorative criteria, many of which are inimical to core premises of liberal justice. Tauri and Morris's starting-point in Chapter 4 is the failure of colonial criminal justice to meet the needs of societies divided by 'race' and ethnicity. And, in the final chapter in Part One, Braithwaite challenges the fundamentally anti-democratic and unrepublican nature of dominant modes of justice.

What links the chapters in Part One (in addition to their challenge to dominant modes of criminal justice) is a recognition of the legitimate interests of the three key parties to any crime – offender, victim, community – and their regard for the future prospects for all parties, as well as for their pasts. Beyond these commonalties, there is much to differentiate them. Their interpretations of all aspects of these elements differ, as do their prescriptions for policy and change. Fundamental tensions about the locus of power in judicial and legal process are visible. Wider social purposes of the changes they propose are disparate. Nonetheless, the central themes of (a) problematizing crime, (b) problematizing the state and criminal justice process and (c) recentring community are present, in all founding propositions of restorative justice outlined here. To these can be added the interesting question of how restorative justice is linked to changing modes of governance.

Problematizing 'crime'

From the various perspectives, 'crime' is seen as more than a breach of state-created criminal laws. 'Crime' is conceptualized relationally in a variety of ways. It is a breakdown of pre-existing relationships between victims, offenders and the community or the abuse of pre-existing relationships among offenders and the community. Or it is the creation, however brief, of a coercive relationship between the offender and the victim, where none existed before.

Many advocates of restorative justice prefer to deploy replacement discourses such as 'harm', 'conflict' and 'dispute' rather then 'crime', recognizing that the way we understand and define human behaviour and actions is open to definition and redefinition. There is nothing inherent about a conflict that would privilege one definition over another. Which definition prevails is largely shaped by the relative power of different social groups at different times. The way we conceptualize a conflict also establishes the criteria against which success and failure is measured. Once an issue is characterized in one way there is an institutional impetus to maintain that characterization. This is particularly true of the criminal justice system. Once the police have defined a given dispute as a criminal offence, the original parties to it are almost powerless to change the definition. The conflict is now under the control of the state. The participants in the dispute may be consulted or they may be asked to provide evidence to the court. The decision on how to proceed with the case is in the hands of the *state* but there is no necessary connection between the interests of the state and the interests of the participants.

Problematizing the criminal justice process

The state is unequivocally identified by all the contributors in Part One as the source of a number of the shortcomings of crime control. The state's relationship to and use of the criminal justice system is a key axis of its power, and is widely regarded as one that both limits and distorts its capacity to secure just and equitable outcomes. Many of the so-called founding propositions of restorative justice, which are explored in later chapters, arise from critical analysis of the role of the state. Indeed, many of its policy prescriptions aim to reconfigure the location and relative power of the state in the administration of justice.

Christie's interpretation of the state's role is an axiomatic founding proposition of restorative justice. As we noted above, the state's legal and professional agents are seen as appropriating conflicts that belong to the victim and the offender. The state substitutes itself for the victim, by claiming that the offender's principal harm is to legal codes. Offenders are therefore obliged to seek comparable legal representation to that of the victim, and are distanced from the proceedings. In effect, conflicts become 'owned' by two sets of contending legal representatives and a supposedly impartial judicial third party. Kay Harris's analysis of the state shares Christie's view that its overarching and centralized power deprives citizens of their powers to resolve conflicts by its insistence on controlling conflict. For both Christie and Harris the state then acts as a barrier to possibilities for enhancing social harmony through participatory modes of conflict resolution. For Christie the source of this tendency is the cadre of professionals who function as a self-interested occupational class. For Kay Harris it is the state's preoccupation with power, the macro-politics of control and the coercive containment of individuals, all of which are associated with characteristically masculine values and behaviours, that drives its dominance.

Similarly, Braithwaite is critical of the state's dominance of the administration and conduct of justice processes. He too points to the prospective collapse of dominant systems. For Braithwaite, however, it is the *adversarial* nature of formal justice in a state-centred system that is the problem, because it removes, dilutes or distorts the critical elements of any judicial system. Moreover, it takes away the capacity to induce genuinely felt shame, from which offenders can then be released through restorative processes that have palliative effects on these feelings and emotions. State-centredness has also denied the democratic nature of judicial processes, disallowing deliberative processes and thereby also undermining the republican qualities of justice.

The readings in Part One present a number of approaches to ways in which the state is a critical source of the problems of criminal justice. Both Christie and Kay Morris offer radical critiques, suggesting approaches to justice that are beyond conceptions that the state could promote. Braithwaite's view has some of this radicalism but it is less the state *per se*, as a dominant force protecting particular interests, than the effects of its processes, such as diluting shame, and inhibiting deliberative democracy, that occasions the need for alternatives. Zehr and Mika's reading extends this continuum, in offering no direct critique of the state, and appearing to favour a harm-led approach rather than to oppose state-centeredness in its own right. If there is a continuum from Christie's vision of the state's misappropriation of conflicts to Zehr and Mika's preferences for a harm-led community-focused approach, the question arises as to whether the state is intrinsically or merely contingently incapable of adopting an essentially restorative approach to crime and justice – however defined.

A closely related theme is the decentring of the criminal justice process. Much of the critique of dominant criminal justice arises from the ways in which state power is articulated and realized through legal process, and in particular through its institutional procedures and practices. Much of the harm done by formal criminal justice occurs, according to most proponents of restorative justice, through the formal state-constituted and regulated procedures of pre-trial, trial and judicial dispositions. Most of the principles and many of the practices of these stages of due process are seen to inhibit forms of response and the consideration of kinds of evidence that would secure more humane and even more defensible justice. While much restorative justice discourse concerns itself primarily with processes and dispositions that follow admission of guilt, this also has clear implications for earlier stages of the criminal justice process.

Numerous aspects of the formal procedures and conventions of criminal justice process are criticized as inherently unrestorative. Criminal justice process is construed by advocates of restorative justice as being preoccupied with principles, consistency, rights, and moral abstractions, at the expense of recognition of circumstance, the well-being of victims and offenders, and moral action. It is viewed as adversarial at the expense of finding consensus, impersonal despite the fundamentally interpersonal character of much crime, preoccupied with rationality and neglectful of the centrality of the affective and emotional to most crimes, and the consequences that flow from them.

Many of these effects are viewed as the direct consequence of the pre-eminent position of a wide range of legal professionals to the detriment of the protagonists and the exclusion of legitimately interested members of their families and communities. Because of professionals' absolute control over proceedings, the possibilities for deliberation are rule bound, highly circumscribed and grounded in the positivistic pursuit of evidence, logical deduction and the conventions of rational discourse. Less formalized, democratic deliberation would give due account to circumstance and allow the expression of emotions that are crucial elements in resolving, as opposed to merely solving, crimes.

Nevertheless, there are both unities and significant differences in the founding propositions of proponents of restorative justice around these broad issues. For Christie, it is the dominance and exclusivity of legal professionals that is one key source of the inadequacy of legal process, because professionals acquire ownership of conflicts. The other source, for him, is the depersonalized nature of legal proceedings, through which participants become identified not as unique, human individuals with feelings and needs, but as anonymous representatives of groups who are seen as 'other' by virtue of social category or cultural difference. For Kay Harris, the injunctions of criminal justice process are essentially to be understood as gendered, notably through their 'characteristically masculine' denial of the centrality of the personal, of the affective, of relationships and interdependency and of the potential for mutuality. For Braithwaite, the source of failure of conventional justice is the intimidating and deadening effects of typical court proceedings in that they fail to trigger the empathy that is the essential pre-requisite of shame and so of restoration.

Variously, the readings in Part One locate their critique in class divisions, gender differences, and the social psychology of support and mutuality. Diverse prescriptions follow, and open up equally diverse critiques of restorative justice.

Restoring the community

A corollary of the critique of the overwhelming power held by state bureaucracies and agencies is restorative justice's view of the role of 'community' in formal legal processes. Marginalization or exclusion of community from the processes of determining outcomes, and its invisibility as both a potentially significant factor in crimes, and as a victim of crimes, explains the failure of statutory legal practices to reduce re-offending, deter others or ameliorate the lasting ill-effects of crime. Restoring the historical place of community is central to the founding propositions of most restorative justice proponents.

It is the exclusion of victim, offender and community from the processes of its resolution that unites all discourses of restorative justice. Three-sided, two-way relations between these three main parties to criminal offences are the key parameters which processes of trial, conviction and disposition must follow if they are to restore damaged individuals and damaged relations, rather than merely attempt closure on harm through retribution. Bonds between these parties through family, social networks and neighbourhood are critical both to understanding crimes, resolving them, and moving on from the harm they inflict. Conflict in one set of relationships is mediated to others, but mutuality in one set may also be similarly mediated in restoring good relations. By excluding the known and immediate community in favour of its remote and anonymous legal representatives, the state entrenches division, leaves conflicts open, and misses critical opportunities for compromise, resolution and restoration. Victims are debarred from expressing their anger and anguish, from dialogue with the offender, and from making an active contribution to forgiveness and rehabilitation. By the same token, offenders are prevented from engaging in direct dialogue with victims to explain their actions, from direct expressions of remorse, and from restoring losses and making good harms.

All founding propositions engage with this set of relations, seen in the context of state dominance and legal process. For many proponents of restorative justice these are the centrepiece of restoration. Their recurring tenets are self-evident truths or common senses, which stop them producing a theoretical critique of dominant models and the probable outcomes of resultant policy prescriptions. In different ways, Christie, Kay Harris and Braithwaite are notable exceptions.

Christie identifies the state's action in supplanting the victim as the injured party as a misplaced intention – underpinned by sectional professional interests – to protect other prospective victims by punitive deterrence. The offender's isolation within legal processes is an escalatory consequence of this misplaced intention, since the offender must match the state's specialist representatives. In turn, tangentially involved citizens lose their rights to participate in decisions about what are acceptable interpretations of codified norms, and to share ownership of them in ways that promote cohesion.

Kay Harris is equally critical of the consequences for all three parties of the state's controlling and highly proceduralized and codified role. For her, supposedly protective state action on behalf of the victim arises from the predominance of values that are coded as masculine. Such action obscures possibilities for the pursuit of security that can come through social harmony. The social rejection of 'unheard' offenders that becomes the corollary of indictment postpones and stores up conflict. And the opportunities for communities to solve problems by democratic deliberative processes outside the bounds of state-sanctioned legal process in ways that build interdependency and mutuality are lost.

John Braithwaite interprets the exclusion of victims, offenders and communities through the theoretical lens of 'disintegration' and 'reintegration'. His emphasis falls on the offender, who is cut off from feelings of empathy and remorse, and from family, friends and neighbours. This double isolation, from self and from community, allows the offender no way back to social acceptance, and as a result entrenches the conditions for prolonged conflict. At the same time, an overactive state and the political endorsement of competitive individualism have damaged the possibilities for deliberative democratic participation in such processes of restoration.

Recentring the community enables restorative justice advocates to re-think what they define as 'the sanctioning process'. Perhaps the most discussed and most controversial alternative to punishment and custodial sentences is John Braithwaite's support for the reintroduction of 'shame', which he argues is one the most powerful tools of informal communal control. For Braithwaite, 'reintegrative shaming' is most likely to work in close-knit communities or in a social setting that combines a dense network of individual interdependencies with strong cultural commitments to mutuality of obligation. Hence, there is the intriguing message in Chapter 5 that many Western societies will have to recreate these communal conditions and bonds if effective crime control is to be realized (see Ahmed *et al.*, 2001).

Reimagining governance

Most of the founding propositions of restorative justice share a critique of criminal justice that recognize it as a critical arm of governance, extending far beyond the immediate concerns of the application of specific criminal laws to offending behaviour. Most recognize that its failure to control crime and establish security is also a failure to 'govern the social'. Modern systems of criminal justice foster the illusion that crime can be controlled by appeal to structures and systems of power and social control that are top down, stratified and built on assumptions about social relations and distributions of power in families, households, neighbourhoods and other micro-social institutions that are increasingly tenuous, and oblivious to major social upheavals of late modernity. In short, they are locked into structural notions of government, and blind to more complex and nuanced post-structural conceptions of governance that look to the diffusion and dispersal of power, and to 'governing at a distance' (see Rose, 2000). (This is a theme we will return to in Part Three.)

In this sense, a defining feature of restorative justice is that it makes claims to redistribute power and disperse decision-making to a much wider and more heterogeneous community. Indeed, in more highly evolved restorative scenarios, the self-managing community, including victims and offenders themselves, would themselves define what is 'justice' as well as how to realize greater safety and security. In most founding propositions this is understood in terms of democratization and the restoration of ownership of crime-induced conflicts to those who are party to them. Most propositions set out in Part One put forward a recognizable version of this view. For Nils Christie 'the community' is the proper location of conflict resolution. For Kay Harris 'community' speaks of a more organic, integrated and socially grounded approach. For Jaun Tauri and Allison Morris 'community' signals the recognition and valuation of indigenous justice. For John Braithwaite 'community' is essentially democratic and republican. In all cases, power over the social is conceived as being redistributed downwards, and dispersed, following a principle of subsidiarity that locates engagement with social problems as near as possible to the origins of these problems.

Part Two: Institutionalizing restorative justice

In the highly sensitive sphere of governmental activity that defines and regulates the intersections between state, civil society and individual citizenship, policy innovation is normally approached with extreme caution. The evidence threshold for proposed policy change is usually set very high and so the advance and penetration of potentially very radical initiatives associated with restorative justice is all the more remarkable. It is undoubtedly the case that the pressure on criminal justice policy-makers to be seen to be 'doing something' to reverse the spiral of decline in public confidence in the criminal justice system, reduce the propensity of offenders to reoffend and increase victim satisfaction has forced the government to explore the possibilities of innovative practices. Hence, as the readings in Part Two demonstrate, a policy space has opened for restorative justice to demonstrate that there are benefits – or at least very few real risks – in reconsidering the dominant retributive justice approach to crime control.

A new global policy network

By posing new sets of concerns and questions, and by illustrating the benefits of thinking beyond the prevailing retributive criminal justice paradigm, proponents of restorative justice have been able to cultivate 'common ground' with victim rights' organizations, campaigners for non-custodial sentences and practitioners involved in diverting young offenders from the formal criminal justice system. What is truly remarkable is the emergence of a very effective global network that popularizes the 'good news' about restorative justice through conferences, seminars, publications, newsletters, websites, and so on. These networks enable the sharing of information and the linking into local, regional, national and international policy debates and initiatives. And maybe because restorative justice writings often do not read much like conventional policy documents in either their style or mode of argument they have, in a similar manner to situational crime prevention theorists, managed to speak *across* the activist/academic/policymaker/practitioner divides. The acute attentiveness of policy-makers and politicians to restorative justice may also lie in its claims not just to reduce re-offending and meet the needs of victims but also to provide communitarian solutions for improving social integration and cohesion in an era of radical and unpredictable social transformation.

The readings in Part Two illustrate that restorative justice has been undergoing intense official interrogation across various jurisdictions to prove its usefulness and usability as an institutionalized governmental practice. Its proponents have had to formalize what is and is not 'restorative justice'. The readings in Part One illustrated that 'restorative justice' originally denoted a set of disparate endeavours to shift understandings of the 'problem of crime' and radically reimagine relations among offender, victim and the community. The strong focus on values, principles and the insistence on restorative justice as a vehicle for the airing of 'eternal truths' has led to considerable stress on it not being a tool-kit of methods or models. Given its diverse roots and far-reaching aspirations as a political project, constructing a formal definition of restorative justice has therefore been highly problematic and controversial. Not surprisingly, many writers have chosen to define restorative justice by contrasting it with a hard definition of retributive or punitive justice (see Daly, Chapter 16). One of the things that would seem to feature in emergent definitions across a variety of jurisdictions is the insistence that 'justice' can only be realized when the stakeholders most directly affected by a specific offence – the victim, the offender and the community – have the opportunity to voluntarily work through the consequences of the offence with the emphasis on repairing the harm and damage done.

Policy-makers have increasingly required advocates not just to do base-line definitional work but to formalize what is and is not a restorative justice practice as well as what it seeks to accomplish practically. As the first two readings in Part Two by Mark Umbreit and Howard Zehr and Gordon Bazemore and Curt Taylor Griffith illustrate, the most discussed restorative justice practices are victim–offender mediation, family group conferences (FGCs) and healing or sentencing circles. Of course, as the authors note, these models do not exhaust the possibilities for practices that might fall within the borders of restorative justice. As they have travelled to different jurisdictions these models have experienced considerable policy translation and adaptation and varying degrees of institutionalization, ultimately giving rise to new locally appropriate conferencing practices.

The restorative conference

In 1989, the family group conference – a structured, voluntary, mediated meeting between offenders, victims and both parties' families and friends – became an integral part of New Zealand's youth justice system in an attempt to avoid the shortcoming of the traditional court-based approach. This provides us with an interesting example of what exactly is being formalized and institutionalized as governmental practice. The roots of FGCs are to be found in Maori criticism of the dominant Western juvenile justice system which had stripped the community of responsibility for dealing with its own youth. Thus, certain commentators view the family group conference as an attempt to 'culturally sensitize' New Zealand's juvenile justice process. Although New Zealand's family group conference was not designed specifically as a restorative justice initiative, it is viewed as encapsulating what must happen for the 'moral centre' of restorative justice to be realized. Supporters argue that the FGC balances the complicated set of emotions, interests and needs embedded in a particular criminal event.

Victims are provided with greater agency and voice, and the opportunity to release pent-up feelings of anger and fear and to seek answers to troubling questions. Reconciliation between the victim and the offender is achieved through the social rituals of remorse, apology, forgiveness and reparations. In addition to emotional catharsis, the restoration of personal dignity and autonomy, and holding offenders to account, victims should also be able to leave a restorative based conference with a satisfactory reparation agreement. For offenders, meanwhile, the encounter offers the opportunity to humanize the relationship with their victims, accept responsibility for their actions, express remorse and ask for forgiveness. Reintegration of offenders within the community is intended to seal the process of healing and closure. In addition, the community is offered the pragmatic benefits of the long-term rehabilitation of offenders who live in its midst and – equally significantly – the fostering of a communal atmosphere of tolerance and understanding.

As the family group conference has travelled it has been modified. Perhaps the most internationally well-known as well as most controversial version of the model was developed in the Wagga Wagga police district in New South Wales to play a central part in an effective police-cautioning scheme for juvenile offenders. It differed from the New Zealand 'original' in that it was a police-led process with officers deciding which cases were appropriate for conferencing as well as convening and facilitating the conference itself. The 'Wagga Wagga model' also opted for formal 'scripts' to ensure consistency of approach and a clear focus on the 'reintegrative shaming' aspects of the conference (see Moore, Forsythe and O'Connell, 1995). This model was imported to the United States by the Pennsylvannia 'Real Justice' organization who view it as a natural extension of already well-established victim–offender mediation programmes. The reading by Richard Young and Benjamin Goold (Chapter 8) details how it was also the inspiration for the innovative restorative-caution programme developed by the Thames Valley police force in the UK as part of its shift to a problem-oriented style of policing.

Young and Goold's case study highlights some of the critical issues associated with transplanting a restorative justice practice into a traditional criminal justice organizational setting. They illustrate some of the difficulties that specially trained police facilitators in Thames Valley police force have had in adhering to core restorative justice values and in realizing its objectives. The dynamics associated with the restorative caution are a considerable advance on the old police caution, which was very often based on humiliation and stigmatization. However, their research points to several problematic features, namely: the dominance of police officers during the conferences; the restrictive nature of the structured script officers are following; outcomes perceived as being disproportionately severe for relative minor offenders; the potential for net-widening; the lack of attention to procedural safeguards; the inappropriate use of shaming; and the ever-present tension between traditional police culture and restorative values. The more fundamental question of whether formal criminal justice professionals should be responsible for convening and facilitating restorative conferences is also raised (see also Ashworth and Cunneen in this volume).

Chapter 9, by Jim Dignan and Peter Marsh, provides a detailed account the development of family group conferences in England and Wales. Initially, these stood outside the formal criminal justice system and this provided restorative justice practitioners with considerable scope for experimentation and innovation. However, it also meant that they were marginalized and lacked adequate funding. Dignan and Marsh's review of the available evidence suggests that across jurisdictions the shift from a 'stand-alone' model to a more integrated one requires the enactment and enforcement of an appropriate legislative framework; the creation or nurturing of an amenable professional culture and the existence or establishment of a supportive institutional setting. In the UK context, the legislative and institutional framework established to deliver New Labour's youth justice agenda at the beginning of the twenty-first century is beginning to inaugurate such a shift.

Dignan and Marsh also note how the increasing institutionalization of restorative justice by criminal and youth justice practitioners has enabled policy-makers to insist on the evaluation of existing programmes and the setting-up of pilot schemes in order to produce a solid evidence base for restorative justice. This has initiated a potentially difficult debate about process and outcomes: which aspects of restorative justice should be evaluated; which methodologies should be employed to research restorative justice; which restorative justice processes are open to research; and what are the most appropriate ways of defining and evaluating restorative justice success. For faith-based restorative justice advocates, this is highly problematic because many of them place considerable weight on personal testimony and bearing witness. These are seen as crucial to the redemptive, virtually sacred nature of the conferencing process. Put simply, are the emotional dynamics and 'story-telling' transactions that are constitutive of restorative conferences amenable to realist evaluation methodologies?

Dignan and Marsh's conclusion points to an increasing focus in the UK at least on identifying outcomes that are measurable and linked directly to the self-stated goals of the New Labour government, namely reducing offending and increasing levels of victim satisfaction. The strong governmental imperative in the UK to acquire evidence of 'what works' to inform the criminal and youth justice policy-making process, and to secure what it defines as continuous improvement in cost effectiveness and performance, means that restorative justice practices could be increasingly disciplined by an extensive set of quantifiable performance indicators, designated targets and standards backed up by a managerialist regime of audit and inspection. There is the very real possibility that a highly technocratic approach to evidence-gathering and evaluation as well as to establishing 'best practice' will lock restorative justice into a pragmatic concentration on crime reduction. It also means that future restorative justice practices, in the UK at least, will be developed within a statutory framework of 'community punishment' orders and governed by a politically volatile law-and-order agenda. This has serious implications for those hoping that the injection of restorative practices can transform the criminal justice system into a fully functioning restorative justice system.

The restorative conference and power differentials

Traditionally, it was held that restorative justice wasn't suited to violent or extreme offenders or crimes involving more than one offender. However, more recently to prove that it is not a 'soft option', and working on the assumption that it works with juveniles, restorative justice is also being asked to cover virtually any sentencing situation and most types of crime.

This is a highly significant development because, even in relation to youth offending, concerns have been raised about its appropriateness for different categories of youth offenders. In Australia there is unease about its use to govern Aboriginal youth (Blagg, 2001). And to date, little attention has been given, for example, to gender-specific issues in the development of restorative practice with young offenders. Christine Alder in Chapter 10 notes that the absence of any reference to gender in most of the literature implies an assumption that the processes and outcomes will be roughly the same for young women as men. Drawing on available research on young women's experience of the youth justice system she argues that complicated issues need to be discussed and addressed if the restorative justice conference is to benefit this category of offender. It cannot be assumed, for example, that community-based conferencing will be benign in outcome or balanced in process for these young women. Community and family censorship and sanctioning of young women who violate dominant notions of gender-appropriate behaviour can be harsh and stigmatizing and the shaming process all consuming rather than reintegrative and restorative. Furthermore, there needs to be recognition of the complex nature and dynamics of young women's motivations for offending and the intricately coded strategies they have developed to protect themselves. This explains the traditional difficulty youth justice workers have had in establishing relations of trust. She concludes by arguing that conferencing needs to include consideration of the special needs and interests of this particular group of offenders, some of whom have been seriously damaged by their family context and contact with the authorities. Alder also draws our attention to the difficult questions of what conference participants think they are doing and what exactly is being internalized in the conference process?

There have also been specific moves to apply restorative justice to cases of violent interpersonal crime, including domestic violence, sexual assault and murder. Although this poses new concerns about what will happen to restorative justice if it becomes embroiled in the 'deep end' of the criminal justice system, it is here that the traumatic impact of offending on victims is greatest and where victims are most in need of closure. In Chapter 11, Allison Morris and Loraine Gelsthorpe consider the different policy interventions for dealing with men's violence against their female partners. The characteristics of this particular form of violence throw into question the appropriateness of traditional criminal justice interventions. Not only does the process not meet the needs of the victims, there is little evidence that available sanctions have any positive effect on the perpetrators or act as a deterrent. After reviewing eight objections, they argue that with the proper safeguards, in the case of family violence, restorative justice programmes could increase women's choices, provide them with a voice and mobilize the support of family and friends in a supportive, organized manner. This suggestion is clearly controversial not least because it begs the obvious question: what is likely to be restored by such a conferencing process? (See Presser and Gaader, 2000.)

Just how far restorative justice principles can be extended is explored in our final reading in Part Two. Michael Levi considers the extent to which shaming can regulate business practices and the extent to which fraudsters are likely to care about the shaming of reputation that might be imposed upon them if they are caught and processed. Here, Levi is engaging with Braithwaite's pioneering work on the differential regulation of corporate crime (Makkai and Braithwaite, 1994). This form of crime also poses problems for traditional criminal justice approaches. There is public and indeed judicial ambivalence towards the offenders and a widespread assumption that business people are members of a normative community governed by informal social controls. Levi's very detailed analysis of Braithwaite's 'reintegrative shaming' thesis concludes that the potential damage to business prospects might remain more significant than shame or the impact of informal sanctions. This conclusion is of particular importance when read against the radical redesign of federal securities laws that took place in the aftermath of the sensational accounting scandals and corporate frauds that surfaced in the USA during 2001–2. Tougher sentencing and punishment of 'rogue traders' also reflect a climate that has become less tolerant of corporate crime.

Part Three: Contesting restorative justice

As we have seen in Part Two, restorative justice is being presented globally to politicians and policy-makers as offering many advantages to victims, offenders and the wider communities. There is a considerable evangelical literature that declares that 'restorative justice is an idea whose time has come'. In Part Three some of its central themes are reconsidered – in particular the implications of problematizing the state and legal process and the identification of 'the community' as a mode of governance. Hence, each chapter in Part Three considers both the *progressive* and *regressive* possibilities of the demand to go beyond state-centred criminal justice.

Some of the contributors are sceptical of restorative justice, but put forward perspectives by which new imaginaries of justice, harm reduction and good governance may be opened up within contemporary criminological thought. They also develop the debate on the role of research, the specificities of theory and politics and managing the process of translation of academic issues into wider public debates on the nature of the 'just society'. This stands in contrast to a tendency towards 'impossibilism' and intellectual foreclosure in some radical critiques of shifts in criminal justice and crime control. As O'Malley (2000) notes, much contemporary criminological analyses of the ongoing late modern shifts in criminal justice have tended to indulge in the tendency towards the production of what he terms 'criminologies of catastrophe'. By this, he means that such analyses envisage a transformation of criminal justice that is over-determined by structural shifts associated with wider social and political transformations allied with the globalization of neo-liberalism. These leave little room for the impact of contestation and resistance in particular sites and contexts.

Restorative justice and social justice

In the first reading, we return to the work of John Braithwaite, arguably the intellectual leader of the restorative justice movement and also a highly influential policy consultant across the world. The reading is based on a public lecture given in Canada, which as we know is one of the most fertile terrains for the realization of the restorative justice agenda (not least by building on the 'traditions' of its indigenous peoples). The piece represents a 'clarion call' for and defence of restorative justice's progressive and transformative potential at the beginning of this century. It assesses whether or not restorative justice can do more good than harm. The three core values of the new social movement – healing, community deliberation, and freedom as 'non-domination' – lead Braithwaite to focus on possible connections between restorative justice and social justice, rather than the more narrowly defined notion of criminal justice. In particular, he addresses three hypotheses, which have been aired about the relationship of restorative justice and social justice, and in so doing seeks to address the criticisms that have been made against restorative justice.

The first hypothesis is that 'restorative justice is unimportant to the struggles for social justice'. This assertion is one which Braithwaite admits to once sharing himself, given that restorative justice does not address the underlying structural factors that generate inequality, discrimination and such like. He uses his response to the other two hypotheses to answer this criticism of restorative justice. The second hypothesis is that 'restorative justice risks the worsening of social justice' because it represents a recolonizing, mono-cultural narrative which enables 'the West' to dominate others around the globe, particularly indigenous peoples. This hypothesis is also tied to what Braithwaite recognizes as arguably the most important critique of restorative justice, namely feminist critiques regarding the oppression of women and children. On both counts Braithwaite argues that restorative justice practices can empower disadvantaged populations and groups although this is by no means inevitable.

Moving on to the third hypothesis, namely that 'restorative justice can be an important strategy for advancing social justice', Braithwaite argues that restorative justice should be justified in terms of 'avoiding harm' rather than 'doing good'. The key role for restorative justice in reducing social injustice in turn lies in its contribution to reducing the impact of imprisonment as the cause of related harms and injustices. Braithwaite concludes by rejecting the first hypothesis and by accepting that the other two hypotheses are still 'up for grabs'. The likelihood of the positive third hypothesis being realized depends on how central the core value of 'non-domination' is to the processes and outcomes of restorative justice. Finally, Braithwaite notes that much will be determined by the battle of competing moral values in civil society, namely those that promote 'hurt begetting hurt' as against those that promote a world where 'help begets help and grace begets grace'. In ending on this note, the explicitly faith-based foundations and aspirations of aspects of the restorative justice movement are once more articulated.

Restorative justice and indigenous justice

The next four readings provide, to varying degrees, critical academic contestation of the claims of restorative justice advocates such as Braithwaite and their promotion of restorative justice as a progressive governmental technique of crime control across the globe. Chapter 16 by Kathleen Daly comes from a proponent of restorative justice who has become increasingly critical of the claims made by the more evangelical advocates in the movement. Daly's contribution is particularly valuable in providing one of the very few sustained deconstructions of the 'story' of restorative justice to date as it is based on a critical and detailed examination of the evidence of what is happening on the ground. More specifically, Daly contends that advocates' claims about restorative justice contain four major 'myths', namely: (1) 'restorative justice is the opposite of retributive justice'; (2) 'restorative justice uses indigenous justice practices and that this was the dominant form of pre-modern justice'; (3) 'restorative justice is a "caring" or feminist response to crime in contrast to a "justice" or masculinist response'; and (4) 'restorative justice can be expected to produce major changes in people'. She then goes on to contend that each of these myths or 'origin stories' does not stand up to critical, empirically informed analysis.

In terms of the first myth, Daly contends that the supposed dualism of restorative justice and retributive justice oversimplifies the complex, inter-dependent relationship between the two modes of justice and says more about the 'sales pitch' of restorative justice advocates than empirical realities on the ground in conferences and such like. In place of this simple dichotomy, Daly highlights the fragmentary and contradictory developments in the field. With regard to the second myth, Daly argues that restorative justice advocates do not provide authoritative histories of justice in the past but rather are indulging in the construction of origin myths about the 'golden days of yore'. Furthermore, like Cunneen (in Chapter 15), she questions the extent to which restorative justice uses indigenous justice practices, pointing to the empirical realities of both fragmented justice forms in such examples as family group conferences in New Zealand, and the tendency of advocates to be 'white-centered, creaming off and homogenizing cultural difference and specificity'. Daly takes issue with the third myth for its simplifying of the gendered dichotomization of 'caring' and 'justice' approaches which in turn underplays the more complex and hybridized mixes which are at work. Myth four is demystified again by means of Daly's scrutiny of practices that fall within the rubric of restorative justice. She notes in particular that the claims of personal and social transformation rely on emotion laden 'stories' and personal testimonies which are employed to denigrate retributive justice, valorize restorative justice and stand both as generalization and inspiration. Overall then, the stories of restorative justice are seen by Daly as being closer to 'fables' rather than based on evidence. Daly concludes by suggesting that the 'real' story of restorative justice is a considerably more qualified one than that propounded by those advocates intent on selling or franchising their 'product' to a wider policy-making audience.

The third reading by Chris Cunneen, written especially for this volume, outlines a concise overview of some of the key critical issues that have emerged in critiques of restorative justice. This chapter focuses both on questions associated with 'what is' restorative justice and more fleetingly on what restorative justice 'might be'. The chapter is particularly important in noting the contradictory character of restorative justice in the wider context of the politics of punishment in contemporary societies. In particular, Cunneen argues that restorative justice continues to sit alongside repressive crime-control strategies whilst at the same time having the potential for critiquing dominant criminal justice systems and offering the possibility of alternative practices. Once again, we note that restorative justice is a site of contestation in the new governance 'post social', bringing with it both dangers to and possibilities for a 'progressive' law and order agenda. In marshalling together his critical overview, Cunneen uses several radical intellectual perspectives – neo-Marxism, post-modernism, feminism, post-colonialism and liberalism – both to critique existing orthodoxies on restorative justice and to inform a more nuanced understanding of this emergent mode of governance of crime, harms and justice. However, the originality of Cunneen's critical appraisal in terms of questions of power and resistance lies predominantly in his elaboration of post-colonial critiques of restorative justice and its impact on indigenous peoples and minority ethnic groups. In the course of his discussion, Cunneen focuses on four main thematic concerns to explore the power relations at work in this field: (1) the state and its agencies; (2) the concepts of globalization and community; (3) the relations of class, 'race', ethnicity and gender; and (4) the rule of law, legal principles and process.

Throughout the chapter, the dominant thrust of the discussion is pessimistic although there are points of argument which give a glimpse of restorative justice's progressive possibilities, not least its continuing potential as a 'replacement discourse' around harm reduction (see Hughes *et al.*, 2002). On the issue of the power of the state and its agencies, Chris Cunneen argues that advocates of restorative justice have been naïve and complacent. In particular Cunneen, like Ashworth, questions the consequences of the expanded role of the police in restorative justice practices and highlights the closer affinity of restorative justice practices to both rehabilitative and retributive elements of penality than its advocates recognize. With regard to the concept of globalization, he suggests that restorative justice may be as much an instance of globalizing force as other western legal forms, whilst the concept of community which plays a central role in the restorative justice discourse is deconstructed in terms of the disjuncture between its rhetoric (consensus/harmony) and its empirical reality (exclusion/oppression). With regard to the relations of gender, 'race', ethnicity and difference Cunneen is sceptical about the extent to which such structural imbalances of power are currently addressed in restorative justice practices. On the final theme, Cunneen touches briefly on the issues addressed more fully by the next reading by Andrew Ashworth, pointing out the potential abuses of power associated with neglect and myopia towards legal process and procedural rights in much restorative justice practices. Especially given the shift in late modernity from social to repressive exercise of power, restorative justice may legitimize the development of a bifurcated system in which retribution and restoration co-exist, according to the assessed risk (and hence the social group) of the offence in question. In conclusion, he argues that the future is still open for a more progressive discourse around restorative justice but that this will be dependent on the development of a 'critical reflexivity' regarding its relationship to other forms of power, both state- and non-state based.

Restorative justice and criminal justice

The fourth reading in Part Three by Andrew Ashworth offers a 'just deserts' and a human-rights-based critique of restorative justice. It also reflects on the as yet unrealized possibilities of criminal justice reform. Ashworth's critique is significant not least for highlighting the continuing power of the rule of law and human rights in the regulation of human conflict. Ashworth's diagnosis identifies two main objections to restorative justice: constitutional or institutional ones and rights-based ones, together with some doubts about the effectiveness of restorative justice in preventing crimes and related harms. Ashworth's constitutional objections focus primarily on the dangers associated with removing the administration of criminal justice from the hands of the legally constituted state and locating it within the para-legal or non-legal community. Despite the claims of some social theorists (Garland, 2001) that the sovereign nation state is in decline under late modern conditions and in the wake of globalization and the arguments of such abolitionists as Nils Christie and Kay Harris, Ashworth makes a strong argument that the state should retain the sovereign power to sentence and punish public wrongs such as crimes rather than leaving them to particular victims and communities. Ashworth's rights-based objections relate to three principles which restorative justice tends to undermine and which a rights-based discourse would defend, namely, independence and impartiality, proportionality, and compensation for wrongs. As the authors throughout this volume have emphasized, victims should be empowered by the handing over of 'state' power to 'communities'. But there are concerns particularly over the power to apply informal sanctions such as 'reintegrative shaming'. Exactly *who* has the power in the communal decision-making process is a central concern for critics of restorative justice such as Ashworth. With regard to victims' rights, Ashworth argues that restorative justice proponents and practitioners are confusing the victim's right to reparation and compensation with the sovereign state's right to punish the offender. Ashworth defends this position by arguing that victims who give evidence should be valued as citizens but that their role should be limited severely. To what extent restorative justice gives the victims a 'good' and fair outcome, and whether the offenders taking part in the process feel fairly treated, are perhaps the crucial aspects of this ongoing debate. Finally, Ashworth's doubts over the effectiveness of restorative justice cover the ground already detailed in Daly's contribution, pointing to the tendency of advocates to 'over-sell' their product on the basis of non-existent or 'soft' evaluation.

Restorative justice and community justice

The fifth and final reading in Part Three (by Adam Crawford and Todd Clear) attempts to relate restorative justice to comparative developments in what is known in the USA as 'community justice' and what is more commonly termed 'community safety' in the UK (see Hughes *et al.*, 2002). Their contribution offers a sceptical assessment of the 'transformative' potentialities of restorative justice in terms of its connections with wider socio-political change and the often-dangerous appeal to that slippery signifier, 'the community'. In so doing, the authors, like other critics in Part Three, draw attention to the ambiguous political implications of restorative justice that were highlighted in our review of Part One. The authors begin by noting the key differences between appeals to 'community justice' and 'restorative justice', with the former viewed as a more radical reform orientation in that community justice 'works' when the quality of life of a 'place' or neighbourhood improves, whereas the criminal 'case'-oriented perspective of restorative justice sees success in terms of participants' experience of the restorative process. Crawford and Clear then examine the themes common to the two models of justice. Not surprisingly they view the growing influence of 'community' as indicative of the global shift towards the neo-liberal governance of crime and disorder, in the context of the decline of the sovereign nation state. This is a complex claim which lies beyond the scope of this introduction. However, is it a coincidence that restorative justice has come to the fore at the moment that the 'market state' is attempting to shift the primary responsibility for the governance of crime onto responsibilized individuals and communities? (See O'Malley, 2000; Rose, 2000.)

For Crawford and Clear, as for some of the other authors in Part Three, 'community' remains a difficult policy construct, because both its impact on daily behaviours and attitudes and its significance in forging progressive transformation remain uncertain. They suggest that restorative justice proponents tend to assume 'strong' communities are unified and speak with a discernible moral voice whilst 'weak', 'disorganized' communities require 'restoration'. The empirical realities of most strong communities are that they are exclusive, hierarchical and potentially authoritarian formations. Given this, they argue that the political project of restorative justice/community justice should be aimed at *transforming* rather than restoring or reintegrating communities. However, in common with other critics, and indeed Braithwaite in Part Three, Crawford and Clear question the feasibility of restorative justice as a radical force for social and political renewal. Restorative justice cannot be transformative on its own because it cannot address structural inequalities and material injustices; it is primarily reactive in nature. Instead they, like Ashworth, point to the continuing importance of the state remaining a key 'power-container' and 'norm-enforcer' in the promotion of 'public goods' rather than more restricted and exclusive 'club goods'. The intriguing but undisguised question of 'distributive justice' lurks around the edges of this line of reasoning. Crawford and Clear's wariness of the possibilities of either restorative justice or community justice engendering a more just, vibrant or inclusive civil society leads them to conclude that a more modest contribution can be made by both models to the realization of more just communities.

Conclusion

If this book were taken as a current snapshot, then it would seem that restorative justice is enjoying a period of increasing recognition and is seeping into public policy. As this collection of readings demonstrates, a broad range of issues are being considered by a diversity of scholars working both within and beyond restorative justice. Although much of the work represented here is intended primarily to focus on the immediate concerns of restorative justice, there is a sense that many writers are conscious of the importance of drawing upon and contributing to a broader discussion on the nature of a 'just society'. Given the present obsession with law and order and what we might describe as the 'hyper-punitive turn' across many societies, it is all too easy for criminologists to accept the idea that their endeavours must be policy relevant. But criminology is perhaps most socially and intellectually purposeful when it rethinks old questions in fundamentally different ways and when it addresses new sets of concerns and issues with new conversational partners. It is also only by refusing to be contained within a criminal justice paradigm and a discourse of insecurity, that criminology can hope to promote a different type of public conversation and encourage transformative agendas to take hold. It is a criminological truism that crime produces highly emotional states most obviously in the case of victims but also offenders and within communities: the emotions unlocked by the problem of crime are multifaceted and call attention to both the nature of the victimization and also the governmental processes through which the criminal act comes to be acknowledged and addressed. Criminology must continue to be supportive of restorative justice because it offers us an analytic framework that insists we would have a lot to say to one another about what 'crime' signifies emotionally, if only we knew *how* and *when* to speak and *how* and *when* to listen.

References

Ahmed, E., Harris, N., Braithwaite, J. and Braithwaite, V. (2001) *Shame, Shame Management and Regulation*, Cambridge, Cambridge University Press.

Blagg, H. (2001) 'Aboriginal youth and restorative justice', in A. Morris and G. Maxwell (eds) *Restorative Justice for Juveniles: Conferencing, Mediation and Circles*, Oxford, Hart Publishing.

Braithwaite, J. (1989) *Crime, Shame and Reintegration*, Cambridge, Cambridge University Press.

Braithwaite, J (1993) 'Shame and modernity', *British Journal of Criminology*, vol.33, pp.1–18.

Braithwaite, J. (2002) *Restorative Justice and Responsive Regulation*, Oxford, Oxford University Press.

De Haan, W. (1990) *The Politics of Redress*, London, Sage.

Etzioni, A. (1998) *The Essential Communitarian Reader*, Lanham, MD, Rowman and Littlefield.

Garland, D. (2001) *The Culture of Control: Crime and Social Order in Contemporary Society*, Chicago, University of Chicago Press.

Hadley, M.L. (2001) *The Spiritual Roots of Restorative Justice*, Albany, NY, SUNY Press.

Hughes, G., McLaughlin, E., and Muncie, J. (2002) *Crime Prevention and Community Safety: New Directions*, London, Sage.

Illich, I. (1977) *Disabling Professions*, London, Boyard Press.

Makkai, T. and Braithwaite, J. (1994) 'Reintegrative shaming and compliance with regulatory standards', *Criminology*, vol.32, pp.361–83.

Mathiesen, T. (1990) *Prison on Trial: A Critical Assessment*, London, Sage.

Moore, D., Forsythe, L., and O'Connell, T. (1995) *A New Approach to Juvenile Justice: An Evaluation of Conferencing in Wagga Wagga*, Sydney, Australian Criminology Council.

O'Malley, P. (2000) 'Criminologies of catastrophe? Understanding criminal justice on the edge of the new millennium', *Australian and New Zealand Journal of Criminology*, vol.33, no.2, pp.153–67.

Pepinsky, H.E. and Quinney, R. (1991) *Criminology as Peacemaking*, Bloomington, Indiana University Press.

Presser, L. and Gaarder, E. (2000) 'Can restorative justice reduce battering? Some preliminary considerations', *Social Justice*, vol.27, no.1, pp.175–95.

Rose, N. (2000) *Powers of Freedom: Reframing Political Thought*, Cambridge, Cambridge University Press.

Strang, H. and Braithwaite, J. (2002) (eds) *Restorative Justice and Family Violence*, Cambridge, Cambridge University Press.

Umbreit, M.S., Bradshaw, W. and Coates, R.B. (1999) 'Victims of severe violence meet the offender: restorative justice through dialogue', *International Review of Victimology*, vol.6, pp.321–43.

Walgrave, L. (ed.) (1998) *Restorative Justice for Juveniles*, Leuven, Leuven University Press.

Weitekamp, E. and Kerner, H.J. (2002) *Restorative Justice: Theoretical Foundations*, Collompton, Willan Press.

Wright, M. (1996) *Justice for Victims and Offenders*, 2nd edn, Winchester, Waterside Press.

Zehr, H. (1985) *Changing Lenses: A New Focus for Criminal Justice*, Scottsdale, PA, Herald Press.

Part One

Conceptualizing Restorative Justice

CHAPTER I

Conflicts as Property

by Nils Christie

Introduction

Maybe we should not have any criminology. Maybe we should rather abolish institutes, not open them. Maybe the social consequences of criminology are more dubious than we like to think.

I think they are. And I think this relates to my topic – conflicts as property. My suspicion is that criminology to some extent has amplified a process where conflicts have been taken away from the parties directly involved and thereby have either disappeared or become other people's property. In both cases a deplorable outcome. Conflicts ought to be used, not only left in erosion. And they ought to be used, and become useful, for those originally involved in the conflict. Conflicts *might* hurt individuals as well as social systems. That is what we learn in school. That is why we have officials. Without them, private vengeance and vendettas will blossom. We have learned this so solidly that we have lost track of the other side of the coin: our industrialised large-scale society is not one with too many internal conflicts. It is one with too little. Conflicts might kill, but too little of them might paralyse. I will use this occasion to give a sketch of this situation. It cannot be more than a sketch. This paper represents the beginning of the development of some ideas, not the polished end-product.

On happenings and non-happenings

Let us take our point of departure far away. Let us move to Tanzania. Let us approach our problem from the sunny hillside of the Arusha province. Here, inside a relatively large house in a very small village, a sort of happening took place. The house was overcrowded. Most grown-ups from the village and several from adjoining ones were there. It was a happy happening, fast talking, jokes, smiles, eager attention, not a sentence was to be lost. It was circus, it was drama. It was a court case.

The conflict this time was between a man and a woman. They had been engaged. He had invested a lot in the relationship through a long period, until she broke it off. Now he wanted it back. Gold and silver and money were easily decided on, but what about utilities already worn, and what about general expenses?

The outcome is of no interest in our context. But the framework for conflict solution is. Five elements ought to be particularly mentioned:

1 The parties, the former lovers, were in *the centre* of the room and in the centre of everyone's attention. They talked often and were eagerly listened to.

2 Close to them were relatives and friends who also took part. But they did not *take over*.

3 There was also participation from the general audience with short questions, information, or jokes.

4 The judges, three local party secretaries, were extremely inactive. They were obviously ignorant with regard to village matters. All the other people in the room were experts. They were experts on norms as well as actions. And they crystallised norms and clarified what had happened through participation in the procedure.

5 No reporters attended. They were all there.

My personal knowledge when it comes to British courts is limited indeed. ... [L]et me keep quiet about your system, and instead concentrate on my own. And let me assure you: what goes on

Source: *British Journal of Criminology* (1977), vol.17, no.1, pp.1–15.

is no happening. It is all a negation of the Tanzanian case. What is striking in nearly all the Scandinavian cases is the greyness, the dullness, and the lack of any important audience. Courts are not central elements in the daily life of our citizens, but peripheral in four major ways:

1 They are situated in the administrative centres of the towns, outside the territories of ordinary people.

2 Within these centres they are often centralised within one or two large buildings of considerable complexity. Lawyers often complain that they need months to find their way within these buildings. It does not demand much fantasy to imagine the situation of parties or public when they are trapped within these structures. A comparative study of court architecture might become equally relevant for the sociology of law as Oscar Newman's (1972) study of defensible space is for criminology. But even without any study, I feel it safe to say that both physical situation and architectural design are strong indicators that courts in Scandinavia belong to the administrators of law.

3 This impression is strengthened when you enter the courtroom itself – if you are lucky enough to find your way to it. Here again, the periphery of the parties is the striking observation. The parties are represented, and it is these representatives and the judge or judges who express the little activity that is activated within these rooms. Honoré Daumier's famous drawings from the courts are as representative for Scandinavia as they are for France.

   There are variations. In the small cities, or in the countryside, the courts are more easily reached than in the larger towns. And at the very lowest end of the court system – the so-called arbitration boards – the parties are sometimes less heavily represented through experts in law. But the symbol of the whole system is the Supreme Court where the directly involved parties do not even attend their own court cases.

4 I have not yet made any distinction between civil and criminal conflicts. But it was not by chance that the Tanzania case was a civil one. Full participation in your own conflict presupposes elements of civil law. The key element in a criminal proceeding is that the proceeding is converted from something between the concrete parties into a conflict between one of the parties and the state. So, in a modern criminal trial, two important things have happened. First, the parties are being *represented*. Secondly, the one party that is represented by the state, namely the victim, is so thoroughly represented that she or he for most of the proceedings is pushed completely out of the arena, reduced to the triggerer-off of the whole thing. She or he is a sort of double loser; first, *vis-à-vis* the offender, but secondly and often in a more crippling manner by being denied rights to full participation in what might have been one of the more important ritual encounters in life. The victim has lost the case to the state.

Professional thieves

As we all know, there are many honourable as well as dishonourable reasons behind this development. The honourable ones have to do with the state's need for conflict reduction and certainly also its wishes for the protection of the victim. It is rather obvious. So is also the less honourable temptation for the state, or Emperor, or whoever is in power, to use the criminal case for personal gain. Offenders might pay for their sins. Authorities have in times past shown considerable willingness, in representing the victim, to act as receivers of the money or other property from the offender. Those days are gone; the crime control system is not run for profit. And yet they are not gone. There are, in all banality, many interests at stake here, most of them related to professionalisation.

Lawyers are particularly good at stealing conflicts. They are trained for it. They are trained to prevent and solve conflicts. They are socialised into a sub-culture with a surprisingly high agreement concerning interpretation of norms, and regarding what sort of information can be accepted as relevant in each case. Many among us have, as laymen, experienced the sad moments of truth when our lawyers tell us that our best arguments in our fight against our neighbour are without any legal relevance whatsoever and that we for God's sake ought to keep quiet about them in court. Instead they pick out arguments we might find irrelevant or even wrong to use. My favourite example took place just after the war. One of my country's absolutely top defenders told with pride how he had just rescued a poor client. The client had collaborated with the Germans. The prosecutor claimed that the client had been one of the key people in the organisation of the Nazi movement. He had been one of the master-minds behind it all. The defender, however, saved his client. He saved him by pointing out to the jury how weak, how lacking in ability, how obviously deficient his client was, socially as well as organisationally. His client could simply not have been one of the organisers among the collaborators; he was without talents. And he won his case. His client got a very minor sentence as a very minor figure. The defender ended his story by telling me – with some indignation – that neither the accused, nor his wife, had ever thanked him, they had not even talked to him afterwards.

Conflicts become the property of lawyers. But lawyers don't hide that it is conflicts they handle. And the organisational framework of the courts underlines this point. The opposing parties, the judge, the ban against privileged communication within the court system, the lack of encouragement for specialisation – specialists cannot be internally controlled – it all underlines that this is an organisation for the handling of conflicts. *Treatment personnel* are in another position. They are more interested in *converting the image of the case from one of conflict into one of non-conflict.* The basic model of healers is not one of opposing parties, but one where one party has to be helped in the direction of one generally accepted goal – the preservation or restoration of health. They are not trained into a system where it is important that parties can control each other. There is, in the ideal case, nothing to control, because there is only one goal. Specialisation is encouraged. It increases the amount of available knowledge, and the loss of internal control is of no relevance. A conflict perspective creates unpleasant doubts with regard to the healer's suitability for the job. A non-conflict perspective is a precondition for defining crime as a legitimate target for treatment.

One way of reducing attention to the conflict is reduced attention given to the victim. Another is concentrated attention given to those attributes in the criminal's background which the healer is particularly trained to handle. Biological defects are perfect. So also are personality defects when they are established far back in time – far away from the recent conflict. And so are also the whole row of explanatory variables that criminology might offer. We have, in criminology, to a large extent functioned as an auxiliary science for the professionals within the crime control system. We have focused on the offender, made her or him into an object for study, manipulation and control. We have added to all those forces that have reduced the victim to a nonentity and the offender to a thing. And this critique is perhaps not only relevant for the old criminology, but also for the new criminology. While the old one explained crime from personal defects or social handicaps, the new criminology explains crime as the result of broad economic conflicts. The old criminology loses the conflicts, the new one converts them from interpersonal conflicts to class conflicts. And they are. They are class conflicts – also. But, by stressing this, the conflicts are again taken away from the directly involved parties. So, as a preliminary statement: Criminal conflicts have either become *other people's property* – primarily the property of lawyers – or it has been in other people's interests to *define conflicts away.*

Structural thieves

But there is more to it than professional manipulation of conflicts. Changes in the basic social structure have worked in the same way.

What I particularly have in mind are *two types of segmentation* easily observed in highly industrialised societies. First, there is the question of segmentation *in space.* We function each day, as migrants moving between sets of people which do not need to have any link – except through the mover. Often, therefore, we know our work-mates only as work-mates, neighbours only as neighbours, fellow cross-country skiers only as fellow cross-country skiers. We get to know them as *roles*, not as total persons. This situation is accentuated by the extreme degree of division of labour we accept to live with. Only experts can evaluate each other according to individual – personal – competence. Outside the speciality we have to fall back on a general evaluation of the supposed importance of the work. Except between specialists, we cannot evaluate how good anybody is in his work, only how good, in the sense of important, the role is. Through all this, we get limited possibilities for understanding other people's behaviour. Their behaviour will also get limited relevance for us. Role-players are more easily exchanged than persons.

The second type of segmentation has to do with what I would like to call our re-establishment of caste-society. I am not saying class-society, even though there are obvious tendencies also in that direction. In my framework, however, I find the elements of caste even more important. What I have in mind is the segregation based on biological attributes such as sex, colour, physical handicaps or the number of winters that have passed since birth. Age is particularly important. It is an attribute nearly perfectly synchronised to a modern complex industrialised society. It is a continuous variable where we can introduce as many intervals as we might need. We can split the population in two: children and adults. But we can also split it in ten: babies, pre-school children, school-children, teenagers, older youth, adults, pre-pensioned, pensioned, old people, the senile. And most important: the cutting points can be moved up and down according to social needs. The concept 'teenager' was particularly suitable ten years ago. It would not have caught on if social realities had not been in accordance with the word. Today the concept is not often used in my country. The condition of youth is not over at nineteen. Young people have to wait even longer before they are allowed to enter the work force. The caste of those outside the work force has been extended far into the twenties. At the same time departure from the work force – if you ever were admitted, if you were not kept completely out because of race or sex attributes – is brought forward into the early sixties in a person's life. In my tiny country of four million inhabitants, we have 800,000 persons segregated within the educational system. Increased scarcity of work has immediately led authorities to increase the capacity of educational incarceration. Another 600,000 are pensioners.

Segmentation according to space and according to caste attributes has several consequences. First and foremost it leads into a *depersonalisation* of social life. Individuals are to a smaller extent linked to each other in close social networks where they are confronted with *all* the significant roles of the significant others. This creates a situation with limited amounts of information with regard to each other. We do know less about other people, and get limited possibilities both for understanding and for prediction of their behaviour. If a conflict is created, we are less able to cope with this situation. Not only are professionals there, able and willing to take the conflict away, but we are also more willing to give it away.

Secondly, segmentation leads to destruction of certain conflicts even before they get going. The depersonalisation and mobility within industrial society melt away some essential conditions for living conflicts; those between parties that mean a lot to each other. What I have particularly in mind is crime against other people's honour, libel or defamation of character. All the Scandinavian countries have had a dramatic decrease in this form of crime. In my interpretation, this is not because honour has become more respected, but because there is less honour to respect. The various forms of segmentation mean that human beings are inter-related in ways where they simply mean less to each other. When they are hurt, they are only hurt partially. And if they are troubled, they can easily move away. And after all, who cares? Nobody knows me. In my evaluation, the decrease in the crimes of infamy and libel is one of the most interesting and sad symptoms of dangerous developments within modern industrialised societies. The decrease here is clearly related to social conditions that lead to increase in other forms of crime brought to the attention of the authorities. It is an important goal for crime prevention to re-create social conditions which lead to an increase in the number of crimes against other people's honour.

A third consequence of segmentation according to space and age is that certain conflicts are made completely invisible, and thereby don't get any decent solution whatsoever. I have here in mind conflicts at the two extremes of a continuum. On the one extreme we have the over-privatised ones, those taking place against individuals captured within one of the segments. Wife beating or child battering represent examples. The more isolated a segment is, the more the weakest among parties is alone, open for abuse. Kinberg, Inghe and Riemer (1943) made the classical study many years ago of a related phenomenon in their book on incest. Their major point was that the social isolation of certain categories of proletarised Swedish farm-workers was the necessary condition for this type of crime. Poverty meant that the parties within the nuclear family became completely dependent on each other. Isolation meant that the weakest parties within the family had no external network where they could appeal for help. The physical strength of the husband got an undue importance. At the other extreme we have crimes done by large economic organisations against individuals too weak and ignorant to be able even to realise they have been victimised. In both cases the goal for crime prevention might be to re-create social conditions which make the conflicts visible and thereafter manageable.

Conflicts as property

Conflicts are taken away, given away, melt away, or are made invisible. Does it matter, does it really matter?

Most of us would probably agree that we ought to protect the invisible victims just mentioned. Many would also nod approvingly to ideas saying that states, or Governments, or other authorities ought to stop stealing fines, and instead let the poor victim receive this money. I at least would approve such an arrangement. But I will not go into that problem area here and now. Material compensation is not what I have in mind with the formulation 'conflicts as property'. It is the *conflict itself* that represents the most interesting property taken away, not the goods originally taken away from the victim, or given back to him. In our types of society, conflicts are more scarce than property. And they are immensely more valuable.

They are valuable in several ways. Let me start at the societal level, since here I have already presented the necessary fragments of analysis that might allow us to see what the problem is. Highly industrialised societies face major problems in organising their members in ways such that a decent quota take part in any activity at all. Segmentation according to age and sex can be seen as shrewd methods for segregation. Participation is such a scarcity that insiders create monopolies against outsiders, particularly with regard to work. In this perspective, it will easily be seen that conflicts represent a *potential for activity, for participation*. Modern criminal control systems represent one of the many cases of lost opportunities for involving citizens in tasks that are of immediate importance to them. Ours is a society of task-monopolists.

The victim is a particularly heavy loser in this situation. Not only has he suffered, lost materially or become hurt, physically or otherwise. And not only does the state take the compensation. But above all he has lost participation in his own case. It is the Crown that comes into the spotlight, not the victim. It is the Crown that describes the losses, not the victim. It is the Crown that appears in the newspaper, very seldom the victim. It is the Crown that gets a chance to talk to the offender, and neither the Crown nor the offender are particularly interested in carrying on that conversation. The prosecutor is fed-up long since. The victim would not have been. He might have been scared to death, panic-stricken, or furious. But he would not have been uninvolved. It would have been one of the important days in his life. Something that belonged to him has been taken away from that victim.

But the big loser is us – to the extent that society is us. This loss is first and foremost a loss in *opportunities for norm-clarification*. It is a loss of pedagogical possibilities. It is a loss of opportunities for a continuous discussion of what represents the law of the land. How wrong was the thief, how right was the victim? Lawyers are, as we saw, trained into agreement on what is relevant in a case. But that means a trained incapacity in letting the parties decide what *they* think is relevant. It means that it is difficult to stage what we might call a political debate in the court. When the victim is small and the offender big – in size or power – how blameworthy then is the crime? And what about the opposite case, the small thief and the big house-owner? If the offender is well educated, ought he then to suffer more, or maybe less, for his sins? Or if he is black, or if he is young, or if the other party is an insurance company, or if his wife has just left him, or if his factory will break down if he has to go to jail, or if his daughter will lose her fiancé, or if he was drunk, or if he was sad, or if he was mad? There is no end to it. And maybe there ought to be none. Maybe Barotse law as described by Max Gluckman (1967) is a better instrument for norm-clarification, allowing the conflicting parties to bring in the whole chain of old complaints and arguments each time. Maybe decisions on relevance and on the weight of what is found relevant ought to be taken away from legal scholars, the chief ideologists of crime control systems, and brought back for free decisions in the court-rooms.

A further general loss – both for the victim and for society in general – has to do with anxiety-level and misconceptions. It is again the possibilities for personalised encounters I have in mind. The victim is so totally out of the case that he has no chance, ever, to come to know the offender. We leave him outside, angry, maybe humiliated through a cross-examination in court, without any human contact with the offender. He has no alternative. He will need all the classical stereotypes around 'the criminal' to get a grasp on the whole thing. He has a need for understanding, but is instead a non-person in a Kafka play. Of course, he will go away more frightened than ever, more in need than ever of an explanation of criminals as non-human.

The offender represents a more complicated case. Not much introspection is needed to see that direct victim-participation might be experienced as painful indeed. Most of us would shy away from a confrontation of this character. That is the first reaction. But the second one is slightly more positive. Human beings have reasons for their actions. If the situation is staged so that reasons can be given (reasons as the parties see them, not only the selection lawyers have decided to classify as relevant), in such a case maybe the situation would not be all that humiliating. And, particularly, if the situation was staged in such a manner that the central question was not meting out guilt, but a thorough discussion of what could be done to undo the deed, then the situation might change. And this is exactly what ought to happen when the victim is re-introduced in the case. Serious attention will centre on the victim's losses. That leads to a natural attention as to how they can be softened. It leads into a discussion of restitution. The offender gets a possibility to change his position from being a listener to a discussion – often a highly unintelligible one – of how much pain he ought to receive, into a participant in a discussion of how he could make it good again. The offender has lost the opportunity to explain himself to a person whose evaluation of him might have mattered. He has thereby also lost one of the most important possibilities for being forgiven. Compared to the humiliations in an ordinary court ... this is not obviously any bad deal for the criminal.

But let me add that I think we should do it quite independently of his wishes. It is not health-control we are discussing. It is crime control. If criminals are shocked by the initial thought of close confrontation with the victim, preferably a confrontation in the very local neighbourhood of one of the parties, what then? I know from recent conversations on these matters that most people sentenced are shocked. After all, they prefer distance from the victim, from neighbours, from listeners and maybe also from their own court case through the vocabulary and the behavioural science experts who might happen to be present. They are perfectly willing to give away their property right to the conflict. So the question is more: are *we* willing to let them give it away? Are we willing to give them this easy way out?

Let me be quite explicit on one point: I am not suggesting these ideas out of any particular interest in the treatment or improvement of criminals. I am not basing my reasoning on a belief that a more personalised meeting between offender and victim would lead to reduced recidivism. Maybe it would. I think it would. As it is now, the offender has lost the opportunity for participation in a personal confrontation of a very serious nature. He has lost the opportunity to receive a type of blame that it would be very difficult to neutralise. However, I would have suggested these arrangements even if it was absolutely certain they had no effects on recidivism, maybe even if they had a negative effect. I would have done that because of the other, more general gains. And let me also add – it is not much to lose. As we all know today, at least nearly all, we have not been able to invent any cure for crime. Except for execution, castration or incarceration for life, no measure has a proven minimum of efficiency compared to any other measure. We might as well react to crime according to what closely involved parties find is just and in accordance with general values in society.

With this last statement, as with most of the others I have made, I raise many more problems than I answer. Statements on criminal politics, particularly from those with the burden of responsibility, are usually filled with answers. It is questions we need. The gravity of our topic makes us much too pedantic and thereby useless as paradigm-changers.

A victim-oriented court

There is clearly a model of neighbourhood courts behind my reasoning. But it is one with some peculiar features, and it is only these I will discuss in what follows.

First and foremost; it is a *victim-oriented* organisation. Not in its initial stage, though. The first stage will be a traditional one where it is established whether it is true that the law has been broken, and whether it was this particular person who broke it.

Then comes the second stage, which in these courts would be of the utmost importance. That would be the stage where the victim's situation was considered, where every detail regarding what had happened – legally relevant or not – was brought to the court's attention. Particularly important here would be detailed consideration regarding what could be done for him, first and foremost by the offender, secondly by the local neighbourhood, thirdly by the state. Could the harm be compensated, the window repaired, the lock replaced, the wall painted, the loss of time because the car was stolen given back through garden work or washing of the car ten Sundays in a row? Or maybe, when this discussion started, the damage was not so important as it looked in documents written to impress insurance companies? Could physical suffering become slightly less painful by any action from the offender, during days, months or years? But, in addition, had the community exhausted all resources that might have offered help? Was it absolutely certain that the local hospital could not do anything? What about a helping hand from the janitor twice a day if the offender took over the cleaning of the basement every Saturday? None of these ideas is unknown or untried, particularly not in England. But we need an organisation for the systematic application of them.

Only after this stage was passed, and it ought to take hours, maybe days, to pass it, only then would come the time for an eventual decision on punishment. Punishment, then, becomes that suffering which the judge found necessary to apply *in addition to* those unintended constructive sufferings the offender would go through in his restitutive actions *vis-à-vis* the victim. Maybe nothing could be done or nothing would be done. But neighbourhoods might find it intolerable that nothing happened. Local courts out of tune with local values are not local courts. That is just the trouble with them, seen from the liberal reformer's point of view.

A fourth stage has to be added. That is the stage for service to the offender. His general social and personal situation is by now well-known to the court. The discussion of his possibilities for restoring the victim's situation cannot be carried out without at the same time giving information about the offender's situation. This might have exposed needs for social, educational, medical or religious action – not to prevent further crime, but because needs ought to be met. Courts are public arenas, needs are made visible. But it is important that this stage comes *after* sentencing. Otherwise we get a re-emergence of the whole array of so-called 'special measures' – compulsory treatments – very often only euphemisms for indeterminate imprisonment.

Through these four stages, these courts would represent a blend of elements from civil and criminal courts, but with a strong emphasis on the civil side.

A lay-oriented court

The second major peculiarity with the court model I have in mind is that it will be one with an extreme degree of lay-orientation. This is essential when conflicts are seen as property that ought to be shared. It is with conflicts as with so many good things: they are in no unlimited supply. Conflicts can be cared for, protected, nurtured. But there are limits. If some are given more access in the disposal of conflicts, others are getting less. It is as simple as that.

Specialisation in conflict solution is the major enemy; specialisation that in due – or undue – time leads to professionalisation. That is when the specialists get sufficient power to claim that they have acquired special gifts, mostly through education, gifts so powerful that it is obvious that they can only be handled by the certified craftsman.

With a clarification of the enemy, we are also able to specify the goal; let us reduce specialisation and particularly our dependence on the professionals within the crime control system to the utmost.

The ideal is clear; it ought to be a court of equals representing themselves. When they are able to find a solution between themselves, no judges are needed. When they are not, the judges ought also to be their equals.

Maybe the judge would be the easiest to replace, if we made a serious attempt to bring our present courts nearer to this model of lay orientation. We have lay judges already, in principle. But that is a far cry from realities. What we have, both in England and in my own country, is a sort of specialised non-specialist. First, they are used *again and again*. Secondly, some are even *trained*, given special courses or sent on excursions to foreign countries to learn about how to behave as a lay judge. Thirdly, most of them do also represent an extremely *biased sample* of the population with regard to sex, age, education, income, class and personal experience as criminals. With real lay judges, I conceive of a system where nobody was given the right to take part in conflict solution more than a few times, and then had to wait until all other community members had had the same experience.

Should lawyers be admitted to court? We had an old law in Norway that forbids them to enter the rural districts. Maybe they should be admitted in stage 1 where it is decided if the man is guilty. I am not sure. Experts are as cancer to any lay body. It is exactly as Ivan Illich describes for the educational system in general. Each time you increase the length of compulsory education in a society, each time you also decrease the same population's trust in what they have learned and understood quite by themselves.

Behaviour experts represent the same dilemma. Is there a place for them in this model? Ought there to be any place? In stage 1, decisions on facts, certainly not. In stage 3, decisions on eventual punishment, certainly not. It is too obvious to waste words on. We have the painful row of mistakes from Lombroso, through the movement for social defence and up to recent attempts to dispose of supposedly dangerous people through predicitions of who they are and when they are not dangerous any more. Let these ideas die, without further comments.

The real problem has to do with the service function of behaviour experts. Social scientists can be perceived as functional answers to a segmented society. Most of us have lost the physical possibility to experience the totality, both on the social system level and on the personality level. Psychologists can be seen as historians for the individuals; sociologists have much of the same function for the social system. Social workers are oil in the machinery, a sort of security counsel. Can we function without them, would the victim and the offender be worse off?

Maybe. But it would be immensely difficult to get such a court to function if they were all there. Our theme is social conflict. Who is not at least made slightly uneasy in the handling of her or his own social conflicts if we get to know that there is an expert on this very matter at the same table? I have no clear answer, only strong feelings behind a vague conclusion: let us have as few behaviour experts as we dare to. And if we have any, let us for God's sake not have any that specialise in crime and conflict resolution. Let us have generalised experts with a solid base outside the crime control system. And a last point with relevance for both behaviour experts and lawyers: if we find them unavoidable in certain cases or at certain stages, let us try to get across to them the problems they create for broad social participation. Let us try to get them to perceive themselves as resource-persons, answering when asked, but not domineering, not in the centre. They might help to stage conflicts, not take them over.

Rolling stones

There are hundreds of blocks against getting such a system to operate within our western culture. Let me only mention three major ones. They are:

1 There is a lack of neighbourhoods.

2 There are too few victims.

3 There are too many professionals around.

With lack of neighbourhoods I have in mind the very same phenomenon I described as a consequence of industrialised living; segmentation according to space and age. Much of our trouble stems from killed neighbourhoods or killed local communities. How can we then thrust towards neighbourhoods a task that presupposes they are highly alive? I have no really good arguments, only two weak ones. First, it is not quite that bad. The death is not complete. Secondly, one of the major ideas behind the formulation 'Conflicts as Property' is that it is neighbourhood-property. It is not private. It belongs to the system. It is intended as a vitaliser for neighbourhoods. The more fainting the neighbourhood is, the more we need neighbourhood courts as one of the many functions any social system needs for not dying through lack of challenge.

Equally bad is the lack of victims. Here I have particularly in mind the lack of personal victims. The problem behind this is again the large units in industrialised society. ... But again I will say: there is not a complete lack of personal victims, and their needs ought to get priority. But we should not forget the large organisations. They, or their boards, would certainly prefer not to have to appear as victims in 5000 neighbourhood courts all over the country. But maybe they ought to be compelled to appear. If the complaint is serious enough to bring the offender into the ranks of the criminal, then the victim ought to appear. A related problem has to do with insurance companies – the industrialised alternative to friendship and kinship. Again we have a case where the crutches deteriorate the condition. Insurance takes the consequences of crime away. We will therefore have to take insurance away. Or rather: we will have to keep the possibilities for compensation through the insurance companies back until in the procedure I have described it has been proved beyond all possible doubt that there are no other alternatives left – particularly that the offender has no possibilities whatsoever. Such a solution will create more paper-work, less predictability, more aggression from customers. And the solution will not necessarily be seen as good from the perspective of the policy-holder. But it will help to protect conflicts as social fuel.

None of these troubles can, however, compete with the third and last I will comment on: the abundance of professionals. We know it all from our own personal biographies or personal observations. And in addition we get it confirmed from all sorts of social science research: the educational system of any society is not necessarily synchronised with any needs for the product of this system. Once upon a time we thought there was a direct causal relation from the number of highly educated persons in a country to the Gross National Product. Today we suspect the relationship to go the other way, if we are at all willing to use GNP as a meaningful indicator. We also know that most educational systems are extremely class-biased. We know that most academic people have had profitable investments in our education, that we fight for the same for our children, and that we also often have vested interests in making our part of the educational system even bigger. More schools for more lawyers, social workers, sociologists, criminologists. While I am *talking* deprofessionalisation, we are increasing the capacity to be able to fill up the whole world with them.

There is no solid base for optimism. On the other hand insights about the situation, and goal formulation, is a pre-condition for action. Of course, the crime control system is not the domineering one in our type of society. But it has some importance. And occurrences here are unusually well suited as pedagogical illustrations of general trends in society. There is also some room for manoeuvre. And when we hit the limits, or are hit by them, this collision represents in itself a renewed argument for more broadly conceived changes.

Another source for hope: ideas formulated here are not quite so isolated or in dissonance with the mainstream of thinking when we leave our crime control area and enter other institutions. I have already mentioned Ivan Illich with his attempts to get learning away from the teachers and back to active human beings. Compulsory learning, compulsory medication and compulsory consummation of conflict solutions have interesting similarities. When Ivan Illich and Paulo Freire are listened to, and my impression is that they increasingly are, the crime control system will also become more easily influenced.

Another, but related, major shift in paradigm is about to happen within the whole field of technology. Partly, it is the lessons from the third world that now are more easily seen, partly it is the experience from the ecology debate. The globe is obviously suffering from what we, through our technique, are doing to her. Social systems in the third world are equally obviously suffering. So the suspicion starts. Maybe the first world can't take all this technology either. Maybe some of the old social thinkers were not so dumb after all. Maybe social systems can be perceived as biological ones. And maybe there are certain types of large-scale technology that kill social systems, as they kill globes. Schumacher (1973) with his book *Small is Beautiful* and the related Institute for Intermediate Technology come in here. So do also the numerous attempts, particularly by several outstanding Institutes for Peace Research, to show the dangers in concept of Gross National Product, and replace it with indicators that take care of dignity, equity and justice. The perspective developed in Johan Galtung's research group on World Indicators might prove extremely useful also within our own field of crime control.

There is also a political phenomenon opening vistas. At least in Scandinavia social democrats and related groupings have considerable power, but are without an explicated ideology regarding the goals for a reconstructed society. This vacuum is being felt by many, and creates a willingness to accept and even expect considerable institutional experimentation.

Then to my very last point: what about the universities in this picture? ... The answer has probably to be the old one: universities have to re-emphasise the old tasks of understanding and of criticising. But the task of training professionals ought to be looked into with renewed scepticism. Let us re-establish the credibility of encounters between critical human beings: low-paid, highly regarded, but with no extra power – outside the weight of their good ideas. That is as it ought to be.

References

Baldwin, J. (1976) 'The social composition of magistracy', *British Journal of Criminology*, vol. 16, pp.171–4.

Gluckman, M. (1967) *The Judicial Process among the Barotse of Northern Rhodesia*, Manchester, Manchester University Press.

Kinberg, O., Inghe, G. and Riemer, S. (1943) *Incest-Problemet i Sverige.*

Newman, O. (1972) *Defensible Space: People and Design in the Violent City*, London, Architectural Press.

Schumacher, E.F. (1973) *Small is Beautiful: A Study of Economics as if People Mattered*, London, Blond and Briggs.

CHAPTER 2

Moving into the New Millennium: Toward a Feminist Vision of Justice

by M. Kay Harris

The approach of the twenty-first century tends to inspire future-oriented thinking. With respect to criminal justice policies and practices, it is disheartening to imagine what the future holds if the current course is maintained. This article argues that moving toward a significantly brighter future requires abandoning conventional frames of thought and practice and adopting a fundamentally different way of thinking and acting. The focus is on exploring what the next century might look like if a feminist orientation toward justice were embraced.

Conventional approaches to criminal justice reform

Most proposals for change in policies directed at crime and criminal justice concerns fall within one of two types. Many proposals are developed from a systems-improvement orientation. This orientation takes for granted existing political, economic, and social institutional structures as well as the values that undergird them, assuming that they are proper or, at least, unlikely to be changed within the foreseeable future. Reform proposals generated from a systems-improvement perspective characteristically are framed as if crime were primarily an individual problem best addressed through more effective or more rigorous enforcement of the law. Thus, they focus on trying to find better means of identifying and intervening with individual offenders and of strengthening and increasing the efficiency of existing criminal justice institutions and agencies.

The other familiar way of framing reform proposals involves a broader crime-prevention/social-reform orientation. Reformers with this orientation emphasize the social and economic underpinnings of crime and the need to address them through policies and programs focused on families, neighborhoods, schools, and other institutions. In recent years, advocates of a prevention/social-reform approach have moved considerably beyond the ameliorative strategies of the 1960s toward proposals for more sweeping social and economic reconstruction, stressing that policies aimed at strengthening families and communities need to be coupled with efforts to promote economic development and full employment. Although they do not excuse individual offenders or ignore possible advances to be made by improving criminal justice practices, these reformers tend to view interventions with identified offenders more as last lines of defense than as promising avenues for reducing crime.

There are significant problems associated with trying to formulate recommendations for the future on the basis of either of these two conventional ways of framing the issues. The systems-improvement approach has the apparent advantage of offering advances in the identification, classification, control, or treatment of offenders and in the operation, efficiency, effectiveness, or accountability of criminal justice agencies. However, this approach ignores the political, economic, and social aspects of crime and has little or nothing to contribute to the overall, long-term development of social life. Furthermore, it offers, at best, only limited, short-term utility in dealing with crime.

Many systems-improvement advocates promise dramatic increases in crime control if only sanctions can be made more frightening, severe, certain, restrictive, or corrective. But such

Source: Pepinsky, H.E. and Quinney, R. (eds) (1991) *Criminology as Peacemaking*, Bloomington, Indiana University Press, pp.83–97.

promises lack both theoretical and scientific support. Current knowledge provides little basis for expecting significant reductions in crime through reshaping policies in hopes of achieving greater deterrent, incapacitative, or rehabilitative effects. Other systems-improvement supporters concede that notable increases in domestic tranquility are unlikely to be secured at the hands of crime-control agents, but argue that until more fundamental changes have been made in social relations and policies, there is no alternative but to continue working toward whatever marginal increases in efficiency, effectiveness, or even-handedness might be achievable.

To date, prevention/social-reform advocates have made scant progress in overcoming the notion that their proposals already have been tried in the War on Poverty/Great Society era and found ineffective. Many who agree that the measures championed by these advocates are prerequisites for dramatic shifts in crime and social relations doubt that the massive changes envisioned are economically or politically feasible. Furthermore, prevention/social-reform advocates have had little influence in ongoing criminal justice policy debates because their recommendations concerning interim criminal justice policies have been meager and uncompelling. They have offered little more than echoes of systems-improvement reform proposals, accompanied by warnings about the risk of simply reinforcing the underclass and increasing the social divisions in society if repressive measures targeted on offenders are pursued too zealously.

Thus, despite widespread dissatisfaction with the results of current policies and their burgeoning costs, it is difficult to find grounds for believing that the future toward which we are heading holds much promise of anything beyond more of the same. If current trends hold the key to seeing what the criminal justice system will look like in the next few decades, we face the prospect of maintaining a punishment system of awesome proportions without being able to expect much relief from the problems it supposedly exists to address.

Iron bars and velvet ankle bracelets: the need for new approaches

Many common citizens, scientists, futurists, and leaders are predicting that the next 25 years portend a series of collisions, conflicts, and catastrophes. Recent world experience with increasing interpersonal violence, terrorism, social injustice, and inequality – along with such growing problems as overpopulation, ecological damage, resource shortages, the continuing arms buildup, and the specter of nuclear holocaust – has generated heightened awareness of the need to think globally and much more creatively about the future. To begin to adequately envision what criminal justice should look like in the year 2012, we need to step outside of the traditional ways of framing the issues and consider approaches that transcend not only conventional criminological and political lines, but also national and cultural boundaries and other limiting habits of the mind. At the same time, 'focusing on the principles and tools of punishment' can help us 'understand the most prevalent way we have chosen to relate to each other in the twentieth century' (Sullivan, 1980, p.14).

Just as the velvet glove only thinly cushions and screens the iron fist, it is important to recognize that 'the velvet ankle bracelet' and its ostensibly more benign brethren 'community penalties' are facilitating the diffusion and expansion of social control through the penal system and augmenting the iron bars rather than replacing them. With little fanfare or protest, we have come to accept levels of state intrusiveness into individual lives, remarkable in a society that professes to value liberty. The nature and direction of the bulk of changes undertaken in the criminal justice system in recent years are such that the most pressing tasks in the coming years necessarily will involve damage control. Massive efforts will need to be devoted to coping with, undoing, and trying to ameliorate the effects of the present blind, determined push for greater punishment and control. Pursuing a more hopeful future requires exploration of alternative visions of justice.

A number of movements, models, and philosophies in various stages of development have arisen in response to the critical problems of the day, ranging from those focused on world order or global transformation to pacificism or peace studies, reconciliation, humanism, feminism, and a wide range of other visions of a better world and a better future. While few have been focused on criminal justice problems, they offer a rich resource for a fundamental rethinking of our approach to crime and justice.

In seeking to escape the fetters on my own thinking and aspirations for the future, I have found much of value in a number of orientations. Indeed, I have been struck by the common themes that emerge across a variety of perspectives with a wide range of labels. This suggests the possibility of articulating a new direction for the future by drawing from many orientations and avoiding attaching any label to the values and concepts discussed. Such an approach would help prevent burdening the ideas with unnecessary baggage or losing the attention of people put off by the images any particular school of thought raises in their minds. For me, however, the most significant breakthroughs in thought and hope came when I began to apply myself to considering what the values and principles of one particular orientation – feminism – would mean in rethinking crime and justice issues. Thus, the rest of this article shares ideas that emerged from this path of exploration, a path that continues to hold increasing meaning and inspiration for me and one that I hope will attract interest from a variety of people who otherwise might not devote attention to these issues. At the same time, it is my hope that people who find themselves more attuned to other orientations, or who see feminism differently, may find it useful to consider how the values described fit with theirs and what a future based on these values might look like, no matter what terms are used to describe it.

Values central to a feminist future

Feminism offers and is a set of values, beliefs, and experiences – a consciousness, a way of looking at the world. Feminism should be seen not merely as a prescription for granting rights to women, but as a far broader vision. There are a number of varying strands within feminist thought, but there are some core values that transcend the differences. Among the key tenets of feminism are three simple beliefs – that all people have equal value as human beings, that harmony and felicity are more important than power and possession, and that the personal is the political (French, 1985).

Feminist insistence on equality in sexual, racial, economic and all other types of relations stems from recognition that all humans are equally tied to the human condition, equally deserving of respect for their personhood, and equally worthy of survival and of access to those things that make life worth living. This is not to argue that all people are identical. Indeed, feminism places great emphasis on the value of difference and diversity, holding that different people should receive not identical treatment, but identical consideration. Feminists are concerned not simply with equal opportunities or equal entitlements within existing social structures, but with creating a different set of structures and relations that are not only nonsexist, but also are nonracist and economically just.

In the feminist view, felicity and harmony are regarded as the highest values. Viewing all people as part of a network on whose continuation we all depend, feminists stress the themes of caring, sharing, nurturing, and loving. This contrasts sharply with an orientation that values power and control above all else. Where the central goal is power, power conceived as 'power over' or control, people and things are not viewed as ends in themselves but as instruments for the furtherance of power. Hierarchical institutions and structures are established both to clarify power rankings and to maintain them. The resulting stratifications create levels of superiority and inferiority, which carry differential status, legitimacy, and access to resources and other benefits. Such divisions and exclusions engender resentment and revolt in various forms, which then are used to justify greater control.

Feminists believe that it is impossible to realize humane goals and create humane structures in a society that values power above all else. A major part of feminist effort involves better identifying and confronting characteristics and values – the political, social, economic, and cultural structures and ideologies – that are not conducive to the full realization of the human potential in individuals or society, the negative values that underlie stereotypes, rationalize discrimination and oppression, and serve only to support the groups in power.

Feminist belief is that the personal is the political, which means that core values must be lived and acted upon in both public and private arenas. Thus, feminists reject the tendency to offer one set of values to guide interactions in the private and personal realms and another set of values to govern interactions in the public worlds of politics and power. Empathy, compassion, and the loving, healthy, person-oriented values must be valued and affirmed not only in the family and the home but also in the halls where public policymaking, diplomacy, and politics are practiced.

Modes of moral reasoning

Research on moral development and on how people construe moral choices has identified two orientations that reflect significant differences (Gilligan, 1982a and b). In a *rights/justice* orientation, morality is conceived as being tied to respect for rules. It is a mode of reasoning that reflects the imagery of hierarchy, a hierarchy of values and a hierarchy of power. It assumes a world comprised of separate individuals whose claims and interests fundamentally conflict and in which infringements on an individual's rights can be controlled or redressed through rational and objective means deducible from logic and rules.

In a *care/response* orientation, morality is conceived contextually and in terms of a network of interpersonal relationships and connection. This mode of reasoning reflects the imagery of a web, a nonhierarchical network of affiliation and mutuality. It assumes a world of interdependence and care among people, a world in which conflicts and injuries can best be responded to by a process of ongoing communication and involvement that considers the needs, interests, and motivations of all involved.

At present, the care/response mode, with its emphasis on contextuality, relationship, and the human consequences of choices and actions, tends to be viewed as representing a lesser stage of moral development – less broadly applicable – than the rights/justice orientation, with its emphasis on standards, rights, and duties (Scharf *et al*., 1981, p.413). This tendency to contrast and rank the differing modes of reasoning has limited the moral and conceptual repertoires with which problems are approached in the worlds of government, science, and world power. Devotion to peacekeeping and nonviolent conflict resolution often are dismissed as irrelevant or less important than devotion to the 'rules of the game' or abstract notions of rights and responsibilities. Thus, the potential contributions of a care/response orientation to dealing constructively with the major global crises of security, justice, and equity have hardly begun to be tapped (Reardon, 1985, pp.89–90).

There is a need for a massive infusion of the values associated with the care/response mode of reasoning into a wide range of contexts from which they have been excluded almost entirely. It would be a mistake, however, to try to simply substitute a care/response orientation for one focused on justice and rights. Especially at present, when there are such vast differences in power among people, we are not in a position to trust that the interests of the less powerful will be protected in the absence of rules designed to insure that protection.

Studies by Carol Gilligan suggest that although most people can and do understand and use both modes of reasoning, they tend to focus more on one or the other in confronting moral issues. In her research, the mode of reasoning around which people tended to center was associated with gender. Men were more likely to employ a rights/justice orientation and women were more likely to reflect a care/response orientation, although responses from women were more mixed than those for men. Given the capacities of both men and women to use both modes of moral reasoning, and because there is no reason to believe that differing emphases or priorities in moral reasoning are innate or biological (see Bleier, 1984), we have an opportunity to explore more fully the contributions each can make to resolving moral dilemmas of all kinds.

Thus, the challenge involves searching for a more complete vision of justice and morality, a vision that encompasses concern for process and outcomes, as well as principles and rules, and for feelings and relationships, as well as logic and rationality. We need to labor to find ways of more fully integrating abstract notions of justice and rights with contextual notions of caring and relationship in both public (political) and private (personal) realms.

The criminal justice context: the dilemmas of defense and protection

The criminal justice system provides a clear picture of the challenges ahead. In the criminal justice arena, there is no attempt to disguise the fact that the goal and purpose of the system is power/control. The stated goal is control of crime and criminals, but it is widely recognized that the criminal justice system serves to achieve social control functions more generally. Law is an embodiment of power arrangements: it specifies a set of norms to be followed – an order – and also provides the basis for securing that order [through] coercive force. Coercive force is seen as the ultimate and the most effective mechanism for social defense. And once the order to be protected and preserved is in place, little attention is given to whether the social system to be defended is just or serves human ends.

It is important to bear in mind that penal sanctions, like crimes, are intended harms. 'The violent, punishing acts of the state ... are of the same genre as the violent acts of individuals. In each instance the acts reflect an attempt to monopolize human interaction to control another person as if he or she were a commodity' (Sullivan, 1980). Those who set themselves up as beyond reproach define *the criminal* as less than fully human. Without such objectification, the routine practice of subjecting human beings to calculated pain infliction, degradation, domination, banishment, and execution clearly would be regarded as intolerable.

Feminist analysis of the war system can be applied to the criminal justice system; the civil war in which we are engaged – the war on crime – is the domestic equivalent of the international war system. One has only to attend any budget hearing at which increased appropriations are being sought for war efforts – whether labeled as in defense of criminals, communists, or other enemies – to realize that the rationales and the rhetoric are the same. The ideologies of deterrence and retaliation; the hierarchal, militaristic structures and institutions; the incessant demand for more and greater weaponry, technology, and fighting forces; the sense of urgency and willingness to sacrifice other important interests to the cause; the tendency to dehumanize and objectify those defined as foes; and the belief in coercive force as the most effective means of obtaining security – all of these and other features characteristic of both domestic and international so-called defense systems suggest not just similarity, but identity. People concerned with international peace need to recognize that supporting the 'war on crime' is supporting the very establishment, ideology, structures, and morality against which they have been struggling.

We are caught in a truly vicious cycle. Existing structures, institutions, relations, and values create the problems that we then turn around and ask them to solve – or rather, control – using the very same structures, forms, and values, which in turn leads to more problems and greater demand for control. We all want to be protected from those who would violate our houses, our persons, and our general welfare and safety; but the protections we are offered tend to reinforce the divisions and distorted relations in society and to exacerbate the conditions that create much of the need for such protections. The complicated issues surrounding self-defense – whether in an immediate personal sense (as when confronted by a would-be rapist or other attacker), in a penal policy sense (as when deciding how to deal with known assaulters), or in even broader terms (as when confronted by powers and structures that seem bound to destroy us) – vividly illuminate the dilemma.

Sally Miller Gearhart vividly describes the dilemma surrounding trying to work toward the future we dream of while living in the present world by citing a science fiction work, *Rule Golden*, in which Damon Knight wipes violence from the face of the earth by having every agent feel in his/her own body and physical action what she/he delivers. 'Kick a dog and feel the boot in your own rib: commit murder and die yourself. Similarly, stroking another in love results in the physical feeling of being lovingly stroked' (Gearhart, 1982, p.266). Such imagery highlights:

> … the necessary connection between *empathy* and *nonviolence*, [the fact that] *objectification* is the necessary, if not sufficient component of any violent act. Thinking of myself as separate from another entity makes it possible for me to 'do to' that entity things I would not 'do to' myself. But if I see all things as myself, or empathize with all other things, then to hurt them is to do damage to me.…
>
> But empaths don't live if the Rule Golden is not in effect. Our world belongs to those who can objectify … and if I want to protect myself from them I learn to objectify and fight back in self-defense. I seem bound to choose between being violent and being victimized. Or I live a schizophrenic existence in which my values are at war with my actions because I must keep a constant shield of protectiveness (objectification) intact over my real self, over my empathy or my identification with others; the longer I keep up the shield the thicker it gets and the less empathic I am with those around me. So every second of protecting myself from violence makes me objectify more and ensures that I am more and more capable of doing violence myself. I am caught always in the violence-victim trap.
>
> (Gearhart, 1982, p.266)

Clearly, the standard approach in recent years has been to seek more control – more prisons, more time in confinement for more people, more surveillance and restriction of those not confined. Our willingness to cede greater and greater power to the institutions of social control is a reflection of a desperate society. But 'no amount of police, laws, courts, judges, prisons, mental hospitals, psychiatrists, and social workers can create a society with relative harmony. The most institutions can do is to impose the appearance of relative harmony …' (French, 1985). To the extent that we acquiesce to continuing escalation of social controls, agents of the state, we reduce correspondingly the prospects for the kind of safety that cannot be achieved through force.

It will not be easy to escape from the cycle in which we find ourselves swirling. Legitimate concerns for safety and protection pose difficult dilemmas for feminists. How can we meet the serious and all-too-real need for protection against violence without violating our peaceful values and aspirations? How can we respond effectively to people who inflict injury and hardship on others without employing the same script and the same means that they do? How can we satisfy immediate needs for safety without elevating those needs over the need to recreate the morality, relations, and conception of justice in our society?

As Marilyn French has put it, 'The major problem facing feminists can be easily summed up: there is no clear right way to move' (French, 1985). However, we can expand the conceptual and practical possibilities for change in criminal justice by re-examining our assumptions and expectations.

> [W]e need to begin picturing the new order in our minds, fantasying it, playing with possibilities. … An exercise in first stepping into a desired future in imagination, then consciously elaborating the structures needed to maintain it, and finally imagining the future history that would get us there, is a very liberating experience for people who feel trapped in an unyielding present. … [S]ocieties move toward what they image. If we remain frozen in the present as we have done since World War II, society stagnates. Imaging the future gives us action ideas for the present.
>
> (Boulding, 1987)

Emerging guides for the future

Identifying values central to feminist belief does not automatically yield a specific formula for better responding to crime and other conflicts, or for resolving the dilemmas with which we are confronted. Indeed, feminists do not see the best way of moving toward a more positive future as involving primarily analytic and abstract efforts to describe specific structures and processes. Such approaches almost never encompass any explicit element of human relations or affective, emotional content, and few display any cultural dimension (Reardon, 1985, pp.89–90). 'We need theory and feeling as rough guides on which to build a next step and only a next step: flexible, responsive emotional theory capable of adjusting to human needs and desires when these create contradictions' (Reardon, 1985, pp.89–90).

Feminist values do offer, however, some beginning guides for approaching the future. A key standard to help in making choices is to ask: What kinds of behavior and responses will achieve the goal of the greatest possible harmony? Thus, the task is not to discover how to eradicate crime, but to discover how to behave as befits our values and desire for harmony.

Acceptance of human equality and recognition of the interdependence of all people requires rejection of several current common tendencies. We need to struggle against the tendency toward objectification, of talking and thinking about crime and criminals as if they were distinct entities in themselves. We also need to reject the idea that those who cause injury or harm to others should suffer severance of the common bonds of respect and concern that bind members of a community. We should relinquish the notion that it is acceptable to try to 'get rid of' another person, whether through execution, banishment, or caging away people about whom we do not care. We should no longer pretend that conflicts can be resolved by the pounding of a gavel or the locking of a cell door.

A feminist orientation leads to greater awareness of the role and responsibility of society, not just the individual, in development of conflict. This suggests that individuals, groups, and societies need to accept greater responsibility for preventing and reducing those conditions, values, and structures that produce and support violence and strife. Removing the idea of power from its central position is key here, and this requires continually challenging actions, practices, and assumptions that glorify power, control, and domination, as well as developing more felicitous alternatives.

Commitment to the principle of equality means striving for interactions that are participatory, democratic, cooperative, and inclusive, characteristics that are incompatible with hierarchy, stratification, and centralized decision making. Thus, rules, which often are substituted for sensitive, respectful engagement of persons in cooperative problem solving, should not be regarded as sacrosanct. And because people learn from the nature of the processes in which they participate, as well as from the objectives of these processes, we should give greater attention to what the process teaches and how it is experienced.

It may be difficult to imagine how some conflicts could be resolved amicably. Especially while we are in the process of transition, we have to contend with all of the effects that our present structures, values, and stratifications have had on people. Thus, we are unlikely to reach soon a stage in which we can expect never to feel the need to resort to exercising control over another person. But we can greatly reduce our current reliance on repressive measures, and we should aim to move continually in the direction of imposing fewer coercive restraints on other people.

Indeed, we need to question and rethink the entire basis of the punishment system. Virtually all discussion of change begins and ends with the premise that punishment must take place. All of the existing institutions and structures – the criminal law, the criminal-processing system, the prisons – are assumed. We allow ourselves only to entertain debates about rearrangements and reallocations within those powerfully constraining givens. We swing among the traditional, tired philosophies of punishment as the weight of the inadequacies of one propels us to turn to another. We swing between attempting *to do something with lawbreakers* – changing, controlling, or making an example of them – and simply striving *to dole out a just measure of pain*. The sterility of the debates and the disturbing ways they are played out in practice underscore the need to explore alternative visions. We need to step back to reconsider whether or not we should punish, not just to argue about how to punish.

We may remain convinced that something is needed to serve the declaratory function of the criminal law, something that tells us what is not to be done. We may conclude that there is a need for some sort of process that holds people accountable for their wrongful actions. We may not be able to think of ways to completely eliminate restraints on people who have done harmful things. But we should not simply assume that we cannot develop better ways to satisfy these and other important interests as we try to create our desired future.

While we are in the transition process, and where we continue to feel that it is necessary to exercise power over other people, we should honor more completely certain familiar principles that are often stated but seldom fully realized. Resort to the restriction of liberty, whether of movement, of association, or of other personal choices, should be clearly recognized as an evil. Whenever it is argued that it is a necessary evil, there should be a strong, nonroutine burden of establishing such necessity. And where it is accepted that some restriction is demonstrably necessary, every effort should be made to utilize the least drastic means that will satisfy the need established. Thus, we should approach restriction and control of others with trepidation, restraint, caution, and care.

In addition, we should recognize that the more we restrict an individual's chances and choices, the greater is the responsibility we assume for protecting that person and preserving his or her personhood. We should no longer accept the routine deprivations of privacy, healthful surroundings, contacts, and opportunities to exercise choice and preference that we have come to treat as standard concomitants of restriction of liberty. Such deprivations are not only unnecessary but also offensive to our values and destructive to all involved.

These principles make it apparent that we should abandon imprisonment, at least in anything like the way we have come to accept the meaning of that word. There is no excuse for continuing to utilize the dungeons of the past nor for replicating the assumptions, ideology, and values that have created their newer, shinier, more modern brethren, those even now being constructed on an astonishing scale. While tiers of human cages stacked one upon another are the most apparently repugnant form, all institutions erected for the purpose of congregate confinement need to be acknowledged as anachronisms of a less felicitous time.

How should we deal with people who demonstrate that, at least for a time, they cannot live peacefully among us unrestrained? Although the answers to that question are not entirely clear, feminist values suggest that we should move toward conceiving restriction of liberty as having less to do with buildings, structures, and walls and more to do with human contacts and relations. Few if any creatures are dangerous to all other creatures at all times, especially to those with whom they are directly and closely connected on an ongoing basis. Perhaps we can fashion some variant of jury duty and of citizens standing up for one another in the tradition of John Augustus, in which a small group of citizens would be asked to assume responsibility for maintaining one person safely for a period of time. A range of compassionate, constructive, and caring arrangements needs to be created. And we should not allow the most difficult cases to stand in the way of more rapidly evolving, better approaches for the rest.

At the same time, we need to stop thinking about issues related to how best to respond to those who caused harm as if they were totally separate from, or in competition with, issues related to how best to respond to those who have been harmed. There is not a fixed quantity of compassion and care, or even of rights, that will be diminished for those who have been victimized as they are extended to those who victimized them.

Many of these ideas may seem foreign, naïve, or beyond our abilities. If they seem foreign, that may be because the ideas of care, community, and mutuality seem foreign. If these dreams for the future seem naïve or out of reach, that may be because we have lost confidence in our capacity to choose, to recreate relations, and to realign priorities. It may be tempting to conclude that no efforts in the directions suggested here will be worthwhile, that nothing can be done until everything can be done, that no one can confront crime humanely until everyone is willing to do so. And it is true that we will never approach making such a vision reality if we focus only on issues of criminal justice. Our energies must be focused on the full panoply of global-peace and social-justice issues. But when we turn our attentions to criminal justice, we should choose and act according to the values and aims we seek more generally and not to increase division, alienation, bitterness, and despair. And every day, we should try to act as we believe would be the best way to act – not just in the future, but in the present.

What is advocated here is radical, but hardly novel. It simply echoes themes that have been heard through the ages, if rarely lived fully. We should refuse to return evil with evil. Although we have enemies, we should seek to forgive, reconcile, and heal. We should strive to find within ourselves outrageous love, the kind of love that extends even to those it is easiest to fear and hate. Love frequently is seen as having little relevance outside the personal realm. Yet the power ethic has failed to serve human happiness. To have a harmonious society, we must act in ways designed to increase harmony, not to further fragment, repress, and control. There is no other way. The means and the end are the same.

References

Bleier, R. (1984) *Science and Gender: A Critique of Biology and its Theories on Women*, New York, Pergamon Press.

Boulding, E. (1987) 'Warriors and saints: dilemmas in the history of men, women and war', Paper presented at the International Symposium on Women and the Military System, Siuntio Baths, Finland, 22–25 January. On file with author.

French, M. (1985) *Beyond Power: On Women, Men and Morals,* New York, Summit Books.

Gearhart, S.M. (1982) 'The future – if there is one – is female', in McAllister, P. (ed.) *Reweaving the Web of Life: Feminism and Nonviolence,* Philadelphia, New Society Publishers.

Gilligan, C. (1982a) *In a Different Voice: Psychological Theory and Women's Development,* Cambridge, Harvard University Press.

Gilligan, C. (1982b) 'New maps of development: new visions of maturity', *American Journal of Orthopsychiatry* (April).

Reardon, B.A. (1985) *Sexism and the War System,* New York, Teachers College Press, Columbia University.

Scharf, P., Kohlberg, L. and Hickey, J. (1981) 'Ideology and correctional intervention: the creation of a just prison community', in Kratcoski, C. (ed.) *Correctional Counseling and Treatment,* Monterey, CA, Duxbury.

Sullivan, D. (1980) *The Mask of Love: Corrections in America (Toward a Mutual Aid Alternative),* Port Washington, NY, Kennikat Press.

CHAPTER 3

Fundamental Concepts of Restorative Justice

by Howard Zehr and Harry Mika

Introduction

A working definition of restorative justice, such as the one we propose, is the product of a great deal of input and deliberation of practitioners and other professionals, who in their own work are attempting to clarify the basic values and indices of restorative justice practice. We are indebted for this breadth of experience and reflection, and the spirit in which we have been engaged. The limitations of our proposal should in no way reflect poorly upon the advice we have been given.

The definition is, as it were, a single side of a coin. Here, we have articulated the component parts of restorative justice practice. Elsewhere, these elements will need to yield measures of restorative practice – a restorative justice yardstick – that are so integral to evaluating justice practice, and improving program design.

The definition is couched within several parameters. First, it is unlikely that any restorative justice practice will incorporate all of the following elements. Further, the critical mass of these elements that would absolutely distinguish between retributive and restorative justice practice seem very hard to specify. Second, we suspect these elements are not static, but are rather dynamic in response to changing needs, changing relationships, and cultural values. Third, this definition is surely a product of largely US experiences in justice programs, most of which have their genesis in community-based practice and initiatives. From time to time, what is now captioned as 'restorative justice' has selectively incorporated innovations in community corrections, informal justice, community service, alternative sentencing, community mediation, victim offender reconciliation, and the like.

A final parameter concerns the lexicon of restorative justice, itself a matter for contemplative critique. From time to time and place to place, the use of certain language forms becomes a barrier to shared meanings and understanding.

For example, the terminology 'victim' suggests to some dependence, resignation, and lack of capacity and competence, the very antithesis of support and advocacy by those who bear the harms of crime. The preference might be to refer to such persons as the 'bereaved' and 'traumatized'. For some, the concept of 'offender' – where it might include persons who break the criminal law – is itself a mechanism for denying the political nature of those behaviors that are intended as antistate actions. 'Combatants', 'political prisoners,' and/or 'prisoners of war' are felt to be more accurate representations. Similarly, the terms 'offender' and 'crime' presuppose that the actions and reactions of those oppressed politically and economically merit punitive intervention, and the conditions that beget such actions or 'crimes' in the first place will not be subject to scrutiny. The idea of 'community' is notoriously difficult to define, and at its worst, may conjure up romantic ideas of a place or a people that do not appear to have much basis in reality. 'Restoration', it is said, may be impossibly ambitious for some bereaved, who might eventually be reconciled to their loss, but never again be whole or restored. The language of this definition is encumbered with difficulties such as these. We are fully cognizant of the limitations of our conventional usages, and intend no offense.

Source: *Contemporary Justice Review* (1997) vol.1, no.1, pp.47–56.

A definition of restorative justice

The elements specified below seek to address the critical components of one vision of restorative justice practice. Organizationally, the definition is composed of three major headings that define crime, obligations and liabilities, and justice practice. Under each of the headings, a number of secondary and tertiary points specify and elaborate on the general themes.

I Crime is fundamentally a violation of people and interpersonal relationships.

Victims and the community have been harmed and are in need of restoration.

1 The primary victims are those most directly affected by the offense but others, such as family members of victims and offenders, witnesses and members of the affected community, are also victims.

2 The relationships affected (and reflected) by crime must be addressed.

3 Restoration is a continuum of responses to the range of needs and harms experienced by victims, offenders and the community.

Victims, offenders and the affected communities are the key stakeholders in justice.

1 A restorative justice process maximizes the input and participation of these parties – but especially primary victims as well as offenders – in the search for restoration, healing, responsibility and prevention.

2 The roles of these parties will vary according to the nature of the offense as well as the capacities and preferences of the parties.

3 The state has circumscribed roles, such as investigating facts, facilitating processes and ensuring safety, but the state is not a primary victim.

II Violations create obligations and liabilities.

Offenders' obligations are to make things right as much as possible.

1 Since the primary obligation is to victims, a restorative justice process empowers victims to effectively participate in defining obligations.

2 Offenders are provided opportunities and encouragement to understand the harm they have caused to victims and the community and to develop plans for taking appropriate responsibility.

3 Voluntary participation by offenders is maximized; coercion and exclusion are minimized. However, offenders may be required to accept their obligations if they do not do so voluntarily.

4 Obligations that follow from the harm inflicted by crime should be related to making things right.

5 Obligations may be experienced as difficult, even painful, but are not intended as pain, vengeance or revenge.

6 Obligations to victims such as restitution take priority over other sanctions and obligations to the state such as fines.

7 Offenders have an obligation to be active participants in addressing their own needs.

The community's obligations are to victims and to offenders and for the general welfare of its members.

1 The community has a responsibility to support and help victims of crime to meet their needs.

2 The community bears a responsibility for the welfare of its members and the social conditions and relationships which promote both crime and community peace.

3 The community has responsibilities to support efforts to integrate offenders into the community, to be actively involved in the definitions of offender obligations and to ensure opportunities for offenders to make amends.

III Restorative justice seeks to heal and put right the wrongs.

The needs of victims for information, validation, vindication, restitution, testimony, safety and support are the starting points of justice.

1 The safety of victims is an immediate priority.

2 The justice process provides a framework that promotes the work of recovery and healing that is ultimately the domain of the individual victim.

3 Victims are empowered by maximizing their input and participation in determining needs and outcomes.

4 Offenders are involved in repair of the harm insofar as possible.

The process of justice maximizes opportunities for exchange of information, participation, dialogue and mutual consent between victim and offender.

1 Face-to-face encounters are appropriate in some instances while alternative forms of exchange are more appropriate in others.

2 Victims have the principal role in defining and directing the terms and conditions of the exchange.

3 Mutual agreement takes precedence over imposed outcomes.

4 Opportunities are provided for remorse, forgiveness and reconciliation.

Offenders' needs and competencies are addressed.

1 Recognizing that offenders themselves have often been harmed, healing and integration of offenders into the community are emphasized.

2 Offenders are supported and treated respectfully in the justice process.

3 Removal from the community and severe restriction of offenders is limited to the minimum necessary.

4 Justice values personal change above compliant behavior.

The justice process belongs to the community.

1 Community members are actively involved in doing justice.

2 The justice process draws from community resources and, in turn, contributes to the building and strengthening of community.

3 The justice process attempts to promote changes in the community to both prevent similar harms from happening to others, and to foster early intervention to address the needs of victims and the accountability of offenders.

Justice is mindful of the outcomes, intended and unintended, of its responses to crime and victimization.

1 Justice monitors and encourages follow-through since healing, recovery, accountability and change are maximized when agreements are kept.

2 Fairness is assured, not by uniformity of outcomes, but through provision of necessary support and opportunities to all parties and avoidance of discrimination based on ethnicity, class and sex.

3 Outcomes which are predominantly deterrent or incapacitative should be implemented as a last resort, involving the least restrictive intervention while seeking restoration of the parties involved.

4 Unintended consequences such as the cooptation of restorative processes for coercive or punitive ends, undue offender orientation, or the expansion of social control, are resisted.

Restorative justice signposts

Any definition of a concept contains the seeds of the values to which it subscribes. Our proposal is no different. Hence, this is obviously a community-oriented perspective, quite different in fundamental respects from other contemporary visions of restorative justice that use as their basic framework a top-down, or state promotion and practice of justice. Equally obvious is the value of including multiple stakeholders in restorative justice processes. Their roles and levels of participation should be dramatically different than those of conventional, retributive justice practice, and their needs and accountability are redefined accordingly. Their roles may continue to change in the future as well. For example, increasingly we want to consider the role of a community of victims, made up of individuals and groups variously affected by crime, safety and victimization issues, for whom some degree of healing and restoration is requisite for an improved quality of communal life.

Where conventional justice is law and punishment oriented, we conceive of restorative justice as a harm-centered approach: the centrality of victims, the obligations of offenders (and the meaning of accountability), the role of the community, and the active engagement of all parties in the justice equation are distinctive elements, we believe, of such an approach. Tony Marshall's (1996) restorative justice definition, as 'a process whereby all the parties with a stake in a particular offence come together to resolve collectively how to deal with the aftermath of the offence and its implications for the future', captures this core idea of restorative justice practice as a collaborative process to resolve harms. Despite the seductiveness of his succinct definition, however, we feel it is important to be more explicit about the elemental features of a restorative approach.

To conclude, we propose a number of simple tests or principles that flow from the definition, that may in turn guide practice. We suggest that we are working toward restorative justice when we:

- focus on the harms of wrongdoing more than the rules that have been broken;
- show equal concern and commitment to victims and offenders, involving both in the process of justice;
- work toward the restoration of victims, empowering them and responding to their needs as they see them;
- support offenders while encouraging them to understand, accept and carry out their obligations;
- recognize that while obligations may be difficult for offenders, they should not be intended as harms and they must be achievable;
- provide opportunities for dialogue, direct or indirect, between victims and offenders as appropriate;
- involve and empower the affected community through the justice process, and increase its capacity to recognize and respond to community bases of crime;
- encourage collaboration and reintegration rather than coercion and isolation;
- give attention to the unintended consequences of our actions and programs; and
- show respect to all parties, including victims, offenders and justice colleagues.

Our definition and these principles imperfectly acknowledge haunting challenges to restorative justice practice. For example, we are ever-mindful of the struggle of sustaining restorative justice ideals and values in a retributive justice context, and how in practice these translate into the serious issues of credibility, legitimacy, program viability, and financial solvency. Similarly, an expanded role for the community, as the locus of trouble and justice, will mean redefining community accountability to both victims and offenders, and a local role in preventing and intervening in those conditions that precipitate conflict and impede its productive resolution. Finally, the definition moves – step, by stagger, by lurch – towards acknowledging the central role that socially structured cleavages play in the practice and realization of justice. As Ruth Morris (1995a, b) instructs us, it is the 'transformative' requisite of restorative justice that is surely its stiffest test.

References

Marshall, T. (1996) *The Evolution of Restorative Justice in Britain*, unpublished manuscript, prepared for the European Committee of Experts on Mediation in Penal Matters.

Morris, R. (1995a) 'Not enough!', *Mediation Quarterly*, vol.12, no.3, pp.285–91.

Morris, R. (1995b) *Penal Abolition: The Tactical Choice*, Toronto, Canadian Scholars Press.

CHAPTER 4

Re-forming Justice: The Potential of Maori Processes

by Juan Tauri and Allison Morris

Setting the scene

Indigenous peoples in a range of countries are over-represented in crime, court and prison statistics and Maori in New Zealand are no exception.[1] For the year ended June 30 1996, 37% of offenders apprehended by New Zealand police were described as Maori (Police National Headquarters, 1996).[2] According to the 1995 Prison Census, 50% of male prisoners and 56% of female prisoners in New Zealand identified themselves as Maori (Ministry of Justice, 1996). Maori make up around 13% of the New Zealand population (Statistics New Zealand, 1996).

It has not always been like this for Maori. Historically, far from the stereotype of a lawless people, Maori were viewed by colonists in the early to mid 19th century as relatively law-abiding in contrast to the influx of European whalers, seamen and the like (Pratt, 1992). This gradually changed: for example, in 1910, Maori made up 5% of the population and 12% of the prison population and by 1950 Maori made up 6% of the population and 18% of the prison population (Pratt, 1992). This increase is generally associated with urbanisation. It is more complicated than that, however.[3]

There was another sense in which Maori were not law-less. Maori did possess recognisable legal structures. Maori society was governed by a set of rules by which the community was expected to live, and a system existed which was employed when these rules were broken (Jackson, 1988). *Tikanga o nga hara*, for example, translates broadly into the law of wrongdoing and many Maori *hapu* (sub-tribes or collections of families) and *iwi* (tribes) possessed *runanga o nga tura* which translates broadly into a council of law or court. These were headed by *tohunga o nga ture*, experts in law, but also contained *kaumatua* or *kuia* (male and female elders), representatives from the offender's family and representatives from the victim's family (see Jackson, 1988; Durie, 1995; Olsen *et al.*, 1995 and Pratt, 1992 for more information).

It is the re-assertion of these traditional processes with which this paper is concerned. Specifically, it explores whether or not it is possible to return to these processes in a modern day context: in part, as a way of addressing the over-representation of Maori in the criminal justice system, in part as a way of contributing to New Zealand's ideal of biculturalism, but in part also as a way of creating a system of justice which better meets the concerns and needs of victims, Pakeha (New Zealander of European origin) and Maori alike, and which better makes offenders, Pakeha and Maori alike, accountable for their offending. In this sense, Maori justice processes could provide a protoype for re-forming New Zealand criminal justice processes since victims would no longer be literally excluded from that process (except when required to give evidence as witnesses)[4] and offenders would no longer be passive observers in the courtroom while the professionals play the key roles.[5]

Maori justice pre-colonisation

We need to say a little more about the practice of Maori justice in pre-colonial times. This discussion is necessarily brief given the focus of this paper (for more information, see Jackson, 1988; Ward, 1995 and Pratt, 1992), but, essentially, Maori justice processes were based on notions that responsibility was collective rather than individual and that redress was due

Source: Australian and New Zealand Journal of Criminology (1997) vol.30, no.2, pp.149–67.

not just to the victim but also to the victim's family. Understanding why an individual had offended was also linked to this notion of collective responsibility. The reasons were felt to lie not in the individual but in a lack of balance in the offender's social and family environment. The causes of this imbalance, therefore, had to be addressed in a collective way and, in particular, the imbalance between the offender and the victim's family had to be restored. For example, the agreed outcome might have been the transfer of the offender's goods to the victim or work by the offender for the victim (Durie, 1995). The role of the *whanau* (the family group which includes parents, children and other close kin) and *hapu* were of paramount importance to the process. Most decisions, whatever their nature, were customarily made by the *whanau* and *hapu* depending on the importance and nature of the decision (Consedine, 1995).

Colonialism, however, all but destroyed indigenous systems of justice in all parts of the British Empire, and New Zealand was no exception (Brennan, 1993; Fitzpatrick, 1983; Griffiths, 1986; Merry, 1992; Pratt, 1992). The relationship between the State and Maoridom as set out in the Treaty of Waitangi and signed by the Crown and some Maori chiefs in 1840 was intended to be a partnership in which Maori sovereignty was preserved, but this did not happen. The culture and values of Maori were not allowed to exist alongside the culture and values of the colonisers. Dismantling these and the subsequent enforced assimilation to 'the British way of life' was what Pratt (1992) ironically calls the 'gift of civilisation'.

To be 'one people' required one set of laws and since the colonisers had the power (first through weapons and later through increased numbers), it was their law which dominated from 1893 (after the Magistrates Court Act of that year introduced a unified criminal justice system). Indeed, silencing Maori law was a powerful mechanism for destabilising the foundations of Maori society. As a result, decisions affecting Maori in such areas as social welfare and criminal justice were made for Maori and with little consultation with Maori. Traditional Maori structures were thereby weakened (Pratt, 1992).

However, this is not to say that Maori justice practices disappeared altogether. Acts such as the Maori Councils Act 1900, the Maori Social and Economic Advancement Act 1945 and the Maori Welfare Act 1962 (now the Maori Community Development Act 1977) established Maori District Committees through which Maori were given the power to exercise Maori customary law by way of by-laws (Wickliffe, 1995). Ethnographic evidence shows that Maori were also practising 'justice' outside these formalised structures (Metge, 1977; Walker, 1975).

Towards Maori justice in modern times

There have been a number of calls for the implementation of a parallel or separate Maori justice system governed by Maori philosophies, concepts and cultural practices (Jackson, 1988, 1995; Wickliffe, 1995). Though this has been consistently rejected by various Governments, recently suggestions have been made which are indicative of some tentative steps in this direction.

The Minister of Justice, for example, was quoted as stating that it might be possible to hold court cases on *marae* (communal gathering place) and that suggestions which Maori made concerning sanctions or punishment in a particular case might be taken into consideration by the presiding judge (*The Dominion,* 1995). His Ministry has since published a discussion paper on 'restorative justice', an approach which has its roots in part in indigenous justice and which includes many of the concepts identified earlier as key for Maori justice such as the participation of the offender, the victim and, where appropriate, their *whanau*; healing the damage that has been caused by the offending and restoring harmony between the offender, the victim and, where appropriate, their *whanau*; and decision-making through agreement rather than sanctions imposed externally (Ministry of Justice, 1995a).

The Labour Party too has announced policies which would give Maori the opportunity to develop separate programmes 'devoted to rehabilitation for first and young offenders' (New Zealand Labour Party, 1996, p.2). It is clear also that there are already examples of Maori justice in existence now.[6] However, many Pakeha in particular but also many Maori do not have a clear picture of what Maori justice processes and practices might look like, how it might relate to the criminal justice system and how perceived difficulties in its implementation might be resolved.

Research questions

To try to take current debates about Maori justice further, we conducted an exploratory study of Maori justice practices (Morris and Tauri, 1995).[7] The research focused on two main broad questions:

> 'How did Maori communities deal with offenders and resolve conflict in the recent past?';

and

> 'How might Maori justice practices work today and in urban areas?'
>
> ...

Sample limitations

The voices of 54 Maori and 12 *iwi*[8] are reflected in the description of the research findings which follows. This is neither a representative nor a random sample; participants were recruited by contacting key informants and we built from there. Progress was initially slow – the research coincided with a period in which other more urgent issues arose for Maori[9] – and the authority and credibility of the interviewer had to be 'tested'.

'How did Maori communities deal with offenders and resolve conflict in the recent past?'

Participants' responses to this first question broadly confirm the accounts already presented in the literature (Walker, 1975; Jackson, 1988; Durie, 1995; Consedine, 1995). However, the offenders dealt with in the relatively recent past were a narrower group than we would find described in historical records (Pratt, 1992; Ward, 1995). They were primarily first time and minor offenders (for example, those involved in minor assault, theft, and drunk and disorderly behaviour), but they were not exclusively so: those involved in sexual assault, incest and family violence were also dealt with within Maori communities.

...

The restoration of communal harmony was presented as the primary aim of sanctions. It was not, however, the only aim. For example, one participant noted that:

> [It is] no good pretending that Maori culture is all *aroha* (love). If you were to rape my daughter the first and only thing on my mind would be to kill you, to have *utu* (revenge). Maori and *marae* justice was not all integration; it could also be punitive and unforgiving.

As we mentioned earlier, by the 1950s, Maori justice practices had been heavily influenced by legislation which restricted both the offences and offenders that could be dealt with by Maori communities. However, the important point made here by participants is that the central justice concepts and philosophies of Maoridom which we identified earlier were sustained. The *marae* was the preferred setting, *kaumatua* were the primary decision makers (though working through tribal or Maori committees), and the restoration of communal harmony was the primary although not the only aim.

'How might Maori justice practices work today and in urban areas?'

When participants were asked this question they overwhelmingly promoted the idea that Maori should deal with Maori offenders. In the words of one interviewee: 'well, we can't do any worse! The bloody courts just send them to prison'. It is quite clear that they perceived it as having failed Maori. Once again, their views paralleled those presented in the literature (Jackson, 1988, 1995; Fleras and Elliot, 1992; Wickliffe, 1995) and provide a powerful argument for reforming current justice practices in New Zealand. They saw the current criminal justice system as relying too heavily on imprisonment as a sanction and as culturally insensitive and inappropriate, as well as exclusive.

> Very cold, unnatural … you go in alone, you stand alone. If you're lucky you get to say what you want, but usually not the way you want to … if you're the victim you seem to get no say. The lawyers, judges, police, they rule everything that goes on … only those with degrees can talk.

> It mishandles Maori offenders. [In what way?] It relies too much on prison, on sending them away. Their families suffer, you know, loss of money; it just makes things worse … the young guys go in and learn crime off the older ones … prisons cause a vicious cycle.

This was contrasted by participants within Maori justice practices in which offenders would be supported by *whanau*, in which victims would have a say and which would emphasise restitution and community service – practices commonly discussed under the framework of restorative justice.

The *marae* was presented as the appropriate 'site' for Maori justice practices. This was seen as particularly important in urban areas where it was thought necessary to establish *marae* as the focus of urban Maori communities. However, participants felt that the focus should be on young, first time and minor offenders and that these offenders were best dealt with by sanctions such as restitution and community service. More serious offenders were thought at this point in time to be best dealt with by the present criminal justice system.

…

A number of points emerge. … First, there is a preference for caution, for building upon experience before tackling more serious or persistent offenders. Second, related to this, dealing with all Maori offenders is viewed as a legitimate long term goal. And third, this belief is tempered with realism (others might describe it as pessimism): 'they [the present criminal justice system] would never let us deal with those offenders anyway.'

Perceived difficulties to be resolved in developing Maori justice practices

Despite overwhelming support for moves toward Maori justice practices, the participants raised a number of concerns.

…

First, Maori in many urban areas do not constitute an identifiable 'community'. Maori communities today are beset by many of the problems that exist in highly industrialised societies, for example, the fragmented nature of modern communities and the difficulties of organising large numbers of individuals to take part in 'communal' activity (Christie, 1977).

…

Second, many of the participants recognised that the inter-*iwi* and *hapu* nature of urban Maori communities could create problems in establishing a single Maori justice system because of historical and contemporary conflicts.

…

Third, related to this but perhaps more problematic, is the question of how Maori justice would deal with cases where either the offender or victim were not Maori.

…

Fourth, participants made the point that if the *marae* is going to be the site for Maori justice then the re-education of Maori may be necessary. Many Maori – particularly the young – know little about *marae* and *marae* protocol and have little skill in *te reo* Maori (Maori language).

…

Participants felt, therefore, that not only *kaumatua*, but also other experts and people of standing from within the Maori community (for example, social workers, probation officers, lawyers, and respected peers) should control a Maori justice process. To some extent this was what happened in Maori committees in the 1960s (Walker 1975; Metge 1977). No explicit mention was made of the specific roles to be played by offenders' *whanau*, victims or victims' *whanau* in this process but their presence was implicit in much of what else was said.

...

Finally, concern was expressed by a number of the participants regarding the issue of 'location of control'. There was concern that Maori justice practices would be used to further the interests of the present criminal justice system, rather than empowering Maori. The dominant view among participants was that they would not be happy with the criminal justice system controlling the decision-making process or the sanctions available.

...

Family group conferences as a case study of Maori justice

Family group conferences which were introduced in New Zealand in 1989 to deal with offending by young people share certain features of Maori justice.[10] Specifically, these include: attempting to heal the damage that has been caused by the offending and to restore harmony between those who have been affected by it, encouraging the participation of those affected by the offending and those able to contribute to effective solutions, and decision-making through consensus. Family group conferences are also intended to provide processes and outcomes which are culturally appropriate. To this extent, the practice of family group conferences provides a case study, and in some ways a test case, of the ability of the present justice system to adapt to the needs of indigenous peoples. We draw here from the research of Maxwell and Morris (1993) and focus, in particular, on the involvement and satisfaction of victims in family group conferences, how families and young people saw this process, the role of professionals in family group conferences and the extent to which family group conferences have provided processes and outcomes which are culturally appropriate.

The involvement and satisfaction of victims in family group conferences

Maxwell and Morris (1993) have shown that, for nearly half the family group conferences in their research, at least one victim or victims' representative was present.[11] When asked, victims gave a range of reasons for welcoming this opportunity.[12] Only 6% of victims said that they did not wish to meet the offender. Maxwell and Morris's research also showed that, when victims were involved, about a quarter said that they felt worse as a result of attending the family group conference. Many more, however, found this a positive process. About 60% of the victims interviewed described the family group conference they attended as helpful and rewarding. Generally, they said that they were effectively involved in the process and felt better as a result of participating. Victims also commented on two other specific benefits for them. First, it provided them with a voice in determining appropriate outcomes. Second, they were able to meet the offender and the offender's family face-to-face so that they could assess their attitude, understand more why the offence had occurred and assess the likelihood of it recurring. There is some preliminary evidence too that factors stemming from the involvement of victims have positive benefits in reducing reconvictions.[13]

The views of families and young people on family group conferences

Families and young people who were part of the former court process saw the court as alien, remote and frustrating, described their participation as rare, their communication as routine and felt that they had wasted their time (Morris and Young, 1987). In contrast, in Maxwell and Morris's research on family group conferences, more than half the families interviewed felt that they had been involved in what happened. In more than two thirds of the cases, parents also identified themselves as the decision-makers and 85% said that they were satisfied with the outcomes. The young people they talked with were less engaged in the decision-making process. Only about a third felt involved and less than a fifth felt that they had been a party to the decision. But this lack of involvement may be because both families and professionals do not allow young people the opportunity to become more involved. On the other hand, 84% of young people expressed satisfaction with the outcome of the family group conference. More importantly, there was little doubt that the families and young people we talked to preferred the process of family group conferences to the process of courts. Their comments highlight the participatory nature of the family group conference process, the greater degree of support available at the family group conference and the stress that accompanies a court appearance. As well as feeling more comfortable at the family group conference, they understood more of what happened and believed that it provided a more realistic forum for decision-making.

The role of professionals in family group conferences

Families, young people and victims are all key decision-makers. However, there is another important decision-maker – the state. It is the professionals who represent the state who make the arrangements for family group conferences, invite the participants to them, manage the process and must agree to the decisions. There is little doubt that the state's interests are being served too. And, despite the positive comments above, there are question marks over the role of some professionals in both shaping and determining outcomes at family group conferences. It is almost invariably the professionals who provide the informational basis for decisions and a disturbing feature in the research by Maxwell and Morris (1993) was that 15% of the families identified the professionals alone as the decision-makers. The police, in particular, were identified as determining the decision.

The cultural appropriateness of family group conferences

The family group conference is an attempt to give a prominent place to culture in reaching decisions. But research (Olsen *et al.*, 1995) has shown that although family group conferences could transcend tokenism and embody a Maori process, they often failed to do so or to enable outcomes to be reached which were in accord with Maori philosophies and values. Nor has there been any discussion at all in this context of how paying one's penalty might be given a cultural meaning and significance. With respect to the provisions of services, the Government, until recently, has failed to honour its commitment to provide *iwi* and cultural services.

Extending family group conferences

It would be a mistake to describe family group conferences as the rejection of a Western criminal justice system in favour of the adoption of an indigenous method of resolution. A distinction must be drawn between a system which attempts to re-establish the indigenous model of pre-European times and a system of justice which is culturally sensitive and appropriate. The new New Zealand system is an attempt to establish the latter, not to replicate the former. As such, it seeks to incorporate many of the features apparent in *whanau* decision-making processes and seen in meetings on *marae* today, but it also contains elements quite alien to indigenous models (for example, the presence of representatives of the state) and other principles which are equally important: the empowerment of families, offenders and victims. Although families and victims had a recognised role in the resolution of disputes in traditional Maori society, their part in the new system is not necessarily identical. However, at the very least, New Zealand's experience with family group conferences has shown that, to some extent, justice systems can be adapted to better meet the needs and demands of Maori.[14]

Maori sovereignty versus Maori self-determination

At the same time, none of these practices or suggestions goes far enough for the participants of our research on Maori justice since control remains located within the criminal justice system and not with Maori. Thus they *appear* to allow Maori communities to retake possession of their conflicts and to deal with their community members but in reality do not.

Current discussions about implementing Maori justice can, therefore, be seen simply as continuing the historical trend whereby whatever form Maori justice practices take is co-opted by the state. Jackson (1995, p.34) makes this point clear when he argues that 'justice for Maori does not mean the grafting of Maori processes upon a system that retains the authority to determine the extent, applicability, and validity of those processes.' In an earlier paper, Jackson also took issue with the idea of moving the court setting to the *marae*. He viewed such initiatives as having the potential to further alienate Maori and contended that merely transferring the alienating nature of the court setting to the *marae* 'runs the very real risk of ... making young Maori associate the injustice and dismissiveness of the court process with the *marae*. The emotional and cultural support of *marae* would clearly be undermined in this situation' (Jackson 1988, pp.237–8).

For control to be invested in Maori – which is what participants in the research wanted – the relationship between Maori and the state would require renegotiation and redefinition. The essential issue here is reflected in current debates surrounding Maori sovereignty – the perspective of many Maori – and Maori self-determination – the Government's perspective (Jackson, 1995; Oliver, 1995).[15]

Any discussion of the construction of a Maori justice system requires entering the ongoing debate on Maori sovereignty between sections of Maoridom and the Government (Wickliffe, 1995). For the Government to allow Maori the form of jurisdictional autonomy that some Maori argue for would mean a refocus on the part of the Government on the texts of the Treaty of Waitangi it uses for the purposes of Treaty interpretation. At present, the Government relies on the English version of the Treaty, within which the Crown was granted sovereignty. This, according to the Government, gives it the sole right to institute and control legal jurisdiction.

However, in the Maori language text, Maori were guaranteed '*tino rangatiratanga*' or 'absolute independence' and the Crown was granted only the limited power of *kawanatanga*, which roughly translates as governance (Kelsey, 1990). For some Maori, this was a recognition of the special status of the *tangata whenua* (people of the land). This recognition included an acknowledgement of the institutions central to Maori society, including their laws (Jackson, 1995). This, then, provides the basis for the call by some Maori for their right to deal with Maori offenders according to Maori processes of social control.

...

Conclusion

Some Maori activists argue that the practical implementation of Maori justice need not be a difficult task. The participants in our research on Maori justice were, as we noted, more cautious, as, indeed, are participants in other research (Ministry of Justice, 1995b). And there are good reasons to be cautious. It has to be recognised, for example, that at this point in time there remain a number of unresolved issues. For example, not all Maori or those of Maori descent may want to participate in a justice system that has its philosophical basis in Maori culture. Comments to this effect were made by participants in the research on youth justice in New Zealand carried out by Maxwell and Morris (1993).

What we would advocate is a reconciliation of Maori and Pakeha justice systems. In some ways, this process has already begun with the development of family group conferences. It seems a good time for this: New Zealand is beginning to move away from the Crown at a political level (for example, through the creation of its own Honours system) and at a legal level (for example, through the proposed removal of the right to appeal to the Privy Council). We need to shift debate from political and ideological rhetoric which in the end analysis serves well neither offenders nor victims (Maori or Pakeha) and to move towards examination and evaluation of the concrete alternative justice practices which many communities and agencies are already using. One of the participants summed up well this need for action:

> In the end we need to be realistic. We are heading towards the 21st century. Maori offending and recidivism are not being reduced and the Pakeha solution – sending our offenders to prison – is

obviously not working, the Pakeha system is a failure. So, just as with *kohanga reo* (language schools for young children) and *te reo*, Maoridom must look to itself for solutions.

Perhaps Pakeha too need to look to Maoridom for solutions.

Notes

1 For example, Australian Aboriginals and North American Indians in both Canada and the United States are over-represented. Indeed, the rate of imprisonment for some of these groups is significantly higher than for Maori (Fleras and Elliott, 1992).

2 Caution has to be exercised when interpreting police figures since one offender apprehended for 300 offences will be counted 300 times, but they are generally accepted as indicative of the characteristics of known offenders.

3 Maori are also over-represented in various indices of social and economic deprivation: high infant mortality rates, low life expectancy rates, high unemployment rates and low incomes (Ministerial Advisory Committee on a Maori Perspective for the Department of Social Welfare, 1986). There is evidence too that young Maori are more likely to come to police attention and to be arrested than young Pakeha in similar situations (Fergusson *et al.*, 1993; Maxwell and Morris, 1993). But understanding why Maori are now over-represented in official data is not the purpose of this paper.

4 There is now a growing focus on the needs and wishes of victims and in most countries in recent years there have been significant changes: the introduction of 'victim impact statements' in court proceedings, the provision of support services for victims and sentences which include reparation (payment of the cost of damage and/or stolen property). However, it remains rare for victims to participate in the sentencing process.

5 Carlen (1976) captures this well in her description of defendants as 'dummy players'. Research by Maxwell, Robertson and Morris (1993) in New Zealand makes clear that defendants there feel similarly excluded.

6 An example is provided by Aroha Terry's work with victims of sexual abuse in the Waikato.

7 This research was funded by the Legal Research Foundation and we appreciate their help with this. This part of the paper has also been published in McElrea (1995).

8 The *iwi* represented were Ngati Awa, Ngati Kahungunu, Ngati Pikiao, Ngati Porou, Ngati Raukawa, Ngati Tuwharetoa, Ngati Whakaue, Rongowhakaata, Taranaki, Te Atiawa, Tuhoe, and Whanau-a-Apanui.

9 The interviews were conducted between mid-January and May 1995. Many of the potential participants in this study were involved in various *hui* organised by the Government to discuss the settlement of Treaty of Waitangi claims.

10 Family group conferences apply not only to Maori but to all young offenders in New Zealand, including young offenders who have committed offences such as sexual violation and serious assault (except those charged with murder or manslaughter). The family group conference is made up of the young person, his or her advocate if one has been arranged (usually only arrest/court cases), members of the family and whoever they invite, the victim(s) or their representative, the police, the social worker if one has been involved with the family and the youth justice co-ordinator (the employee of the Department of Social Welfare responsible for managing the youth justice process). The family and those it invites are entitled to deliberate in private during the family group conference or can ask for the meeting to

be adjourned to enable discussions to continue elsewhere. Family group conferences can take place wherever the family wish, provided (since 1994) the victim agrees. Common venues include facilities of the Department of Social Welfare, the family's home, community rooms or *marae* (meeting houses). The jurisdiction of the family group conference is limited to the disposition of cases where the young person has not denied the alleged offences or has already been found guilty. The family group conference has responsibility to formulate a plan about how best to deal with the offending. The range of possibilities here are limitless (as long as they are agreed by the parties) but could include an apology, community work, reparation or involvement in some programme. The plans and decisions are binding when they have been agreed to by a family group conference, and, for court referred cases, accepted by the court.

11 Eighty-five per cent of the victims who did not attend a family group conference gave reasons which related to poor practice: they were not invited, the time was unsuitable for them or they were given inadequate notice of the family group conference.

12 Some victims stressed the value of expressing their feelings to the offender and of making sure that the offender learned from the experience. Other victims wanted to contribute to the offender's rehabilitation or to show their support for the process or for offenders of their cultural group. Yet other victims emphasised their own interests: they wanted to make sure things were done properly and to get reparation.

13 Morris and Maxwell (1997) found that the factor 'victim satisfaction' was least often reported for a sample of young people who had been involved in family group conferences but who had become persistent recidivists and regression analysis suggested that those young offenders who failed to apologise to victims were three times more likely to be reconvicted than those who had apologised.

14 There have now been suggestions that 'community group conferences' could be held for adult offenders at which offenders, victims and their 'communities of interest' could attempt to come to a decision about how best to deal with the offending and the hurt caused by it (McElrea, 1995).

15 There are other difficulties. For example, there has been little discussion of the entry point to a Maori justice system. Unless it is intended also to have a separate Maori police system (which seems unlikely and unworkable) there would have to be a close working relationship between a Maori justice system and the current criminal justice system – there is no other option.

References

Brennan, F. (1993) 'Self-determination: the limits of allowing Aboriginal communities to be a law unto themselves', *University of New South Wales Law Journal*, vol.16, pp.245–64.

Carlen, P. (1976) *Magistrates' Justice*, London, Martin Robertson.

Christie, N. (1977) 'Conflicts as property', *British Journal of Criminology*, vol.17, pp.1–15.

Consedine, J. (1995) *Restorative Justice: Healing the Effects of Crime*, Lyttelton, New Zealand, Ploughshares Publications.

Durie, E. (1995) 'Custom law', unpublished manuscript.

Fergusson, D., Horwood, L. and Lynskey, M. (1993) 'Ethnicity, social background and young offending: a 14-year longitudinal study', *Australian and New Zealand Journal of Criminology*, vol.26, pp.155–70.

Fitzpatrick, P. (1983) 'Law, plurality and underdevelopment', in Sugarman, D. (ed.) *Legality, Ideology and the State*, London, Academic Press.

Fleras, A. and Elliot, J. (1992) *The Nations Within: Aboriginal–State Relations in Canada, the USA and New Zealand*, Toronto, Oxford University Press.

Griffiths, A. (1986) 'The problem of informal justice: family dispute processing among the Bakevena – a case study', *International Journal of the Sociology of Law*, vol.14, pp.359–76.

Jackson, M. (1988) *Maori and the Criminal Justice System: He Whaipaanga Hou: A New Perspective Part 2*, Department of Justice, Wellington.

Jackson, M. (1995) 'Cultural justice: a colonial contradiction or a rangatiratanga reality?', in McElrea, F. (ed.), *op.cit.*

Kelsey, J. (1990) 'Economic libertarianism versus Maori self-determination: Aotearoa/New Zealand in crisis', *International Journal of the Sociology of Law*, vol.18, pp.239–58.

Maxwell, G. and Morris, A. (1993) *Family, Victims and Culture: Youth Justice in New Zealand*, Social Policy Agency and the Institute of Criminology, Wellington, Victoria University of Wellington.

Maxwell, G., Robertson, J. and Morris, A. (1993) 'Giving victims a voice: a New Zealand experiment', *The Howard Journal*, vol.32, pp.304–21.

McElrea, F. (1995) 'Accountability in the community: taking responsibility for offending', in McElrea, F. (ed.) *Rethinking Criminal Justice (vol.1): Justice in the Community*, Auckland, Legal Research Foundation.

Merry, S. (1992) 'Anthropology, law, and transnational processes', *Annual Review of Anthropology*, vol.21, pp.357–79.

Metge, J. (1977) *The Maori of New Zealand: Ruatahi,* revised edn, London, Routledge and Kegan Paul.

Ministerial Advisory Committee on a Maori Perspective for the Department of Social Welfare (1986) *Puao-te-ata-tu: (Daybreak). The Report of the Ministerial Advisory Committee on a Maori Perspective for the Department of Social Welfare*, Wellington, Department of Social Welfare.

Ministry of Justice (1995a) *Restorative Justice: A Discussion Paper*, Wellington, Ministry of Justice.

Ministry of Justice (1995b) *Public Attitudes towards Restorative Justice*, Wellington, Ministry of Justice.

Morris, A. and Tauri, J. (1995) 'Maori justice: possibilities and pitfalls, in McElrea, F. (ed.), *op.cit.*

New Zealand Labour Party (1996) *Labour on Whanau/Hapu Development*, Wellington, New Zealand Labour Party.

Oliver, B. (1995) 'Pandora's envelope: it's all about power', *New Zealand Books*, vol.5, pp.18–20.

Olsen, T., Maxwell, G. and Morris, A. (1995) 'Maori and youth justice in New Zealand', in Hazlehurst, K. (ed.) *Popular Justice and Community Regeneration: Pathways to Indigenous Reform*, Westport, Praeger.

Police National Headquarters (1996) Unpublished Police Statistics, Wellington, New Zealand.

Pratt, J. (1992) *Punishment in a Perfect Society: The New Zealand Penal System 1840–1939*, Wellington, Victoria University Press.

Statistics New Zealand (1996) *New Zealand Now: Crime Statistics*, Wellington, New Zealand.

Walker, R. (1975) *Nga Tau Tohetohe: Years of Anger*, Auckland, Penguin Books.

Ward, A. (1995) *A Show of Justice: Racial 'Amalgamation' in Nineteenth Century New Zealand*, 2nd edn, Auckland, Auckland University Press.

Wickliffe, C. (1995) 'A Maori criminal justice system' in McElrea, F. (ed.), *op.cit.*

CHAPTER 5

Restorative Justice and a Better Future

by John Braithwaite

I want you to imagine two robbers. First, a teenager is arrested in Halifax for a robbery. The police send him to court where he is sentenced to six months incarceration. As a victim of child abuse, he is both angry with the world and alienated from it. During his period of confinement he acquires a heroin habit and suffers more violence. He comes out more desperate and alienated than when he went in, sustains his drug habit for the next twenty years by stealing cars, burgles dozens of houses and pushes drugs to others until he dies in a gutter, a death no one mourns. Probably someone rather like that was arrested in Halifax today, perhaps more than one.

Tomorrow, another teenager, Sam, is arrested in Halifax for a robbery. He is a composite of several Sams I have seen. The police officer refers Sam to a facilitator who convenes a restorative justice conference. When the facilitator asks about his parents, Sam says he is homeless. His parents abused him and he hates them. Sam refuses to cooperate with a conference if they attend. After talking with the parents, the facilitator agrees that perhaps it is best not to involve the parents. What about grandparents? No, they are dead. Brothers and sisters? No, he hates his brothers too. Sam's older sister, who was always kind to him, has since left home. He has no contact with her. Aunts and uncles? Not keen on them either, because they would always put him down as the black sheep of the family and stand by his parents. Uncle George was the only one he ever had any time for, but he has not seen him for years. Teachers from school? Hates them all. Sam has dropped out. They always treat him like dirt. The facilitator does not give up: 'No one ever treated you okay at school?' Well, the hockey coach is the only one Sam can ever think of being fair to him. So the hockey coach, Uncle George and older sister are tracked down by the facilitator and invited to the conference along with the robbery victim and her daughter, who comes along to support the victim through the ordeal.

These six participants sit on chairs in a circle. The facilitator starts by introducing everyone and reminding Sam that while he has admitted to the robbery, he can change his plea at any time during the conference and have the matter heard by a court. Sam is asked to explain what happened in his own words. He mumbles that he needed money to survive, saw the lady, knocked her over and ran off with her purse. Uncle George is asked what he thinks of this. He says that Sam used to be a good kid. But Sam had gone off the rails. He had let his parents down so badly that they would not even come today. 'And now you have done this to this poor lady. I never thought you would stoop to violence,' continues Uncle George, building into an angry tirade against the boy. The hockey coach also says he is surprised that Sam could do something as terrible as this. Sam was always a troublemaker at school. But he could see a kindly side in Sam that left him shocked about the violence. The sister is invited to enter the conversation, but the facilitator moves on to the victim when Sam's sister seems too emotional to speak.

The victim explains how much trouble she had to cancel the credit cards in the purse, how she had no money for the shopping she needed to do that day. Her daughter explains that the most important consequence of the crime was that her mother is now afraid to go out on her own. In particular, she is afraid that Sam is stalking her, waiting to rob her again. Sam sneers

Source: *The Dalhousie Review* (1997) vol.76, no.1, pp.9–31.

at this and seems callous throughout. His sister starts to sob. Concerned about how distressed she is, the facilitator calls a brief adjournment so she can comfort her, with help from Uncle George. During the break, the sister reveals that she understands what Sam has been through. She says she was abused by their parents as well. Uncle George has never heard of this, is shocked, and not sure that he believes it.

When the conference reconvenes, Sam's sister speaks to him with love and strength. Looking straight into his eyes, the first gaze he could not avoid in the conference, she says that she knows exactly what he has been through with their parents. No details are spoken. But the victim seems to understand what is spoken of by the knowing communication between sister and brother. Tears rush down the old woman's cheeks and over a trembling mouth.

It is his sister's love that penetrates Sam's callous exterior. From then on he is emotionally engaged with the conference. He says he is sorry about what the victim has lost. He would like to pay it back, but has no money or job. He assures the victim he is not stalking her. She readily accepts this now and when questioned by the facilitator says now she thinks she will feel safe walking out alone. She wants her money back but says it will help her if they can talk about what to do to help Sam find a home and a job. Sam's sister says he can come and live in her house for a while. The hockey coach says he has some casual work that needs to be done, enough to pay Sam's debt to the victim and a bit more. If Sam does a good job, he will write him a reference for applications for permanent jobs. When the conference breaks up, the victim hugs Sam and tearfully wishes him good luck. He apologizes again. Uncle George quietly slips a hundred dollars to Sam's sister to defray the extra cost of having Sam in the house, and says he will be there for both of them if they need him.

Sam has a rocky life punctuated by several periods of unemployment. A year later he has to go through another conference after he steals a bicycle. But he finds work when he can, mostly stays out of trouble and lives to mourn at the funerals of Uncle George and his sister. The victim gets her money back and enjoys taking long walks alone. Both she and her daughter say that they feel enriched as a result of the conference, have a little more grace in their lives. I will return to the meanings of this story.

Institutional collapse

Few sets of institutional arrangements created in the West since the industrial revolution have been as large a failure as the criminal justice system. In theory it administers just, proportionate corrections that deter. In practice, it fails to correct or deter, just as often making things worse as better. It is a criminal *injustice* system that systematically turns a blind eye to crimes of the powerful, while imprisonment remains the best-funded labour market program for the unemployed and indigenous peoples. It pretends to be equitable, yet one offender may be sentenced to a year in a prison where he will be beaten on reception and then systematically bashed thereafter, raped, even infected with AIDS, while others serve twelve months in comparatively decent premises, especially if they are white-collar criminals. While I do believe that Canada's criminal justice system is more decent than ours in Australia, all western criminal justice systems are brutal, institutionally vengeful, and dishonest to their stated intentions. The interesting question is why are they such failures. Given that prisons are vicious and degrading places, you would expect fear of ending up in them would deter crime.

There are many reasons for the failures of the criminal justice system to prevent crime. I will give you just one, articulated in the terms of my theory in *Crime, Shame and Reintegration.*[1] The claim of this theory is that the societies that have the lowest crime rates are the societies that shame criminal conduct most effectively. There is an important difference between reintegrative shaming and stigmatization. While reintegrative shaming prevents crime, stigmatization is a kind of shaming that makes crime problems worse. Stigmatization is a kind of shaming that creates outcasts; it is disrespectful, humiliating. Stigmatization means treating criminals as evil people who have done evil acts. Reintegrative shaming means disapproving of the evil of the deed while treating the person as essentially good. Reintegrative shaming means strong disapproval of the act but doing so in a way that is respecting of the person. Once we understand this distinction, we can see why putting more police on the street can actually increase crime. More police can increase crime if they are systematically stigmatizing in the way they deal with citizens. More police can reduce crime if they are systematically reintegrative in the way they deal with citizens.

We can also understand why building more prisons could make the crime problem worse. Having more people in prison does deter some and incapacitates others from committing certain crimes, like bank robberies, because there are no banks inside the prison for them to rob, though there certainly are plenty of vulnerable people to rape and pillage. But because prisons stigmatize, they also make things worse for those who have criminal identities affirmed by imprisonment, those whose stigmatization leads them to find solace in the society of the similarly outcast, those who are attracted into criminal subcultures, those who treat the prison as an educational institution for learning new skills for the illegitimate labour market. On this account, whether building more prisons reduces or increases the crime rate depends on whether the stigmatizing nature of a particular prison system does more to increase crime than its deterrent and incapacitative effects reduce it.

A lack of theoretical imagination among criminologists has been one underrated reason for the failure of the criminal justice system. Without theorizing why it fails, the debate has collapsed to a contest between those who want more of the same to make it work and those who advance the implausible position that it makes sense to stigmatize people first and later subject them to rehabilitation programs inside institutions. With juvenile justice in particular, the debate throughout the century has see-sawed between the justice model and the welfare model. See-sawing between retribution and rehabilitation has got us nowhere. If we are serious about a better future, we need to hop off this see-saw and strike out in search of a third model.

For me, that third model is restorative justice. …

It has become the slogan of a global social movement. For those of us who see constructive engagement with social movement politics as crucial for major change, labels that carry meaning for activists matter. In this spirit, I now wish that I had called reintegrative shaming, restorative shaming.

What is restorative justice?

Restorative justice means restoring victims, a more victim-centred criminal justice system, as well as restoring offenders and restoring community. First, what does restoring victims mean? It means restoring the *property lost* or the *personal injury*, repairing the broken window or the broken teeth. It means restoring a *sense of security*. Even victims of property crimes such as burglary often suffer a loss of security when the private space of their home is violated. When the criminal justice system fails to leave women secure about walking alone at night, half the population is left unfree in a rather fundamental sense.

Victims suffer loss of dignity when someone violates their bodies or shows them the disrespect of taking things which are precious to them. Sometimes this disrespectful treatment engenders victim shame: 'He abused me rather than some other woman because I am trash,' 'She stole my dad's car because I was irresponsible to park it in such a risky place.' Victim shame often triggers a shame-rage spiral wherein victims reciprocate indignity through vengeance or by their own criminal acts.

Disempowerment is part of the indignity of being a victim of crime. According to Pettit and Braithwaite's republican theory of criminal justice,[2] a wrong should not be defined as a crime unless it involves some domination of us that reduces our freedom to enjoy life as we choose. It follows that it is important to *restore any lost sense of empowerment* as a result of crime. This is particularly important where the victim suffers structurally systematic domination. For example, some of the most important restorative justice initiatives we have seen in Australia have involved some thousands of Aboriginal victims of consumer fraud by major insurance companies.[3] In these cases, victims from remote

Aboriginal communities relished the power of being able to demand restoration and corporate reform from 'white men in white shirts.'

The way that western legal systems handle crime compounds the disempowerment that victims feel, first at the hands of offenders and then at the hands of a professional, remote justice system that eschews their participation. The lawyers, in the words of Nils Christie, 'steal our conflict.'[4] The western criminal justice system has, on balance, been corrosive of deliberate democracy, though the jury is one institution that has preserved a modicum of it. Restorative justice is deliberative justice; it is about people deliberating over the consequences of a crime, how to deal with them and prevent their recurrence. This contrasts with the professional justice of lawyers deciding which rules apply to a case and then constraining their deliberation within a technical discourse about that rule-application. So restorative justice restores the *deliberative control of justice by citizens.*

Restorative justice aims to *restore harmony based on a feeling that justice has been done.* Restoring harmony alone, while leaving an underlying injustice to fester unaddressed, is not enough. 'Restoring balance' is only acceptable as a restorative justice ideal if the 'balance' between offender and victim that prevailed before the crime was a morally decent balance. There is no virtue in restoring the balance by having a woman pay for a loaf of bread she has stolen from a rich man to feed her children. Restoring harmony between victim and offender is only likely to be possible in such a context on the basis of a discussion of why the children are hungry and what should be done about the underlying injustice of their hunger.

Restorative justice cannot resolve the deep structural injustices that cause problems like hunger. But we must demand two things of restorative justice here. First, it must not make structural injustice worse (in the way, for example, that the Australian criminal justice system does by being an important cause of the unemployability and oppression of Aboriginal people). Indeed, we should hope from restorative justice for micro-measures that ameliorate macro-injustice where this is possible. Second, restorative justice should restore harmony with a remedy grounded in dialogue which takes account of underlying injustices. Restorative justice does not resolve the age-old questions of what should count as unjust outcomes. It is a more modest philosophy than that. It settles for the procedural requirement that the parties talk until they feel that harmony has been restored on the basis of a discussion of all the injustices they see as relevant to the case.

Finally, restorative justice aims to *restore social support.* Victims of crime need support from their loved ones during the process of requesting restoration. They sometimes need encouragement and support to engage with deliberation toward restoring harmony. Friends sometimes do blame the victim, or more commonly are frightened off by a victim going through an emotional trauma. Restorative justice aims to institutionalize the gathering around of friends during a time of crisis.

Restoring offenders, restoring community

In most cases, a more limited range of types of restoration is relevant to offenders. Offenders have generally not suffered property loss or injury as a result of their own crime, though sometimes loss or injury is a cause of the crime. Dignity, however, is generally in need of repair after the shame associated with arrest. When there is a victim who has been hurt, there is no dignity in denying that there is something to be ashamed about. Dignity is generally best restored by confronting the shame, accepting responsibility for the bad consequences suffered by the victim and apologizing with sincerity.[5] A task of restorative justice is to institutionalize such *restoration of dignity* for offenders.

The sense of insecurity and disempowerment of offenders is often an issue in their offending, and in discussion about what is to be done to prevent further offending. Violence by young men from racial minorities is sometimes connected to their feelings of being victims of racism. For offenders, *restoring a sense of security and empowerment* is often bound up with employment, the feeling of having a future, achieving some educational success, sporting success, indeed any kind of success.

Many patches are needed to sew the quilt of deliberative democracy. Criminal justice deliberation is not as important a patch as deliberation in the parliament, in trade unions, even in universities. But to the extent that restorative justice deliberation does lead ordinary citizens into serious democratic discussion about racism, unemployment, masculinist cultures in local schools and police accountability, it is not an unimportant element of a deliberatively rich democracy.

The mediation literature shows that satisfaction of complainants with the justice of the mediation is less important than the satisfaction of those who are complained against in achieving mutually beneficial outcomes.[6] Criminal subcultures are memory files that collect injustices.[7] Crime problems will continue to become deeply culturally embedded in western societies until we reinvent criminal justice as a process that restores a sense of procedural justice to offenders.[8]

Finally, Francis T. Cullen has suggested that there could be no better organizing concept for criminology than *social support*, given the large volume of evidence about the importance of social support for preventing crime.[9] The New Zealand Maori people see our justice system as barbaric because it requires the defendant to stand alone in the dock without social support. In Maori thinking, civilized justice requires the offender's loved ones to stand beside him during justice rituals, sharing the shame for what has happened. Hence the shame the offender feels is more the shame of letting his loved ones down than a western sense of individual guilt. The shame of letting loved ones down can be readily transcended by simple acts of forgiveness from those loved ones.

Restoring community is advanced by a proliferation of restorative justice rituals in which social support around specific victims and offenders is restored. At this micro level, restorative justice is an utterly bottom-up approach to restoring community. At a meso level, important elements of a restorative justice package are initiatives to foster community organization in schools, neighbourhoods, ethnic communities, churches, through professions and other NGOs who can deploy restorative justice in their self-regulatory practices. At a macro level, we must better design institutions of deliberative democracy so that concern about issues like unemployment and the effectiveness of labour market programs have a channel through which they can flow from discussions about local injustices up into national economic policy-making debate.

The universality of restorative traditions

I have yet to discover a culture which does not have some deep-seated restorative traditions. Nor is there a culture without retributive traditions. Retributive traditions once had survival value. Cultures which were timid in fighting back were often wiped out by more determinedly violent cultures. In the contemporary world, as opposed to the world of our biological creation, retributive emotions have less survival value. Because risk management is institutionalized in this modern world, retributive emotions are more likely to get us into trouble than out of it, as individuals, groups and nations.

The message we might communicate to all cultures is that, in the world of the twenty-first century, you will find restorative traditions a more valuable resource than retributive traditions. Yet sadly, the hegemonic cultural forces in the contemporary world communicate just the opposite message. Hollywood hammers the message that the way to deal with bad guys is through violence. Political leaders frequently hammer the same message. Yet many of our spiritual leaders are helping us to retrieve our restorative traditions – the Dalai Lama, for example. Archbishop Desmond Tutu, in his Foreword to Jim Consedine's forthcoming new edition of *Restorative Justice*, correctly sees a 'very ancient yet desperately needed truth' as underlying restorative justice processes, 'rooted as they are in all indigenous cultures, including those of Africa.' He sees his Truth and Reconciliation Commission as an example of restorative justice.

The restorative values I have been describing are cultural universals. All cultures value repair of damage to our persons and property, security, dignity, empowerment, deliberative democracy, harmony based on a sense of justice and social support. They are universals because they are all vital to our emotional survival as human beings and vital to the possibility of surviving without constant fear of violence. The world's great religions recognize that the desire to pursue these restorative justice values is universal, which is why some of our spiritual leaders are a hope against those political leaders who wish to rule through fear and by crushing deliberative democracy. Ultimately, those political leaders will find that they will have to reach an accommodation with the growing social movement for restorative justice, just as they must with the great religious movements they confront. Why? Because the evidence is now strong that ordinary citizens like restorative justice.[10] When the major political parties did their door-knocking during our last election in Canberra, they found that the thousands of citizens who had participated in a restorative justice conference mostly liked the justice they experienced.

It is true that the virtues restorative justice restores are viewed differently in different cultures and that opinion about the culturally appropriate ways of realizing them differ greatly. Hence, restorative justice must be a culturally diverse social movement that accommodates a rich plurality of strategies in pursuit of the truths it holds to be universal. It is about different cultures joining hands as they discover the profound commonalities of their experience of the human condition; it is about realizing the value of diversity, of preserving restorative traditions that work because they are embedded in a cultural past. Scientific criminology will never discover any universally best way of doing restorative justice. The best path is the path of cultural plurality in pursuit of culturally shared restorative values.

A path to culturally plural justice

A restorative research agenda to pursue this path has two elements:

1. Culturally-specific investigation of how to save and revive the restorative justice practices that remain in all societies.
2. Culturally-specific investigation of how to transform state criminal justice both by making it more restorative and by rendering its abuses of power more vulnerable to restorative justice.

On the first point, I doubt that neighbourhoods in our cities are replete with restorative justice practices that can be retrieved, though there are some. Yet in the more micro context of the nuclear family, the evidence is overwhelming from the metropolitan US that restorative justice is alive and well and that families who are more restorative are likely to have less delinquent children than families who are punitive and stigmatizing.[11]

Because families so often slip into stigmatization and brutalization of their difficult members, we need restorative justice institutionalized in a wider context that can engage and restore such families. In most societies, the wider contexts where the ethos and rituals of restorative justice are alive and ready to be piped into the wider streams of society are schools, churches and remote indigenous communities. If it is hard to find restorative justice in the disputing practices of our urban neighbourhoods, the experience of recent years has been that they are relatively easy to locate in urban schools.[12] This is because of the ethos of care and integration which is part of the western educational ideal (which, at its best, involves a total rejection of stigmatization) and because the interaction among the members of a school community tends to be more intense than the interaction among urban neighbours. Schools, like families, have actually become more restorative and less retributive than the brutal institutions of the nineteenth century. This is why we have seen very successful restorative conferencing programs in contemporary schools.[13] We have also seen anti-bullying programs with what I would call a restorative ethos which have managed in some cases to halve bullying in schools.[14]

More of the momentum for the restorative justice movement has come from the world's churches than from any other quarter. Even in a nation like Indonesia where the state has such tyrannical power, the political imperative to allow some separation of church and state has left churches as enclaves where restorative traditions could survive. Religions like Islam and Christianity have strong retributive traditions as well, of course, though they have mostly been happy to leave it to the state to do the 'dirty work' of temporal retribution.

When I spoke at a conference on restorative justice in Indonesia, I was struck in a conversation with three Indonesians – one Muslim, one Hindu and one Christian – that in ways I could not understand as an agnostic, each was drawing on a spirituality grounded in their religious experience to make sense of restorative justice. Similarly, I was moved by the spirituality of Cree approaches to restorative justice when a number of Native Canadians visited Canberra this year. There is something important to learn about native North-American spirituality and how it enriches restorative justice.

Your Canadian indigenous communities are a cultural resource for the whole world. Because they have not been totally swamped by the justice codes of the West, they are a cultural resource, just as the biodiversity of your continent supplies the entire world a genetic resource. The very people who by virtue of their remoteness have succumbed least to the western justice model, who have been insulated from Hollywood a little more and for a little longer, the very people who are most backward in western eyes, are precisely those with the richest cultural resources from which the restorative justice movement can learn.

Important scholarly work is being done to unlock the cultural codes of restorative justice in your indigenous communities. 'Healing circles', what a profound cultural code that is to unlock for the rest of the world.[15] How much we all have to learn from the experience of the Hollow Water community in dealing with an epidemic of child abuse through healing circles. Thérèse Lajeunesse's report on Hollow Water is already a wonderful resource for the world.[16] Joan Pennell and Gale Burford[17] have done a splendid job in their reports which document the conferences for dealing with family violence in Newfoundland, which are quite distinctive from, and doubtless superior to, the conferencing models we have applied in the southern hemisphere. I have already remonstrated with them about the need to pull all this illuminating research together into a book that can also have a massive effect internationally, as could a book on Hollow Water. So point one of the reform agenda of restorative justice is a research program to retrieve the restorative justice practices of not only native communities, but also of the schools and churches of dominant urban cultures. Scholars like Carol LaPrairie and Don Clairmont are among the Canadian scholars who are doing vital work in advancing point one of this agenda.

Point two of the agenda is to explore how to transform state criminal justice. In our multicultural cities I have said that we cannot rely on spontaneous ordering of justice in our neighbourhoods. There we must be more reliant on state reformers as catalysts of a new urban restorative justice. In our cities, where neighbourhood social support is least, where the loss from the statist takeover of disputing is most damaging, the gains that can be secured from restorative justice reform are greatest. When a police officer with a restorative justice ethos arrests a youth in a tightly knit rural community who lives in a loving family, who enjoys social support from a caring school and church, that police officer is not likely to do much better or worse by the child than a police officer who does not have a restorative justice ethos. What ever the police do, the child's support network will probably sort the problem out so that serious reoffending does not occur. But when a metropolitan police officer with a restorative justice ethos arrests a homeless child like Sam, who hates parents who abused him, who has dropped out of school and is seemingly alone in the world, it is there that the restorative police officer can make a difference that will render him more effective in preventing crime than the retributive police officer. At least that is my hypothesis, one we can test empirically and are testing empirically.

In the alienated urban context where community is not spontaneously emergent in a satisfactory way, a criminal justice system aimed at restoration can construct a community of care around a specific offender or a specific victim who is in trouble. That is what the story of Sam is about. With the restorative justice conferences being convened in multicultural metropolises like Auckland, Adelaide, Sydney and Singapore, the selection principle as to who is invited to the conference is the opposite to that with a criminal trial. We invite to a criminal trial those who can inflict most damage on the other side. With a conference we invite those who might offer most support to their own side – Sam's sister, uncle and hockey coach, the victim's daughter.

In terms of the theory of reintegrative shaming, the rationale for who is invited to the conference is that the presence of supporters on the victim's side structures shame into the conference, the presence of supporters on the offender's side structures reintegration into the ritual. Conferences can be run in many different ways from the story of Sam's conference. Maori people in New Zealand tend to want to open and close their conferences with a prayer. The institutions of restorative justice we build in the city must be culturally plural, quite different from one community to another depending on the culture of the people involved. It is the empowerment principle of restorative justice that makes this possible – empowerment with process control.

From a restorative perspective, the important thing is that we have institutions in civil society which confront serious problems like violence rather than sweep them under the carpet, yet do so in a way that is neither retributive nor stigmatizing. Violence will not be effectively controlled by communities unless the shamefulness of violence is communicated. This does not mean that we need criminal justice institutions that set out to maximize shame. On the contrary, if we set out to do that we risk the creation of stigmatizing institutions.[18] All we need to do is nurture micro-institutions of deliberative democracy that allow citizens to discuss the consequences of criminal acts, who is responsible, who should put them right and how. Such deliberative processes naturally enable those responsible to confront and deal with the shame arising from what has happened. And if we get the invitation list right by inviting along people who enjoy maximum respect and trust on both the offender and victim side, then we maximize the chances that shame will be dealt with in a reintegrative way.

Decline and revival in restorative traditions

The traditions of restorative justice that can be found in all the world's great cultures have been under attack during the past two centuries. Everywhere in the world, restorative ideals have suffered serious setbacks because of the globalization of the idea of a centralized state that takes central control of justice and rationalizes it into a punitive regime. Control of punishment strengthened the power and legitimacy of rulers.[19] So did control of mercy, the power of royal or presidential pardon. What rulers really wanted was the political power of controlling the police, the prisons and the courts. Yet abuse of that power proved at times such a threat to their legitimacy that they were forced by political opponents to institutionalize certain principles of fairness and consistency into the state system. Of course, the new democratic rulers were no more enthusiastic about returning justice to the people than were the tyrants they succeeded; the secret police continued to be important to combating organized threats to the state monopoly of violence, the regular police to disorganized threats. The pretence that the state punished crime in a consistent, politically even-handed way was part of the legitimation for democratically centralized justice. Citizens continue to see this as a pretence. They realize that whatever the law says, the reality is one law for the rich, another for the poor; one set of rules for the politically connected, another for the powerless. Philip Pettit and I have sought to show that proportionality in practice is proportional punishment for the poor and impunity for the white-collar criminals.[20] Restorative justice, we contend, has a better chance of being made equitably available to rich and poor than just deserts.

While it is a myth that centralized state law enabled greater consistency and lesser partiality than community-based restorative justice, it is true that abuse of power always was and still is common in community justice, as Carol La Prairie's work shows for Canada.[21] And it is true that state oversight of restorative justice in the community can be a check on abuse of rights in local programs, local political dominations and those types of unequal treatment in local programs that are flagrantly unacceptable.[22] Equally it is true that restorative justice can be a check on abuse of rights by the central state. We see it in restorative justice conferences in Canberra when a mother asks during the conference that something be done about the police officers who continue to use excessive force in their dealings with her son, who continue to victimize her son for things done by others. The restorative justice ideal could not and should not be the romantic notion of shifting back to a world where state justice is replaced by local justice. Rather, it might be to use the existence of state traditions of rights, proportionality and rule of law as resources to check abuse of power in local justice and to use the revival of restorative traditions to check abuse of state power. In other words, restorative justice constitutionalized by the state can be the stuff of a republic with a richer separation of powers,[23] with less abuse of power, than could be obtained either under dispute resolution totally controlled by local politics or disputing totally dominated by the state.

The key elements of North Atlantic criminal justice that have globalized almost totally during the past two centuries are:

1 Central state control of criminal justice;

2 The idea of crime itself and that criminal law should be codified;

3 The idea that crimes are committed against the state (rather than the older ideas that they were committed against victims or God);

4 The idea of having a professionalized police who are granted a monopoly over the use of force in domestic conflicts;

5 The idea of moving away from compensation as the dominant way of dealing with crime by building a state prisons system to systematically segregate the good from the bad;

6 The idea that fundamental human rights should be protected during the criminal process.

Like abolitionists,[24] restorative justice theorists see most of these elements of the central state takeover of criminal justice as retrograde. However, unlike the most radical versions of abolitionism, restorative justice sees promise in preserving a state role as a watchdog of rights and concedes that for a tiny fraction of the people in our prisons it may actually be necessary to protect the community from them by incarceration. While restorative justice means treating many things we presently treat as crime simply as problems of living, restorative justice does not mean abolishing the concept of crime. In restorative justice rituals, being able to call wrongdoing a crime can be a powerful resource in persuading citizens to take responsibility, to pay compensation, to apologize, especially with corporate criminals who are not used to thinking of their exploitative conduct in that way.[25] Restorative justice does not mean abolishing the key elements of the state criminal justice system that has globalized so totally this century; it means shifting power from them to civil society, keeping key elements of the statist revolution but shifting power away from central institutions and checking the power that remains by the deliberative democracy from below that restorative justice enables.

So you see I have an analysis that is unfashionably universal. I believe that restorative justice will come to be a profoundly influential social movement throughout the world during the next century, first because it appeals to values that are shared universally by humanity, secondly because it responds to the defects of a centralized state criminal justice model that itself has totally globalized and utterly failed in every country where it gained the ascendancy. Everywhere it has failed, there are criminologists or lawyers within the state itself who are convinced of that failure. And given the global imperatives for states to be competitive by being fiscally frugal, large state expenditures that do not deliver on their objectives are vulnerable to social movements that claim they have an approach which will be cheaper, work better and be more popular with the people in the long run. Hence we should not be surprised at the irony that some of the most savvy conservative governments in the world, who are most imbued with the imperatives for fiscal frugality, like New Zealand and Singapore, are early-movers in embracing the restorative justice movement against the grain of their traditional commitment to state punitiveness. In August of 1996, we even saw a US Assistant Attorney-General espousing a need to reinvent justice as restorative justice.

While I am cautiously optimistic that the empirical evidence will continue to be encouraging about the efficacy and decency of restorative justice compared with retributive justice, the evidence is also clear that restorative justice often fails. Victims sometimes resent the time involved in deliberation; sometimes they experience heightened fear from meeting offenders; sometimes they are extremely vengeful, though more often I am moved by how forgiving they are when genuinely empowered with process control. We need quality research on when and why restorative justice fails and how to cover the weaknesses of restorative justice with complementary strengths of deterrence and incapaciation.[26]

Beyond communitarianism versus individualism

Some criminologists in the West are critical of countries like Singapore, Indonesia and Japan, where crime in the streets is not a major problem, because they think individualism in these societies is crushed by communitarianism or collective obligation. Their prescription is that Asian societies need to shift the balance away from communitarianism and allow greater individualism. I don't find that a very attractive analysis.

Some Asian criminologists are critical of countries like the US and Australia because they think these societies are excessively individualistic, suffering much crime and incivility as a result. According to this analysis, the West needs to shift the balance away from individualism in favour of communitarianism, shift the balance away from rights and toward collective responsibilities. I don't find this a very attractive analysis either.

Both sides of this debate can do a better job of learning from each other. We can aspire to a society that is strong on rights and strong on responsibilities, that nurtures strong communities and strong individuals. Indeed, in the good society strong communities constitute strong individuals and vice versa. Our objective can be to keep the benefits of the statist revolution at the same time as we rediscover community-based justice. Community justice is often oppressive of rights, often subjects the vulnerable to the domination of local elites, subordinates women, can be procedurally unfair and tends to neglect structural solutions. Mindful of this, we might reframe the two challenges posed earlier in the paper:

1 Helping indigenous community justice to learn from the virtues of liberal statism – procedural fairness, rights, protecting the vulnerable from domination.

2 Helping liberal state justice to learn from indigenous community justice – learning the restorative community alternatives to individualism.

This reframed agenda resonates with the writing of Canadians such as Donald Clairmont[27] and Marianne Nielsen, who writes that native communities 'will have the opportunity of taking the best of the old, the best of the new and learning from others' mistakes so that they can design a system that may well turn into a flagship of social change.'[28] Together these two questions ask how we save and revive traditional restorative justice practices in a way that helps them become procedurally fairer, in a way that respects fundamental human rights, that secures protection against domination. The liberal state can be a check on oppressive collectivism, just as bottom-up communitarianism can be a check on oppressive individualism. A healing circle can be a corrective to a justice system that can leave offenders and victims suicidally alone; a Charter of Rights and Freedoms a check on a tribal elder who imposes a violent tyranny on young people. The bringing together of these ideals is an old prescription – not just liberty, not just community, but liberté, égalité, fraternité. Competitive individualism has badly fractured this republican amalgam. The social movement for restorative justice does practical work to weld an amalgam that is relevant to the creation of contemporary urban multicultural republics. Day-to-day it is not sustained by romantic ideals in which I happen to believe, like deliberative democracy. They want to do it for Sam and for an old woman whom Sam pushed over one day. That is what enlists them to the social movement for restorative justice; in the process they are, I submit, enlisted into something of wider political significance.

Notes

1 John Braithwaite (1989) *Crime, Shame and Reintegration*, Cambridge, Cambridge UP.

2 Pettit and Braithwaite (1990) *Not Just Deserts: A Republican Theory of Criminal Justice.*

3 See Brent Fisse and John Braithwaite (1993) *Corporations, Crime and Accountability*, Cambridge, Cambridge UP, pp.218–23.

4 Nils Christie (1978) 'Conflicts as property', *British Journal of Criminology*, no.17, pp.1–15.

5 On this issue, especially the question of by-passed shame, see Tom Scheff and Suzanne Retzinger (1991) *Emotions and Violence: Shame and Rage in Destructive Conflicts*, Lexington, Lexington Books.

6 Dean G. Puritt (1995) 'Research report: process and outcome in community mediation', *Negotiation Journal*, Oct., p.374.

7 David Matza (1964) *Delinquency and Drift*, New York, Wiley, p.102.

8 Tom Tyler (1990) *Why People Obey the Law*, New Haven, Yale UP.

9 Francis T. Cullen (1994) 'Social support as an organizing concept for criminology: presidential address to the Academy of Criminal Justice Sciences', *Justice Quarterly*, vol.11, no.4, pp.527–9.

10 See, for example, Allison Morris and Gabrielle Maxwell (1992) 'Juvenile justice in New Zealand: a new paradigm', *Australia and New Zealand Journal of Criminology*, no.26, pp.72–90; Mary Hyndman, Margaret Thorsborne and Shirley Wood (1996) *Community Accountability Conferencing: Trial Report*, Department of Education, Queensland; Tim Goodes, 'Victims and Family Conferences: Juvenile Justice in South Australia,' unpublished paper; David Moore with Lubica Forsaythe (1995) *A New Approach to Juvenile Justice: An Evaluation of Family Conferencing in Wagga Wagga: A Report to the Criminology Research Council*, Wagga Wagga, The Centre for Rural Social Research, 1995; Donald Clairmont (1994) 'Alternative justice issues for Aboriginal justice', unpublished paper, Atlantic Institute of Criminology, Nov.

11 See the discussion of the evidence on this in Braithwaite, *Crime, Shame and Reintegration*, pp.54–83.

12 Mary Hyndman, Margaret Thorsborne and Shirley Wood, *op. cit.*

13 *Ibid.*

14 Dan Olweus (1994) 'Annotation: bullying at school: basic facts and effects of a school based intervention program', *Journal of Child Psychology and Psychiatry*, no.35, pp.1171–90; David P. Farrington (1993) 'Understanding and preventing bullying', in Tonry, M. (ed.) *Crime and Justice: Annual Review of Research*, vol.17, Chicago, University of Chicago Press; John Pitts and Philip Smith (1995) *Preventing School Bullying*, Police Research Group, Crime Detection and Prevention Series Paper 63, London, Home Office; Debra J. Pepler, Wendy Craig, Suzanne Ziegler, and Alice Charach (1993) 'A school-based antibullying intervention', in Tattum, D. (ed.), *Understanding and Managing Bullying*, London: Heinemann.

15 A.P. Melton (1995) 'Indigenous justice systems and tribal society', *Judicature*, vol.79, no.3, pp.126–33; Four Worlds Development Project (1984) *The Sacred Tree*, Alberta, Four Worlds Development Press.

16 Thérèse Lajeunesse (1993) *Community Holistic Circle Healing: Hollow Water First Nation*, Solicitor General, Ministry Secretariat.

17 Gale Burford and Joan Pennell (1995) *Family Group Decision Making: New Roles for 'Old' Partners in Resolving Family Violence*, St John's, Memorial University of Newfoundland; Joan Pennell and Gale Burford (1994) 'Attending to context: family group decision making in Canada', in Hudson, J. *et al.* (eds) *Family Group Conferences: Perspectives on Policy and Practice*, Monsey, NY, Criminal Justice Press; Joan Pennell and Gale Burford, 'Widening the circle: family group decision making' *Journal of Child and Youth Care*, vol.9, no.1, pp.1–11; Gale Burford and Joan Pennell (forthcoming) 'Family group decision making: an innovation in child and family welfare', in Galaway, B. and Hudson, J. (eds) *Child Welfare Systems: Canadian Research and Policy Implications.*

18 Suzanne Retzinger and Tom Scheff (1996) 'Strategy for community conferences: emotions and social bonds', in Galaway, B. and Hudson, J. (eds) *Restorative Justice: International* Perspectives, Monsey, NY, Criminal Justice Press.

19 See, for example, Michel Foucault (1977) *Discipline and Punish: The Birth of the Prison*, trans. Alan Sheridan, London, Allen Lane.

20 *Not Just Deserts: A Republican Theory of Criminal Justice*, ch. 9.

21 Carol La Prairie (1993), 'Community justice or just communities: Aboriginal communities in search of justice'.

22 Jeremy Webber makes this point in the Canadian context: 'the challenge is to reinvent aboriginal institutions so that they draw upon indigenous traditions and insights in a manner appropriate to the new situation. This may mean inventing checks to prevent abuse that were unnecessary two hundred years ago or which existed in a very different form.' See 'Individuality, equality and difference: justification for a parallel system of Aboriginal justice', in Silverman, R. and Nielsen, M. (1992) (eds) *Aboriginal Peoples and Canadian Criminal Justice*, Toronto, Butterworths, pp.147.

23 John Braithwaite (1996) 'On speaking softly and carrying sticks: neglected dimensions of a Republican separation of powers', unpublished paper.

24 Herman Bianchi and Rene van Swaaningen (1986) (eds), *Abolitionism: Towards a Non-Repressive Approach to Crime*, Amsterdam, Free University Press; Nils Christie (1982) *Limits to Pain*, Oxford, M. Robertson.

25 See John Braithwaite (1995) 'Corporate crime and Republican criminology praxis', in Pearce, F. and Snider, L. (eds) *Corporate Crime: Ethics, Law and the State*, Toronto, University of Toronto Press.

26 John Braithwaite (1993) 'Beyond positivism: learning from contextual integrated strategies', *Journal of Research in Crime and Deliquency*, vol.30, pp.383–99.

27 Donald Clairmont (1994) 'Alternative justice issues for Aboriginal justice', unpublished paper, Atlantic Institute of Criminology, Nov.

28 Marianne Nielsen (1992) 'Criminal justice and native self-government', in Silverman, R. and Nielsen, M. (eds) *Aboriginal Peoples and Canadian Criminal Justice*, Toronto, Butterworths, p.255.

Part Two

Institutionalizing Restorative Justice

CHAPTER 6

Restorative Family Group Conferences: Differing Models and Guidelines for Practice

by Mark Umbreit and Howard Zehr

The concept of restorative justice has been receiving increasing attention from juvenile justice officials and citizens throughout the country during the past several years. With its focus upon understanding crime as primarily against individuals and communities (rather than only the state), elevating the role of crime victims and communities in the justice process, and emphasizing the importance of offenders being held directly accountable to their victims by making amends in some form, restorative justice appears to be addressing a number of unmet needs facing those most affected by crime (Zehr, 1990). Juvenile justice systems in at least 10 states are engaged in redefining their mission and restructuring their activities in order to promote a far more balanced and restorative juvenile justice system based on understanding that victims and communities, along with offenders, are their clients and must be given opportunities for active involvement in the justice process. The BARJ Project (Balanced and Restorative Justice), supported by the Office of Juvenile Justice and Delinquency Prevention of the US Department of Justice, has played a major role in responding to the growing nationwide interest in restorative justice by providing technical assistance and training.

While adopting a restorative justice vision requires major systematic change in our nation's juvenile justice systems (Umbreit and Carey, 1995), far more creative and effective interventions and programs also are required. One of the most promising new interventions to emerge in North America, with great potential for restorative justice practice, is the family group conference (FGC) model. Through a process that employs a facilitated meeting and dialogue, FGCs can meet the needs of crime victims and their families and offenders and their families in a manner that few other interventions can provide.

During the past 18 months, family group conferencing models coming out of New Zealand and Australia have received considerable attention in North America. Representatives from both countries have lectured and provided training workshops throughout the United States and Canada. Audiences have ranged from persons in the victim–offender mediation and restorative justice movement to – more surprisingly – many law enforcement officers and school officials with little prior background in the field. The conference model is also receiving attention in literature, and a scholarly book on FGCs is scheduled for publication by Criminal Justice Press this year. National media also are planning to cover this new approach.

All this attention is bearing fruit. A number of pilot projects and new program initiatives that incorporate some form of this approach are underway. One Pennsylvania-based organization, *Real* Justice (Wachtel, 1994), is vigorously promoting a specific police- and school-based model that originated in Wagga Wagga, Australia. *Real*Justice (McDonald *et al.*, 1995) has trained hundreds of police officers and school personnel and is working to replicate this Australian model in a number of sites including the Bethlehem, Pennsylvania, police department. The Minnesota Bureau of Criminal Apprehension has committed itself to a model combining family group conferencing and victim–offender mediation.

Rarely has a new criminal justice idea

Source: *Federal Probation*, vol.60, no.3, pp.24–9.

received such quick exposure and interest from audiences as widespread as activists, professionals, and the general public. No other restorative justice approach has so quickly brought such numbers of law enforcement officials 'to the table' as active stakeholders in the restorative justice movement.

The FGC is intuitively appealing to restorative justice advocates here in North America and may contain some important suggestions for victim–offender mediation. At the same time, there are a number of unresolved issues and potential dangers in adapting this model to North American culture with its strong commitment to retributive principles of doing justice. The purpose of this article is to move beyond the current promotion of conferencing and to encourage a serious discussion of both the potential opportunities and pitfalls presented by this process.

Family group conferencing originated in New Zealand as a way to address the failures of traditional, juvenile justice and to incorporate indigenous Maori values that emphasized the role of family and community in addressing wrongdoing. Institutionalized in law in 1989, FGCs are now the norm for processing juvenile cases in New Zealand. Australia then picked up the idea and has implemented a number of models in various communities. As with victim–offender mediation in North America, implementation has been piecemeal in Australia and the model varies with the community.

All juvenile cases in New Zealand, with a few exceptions such as homicide cases, are diverted by courts to FGCs. Consequently, judges report drops in caseloads of up to 80 percent. These conferences are then put together and facilitated by a youth justice worker employed not by criminal justice but by the welfare/social service sector. The conferences aim to be inclusive. In addition to the offender, major effort is put into including as many of the offender's family members as possible including extended family. Victims and their supporters are invited as are any professional caregivers who have been involved with the parties. A lawyer/advocate for the offender is invited, and a representative of the police (who serve as prosecutors) is present. This group, which includes participants usually assumed to be adversaries, is expected to come to a consensus on the entire outcome for the case, not just on a restitution agreement. Goals include accountability, healing, and prevention. Facilitator roles are broadly and loosely defined including but not limited to mediation.

Restorative justice theory did not play a large part in the origin of FGCs but was later used to help conceptualize and fine tune the approach, resulting, for instance, in a greater appreciation of the centrality of victims' roles. Now New Zealand Judge F.W.M. McElrea terms the approach the first truly restorative system institutionalized within a Western legal system.

FCGs were adopted and adapted in Australia in a variety of forms, but the model most often promoted in North America was developed in the Wagga Wagga police department. It differs from the New Zealand model in that it uses police officers, usually in uniform, or school officials to set up and facilitate meetings and does not normally use separate caucuses during the mediation sessions. Developments here were much influenced by John Braithwaite's (1989) work on reintegrative shaming, resulting in an important emphasis on changing offender behavior. Table 1 compares the development of family group conferencing in Australia and New Zealand.

Family group conferencing seems to be a natural expansion of the dominant model of victim–offender mediation currently being used by most of the more than 175 programs in North America and an even larger number of programs in Europe. The vast majority of these programs in North America are operated by private community-based organizations that mobilize and train volunteers to serve as mediators. While parents are informed of the program from the beginning and their support is crucial, the victim–offender mediation session most often involves only the involved victim and offender, along with the mediator. Some programs more actively involve parents in the mediation process as well.

Similar to victim–offender mediation (Umbreit, 1994), FGCs provide victims [with] an opportunity to express what impact the crime had upon their lives, to receive answers to any lingering questions about the incident, and to participate in holding offenders accountable for their actions. Offenders can tell their story of why the crime occurred and how it has affected their lives and are given an opportunity to make things right with victims through some form of compensation. FGCs, while emphasizing work with juvenile offenders who commit property crimes, have also been used with juvenile violent crime and adult offender cases. This is consistent with the experience of victim–offender mediation in North America over the past 20 years. A small, but growing, amount of research has emerged in North America (Coates and Gehm, 1989; Galaway and Hudson, 1990; Nugent and Paddock, 1995; Umbreit, 1989, 1991, 1994, 1995; Umbreit and Coates, 1992, 1993) and Europe (Dignan, 1990; Marshall and Merry, 1990) that has fairly consistently validated the effectiveness of victim–offender mediation programs, particularly related to client satisfaction, perceptions of fairness, reduction of fear among victims, greater likelihood of restitution completion, and a reduced likelihood of further criminal behavior.

FGCs, however, use public officials rather than trained volunteers as facilitators. While the roles include mediation, they are much more broadly defined, combining mediation with other roles and allowing for more directed facilitation. The FGC process also casts the circle of participants much wider than victim–offender mediation. This approach has potential advantages over current victim–offender mediation practice (Umbreit and Stacey, 1996) in that it:

- Involves more people in the community in the meeting called to discuss the offense, its effects, and how to remedy the harm, thus contributing to the empowerment and healing of the overall community.
- Acknowledges a wider range of people as being victimized by the offense and explores the effects on those people: the primary victim, people connected to the victim, the offender's family members, and others connected to the offender.
- Gets a wider range of participants to express their feelings about the impact of the crime and potentially to be involved in assisting with the reintegration of the offender into the community and the healing of the victim.
- Acknowledges and regularizes the important role of the family in a juvenile offender's life.

While the FGC model has tremendous potential for enhancing the practice of restorative justice in North America and developing new stakeholders in the movement (police, school officials, and probation), a number of potential dangers also exist that could result in consequences that are far from the intended restorative justice impact. Based upon the nearly 20-year experience of victim–offender mediation programs in North America, it would be naïve to ignore these possible dangers and unanticipated outcomes.

There are at least six potential dangers in the current FGC approach, and particularly the Australian form, as follows:

1 Inadequate preparation

Preparing the primary parties, before the joint conference, is crucial to the process of building rapport and trust with the involved parties, preparing them for participation in a dialogue in which the mediator is not dominating the conversation, assessing their needs/expectations, and gaining a far more human context of the crime that occurred. Meeting in person with the parties before a joint meeting has long been recognized by most victim–offender mediation programs as the preferred process. While the New Zealand FGC model always involves prior meetings with the offender and family, it does not always involve prior in-person meetings with the victim and family. The Australian FGC model routinely uses phone contact with the parties and only occasionally conducts in-person meetings. Eliminating in-person meetings before the actual FGC may significantly limit the impact of the FGC in humanizing the process in such a manner that the parties feel safe and prepared to attend and participate freely in a genuine dialogue.

Table 1 Family group conferencing: comparison of New Zealand and Australian (Wagga Wagga) models

	New Zealand Family Group Conferencing	Australian (Wagga Wagga) Family Group Conferencing
Convened by:	New Zealand Children and Young Persons Services – Youth Justice Coordinator.	Law enforcement officers, school personnel.
Participants:	Youth Justice Coordinator, offender, offender's counsel, offender's family and support system, victim, victim's family and support system, social services, police.	Family group conference coordinator, offender, offender's family and support system, victim, victim's family and support system, investigating officer.
Purpose:	Clarify facts of incident, expression of plea ('yes I did it' or 'no I did not'), reveal effects of incident on all present, determine measures to make amends, decision making relating to other penalties.	Reveal effects of incident on all present, express emotional impact, determine measures to make.
Selection of community members:	Youth justice coordinator/family of offender identify key people to be involved; victim identifies support system.	Coordinator identifies key people involved, victim identifies support system.
Decision making:	Consensus.	Consensus.
Victim role:	Chooses participants for support, expresses feelings about the crime, describes impact on him or her, approves plan to make amends that is submitted by offender's family.	Chooses participants for support, expresses feelings about the crime, describes impact on him or her, provides input to plan to make amends.
Time in operation:	Legislatively mandated in 1989.	Since 1991.
Targeted offenders:	All juvenile offenders, except murder and manslaughter.	Juvenile offenders, property offenses and assaults.
Size of group in conference:	Typically 12–15; can be 40–50.	Typically 12–15; can be 40–50.
Preparation of participants:	Face-to-face visit with offender and family before meeting; phone contact to explain process to victim and other participants and personal visit to victim if needed.	Phone contacts (as the norm) with all participants to explain the process. Occasional personal visits, if determined to be necessary.
Gatekeeper/access to program:	Statutes that provide a family group conference as a right for victims of all juvenile offenses other than murder and manslaughter and require offender participation.	Discretionary judgment of law enforcement officials or school officials.
Conceptual framework:	Clearly based on restorative justice principles, with explicit reference to the more lengthy experience of victim–offender reconciliation and mediation programs.	Clearly grounded in the theory of reintegrative shaming by John Braithwaite, as well as Silvan Tomkins' affect theory. Not explicitly grounded in restorative justice principles and not explicitly drawing upon lengthy experience of victim–offender reconciliation and mediation programs.

2 Victim insensitivity and coercion

The FGC model emphasizes the importance of involving and serving victims. However, by routinely beginning with the offender's story and, in the Australian model, seating the offender's group before bringing in the victim's group, by limiting choices presented to victims (such as where they would feel the safest or most comfortable to meet or whether they would prefer to begin the conference with their story), and by very aggressively selling the program and even telling the victim to just 'trust them (FGC coordinators),' the model inadvertently may mirror the dominant criminal justice system with its totally offender-driven nature and use of victims as 'props.' Many victim–offender mediation programs for many years have allowed victims to tell their story first in the mediation and have developed procedures to enhance the overall victim sensitivity of the process. If the FGC model becomes experienced or even perceived as not being sensitive to the emotional, informational, and participation needs of victims, it defeats one of its main purposes and is likely to trigger needless but understandable resistance from the larger victim movement.

3 Young offenders feeling intimidated by adults

The presence of so many adults in the FGC, including a police officer in uniform, may be so intimidating to young offenders that they may not feel safe enough or comfortable enough to open up and share their feelings and thoughts. This is precisely why in many victim–offender mediation sessions there are usually, but not always, no parents present. It has long been recognized in the victim–offender mediation movement that the presence of parents, not to mention additional adults, can interfere with the process of juvenile offenders truly 'owning up' to their criminal behavior and feeling comfortable enough to talk about it in a genuine way. FGCs can help us take seriously the important role of family in support and accountability. However, as the model is adapted for use in the United States, it will be important to ensure that the process truly creates an environment in which young persons feel safe enough to participate actively and express their feelings instead of the conference being dominated by adults talking at or about the offenders.

4 Lack of neutrality – shaming of offender

Police officers, probation officers, and/or school officials play a particularly critical role in the FGC model, especially in the Australian form, as 'coordinators' of the actual sessions (a role that is actually quite similar to that of facilitators or even mediators). Precisely because of this, it is extremely important that these public officials be trained in conflict resolution and mediation skills so that they can consistently suspend or put aside their normal highly authoritarian role as a public official. The ability of public officials (such as police or probation officers) to serve in a more neutral and facilitative role could be a problem and needs to be closely monitored as FGC programs begin developing in more communities throughout the United States, especially given the retributive climate of American criminal justice. If conference coordinators fall into more authoritarian leadership and communication patterns, the process actually could lead to offenders experiencing conferences as 'shaming and blaming' or even as a process of 'breaking down kids and then trying to build them up' rather than as 'reintegrative shaming' in which criminal behavior is denounced but offenders are treated with respect and feel safe enough in the presence of so many adults to open up and express themselves.

5 Inflexibility and assumed cultural neutrality of process

While the New Zealand FGC model appears to allow for a great deal of flexibility in the process, the Australian model that is being widely promoted in the United States seems to be a very prescriptive, script-driven process. In the *Real* Justice training manual and newsletter, the ıe of 'KTSS' is emphasized: 'Keep to the , stupid.' In other words, one is encouraged .o worry about whether the process should bւ adapted to different cultural needs and preferences within a community. According to *Real*Justice, the FGC model (based on the Wagga Wagga experience in Australia) is remarkably resilient and beneficial if one simply sticks to the script and if the participants just trust the coordinator. The inflexibility of this Australian model may present a serious obstacle to being a truly restorative process, particularly in diverse and multi-cultural communities.

6 Net-widening

Because the FGC model is so closely linked to early intervention by police or school officials (particularly the Australian model developed in Wagga Wagga), it could easily fall prey to the frequent and well-documented American pattern of new and alternative juvenile justice programs taking the easy cases, many of which would have dropped out of the system in the first place. This concern of probable 'net-widening,' identifying and labeling very minor cases that would have largely self-corrected on their own with little intervention by the justice system, is particularly appropriate within the United States, which has a long history of net-widening in new early intervention juvenile justice programs.

It is our belief that as family group conferencing begins to develop more extensively throughout North America in the coming years, the following could serve as initial guiding principles which will maximize the likelihood of it truly being a restorative intervention (Zehr, 1990) for victims, offenders, families and communities. The following guiding principles are based upon a consensus that emerged from a group of individuals who participated in the FGC training provided by the *Real*Justice organization in Pennsylvania. This group represented educators, law enforcement, victim–offender mediation programs, and communities in Minnesota. It was convened by the Center for Restorative Justice & Mediation at the University of Minnesota School of Social Work.

Guiding principles for restorative FGCs:

1. The process must be clearly and explicitly grounded in restorative justice values.
2. If public agencies such as police or probation are initiating family group conferencing, the actual sessions should be co-facilitated by a trained community person.
3. If a local victim–offender mediation or reconciliation program exists, a new FGC program should be developed as a collaborative effort including the use of victim–offender mediation volunteer mediators as co-facilitators.
4. FGC coordinators/facilitators should be trained in mediation and conflict resolution skills.
5. FGC coordinators/facilitators should be trained in understanding the experience and needs of crime victims and offenders.
6. The family group conferencing process should be conducted in the most victim-sensitive manner possible including providing victims with a choice of when and where to meet and allowing them to present their story first if they so desire. In approaching victims to consider the process, coordinators should inform them of both the potential benefits and risks. Victims should not be pressured into a conference or told just to trust the coordinator's judgment.
7. In-person preparation of the primary participants in a conference (victim, victim's immediate family, offender, offender's immediate family) should take place in order to connect with the parties, build rapport and trust, provide information, encourage participation, and, should the parties choose, prepare them for the conference so that they will feel safe enough to participate in a genuine dialogue with each other, with the coordinator/facilitator being as nondirective as possible.

8 FGC coordinators/facilitators should be trained in cultural and ethical issues that are likely to affect the conferencing process and participants.

FGCs are an exciting development in the field of restorative justice. They raise important challenges to the classic pairing of usually only the victim and the offender in most victim–offender mediation programs: Can ways be found to involve the family and community in the victim–offender mediation process? Could mediation begin to focus not just on restitution but on the full outcome of our cases? At the same time, like all innovations, the development of family group conferencing in North America presents potential pitfalls that must be considered. We urge those of us committed to reforming our nation's juvenile justice systems through interventions such as FGCs and victim–offender mediation to continue the dialogue as we seek ways to open new opportunities for restorative justice practice.

References

Braithwaite, J. (1989) *Crime, Shame and Reintegration*, New York, Cambridge University Press.

Coates, R.B. and Gehm, J. (1989) 'An empirical assessment', in Wright, M. and Galaway, B. (eds) *Mediation and Criminal Justice*, London, Sage Publications, pp.251–63.

Dignan, J. (1990) *Repairing the Damage*, Sheffield, Centre for Criminological and Legal Research, University of Sheffield.

Galaway, B. and Hudson, J. (eds) (1990) *Criminal Justice, Restitution, and Reconciliation*, Monsey, NY, Criminal Justice Press.

Marshall, T.F. and Merry, S. (1990) *Crime and Accountability*, London, Home Office.

McDonald, J., Moore, D., O'Connell, T. and Thorsborne, M. (1995) *Real Justice Training Manual: Coordinating Family Group Conferences*, Pipersville, PA, The Piper's Press.

Nugent, W.R. and Paddock, J.B. (1995) 'The effect of victim–offender mediation on severity of reoffense', *Mediation Quarterly*, vol.12, no.4, pp.353–67.

Umbreit, M.S. (1989) 'Crime victims seeking fairness, not revenge: Toward restorative justice', *Federal Probation*, vol.53, no.3, pp.52–7.

Umbreit, M.S. (1991) 'Minnesota mediation center gets positive results', *Corrections Today*, August, pp.194–7.

Umbreit, M.S. (1994) *Victim Meets Offender: The Impact of Restorative Justice and Mediation*, Monsey, NY, Criminal Justice Press.

Umbreit, M.S. (1995) *Mediating Interpersonal Conflicts: A Pathway to Peace*, West Concord, MN, CPI Publishing.

Umbreit, M.S. and Carey, M. (1995) 'Restorative justice: implications for organizational change', *Federal Probation*, vol.59, no.1, pp.47–54.

Umbreit, M.S. and Coates, R.B. (1992) 'The impact of mediating victim–offender conflict: an analysis of programs in three states', *Juvenile and Family Court Journal*, no.43, pp.21–8.

Umbreit, M.S. and Coates, R.B. (1993) 'Cross-site analysis of victim–offender mediation in four states', *Crime and Delinquency*, vol.39, no.4, pp.565–85.

Umbreit, M.S. and Stacey, S. (1996) 'Family Group Conferencing comes to the US: a comparison with victim–offender mediation', *Juvenile and Family Court Journal*, vol.47, no.2, pp.29–38.

Wachtel, T. (1994) 'Family Group Conferencing: restorative justice in practice', *Juvenile Justice Update*, vol.1, no.4.

Zehr, H. (1990) *Changing Lenses: A New Focus for Crime and Justice*, Scottsdale, PA, Herald Press.

CHAPTER 7

Conferences, Circles, Boards, and Mediations: The 'New Wave' of Community Justice Decisionmaking

by Gordon Bazemore and Curt Taylor Griffiths

Case 1 – After approximately 2 hours of at times heated and emotional dialogue, the mediator felt that the offender and victim had heard each other's story and had learned something important about the impact of the crime and about each other. They had agreed that the offender, a 14-year-old, would pay $200 in restitution to cover the cost of damages to the victim's home resulting from a break-in. In addition, he would be required to reimburse the victims for the cost of a VCR he had stolen estimated at $150. A payment schedule would be worked out in the remaining time allowed for the meeting. The offender also had made several apologies to the victim and agreed to complete community service hours working in a food bank sponsored by the victim's church. The victim, a middle-aged neighbor of the offender, said that she felt less angry and fearful after learning more about the offender and the details of the crime and thanked the mediator for allowing the mediation to be held in her church basement.

Case 2 – After the offender, his mother and grandfather, the victim, and the local police officer who had made the arrest had spoken about the offense and its impact, the youth justice coordinator asked for any additional input from other members of the group of about 10 citizens assembled in the local school (the group included two of the offender's teachers, two friends of the victim, and a few others). The coordinator then asked for input into what should be done by the offender to pay back the victim, a teacher who had been injured and had a set of glasses broken in an altercation with the offender, and to pay back the community for the damage caused by his crime. In the remaining half hour of the approximately hour-long conference, the group suggested that restitution to the victim was in order to cover medical expenses and the cost of a new pair of glasses and that community service work on the school grounds would be appropriate.

Case 3 – The victim, the wife of the offender who had admitted to physically abusing her during two recent drunken episodes, spoke about the pain and embarrassment her husband had caused her and her family. After she had finished, the ceremonial feather (used to signify who would be allowed to speak next) was passed to the next person in the circle, a young man who spoke about the contributions the offender had made to the community, the kindness he had shown toward the elders by sharing fish and game with them, and his willingness to help others with home repairs. An elder then took the feather and spoke about the shame the offender's behavior had caused his clan – noting that in the old days, he would have been required to pay the woman's family a substantial compensation as a result. Having heard all this, the judge confirmed that the victim still felt that she wanted to try to work it out with her estranged husband and that she was receiving help from her own support group (including a victim's advocate). Summarizing the case by again stressing the seriousness of the offense and repeating the Crown Counsel's opening remarks that a jail sentence was

Source: *Federal Probation*, vol.61, no.2, pp.25–37.

required, he then proposed to delay sentencing for 6 weeks until the time of the next circuit court hearing. If during that time the offender had: met the requirements presented earlier by a friend of the offender who had agreed to lead a support group and had met with the community justice committee to work out an alcohol and anger management treatment plan; fulfilled the expectations of the victim and her support group; and completed 40 hours of service to be supervised by the group, he would forgo the jail sentence. After a prayer in which the entire group held hands, the circle disbanded and everyone retreated to the kitchen area of the community center for refreshments.

Case 4 – The young offender, a 19-year-old caught driving with an open can of beer in his pick-up truck, sat nervously awaiting the conclusion of a deliberation of the Reparative Board. He had been sentenced by a judge to Reparative Probation and did not know whether to expect something tougher or much easier than regular probation. About a half hour earlier before retreating for their deliberation, the citizen members of the Board had asked the offender several simple and straightforward questions. At 3 p.m. the chairperson explained the four conditions of the offender's contract: 1) begin work to pay off his traffic tickets; 2) complete a state police defensive driving course; 3) undergo an alcohol assessment; and 4) write a three-page paper on how alcohol has negatively affected his life. After the offender had signed the contract, the chairperson adjourned the meeting.

Introduction

What do these cases have in common? Each of the above scenarios illustrates a successful conclusion of one variety of a non-adversarial, community-based sanctioning process now being carried out with some regularity in North America, Australia, New Zealand, and parts of Europe. As decisionmaking models, these processes represent one component of what appears to be a new community justice movement in the 1990s concerned with bringing less formal justice processes closer to neighborhoods and increasing the involvement of citizens in the justice process (e.g. Travis, 1996; Barajas, 1995; Bazemore and Schiff, 1996; Griffiths and Hamilton, 1996). Referred to by such terms as *restorative justice* (e.g. Zehr, 1990; Hudson *et al.*, 1996; Bazemore and Umbreit, 1995), *community justice* (Griffiths and Hamilton, 1996; Stuart, 1995a; Barajas, 1995), and *restorative community justice* (Young, 1995; Bazemore and Schiff, 1996), these initiatives are becoming a topic of high-level national and cross-national discussion and debate in the US and Canada (NIJ, 1996a, 1996b; Depew, 1994) and have already had significant state/provincial, territorial, regional, and even national policy impact.[1] While they by no means exhaust the range of approaches to citizen involvement in the sanctioning process, together the four case examples illustrate some of the diversity, as well as common themes, apparent in what appears to be an emerging 'new wave' of approaches to community justice decisionmaking.

The first case is drawn from the files of one of approximately 500 *victim–offender mediation* (VOM) programs in the US and Canada. Offenders and victims who have agreed to participate meet in these sessions with a third party mediator to arrive at a reparative agreement and allow victims to tell their story and get information about the offense (Umbreit, 1994). Though still unfamiliar to some mainstream criminal justice audiences and marginal to the court process in many jurisdictions where they do operate, VOM programs – originally, and still frequently, referred to as Victim–Offender Reconciliation Programs (VORPs) – now have a long and respectable 25-year track record in Europe, Canada and the US.

The second example describes a typical conclusion of a *family group conference* (FGC). This new model in its modern form was adopted into national legislation in 1989, making it (at least in New Zealand) the most systemically institutionalized of any of the four approaches. By most accounts, it would appear that dispositional decisions in all but the most violent and serious delinquency cases in New Zealand are made in an FGC (Maxwell and Morris, 1993; Alder and Wundersitz, 1994; McElrea, 1993). Based on the centuries old sanctioning and dispute resolution traditions of the New Zealand

Maori and now widely used in modified form as a police-initiated diversion approach in South Australia, FGCs are now also being implemented in cities in Minnesota, Pennsylvania, Montana, and parts of Canada.

The third scenario describes a *circle sentencing* (CS) conference, an updated version of the traditional sanctioning and healing practices of Canadian Aboriginal peoples and indigenous peoples in the Southwestern United States (Stuart, 1995a; Melton, 1995). Circle sentencing was resurrected in 1991 by supportive judges and community justice committees in the Yukon Territory, Canada, and other northern Canadian communities. The strategy is designed not only to address the criminal behavior of offenders, but also to consider the needs of crime victims, families, and communities within a holistic, reintegrative context. Within the circle, crime victims, offenders, justice, and social service personnel, as well as community residents, are allowed to express their feelings about the crime and the offender as well as to offer their suggestions as to how the offense and the needs of the victim and the community can best be addressed. The significance of the circle is more than symbolic: all persons in the circle – police officers, lawyers, the judge, the victim, the offender, and community residents – participate in the case deliberations. Through this community–system partnership, a determination is made as to the most appropriate action to take in addressing the needs of the victim and the offender.

Finally, the fourth case is taken from the files of the *reparative probation program*, a Vermont innovation in which nonviolent offenders are sentenced by the court to a hearing before a community reparative board (RB) composed of local citizens. These boards became operational early in 1995 as part of a newly mandated separation of probation into Community Corrections Service Units (designed to provide supervision to more serious cases) and Court and Reparative Service Units (that coordinate and provide administrative support to the boards). Composed of five local citizens, the boards now make dispositional decisions for eligible probation cases referred by the courts, and if the target goals of state correctional administrators are met, may soon be hearing an estimated 60 per cent of these eligible cases (Dooley, 1995, 1996).

The purpose of this article is to describe the four new decisionmaking models and examine how each involves citizens and community groups in several critical components of the sanctioning process. In doing so, we compare and contrast these models on a number of key operational dimensions with the objective of providing a general framework within which the myriad of alternative justice practices currently being described by at times ill-defined and vague terms such as 'community justice' and/or 'restorative justice' can be categorized and objectively analyzed.

Background and literature review

Table 1 describes the origins and current application of the four decisionmaking models and summarizes several differences and similarities between them in administration and process. While the models share a nonadversarial, community-based sanctioning focus on cases in which offenders either admit guilt or have been found guilty of crimes or delinquent acts, they vary along several of these dimensions of staffing, eligibility, and point in the system at which referrals are made. Notably, eligibility ranges from minor first offenders to quite serious repeat offenders (in the case of circle sentencing), and the models differ in point of referral and structural relationship to formal court and correctional systems. With the exception of the Vermont reparative boards, decisionmaking is by consensus, but the process and dispositional protocol vary substantially – ranging from ancient rituals involving passing of the 'talking stick' or feather in the case of circle sentencing (Stuart, 1995a) to the more deliberative agenda followed in the hearings of community boards (Dooley, 1995).

What's new and what's important?

Although the impact of these administrative and process differences should not be underestimated, except for victim–offender

Table 1 Community decisionmaking models: administration and process

	Circle Sentencing	**Family Group Conferencing**	**Reparative Probation**	**Victim–Offender Mediation**
Time in Operation	Since approximately 1992	New Zealand (NZ) – 1989; Australia – 1991	Since 1995	Since mid-1970s
Where Used	Primarily the Yukon, sporadically in other parts of Canada	Australia, NZ, cities and towns in Montana, Minneapolis, and Pennsylvania	Vermont	Throughout North America and Europe
Point in System	Used at various stages; may be diversion or alternative to formal court hearings and correctional process for indictable offenses	NZ – throughout juvenile justice system; Australia Wagga-Wagga model – police diversion	One of several probation options	Mostly diversion and probation option but some use in residential facilities for more serious cases
Eligibility and Target Group	Offenders who admit guilt and express willingness to change; entire range of offenses and offenders eligible; chronic offenders targeted	NZ model – all juvenile offenders eligible except murder and manslaughter charges; Wagga-Wagga model – determined by police discretion or diversion criteria	Target group is nonviolent offenders; eligibility limited to offenders given probation and assigned to the boards (some boards have been given discretion to accept violent offenders)	Varies, but primarily diversion cases and property offenders; in some locations, used with serious and violent offenders (at victim's request)
Staffing	Community Justice Coordinator	Community Justice Coordinator	Reparative Coordinator (probation staff)	Mediator – other positions vary
Setting	Community center, school, or public building	Social welfare office, school, community building. Police facility (occasionally)	Public building or community center	Neutral setting such as meeting room in library, church, or community center; occasionally in victim's home if approved by other parties
Nature and Order of Process	After judge, justice of the peace, or keeper opens session, each participant allowed to speak when feather or 'talking stick' is passed to him or her; victim(s) generally speak first; consensus decisionmaking	Coordinator follows 'script' in which offender speaks first to board followed by victim and other participants; consensus decisionmaking	Mostly private deliberation by board after questioning offender and hearing statements; some variation emerging	Victim speaks first; mediator facilitates but encourages victim and offender to speak; does not adhere to script or force consensus

mediation, the other models are relatively new – at least to the modern Western world (Melton, 1995; McElrea, 1993) – and thus may be expected to continue to evolve as they are adapted to local circumstances. Currently, then, more important than these distinctions are *common elements* that distinguish these 'new wave' decisionmaking models from both current and past attempts to 'devolve' justice process to local neighborhoods. These elements grow out of the shared association with the principles and practice of restorative and community justice.

Focused on changing the primary goal of justice intervention from punishment or treatment to reparation of harm and altering the justice process to include and meet the needs of victims, communities, and offenders (Zehr, 1990; Van Ness, 1993; Bazemore and Umbreit, 1995), restorative justice has been generally associated with practices and processes such as restitution, community service, victim–offender mediation, victim services, and a variety of conflict resolution processes. The term 'community justice' is being used by some officials in both Canada and the US as a broader umbrella concept which also encompasses community policing, neighborhood courts and justice centers, community development and 'community-building' interventions, 'beat probation,' and a variety of delinquency prevention programs (NIJ, 1996a; Barajas, 1995).

Depending upon who is describing it, the group of interventions currently being labeled as 'community justice' or 'restorative community justice' may therefore refer to a wide array of programs, practices, and 'community-based initiatives' including community policing, 'weed and seed' programs, neighborhood revitalization, and drug courts, as well as the sanctioning and victim reparation programs and processes now commonly associated with restorative justice (Young, 1995; Travis, 1996; Robinson, 1996; Barajas, 1995; Klein, 1995; Bazemore and Schiff, 1996; NIJ, 1996b).[2] Such programmatic approaches to implementing community justice have often been useful in demonstrating innovative intervention strategies not easily initiated in existing bureaucracies and bringing policing, delinquency prevention, courts, and corrections services closer to neighborhoods. However, defining community justice as a 'program' may limit the vision and practical application of a distinctive, more holistic response to crime to a specialized unit or individual assigned a specific function (e.g. Goldstein, 1987). The programmatic emphasis also may increase both jurisdictional and professional insularity and ultimately result in little or no systemic impact on justice agencies and their relationship to neighborhoods and citizen groups. Given the diversity of programs and initiatives being discussed under the banner of community justice, it is first important to place the new decisionmaking models in the somewhat more limited category of efforts to promote citizen involvement in sanctioning and dispute resolution.

Dimensions of community justice and community decisionmaking

Efforts to increase community participation in sanctioning and the dispositional decisionmaking process are nothing new, even in recent criminal justice history. In the late 1970s, the Law Enforcement Assistance Administration (LEAA) of the US Department of Justice supported 'neighborhood justice centers,' also referred to as 'dispute resolution centers,' in several US cities (McGillis and Mullen, 1977; Garafalo and Connelly, 1980). The four new-wave models also should be viewed in the context of a more recent effort to bring courts, prosecution units, and defense teams to local neighborhoods. A recent publication of the National Institute of Justice (NIJ, 1996b), for example, describes a variety of initiatives to locate prosecution and defense services – as well as entire courts – in neighborhoods and adapt their service to provide a better fit with the needs of local citizens (NIJ, 1996b).

Both the older dispute resolution approaches and the new community court and court units often have been effective in increasing accessibility of justice services to citizens by changing the *location* of programs or services so that they are geographically available to neighborhoods, increasing *flexibility* of service delivery (e.g. better hours, more diversity), and encouraging *informality* in the decisionmaking process – relying whenever possible on dispute resolution, negotiation, and mediative practices rather than legal rules and procedures (Harrington and Merry, 1988; Rottman, 1996). As the experience with community corrections clearly illustrates, however, when facilities or service centers are merely located in a neighborhood without the involvement of local residents, the result is an isolated program or process that may be said to be *in*, but not *of*, the community (Byrne, 1989; Clear, 1996). Similarly, increasing flexibility and breaking down formal barriers may increase citizens' willingness to seek and receive assistance, but it does not necessarily increase their involvement as participants in the justice process, or even necessarily allow them to determine what services they would like in their neighborhoods.

Unfortunately, the emphasis on programs and accessibility of services has contributed to a one-dimensional definition of community justice. Ultimately, neither developing programs nor increasing access will alone change the role of neighborhood residents from service recipients to decisionmakers with a stake in, or feeling of ownership in, what services are provided and how they are delivered. Hence, what appears to be most *new* and significant about the four new models is that in defining distinctive roles for citizens in determining what the criminal sanction will be, as well as how it may be carried out, they add an important dimension to both earlier and ongoing community justice initiatives (e.g. McGillis and Mullen, 1977; NIJ, 1996a).

What is the relevance of these apparently esoteric sanctioning and decisionmaking models to probation and parole, victim advocates, treatment providers, and other intervention professionals? Notably, an increasing number of state departments of corrections, probation and parole services, and juvenile corrections systems and probation services are adopting one or more aspects of community and restorative justice policy (e.g. Dooley, 1995; Pranis, 1995). What appear on the surface to be simply informal alternatives to court are therefore being viewed by some administrators as having greater significance to the objectives of probation and parole. This is because they may offer a new avenue for achieving a wide and deeper level of citizen involvement in the rehabilitative, sanctioning, and surveillance missions of community corrections that has been difficult to attain through a focus on offender supervision alone. The prospects for increasing community involvement, the *nature* of the process of engaging citizens, and the role(s) assigned to the community are therefore the most crucial dimensions for contrasting approaches to community decisionmaking.

Contrasting the models: engaging communities in community justice

Community is an amorphous concept that is unfortunately often used in such a way as to obfuscate, rather than clarify, issues of citizen involvement in government-sponsored processes. As Gardner (1990) points out, however, it is not difficult to be more specific in breaking down 'the community' into component parts for purposes of discussion about citizen involvement and participation. Community may be defined, for example, as a neighborhood, a church, a school, a labor union, a civic or fraternal organization, an extended family, an Aboriginal band or tribe, a support group, or other entity.

As Table 2 suggests, the way community is defined in justice decisionmaking models is a critical factor affecting the nature and extent of citizen involvement and ownership. In the case of victim–offender mediation (VOM), for example, the community is defined for all intents and purposes as the victim–offender dyad. In circle sentencing (CS), on the other hand, the community is defined as all residents of a local neighborhood, village, or Aboriginal band. In addition, the list of characteristics in Table 2 addresses several general questions about community justice decisionmaking which provide useful points of comparison between each model. We examine two of these issues in detail in the remainder of this section.

First, what is the role and function of crime victims, relative to offenders and the community, in the process? In the formal justice system, the bulk of attention is directed toward the offender, first with regard to his or her guilt or innocence and second with regard to appropriate punishment, treatment, or monitoring. The community is an increasingly important, albeit distant, concern (e.g. Barajas, 1995; Clear, 1996). Because victims have been so neglected as a client of both formal and community justice approaches, it is important to examine the role of crime victims, *vis à vis* the role of community and offender, in each community justice process.

Second, one of the most interesting and important differences between the community decisionmaking models is the extent to which preparation before the process and follow up is viewed as vital to success. Put differently, community decisionmaking models may vary a great deal in the view of the decisionmaking ceremony itself as primary (and thus spontaneous) or merely one step in an ongoing process that will hopefully result in a complete response to crime. Clearly, the preparation stage of community decisionmaking offers perhaps the greatest opportunity to engage citizens in the process and to ensure their meaningful participation (Stuart, 1995a; Umbreit, 1994). In addition, even more at issue among some critics of these models (Alder and Wundersitz, 1994) is the enforcement and follow-up approach for sanctioning plans and agreements that result from each process (see Table 2). Moreover, the focus on sanctioning, monitoring, and enforcement in these decisionmaking processes provides the most critical linkage with, and has the greatest implications for, community corrections.

Victim–offender mediation

Role of the victim and other coparticipants.

Increasingly, modern VOM programs seek to give first priority to meeting the needs of crime victims (Umbreit, 1994). Specifically, victims are given maximum input into the sanction, referred for needed help and assistance, allowed to tell the offender how the crime has affected them and request information about the crime, and, to the greatest extent possible, are repaid for their losses. As shown earlier in Table 1, to ensure that the victim feels empowered, or at a minimum is not more abused or overwhelmed by the process, victims speak first in mediation sessions. While both victim and offender needs receive priority over the needs of other potential players in the community justice process (parents, relatives, other citizens), in an important sense the victim is also the primary client. The victim must, after all, consent to the process while the offender is often a less than willing participant (Belgrave, 1995). Hence, in contrast to other models, most research studies report that victim satisfaction with VOM has been uniformly high (e.g. Umbreit and Coates, 1993; Belgrave, 1995).

Monitoring, enforcement, and preparation.

In VOM, there is apparently some degree of variation between programs in monitoring and enforcement. In many programs, it is common for the mediator to assist offender and victim in devising a schedule for reparation, and the mediator may even ask that the participants agree to a follow-up meeting to review progress (Umbreit, 1994). In other programs, probation or diversion staff may follow up, depending on the offender's court status; other mediation programs may have paid staff who are charged with monitoring functions, or VOM may be one part of a larger restitution program responsible for development and enforcement of the reparative agreement (Schneider, 1985; Belgrave, 1995). On the front-end, VOM practitioners are perhaps the most adamant of any community justice advocates about the importance of extensive victim and offender preparation before the mediation session. The most widely accepted model encourages extensive pre-mediation discussion with both offender and victim involving at least one face-to-face contact (Umbreit, 1994). In fact, many practitioners argue that up-front preparation is often more important than the session itself in bringing about a successful result (Umbreit and Stacey, 1996).

Table 2 Community decisionmaking models: community role and involvement

	Circle Sentencing	Family Group Conferencing	Reparative Board	Victim–Offender Mediation
Who Participates? ('The Community')	Judge, prosecutor, defense counsel participate in serious cases. Victim(s), offender(s), service providers, support group present. Open to entire community. Justice Committee ensures participation of key residents	Coordinator identifies key people; close kin of victim and offender targeted, as well as police, social services	Reparative coordinator (probation employee); Community Reparative Board	Mediator, victim, offender are standard participants (family and others allowed on rare occasions)
Victim Role	Participates in circle and decisionmaking; gives input into eligibility of offender; chooses support group	Victim expresses feelings about crime; gives input into reparative plan	Input into plan sought by some boards; inclusion of victims currently rare but being encouraged and considered	Major role in decision re: offender obligation and content of reparative plan; express feelings regarding crime and impact
Gatekeepers	Community Justice Committee	NZ – court and Criminal Justice Coordinator; Australia and US law enforcement and school officials	Judge	Victim has ultimate right of refusal; consent is essential
Role and Relationship to System	Judge, prosecution, court officials share power with community, i.e. selection, sanctioning, follow-up; presently, minimal impact on court caseloads	NZ – primary process of hearing juvenile cases; required ceding of disposition power. Major impact on court caseloads. Australia – police driven. Variable impact on caseloads; concern regarding net-widening	One of several probation options for eligible low-risk offenders with minimal services needs; plans to expand; some impact on caseloads anticipated	Varies on continuum from core process in diversion and disposition to marginal programs with minimal impact on court caseloads
Preparation	Extensive work with offender and victim before circle; explain process and rules of circle	Phone contact with all parties to encourage participation and explain process; NZ model requires offender and family have face-to-face visits	Preservice training provided by boards; no advance preparation for individual hearings	Typically face-to-face with victim and offender to explain process; some programs use phone contact

Table 2 *(continued)*

	Circle Sentencing	Family Group Conferencing	Reparative Board	Victim–Offender Mediation
Enforcement and Monitoring	Community Justice Committee; judge may hold jail sentence as incentive for offender to comply with plan	Unclear; police in Australian Wagga-Wagga model, coordinator in NZ model	Condition of probation; coordinator monitors and brings petition of revocation to board, if necessary	Varies; mediator may follow up; probation or other program staff may be responsible
Primary Outcome Sought	Increase community strength and capacity to resolve disputes and prevent crime; develop reparative and rehabilitative plan; address victim's concerns and public safety issues; assign victim and offender support group responsibilities and identify resources	Clarify facts of case; shame/denounce crime while affirming and supporting offender; restore victim loss; encourage offender reintegration; focus on 'deed, not need'	Engage and involve citizens in decisionmaking process; decide appropriate reparative plan for offender; require victim awareness education and other activities that address ways to avoid reoffending in the future	Allow victim to relay impact of crime to offender; express feelings and needs; victim satisfied with process; offender increase awareness of harm; gain empathy; agreement on reparative plan

Reparative boards

Role of the victim and other coparticipants. In the early months of operation, victim involvement in most Vermont RBs has been minimal (Dooley, 1996). While their participation has been strongly encouraged by state officials who developed and now monitor the programs, it remains to be seen to what extent citizen board members will want to take on the at times demanding task of contacting and engaging crime victims in the justice process. RBs have been informed to a large extent by a restorative justice model (Dooley, 1995; 1996). Moreover, the strong commitment on the part of some local boards to seeing that victims are repaid by offenders ultimately may provide greater motivation for increasing involvement when it becomes more clear what value mediation or other forms of victim–offender dialogue may have in improving completion rates (Umbreit and Coates, 1993). Boards have also been encouraged by administrators to refer offenders and victims to victim–offender mediation programs in communities where they are available and when victims agree to participate.

Monitoring, enforcement, and preparation. As Table 2 suggests, enforcement responsibilities in the form of recommending revocation or termination of the 90-day offender contract are assigned to the board members themselves although the final decision is apparently made by a probation administrator who may recommend violation to the court if conditions are not met or require additional corrective actions. The reparative coordinator, a probation employee, is responsible for monitoring contract compliance (Reparative Board Program Description, 1995). While monitoring procedures and policy are perhaps the most formally developed in RBs, case preparation is apparently limited to a brief intake interview with the offender to gather information about the offense for the board. Victims may or may not be contacted though presumably less information is required for the hearings and may be provided from police records via court or probation.

Family Group Conferences

Role of the victim and other coparticipants.

The complexity of the challenge of victim protection and empowerment when one moves beyond the small group or dyad to the larger community is even more apparent in FGCs. FGCs are perhaps the strongest of all the models in their potential for educating offenders about the harm their behavior causes to victims. From a restorative perspective, however, the concern is that the priority given to offender education will – as appears to be the case when conferences are held with little or no victim input or involvement (Maxwell and Morris, 1993; Alder and Wundersitz, 1994) – overshadow or trivialize the concern with meeting victim needs (Belgrave, 1995; Umbreit and Zehr, 1996). In direct contrast to both VOM and CS, the standard protocol for FGCs requires that offenders speak first. This is believed to increase the chance that young offenders will speak *at all* in the presence of family and other adults. In addition, speaking first is said by FGC supporters to help offenders 'own' their behavior early in the session, to let their support group know what happened, to give the victim a different perspective on the crime and on the offender, and even put the victim at ease (McDonald *et al.*, 1995).[4]

The centrality of concern in FGCs with shaming and reintegrating offenders, however, may lead to some interesting twists in terms of how positive victim outcomes are conceptualized and thought to be best achieved. As one recent Australian attempt to evaluate victim outcomes illustrates, even objective observers may become vulnerable to giving primary focus to offender outcomes:

> Conferencing engenders in the *offenders* and their supporters a sense of shame through providing the victims with a forum to explain directly to all experienced in the process. [Such an explanation] is sufficient for the expression of a sincere apology for the harm flowing from the offence. In a successful conference, the shame [experienced by] offenders, in turn, gives rise to the *expression of forgiveness by victims*, while the outcome can provide for material restitution.
>
> (Strang, 1995, p.3) (emphasis added)

As suggested in this explanation, the essential 'business' of the conference appears to be on getting offenders to experience shame (cf. Alder and Wundersitz, 1994). The 'benefit' to the victim is an apology and perhaps material restitution. While either or both may meet the primary needs of many victims, other concerns may be neglected or not even considered. Moreover, if the ultimate motive is forgiveness for the offender, the process may be slanted in the direction of eliciting an apology from the offender, and victims may feel pressured to forgive the offender or become so resentful at the implication that they *should* that they refuse to participate (Umbreit and Stacey, 1996). Others have expressed concern in FGCs about the lack of concern with victim empowerment, protection against abuse or retaliation, and use of victims as 'props' or to meet offender needs (Umbreit and Zehr, 1996). While victim participation and victim satisfaction has been an ongoing problem in FGCs (Maxwell and Morris, 1993), it is unfair to conclude that most FGC advocates are not concerned with victim needs (see Moore and O'Connell, 1995; Braithwaite and Mugford, 1994). Moreover, like all such criticisms of alternative community models, the critique of FGC from the victim's perspective should be made first with reference to the extent of reparation, empowerment, and support available within the *current*, formal system (Stuart, 1995b). However, as FGC models evolve, it will be important to examine the extent to which the priority commitment to offender shaming and reintegration may diminish the capacity of FGCs to involve and attend to the needs of crime victims.

Monitoring, enforcement, and preparation.

FGCs also are responsible for preconference preparation and play a major role in enforcement. In New Zealand, preparation is viewed as critical, and face-to-face meetings are now generally held with the offender and family, with phone contacts made to the victim (Hakiaha, 1995). In the Australian model, by contrast, practitioners rely primarily on phone contacts to explain the process to both offenders and victims and apparently place much less emphasis on preconference preparation. This lack of preparation appears to be based on the belief that spontaneity is best. Some coordinators, for example, argue that hearing the victim's and offender's stories before the conference may even diminish the impact and focus of these stories (Umbreit and Stacy, 1996). Recently, however, some proponents of the Australian model appear to be placing greater emphasis on the need for ensuring accuracy of facts, checking with participants, developing a plan, and ensuring that key participants and their support groups are present at conferences (McDonald *et al.*, 1995). As is the case in courts that lack programmatic approaches to restitution and community service, compliance with reparative obligations appears to be generally left to the offender (Moore and O'Connell, 1994) although in the New Zealand model conferences can be reconvened for failure to comply (Maxwell and Morris, 1993). Monitoring and enforcement responsibilities are not made explicit although the Australian model appears to anticipate that police officers are ultimately responsible for enforcement (Alder and Wundersitz, 1994).

Circle sentencing

Role of victim and other coparticipants.

As with VOM, proponents of the circle sentencing process are concerned with protecting the victim, providing support, and hearing the victim's story. In sentencing circles, after the prosecutor has presented the case against the offender, victims and/or their advocates generally speak first. In the circle this is done to avoid an 'imbalanced focus on the offender's issues,' which may cause the victim to withdraw or react by challenging offenders (Stuart, 1995b, p.7). The telling of the victim's story is viewed as important, not only for the victim, the offender, and their supporters, but also for the community as a whole. CS advocates may encourage a friend or relative to speak on behalf of the victim when he or she is not willing, but they emphasize the value of residents hearing the victim's story firsthand whenever possible (Stuart, 1995b). Because the process is so open and community-driven, however, a potential concern is that the importance given to the victim's needs and the victim's point of view in circle sentencing may vary widely. As appears also to occur in some FGCs, the seriousness of offender needs may slant the focus of the group to execution of the rehabilitative and offender service/support plan rather than toward meeting the reparative and other needs of the victim (Maxwell and Morris, 1993; Umbreit and Stacey, 1996). In addition, the extent of effort required on the part of the offender before the event itself (discussed in the following section) may result in circles stacked with offender supporters who have little relationship to victims. Achieving appropriate balance between victim, offender, and community needs and representation in the circle is a task left to the Community Justice Committee. In this regard, an innovation of CS not apparent in any of the other processes is the victim support group (Stuart, 1995b). This group is formed by the Community Justice Committee, generally at the time the offender petitions for admission to the circle, but may develop or be enhanced at any time including during the circle ceremony itself.

Monitoring, enforcement, and preparation.

Perhaps because its community empowerment and healing goals are most ambitious, the circle sentencing model appears to demand the most extensive pre-process preparation. The admission process generally requires, as a condition of admission to a circle, that an offender petition the Community Justice Committee, visit an elder or other respected community member for a conference to begin work on a reparative plan which may involve some restitution to the victim and community service, and identify a community support group (Stuart, 1995b). While circles may be convened in some cases without these requirements being met (with the special approval of the Community Justice Committee), the preconference process is generally viewed as a screening device and a key indicator to circle participants that the offender is serious about personal change. Hence, it is not uncommon that conferences are canceled or postponed when these steps have not been taken (Stuart, 1995b). When the preliminary screening process works well and offenders meet the preconference obligations, however, a circle sentencing session can actually seem less like a hearing about dispositional requirements than a celebration of the offender's progress, as well as an opportunity for victims and offenders to tell their stories.

This preparation and support on the front end appear also to extend to follow up on the back end. In this regard, monitoring and enforcement of the conditions of the circle sentence, which often include an extensive list of reparative responsibilities, treatment requirements, and (in Aboriginal communities) traditional healing and community building rituals, is assigned to the circle participants. Offender and victim support groups formed through the Community Justice Committee also monitor offenders and advocate for victims to ensure that agreements made within the circle are carried out. In the case of sentencing circles, agreements are subject to review by a judge, who will ask for routine reports from the justice committee and the support groups. Judges may strengthen the enforcement process at the conclusion of the circle by assigning or reaffirming the assignment of community monitoring responsibilities and may withhold a final decision about jail terms or other sanctions pending completion of obligations to be verified at the follow-up hearing.

Discussion

> So we make mistakes – can you say – you (the current system) don't make mistakes ... if you don't think you do, walk through our community, every family will have something to teach you .... By getting involved, by all of us taking responsibility, it is not that we won't make mistakes .... But we would be doing it together, as a community, instead of having it done to us. We need to find peace within our lives ... in our communities. We need to make *real differences* in the way people act and the way we treat others .... Only if we empower them and support them can they break out of this trap.
>
> (Rose Couch, community justice coordinator, Kwanlin Dun First Nations, Yukon, Canada, cited in Stuart, 1995b).

The perpetual absence of 'the community in community corrections,' either as a target of intervention or as a coparticipant in the justice process (e.g. Byrne, 1989; Clear, 1996), may be due in part to the inability to identify meaningful roles for citizens in sanctioning crime. This article has described four alternative community decisionmaking models and contrasted the way each defines and operationalizes the role of citizens and community groups in the response to crime. As illustrated by the examples of the Vermont Reparative Boards and as a growing number of community justice initiatives being initiated and led by corrections departments in states such as Minnesota and Maine indicate (Pranis, 1995; Maine Council of Churches, 1996), such citizen involvement in community sanctioning processes may have significant implications for community corrections. In the processes discussed here, there appears to be significant potential for changing the current dynamic in which the community is viewed by justice agencies as a passive participant. When probation and parole professionals can identify citizens willing to participate in a community sanctioning process, they may also have identified a small support group willing to assist with offender reintegration as well as victim support.

'Riding the wave': critical issues in community justice decisionmaking

As restorative and community justice decisionmaking assumes an ever higher profile at senior governmental policy levels, there are a number of critical issues which must be addressed. Because these new decisionmaking structures and processes, like all criminal justice innovations, are likely to come under close scrutiny, the failure to address several concerns could prove fatal.

The need to evaluate community justice decisionmaking initiatives

Despite the proliferation of restorative and community justice programs, there is a paucity of evaluation research which would provide an empirical basis for determining whether these initiatives are successful in achieving their stated objectives. Critics of circle sentencing (cf. LaPrairie, 1994), for example, point out that there have been no empirical analyses of the extent to which sentencing circles prevent and/or reduce crime and disorder in communities or whether sentencing circles function to reduce recidivism rates among offenders processed through the circles. In an extensive critique of circle sentencing, LaPrairie (1994, pp.82–3) states:

> It has been claimed that sentencing circles have the following benefits: (a) they reduce recidivism, (b) prevent crime, (c) reduce costs, (d) advance the interests of victims, and (e) promote solidarity among community members. These are all measurable and should be put to the empirical test.

Many restorative and community justice initiatives have objectives that are far more holistic than traditional crime control responses, which have typically utilized recidivism rates as a primary outcome measure. An evaluative framework for these approaches would, therefore, have to include measurable criteria to assess outcomes of 'community empowerment and solidarity,' 'victim interests,' and 'crime prevention.' The relative importance assigned to such outcomes as community and victim involvement, offender shaming, reparation to victims, dispute resolution, and healing will also determine how one gauges the effectiveness of any model. However, as new, more appropriate standards emerge for evaluating the impact of community justice, the most important concern, as suggested by the quote from one of the key practitioners of community justice at the beginning of this section, is that the basis for comparison be the reality of the current system rather than an idealized version of its performance.

Discretionary decisionmaking: ensuring accountability in community justice

The community justice decisionmaking models discussed in this article are often proposed as alternatives to the legal-procedural approach to dispositions and sanctioning assumed by the formal justice process. However, the capacity to determine guilt or innocence has not been developed within these models as it has in the formal criminal justice system. Further, concerns have been raised as to the mechanisms of accountability in community justice decisonmaking.

Griffiths and Hamilton (1996, pp.187–188), in considering the development of justice programs in Aboriginal Communities, have therefore cautioned:

> Care must be taken to ensure that family and kinship networks and the community power hierarchy do not compromise the administration of justice. As in any community, there is a danger of a tyranny of community in which certain individuals and groups of residents, particularly those who are members of vulnerable groups, find themselves at the mercy of those in positions of power and influence.

The often dramatic and dysfunctional power differentials within communities may make true participation justice difficult to achieve and may instead produce harmful side effects in some settings (Griffiths and Hamilton, 1996). Ironically, those communities most in need of holistic, restorative-based justice programs that encourage community residents to become involved in the disposition and sanctioning process are often precisely those communities that are the most dysfunctional and may have only limited interest in and/or capacity for such involvement. Specific attention must be given to the development of strategies for empowering communities and recruiting and retaining the participation of community residents.

Protecting the rights and needs of crime victims

Ensuring that the rights of victims are protected is a critical, but potentially divisive, issue in any community justice process. While victim alienation and exclusion from the formal justice system has been a primary catalyst in the search for alternative forums for responding to crime and disorder (e.g. Young, 1995; Umbreit, 1994), concern has been expressed by many observers that community justice decisionmaking models may not give adequate attention to the rights and needs of vulnerable groups, particularly women and female adolescents.

In Canada, Aboriginal women have voiced concerns about the high rates of sexual and physical abuse in communities and have questioned whether local justice initiatives can provide adequate present and future protection for victims (Griffiths and Hamilton, 1996). Additional concerns as to whether the sanctions imposed on offenders by community justice structures were appropriate also have been voiced. In a study of violence against women in the Canadian Northwest Territories, Peterson (1992, p.75) found that Aboriginal and Inuit women were concerned about the attitudes toward violence held by community residents and how this would impact the operation of community justice initiatives: '[T]here can be differences that develop along generational lines ... older people may evidence a tolerance of violence against women that is no longer acceptable to young women.' Unfortunately, the failure to address these critical points has led to situations in which community justice initiatives undertaken by Aboriginal bands have been first criticized by Aboriginal women and then discredited in their entirety.

The formal justice system: collaboration or cooptation?

A critical issue surrounding the development and implementation of community justice decisionmaking models is 'who controls the agenda?' Traditionally, the formal justice system has maintained a tight rein on initiatives that have been designed as 'alternatives' to the criminal justice process. This is evident in the origins and evolution of youth and adult diversion programs, which appear to have become another appendage to the formal justice process. The inability or unwillingness of decisionmakers in the formal criminal justice system to share power with communities is likely to result in net-widening, rather than the development of more effective alternative decisionmaking processes (Blomberg, 1983; Polk, 1994).

If the new decisionmaking models follow the pattern of development of earlier neighborhood dispute resolution – and to a lesser extent the pattern of VOM as the oldest of the new models – one would anticipate a significant addition to the richness and diversity possible in alternative sanctioning but little impact on the formal system. Both VOM and FGCs (with the exceptions of those in New Zealand) are ultimately dependent on system decisionmakers for referrals, and the potential for power sharing is minimal. If these models are to avoid these now traditional fates for such programs, community advocates will need to begin to work with sympathetic justice professionals who are also committed to community-driven systemic reform in what have become intransigent, top-down, rule-driven criminal justice bureaucracies.

But while a primary objective of proponents of community justice decisionmaking is to have such initiatives institutionalized as part of the justice process, the danger is that system control will lead to the top-down development of generic models of community decisionmaking. Hence, the degree of institutionalization that some of these approaches have been able to achieve in a relatively short time and the rather dramatic results in terms of system/community collaboration (especially in CS) that appear to be possible is both promising and risky. While the high profile given to community justice initiatives may result in grant funding for research and programs, such system support is no guarantee of long-term impact of the type envisioned in the community and restorative justice literature. Moreover, in the absence of substantive community input at the design and implementation phases of specific initiatives, this administrative focus may even result in cooptation or watering down of these approaches in ways that ultimately function to undermine the philosophy and objectives of community justice initiatives (Van Ness, 1993). From a community justice perspective, perhaps the biggest challenge to reparative boards, for example, is the fact that they have been implemented in the system itself. On the one hand, RBs may have the greatest potential for significant impact on the response of the formal system to nonviolent crimes. Moreover, the commitment of administrators to local control may also result in the community assuming and demanding a broader mandate. On the other hand, as a creation of the corrections bureaucracy, RBs may expect to be at the center of an ongoing struggle between efforts to give greater power and autonomy to citizens and the needs of the system to maintain control or ensure system accountability. Ultimately, board members also may be challenged to decide the extent to which their primary client is the community or probation and the court system.

In this regard, of the four models, circle sentencing appears most advanced in an implicit continuum of the importance given to the decisionmaking role of communities. As such, this model provides the most complete example of power sharing in its placement of neighborhood residents in the gatekeeper role (see Table 2). Acting through the Community Justice Committee, the community is clearly the 'driver' in determining which offenders will be admitted to the circle. Eligibility in circles is apparently limited only by the ability of the offender to demonstrate to the Community Justice Committee her or his sincerity and willingness to change. Surprisingly, the most promising lesson of circle sentencing has been that when given decisionmaking power, neighborhood residents often choose to include the *most*, rather than the *least*, serious offenders in community justice processes (Stuart, 1995b; Griffiths and Hamilton, 1996). As a result, however, courts and other agencies in Canadian communities experimenting with circle sentencing have experienced ongoing tension over the extent to which power sharing with the community should be limited and whether statutes are being violated.

Implications and conclusions

Systemic reform toward community justice must not begin and end with new programs or staff positions, but with new values which articulate new roles for victims, offenders, and communities as both clients and coparticipants in the justice process, and, accordingly, create and perpetuate new decisionmaking models that meet their needs for meaningful involvement. As is fundamental to the principles and values of restorative justice, the capacity of these models to impact and even transform formal justice decisionmaking, and ultimately correctional practices, seems to lie in the potential power of these coparticipants, if fully engaged in meaningful decisionmaking processes. For this to occur, however, a rather dramatic change must also occur in the role of professionals from one of sole decisionmaker, to one of facilitator of community involvement and resource to the community (Bazemore and Schiff, 1996).

One limitation of this article has been that in describing these four processes as independent models, we have perhaps exaggerated distinctions between processes that are in fact borrowing insights from each other as they are adapted to meet local needs. Hence, it is important not to impose restrictive definitions on what is clearly a dynamic and evolving movement. However, a primary purpose of this article has been to provide a general framework for describing the dimensions of community justice decisionmaking in order to avoid indiscriminate and arbitrary, all inclusive, groupings of programs and practices under what are, for the most part, ill-defined terms such as 'community justice.' The importance of such comparative discussions at this relatively early stage of the development of the various programs and strategies is to highlight similarities and differences across the four emerging models and to prevent, or at least minimize, the 'community-policing syndrome': the widespread application (and misapplication) of a generic term to a broad range of initiatives without a clear understanding of the differences among interventions or benchmark criteria that can be used to assess consistency with fundamental principles (e.g. Mastrofsky and Ritti, 1995). In the absence of an effort to distinguish what should and should *not* be included under the umbrella of community and restorative justice, and to further define success in these interventions, a unique and valuable opportunity to develop more effective methods for enhancing citizen involvement in the response to crime and disorder will have been missed.

Notes

1 The most concrete impact in the US can be seen in Vermont itself, where reparative boards based on the restorative justice perspective are now state policy. Other states that have adopted restorative justice as the mission for their corrections departments include Minnesota and Maine. State juvenile justice systems in Pennsylvania, Florida, New Mexico, and Montana, among others, have adopted restorative justice principles in policy or statute. In the US a series of high-level work group meetings have recently been held within the Office of Justice Programs at the request of the Attorney General, which in turn have sparked several national and cross-national forums on community and restorative justice (NIJ, 1996a; Robinson, 1996).

2 For the remainder of this article, we use, for convenience, the generic term 'community justice', to describe this overall movement and set of philosophies. However, this does not reflect a preference for this term, and, in fact, as the discussion here suggests, community justice may well be too broad to reflect the more specific influence of restorative justice on decisionmaking models. While restorative justice, or community restorative justice, thus more accurately may characterize the interventions of interest here, the issue of terminology is somewhat political and often less relevant than the nature of the interventions being described. Community justice also is frequently associated in Canada with a political transfer of justice decisionmaking power to local communities or indigenous groups (Depew, 1994; Griffiths and Hamilton, 1996).

3 The original group of neighborhood dispute resolution centers differed from the new models in that they generally dealt with a more narrow range of cases, focusing primarily on domestic and neighborhood disputes rather than crimes *per se* and also appear to have been motivated primarily by an attempt to relieve overcrowded court dockets (Garafalo and Connelly, 1980).

4 Critics of this approach suggest that it is symbolically important that the victim speak first, and one compromise that has been proposed gives the victim a choice of whether he or she precedes or follows the offender (Umbreit and Stacey, 1996). FGC advocates argue that the facilitator can avoid situations in which an offender speaking first might anger a victim by a less than repentant, or less than accurate, portrayal of the incident by coaching the offender and possibly challenging aspects of the offender's story in advance. Facilitators are also encouraged to prepare the victim for what he or she may feel is an unfair account of the incident by the offender (Moore and O'Connell, 1995).

References

Alder, C. and Wundersitz, J. (1994) *Family Group Conferencing and Juvenile Justice Act: The Way Forward or Misplaced Optimism?*, Canberra, ACT, Australian Institute of Criminology.

Barajas, E. Jr (1995) 'Moving toward community justice', *Topics in Community Corrections*, Washington, DC, National Institute of Corrections.

Bazemore, G. and Schiff, M. (1996) 'Community justice/restorative justice: prospects for a new social ecology for community corrections', *International Journal of Comparative and Applied Criminal Justice*, vol.20, no.2, pp.311–34.

Bazemore, G. and Umbreit, M. (1995) 'Rethinking the sanctioning function in juvenile court: retributive or restorative responses to youth crime', *Crime and Delinquency*, vol.41, no.3, pp.296–316.

Belgrave, J. (1995) 'Restorative justice', Discussion paper, Wellington, New Zealand, New Zealand Ministry of Justice.

Blomberg, T. (1983) 'Diversion's desperate results and unresolved questions: an integrated evaluation perspective', *Journal of Research in Crime and Delinquency*, vol.20, no.1, pp.24–38.

Braithwaite, J. and Mugford, S. (1994) 'Conditions of successful reintegration ceremonies', *British Journal of Criminology*, vol.34, no.2, pp.139–71.

Byrne, J.M. (1989) 'Reintegrating the concept of community into community-based correction', *Crime and Delinquency*, no.35, pp.471–9.

Clear, T.R. (1996) 'Toward a corrections of "place": The challenge of "community" in corrections', *National Institute of Justice Journal*, August, pp.52–6.

Depew, R.C. (1994) *Popular Justice in Aboriginal Communities*, Monograph, Ottawa, Department of Justice, Aboriginal Justice Division.

Dooley, M.J. (1995) *Reparative Probation Program*, Waterbury, VT, Vermont Department of Corrections.

Dooley, M.J. (1996) *Restoring Hope Through Community Partnerships: The Real Deal in Crime Control*, Monograph, American Probation and Parole Association.

Galaway, B. and Hudson, J. (eds) (1996) *Restorative Justice: International perspectives*, Monsey, NY, Kugler Publications.

Garafalo, J. and Connelly, K. (1980) 'Dispute resolution centers part I: Major features and processes', *Criminal Justice Abstracts*, December.

Gardner, J. (1990) *On Leadership*, New York, The Free Press.

Goldstein, H. (1987) 'Toward community-oriented policing: potential, basic requirements and threshold questions', *Crime and Delinquency*, no.33, pp.6–30.

Griffiths, C.T. and Hamilton, R. (1996) 'Spiritual renewal, community revitalization and healing: Experience in traditional aboriginal justice in Canada', *International Journal of Comparative and Applied Criminal Justice*, vol.20, no.2, pp.289–311.

Hakiaha, M. (1995) *Presentation to staff of the Territorial Court of the Yukon*, Whitehouse, Yukon, May.

Harrington, C. and Merry, S. (1988) 'Ideological production: the making of community mediation', *Law and Society Review*, vol.22, no.4.

Hudson, J., Galaway, B., Morris, A. and Maxwell, G. (1996) 'Research on family group conferencing in child welfare in New Zealand', *Family Group Conferences: Perspectives on Policy and Practice*, Monsey, NY, Criminal Justice Press, pp.1–16.

Klein, A. (1995) 'Community probation: acknowledging probation's multiple clients', *Topics in Community Corrections*, Washington, DC, National Institute of Corrections, Community Division.

LaPrairie, C. (1994) *Community Justice or Just Communities? Aboriginal Communities in Search of Justice*, Unpublished paper, Ottawa, Department of Justice.

Maine Council of Churches (1996) 'DOC hires victim services coordinator', *Kaleidoscope of Justice*, vol.1, no.3, p.4, September.

Mastrofsky, S. and Ritti, R. (1995) 'Making sense of community policing: a theory-based analysis', Paper presented at the annual meeting of the American Society of Criminology, November.

Maxwell, G. and Morris, A. (1993) *Family Participation, Cultural Diversity and Victim Involvement in Youth Justice: A New Zealand Experiment*, Wellington, New Zealand, Victoria University.

McDonald, J., Thorsborne, M., Moore, D., Hyndman, M. and O'Connell, T. (1995) *Real Justice Training Manual: Coordinating Family Group Conferences*, Pipersville, PA, Piper's Press.

McElrea, F.W.M. (1993) 'A new model of justice', in Brown, B.J. (ed.) *The Youth Court in New Zealand: A New Model of Justice*, Auckland, New Zealand, Legal Research Foundation.

McGillis, D. and Mullen, J. (1977) *Neighborhood Justice Centers: An Analysis of Potential Models*, Washington, DC, National Institute of Law Enforcement and Criminal Justice, Law Enforcement Assistance Administration.

Melton, A. (1995) 'Indigenous justice systems and tribal society', *Judicature*, vol.70, no.3, pp.126–33.

Moore, D.B. and O'Connell, T. (1995) 'Family conferencing in Wagga-Wagga: A communitarian model of justice', in Adler, C. and Wundersitz, J. (eds) *Family Conferencing and Juvenile Justice: The Way Forward or Misplaced Optimism?*, Canberra, Australian Institute of Criminology.

(NIJ) National Institute of Justice (1996a) *National Symposium on Restorative Justice Proceedings*, Washington, DC.

(NIJ) National Institute of Justice (1996b)

Communities Mobilizing against Crime: Making Partnerships Work, Washington, DC.

Peterson, K.R. (1992) *The Justice House – Report of the Special Advisor on Gender Equality*, Yellow Knife, Canada, Department of Justice, Government of the Northwest Territories.

Polk, K. (1994) 'Family conferencing: theoretical and evaluative questions', in Alder, C. and Wundersitz, J. (eds) *Family Conferencing and Juvenile Justice: The Way Forward or Misplaced Optimism?*, Canberra, Australian Institute of Criminology, pp.155–68.

Pranis, K. (1995) 'Building community support for restorative justice: principles and strategies', Unpublished paper, Minnesota, Department of Corrections.

Reparative Board Program Description (1995) Vermont Department of Corrections.

Robinson, J. (1996) 'Research on family group conferencing in child welfare in New Zealand', in Hudson, J., Galaway, B., Morris, A. and Maxwell, G. (eds) *Family Group Conferences: Perspectives on Policy and Practice*, Monsey, NY, Criminal Justice Press, pp.49–64.

Rottman, D. (1996) 'Community courts: Prospects and limits in community justice', *National Institute of Justice Journal*, pp.50–1.

Schneider, A. (ed.) (1985) *Guide to Juvenile Restitution*, Washington, DC, Office of Juvenile Justice and Delinquency Prevention.

Strang, H. (1995) *Family Group Conferencing: The Victims' Perspective*, Paper presented at the American Society of Criminology annual meeting, Boston, MA, November.

Stuart, B. (1995a) 'Sentencing circles – making "real" differences', Unpublished paper, Territorial Court of the Yukon.

Stuart, B. (1995b) 'Circle sentencing mediation and consensus – turning swords into ploughshares', Unpublished paper, Territorial Court of the Yukon.

Travis, J. (1996) 'Lessons for the criminal justice system from twenty years of policing reform', Keynote address at the First Annual Conference of the New York Campaign for Effective Crime Policy, New York.

Umbreit, M. (1994) *Victim Meets Offender: The Impact of Restorative Justice in Mediation*, Monsey, NY, Criminal Justice Press.

Umbreit, M. and Coates, R. (1993) 'Cross-site analysis of victim–offender conflict: An analysis of programs in these three states', *Juvenile and Family Court Journal*, vol.43, no.1, pp.21–8.

Umbreit, M. and Stacey, S. (1996) 'Family group conferencing comes to the US: a comparison with victim offender mediation', *Juvenile and Family Court Journal*, pp.29–39.

Umbreit, M. and Zehr, H. (1996) 'Restorative family group conferences: differing models and guidelines for practice', *Federal Probation*, vol.60, no.3, pp.24–9.

Van Ness, D. (1993) 'New wine and old wineskins: four challenges of restorative justice', *Criminal Law Forum*, vol.4, no.2, pp.251–76.

Young, M. (1995) *Restorative Community Justice: A Call to Action*, Washington, DC, Report for National Organization for Victim Assistance.

Zehr, H. (1990) *Changing Lenses: A New Focus for Crime and Justice*, Scottsdale, PA, Herald Press.

CHAPTER 8

Restorative Police Cautioning in Aylesbury – from Degrading to Reintegrative Shaming Ceremonies?

by Richard Young and Benjamin Goold

Introduction

Virtually all cautions in the Aylesbury police area are administered by the Restorative Cautioning Unit, consisting of two Thames Valley Police constables (one of whom works part-time) and one civilian support worker.[1] The most distinctive feature of the Unit's cautioning process lies in its commitment to invite those affected by an offence, most notably the victim, to attend and take part in the cautioning session. The cautioning police officer seeks to facilitate discussion of the harm caused by the offence and of how any of the interests or relationships damaged might be restored by the offender.

The process is inspired by a cluster of ideas that have become known as 'restorative justice', the central tenet of which is that crime should be conceptualised as primarily a matter concerning the individuals affected by an offence rather than as a breach of a more abstract 'public interest'. In cases where an offender is apprehended, the achievement of a reparative outcome is given priority over any more 'objective' standard of justice.[2] The process is also based on the criminological theory of John Braithwaite known as 'reintegrative shaming'.[3] This argues that crime is most effectively controlled by making offenders ashamed of their behaviour but in a way which promotes their reintegration into their community.[4] In essence, the Aylesbury cautioning process seeks to achieve restorative outcomes through a process of reintegrative shaming.

The Unit in Aylesbury has attracted much attention, including that of the Home Secretary, Jack Straw, who observed one of its cautions in September 1997. There is no doubt that the media interest has centred on the apparent impact of restorative cautioning on recidivism.[5] This article represents the first attempt, however, to subject the work of the Restorative Cautioning Unit to independent evaluation. It is not our intention here to present a critical discussion of the theories underlying restorative justice and reintegrative shaming. Rather, on the basis of a small-scale empirical study conducted in 1997, the aim is to examine the extent to which the Aylesbury cautioning process is consistent with these theories and to explore its impact on those who experience it. The research reported here helped pave the way for a three-year study of restorative cautioning as practised by Thames Valley Police,[6] and the discussion in this article is necessarily of an exploratory and preliminary nature.

Research methodology

We carried out the bulk of our study in the months of July and August 1997. The staff of the Restorative Cautioning Unit agreed to provide whatever information we required, including unfettered access to the Unit's filing system and database. We concentrated our efforts on exploring in detail a small number of cases from a variety of perspectives. We selected the cases to be studied ourselves to avoid any risk of being invited to attend only on days when the Unit expected the cautions to be successful, dramatic, difficult or otherwise 'interesting'. The key selection criterion was that the cautions observed

Source: Criminal Law Review (1999), pp.126–38, February.

should be broadly representative of the caseload of the Unit whilst allowing us to observe both police officers at work.[7]

We secured the permission of all participants to our observing and tape-recording the 15 cautioning sessions.[8] Immediately after each caution, we talked in confidence with the key participants, interviewing 15 of the 17 offenders observed, all six victims[9] and 10 other participants (all were offenders' supporters – no victims' supporters attended the observed cautions).[10] Everyone we approached for permission to conduct a tape-recorded interview agreed to grant it. In all 15 cases we carried out a tape-recorded interview with the cautioning police officer.

After transcribing the tapes of the 44 completed interviews, data analysis was carried out by both authors independently of one another, as a way of checking whether there was agreement about the major themes and issues emerging from the data. Having satisfied ourselves that this was so, we then identified the cases which would best illustrate these major themes and issues. In the next section we examine the nature of what we shall refer to as 'old-style' police cautioning, thus allowing us to highlight subsequently how 'restorative cautioning' differs from previous practice.

The police caution as degradation ceremony

A caution is administered in person by a police officer, usually at a police station, and Home Office guidelines envisage it taking the form of an explanatory warning:

> The significance of the caution must be explained: that is, that a record will be kept of the caution, that the fact of a previous caution may influence the decision whether or not to prosecute if the person should offend again, and that it may be cited if the person should subsequently be found guilty of an offence by a court.[11]

One of the theories underlying the evolution of police cautioning has been that this type of low-key response to a relatively minor offence avoids the risk of a courtroom appearance degrading offenders and ultimately confirming them in a deviant self-identity.[12] The widespread assumption that cautioning operates to protect offenders from degradation was challenged by Maggy Lee in the only extensive research on the process of cautioning as experienced by offenders.[13] She argued that a punitive ethos permeated the cautioning process, centred on a belief in individual and parental culpability for offending behaviour. Drawing on the work of Garfinkel,[14] Lee contended that cautioning sessions functioned as 'degradation ceremonies', and that 'the degrading tactics were directed towards the parents as much as the young people'.[15]

She highlighted five key features of the cautioning process that contributed to this degradation. First, it was impressed upon offenders that they were being given a second chance by not being taken to court and that any subsequent offending would result in automatic prosecution. Thus, rather than the caution being presented as a proportionate, fair response to relatively trivial wrongdoing, an attempt was made to make those cautioned appreciate their good fortune in escaping 'real punishment'. Secondly, in asking questions about the offence and the background of the offender, the police looked for respect for private property and authority from parents and offenders alike, and made it obvious that they were dissatisfied with the level of respect displayed by those in front of them. Thirdly, the police would seek to stage the caution in such a way that would most effectively 'dress-down' and maximise the discomfort of the offender, as by forcing eye-contact or by manipulating the spacing arrangements. As one officer told Lee: 'If it is a first-time offender, I'll sit on a chair, make him or her stand in front of me, parents behind so the child won't be distracted.'[16] Fourthly, the cautioning officer would seek a 'heart-to-heart talk', focusing in particular on how a criminal record would disadvantage a young person in the employment market. Fifthly, the young person's status was condemned as criminal, as in the following example Lee quotes[17] from her research notes:

> Inspector: So [this offence] makes you what?
>
> P: A thief [Almost in tears]
>
> Inspector: A thief, ugh!

To the extent that one can generalise from Lee's findings,[18] labelling theory would suggest that cautioning is an effective intervention (in the sense of minimising the risk of reoffending) *despite* the manner in which it is administered. John Braithwaite's important contribution to theoretical thinking in this area was not discussed by Lee, however.[19] Whilst accepting that stigmatising degradation ceremonies can increase the risk of reoffending, he rejects the view that moral condemnation of criminal behaviour is therefore best avoided. To ensure that such condemnation has positive consequences it is necessary that it is bounded rather than of open-ended duration and that efforts are made 'to maintain bonds of love or respect throughout the finite period of suffering shame'.[20]

Braithwaite's work has provided theoretical inspiration for a number of cautioning schemes seeking to promote dialogue between those affected by an offence, most notably the police-led 'community conferencing' initiative in Wagga Wagga, Australia.[21] Based on their observation of a small number of 'community conferences', Braithwaite and Mugford have argued that it is possible to identify a number of key conditions under which degradation ceremonies can be transformed into successful reintegrative ceremonies.[22] These conditions include ensuring that the offence, and not the offender, is made the focus of condemnation, as well as giving victims and other participants (such as the offender's supporters) control over the process of reintegration and the conduct of the ceremony. It was these insights that underpinned the Aylesbury Unit's aspiration to replace 'old-style' cautioning with 'restorative cautioning'.

The Aylesbury cautioning process

All cases considered as suitable for a caution by the multi-agency panel in Aylesbury[23] are passed to the Restorative Cautioning Unit for it to make the arrangements for the cautioning session.[24] On arrival at the Unit's premises, participants are shown into a large room containing a circle of office chairs, and the cautioning police officer invites each party to speak in turn according to a script derived from the Wagga Wagga model.

Although the cautioning officer attempted to structure all cautions in a similar way, we noted that in practice the style of cautioning differed according to the age of the offender. Where offenders were adults, the cautioning sessions more frequently took the form of a dialogue and the cautioning officer's role was less prominent and less directive. For example, in three of the eight adult cautions (including two where victims were present) spirited discussion took place concerning the background to the offence and the fairness of the offender taking all the blame for what had happened. In these sessions the police officer's role drifted away from that envisaged by the standard script for facilitating a restorative caution towards that of an impartial mediator. Even where the offence was clear-cut (for example, the three adult cautions for possession of cannabis) the police officer and the offender tended to talk to one another in a conversational manner: reintegrative shaming techniques were not a prominent feature of these exchanges.

Where the cautioning sessions involved young offenders, by contrast, the role of the police officer was more dominant and the shaming of the offending behaviour more obvious, clear-cut and uncontested. Offenders said comparatively little in these sessions, and their contributions were prompted by directive questioning by the police officer. Even where victims and supporters of offenders were present, there was little in the way of dialogue not involving the police officer. The dominance of the police officer in these sessions was confirmed by a rudimentary form of content analysis in which we examined the spoken contributions of each participant. In six of the seven juvenile cautions the police officer's questioning and comments accounted for between 58 and 70 per cent of the words spoken.[25] By contrast, in six of the seven taped adult cautions the officer's contributions took up between 21 and 53 per cent of words.[26] Of course, the dominance of the police officer was affected by other factors such as the number of persons present at the cautioning session, and whether victims were present, but by far the most important factor appeared to be the age of the offender. Thus, for example, in two adult criminal damage cautioning sessions involving five and three participants, the police officer's 'dominance factor' was 31 and 21 per cent respectively, compared with 58 per cent in a juvenile criminal damage case involving six participants.

In the rest of this article we focus primarily on the cautioning process as experienced by young offenders. This is for three reasons: first, the great majority of those cautioned nationally (and in Aylesbury) are juveniles; secondly, Lee's study of 'old-style' cautioning was restricted to young offenders, thus providing us with a basis for comparison only in relation to those offenders; and thirdly, the core sequence observed in juvenile cautions was much more consistent than in the adult cautions, thus allowing us to describe the process in a reasonably succinct manner.

One striking difference between 'old-style' cautions and restorative cautions for young offenders is the elaborate structure of the latter, usually running to 30–40 minutes in length, and sometimes much longer. Usually the officer began with some words of welcome, designed to put the offender at ease and to describe the purpose and informality of the meeting. Then the offender was asked to provide 'their side of the story'. In the majority of the juvenile conferences we observed, the offender readily provided this, if somewhat nervously at first. These 'stories' were for the most part largely factual – none of the offenders we saw cautioned denied that they had committed the offence. The facilitators used questions to draw out the details of the story, to clarify certain points and to focus the session on the harm caused. A typical sequence of questions was as follows:

> Facilitator: OK. So interviewed, on tape? Finger-printed, photographs, DNA test?
>
> Offender: Yeah.
>
> Facilitator: OK. What was all that like for you?
>
> Offender: I didn't really know what was going on, because I didn't really think I'd done that much wrong. But like I was being treated like a criminal. But, you know, it was a foolish thing to do, but I didn't feel like I was a criminal.
>
> Facilitator: How did the interview go?
>
> Offender: Well, I answered the questions and I felt sorry after, especially seeing my mum as well.
>
> Facilitator: Mum was upset was she?
>
> Offender: Mmmn.
>
> Facilitator: Who do you think you caused harm to, by what you did?
>
> Offender: Um, the people who were scared by what I did.
>
> Facilitator: Anybody else
>
> Offender: My friend who was there and …mum and dad.
>
> Facilitator: I think there's one other person that you've left out, but I'll come on to that in a minute. (Case 9)

At this stage the police officer used similar questions to encourage any victims present to explain how the offence had caused harm to them and, where appropriate, their family or friends. On those occasions where the victim had chosen not to attend, the officer attempted to present their point of view, often stressing the extent of the victim's anger, dismay, and the harm caused by the offence. The various supporters present (typically the parents of the offender) were then invited to explain how the incident had affected them. On those occasions where they expressed a sense of responsibility for an offender's behaviour the officer stressed that they should not blame themselves. Where possible, the facilitator attempted to draw out comments on the extent to which the offending behaviour had caused them to feel hurt or disappointment. In all but one of the conferences we observed where an offender's supporter was present, at least one of those supporters indicated that they would find it difficult to trust the offender in the future. The following extract from Case 13 demonstrates this point well:

> Supporter: If I thought I could do something that'd stop him, then I'd be happier, but I don't know that I could.
>
> Facilitator: So how's this affected you?
>
> Supporter: I've just been watching him all the time.

Facilitator: Why?

Supporter: Because I don't know what he's going to do. Because [when] he's done one thing you worry that he's going to do something else.

Immediately after all participants had spoken in turn, the facilitator attempted to impress upon the offender the nature and extent of the harm that he or she had caused. If the offender had failed earlier in the conference to identify themselves as one of those who had suffered as a consequence of their behaviour, then the facilitator now expressed the view that the offender must have experienced stress as a result of being caught up in the criminal process. Following on from this, the facilitator would ask the offender whether there was anything they wanted to say to anyone present. On those occasions where an apology or expression of regret was not offered, no further effort was made by the facilitator to extract one from the offender. Where the offender did apologise, however, the facilitator was quick to acknowledge this: 'I've got to say this, I've had people in here who couldn't even apologise, who aren't as big a man as you are. And just couldn't do it. But, you know, more power to you. Because you're able to do it' (Case 8).

In all of the cases we observed, the facilitator at this point shifted the focus of the conference to the question of what could be done to repair the harm caused to both the victim and the offender's relationship with their supporters. Supporters were asked what they most wanted to get out of the sessions, and the usual answer was some reassurance that no further offence would be committed. The offender was encouraged by the police officer to identify ways of keeping out of trouble and regaining the respect or trust of their supporters, such as more frequent attendance at school. Where an identifiable victim was involved, an agreement to make some form of compensation or to offer a written apology was often negotiated at this stage. Finally, the facilitator addressed the offender directly for several minutes, and in the tone of a 'heart-to-heart talk', developed a number of key themes, most notably:

(i) *You have begun the process of putting things right*: 'Thanks, all of you. It's not been easy, but I certainly think you've gone some way to repairing the harm. I mean there's still a lot of work to do. Your mum's very upset, she said the trust has gone a bit, and she worries even more. You've got to work hard to put that right, and it won't be easy'. (Case 9)

(ii) *You are in a web of caring relationships*: 'You're lucky, because you've got all this help. People are desperate to help and guide you. Because they care about you. If they didn't care, they wouldn't be here. And you obviously care too because I can see that you're upset.' (Case 11)

(iii) *You're not stupid, but you did something dumb*: 'You can turn this around because I'm not looking at some dumb knuckle-dragging kid. I'm looking at a bright intelligent kid who's made a mistake, that's all.' (Case 9)

The officer concluded the cautioning session by explaining the legal aspects of the caution, and the offender was asked to sign a form to acknowledge that this explanation had been given. It was emphasised that any further offence would result in automatic prosecution and a criminal conviction, and that this might make travelling abroad problematic and obtaining a job nigh impossible. Finally, the officer gave all the participants a short questionnaire form seeking views on the cautioning session.

Observations on the Aylesbury process

By comparison with 'old-style' cautioning, typically delivered by officers using idiosyncratic and often highly questionable methods, the Aylesbury process represents a significant and welcome shift in policing practices. Consistent with the theory of reintegrative shaming, central to all of the cautions observed was a commitment on the part of the facilitator to ensure that it was the criminal behaviour which was the focus of shaming, and not the offenders themselves. Moreover, we saw no instance of a police officer seeking deference from offenders by telling them, for example, to 'speak up', 'sit up straight' or 'look at me when you're talking'. The officers appeared to us to be genuinely concerned with the future welfare of these young people and were committed and dedicated in their approach. All of those present at the cautioning session were treated with respect and invited to take part in the process.

It is also possible, however, to point to a number of similarities between the restorative approach practised in Aylesbury and the 'old-style' cautions observed by Lee. Perhaps most significantly, the police officer remains the dominant figure in the process. This is despite the fact that, according to the theory of reintegrative shaming, it is essential for those with a direct stake in the resolution of the offence and its aftermath to be given 'centre stage' if any meaningful or lasting impression is to be made upon the offender. On occasion, it was apparent that the facilitator was attempting to mould the comments and interactions of the participants to conform to an ideal envisaged by the 'cautioning script' rather than allowing them to express themselves freely or communicate directly with one another. This sometimes provoked forms of resistance, as in the following example taken from Case 13:

> Facilitator: So what's it been like since you knew you were going to get a caution?
>
> Offender: Nothing really, just acted like normal and tried to get it out of my mind.
>
> Facilitator: But it's always come back? [Asked rhetorically]
>
> Offender: Occasionally. Not much.
>
> Facilitator: But enough.
>
> Offender: Mmm. [Not really agreeing with this]
>
> Facilitator: Mmm, so it's been a constant worry, and stress on you and …
>
> Offender: [Interrupting] Not really stress.
>
> Facilitator: No?
>
> Offender: Not really, it didn't really bother me that much.

Another similarity with old-style cautioning was the emphasis placed on the consequences of any further offence. While the facilitator would often be at pains to distinguish between the offender and his or her behaviour, it was invariably underscored (and this was true of adult cautions too) that although on this occasion offenders had been 'given a break', the next time they would be prosecuted, regardless of the seriousness of any future offence. This seemed to us to send a mixed message. Offenders were told on the one hand that they had made an out-of-character stupid mistake whilst on the other they were treated as if requiring stern individual deterrent messages. This deterrent aspect to the cautioning session could also be seen in the way in which the facilitator sought to 'talk up' the harm caused by the offence, as in the exchange quoted above. Another example of such apparent exaggeration was seen in a case of criminal damage caused by two youths kicking a fence (Case 6). The police file recorded the victim's views (as expressed to the arresting officer) in the following manner: 'The complainant wanted the youths in question to be spoken to and given a stern warning. He wasn't bothered about making a formal complaint re: the minor damage. (However, I'm sure he could be persuaded to …)'. This victim chose not to attend the caution, and his views were summarised by the facilitating police officer as follows:

> Well, he didn't want nothing to do with it, because the people who own the fence are absolutely *gutted* by your behaviour because, you know, as both your mums have pointed out, you aren't kids, you are not stupid little morons, you are young adults, who know better and shouldn't have done it and they *do not* want to see you, they are *that* angry. In fact I don't think, in all the time I've been doing this kind of work, I've come across people who are more angry. I've dealt with you know, incredible things, but they're *absolutely* livid, because it's where they live and they don't feel safe by what you've done. (original emphasis).

There was, in other words, an element of 'case construction' in the practice of the Restorative Cautioning Unit. A number of studies have explored the social processes by which police and prosecutors assemble cases for or against prosecution, for example by emphasising or filtering out certain 'facts'.[27] What we observed in Aylesbury was the constructing of cautions with a view to making the greatest possible impression on young offenders. This strategy is, we think, ethically questionable, and, as we explore below, it may even be counter-productive in that it could undermine the legitimacy of the process in young offenders' minds.

Assessments of the cautioning process by offenders, victims and other participants

Taken as a whole, assessments of the restorative cautioning sessions as expressed to us in interview were clearly positive. For example, when participants (other than the facilitator) were asked to say which of a limited number of pre-coded answers best described their views about the caution the answers given were mainly favourable. This was true of both adult and juvenile cautions and we have accordingly aggregated the responses of all our interviewees.[28] Eighteen interviewees said they were 'very positive' or 'positive' in their attitude to the meeting, seven had 'mixed' feelings, three were 'negative' and one 'very negative'. Attitudes towards the police officer who handled the caution were overwhelmingly positive with 20 out of 29 interviewees declaring themselves 'very satisfied' (all eight of the supporters, five of the six victims and seven of the 15 offenders), a further seven interviewees as 'satisfied' (six offenders, one victim), whilst two offenders had 'no attitude'. It was clear from the answers to our more open-ended questions that the sources of any dissatisfaction varied from caution to caution and defied extensive generalisation. It did appear, however, that the most common source of discontent was a feeling amongst young offenders that they had not been given enough explanation about the process before coming to the caution.[29] Whereas they generally expected to be shouted at and told off, they found themselves instead being asked a long series of questions. Despite finding it difficult to formulate answers when 'put on the spot' like this, they considered the process overall to be considerably less punitive than they had feared, as in the following example.

> [Beforehand] I was scared, frightened and that ... because I thought they would like shout and have a go at you and stuff like that. But they didn't. Then I thought, that's *amazing* isn't it?! I think to be honest that's what they normally do don't they, 'Get in there!' and all that ... Mmm. It was a surprise, I thought, they done a good job and that, hadn't they? ... [The officer] was very kind. (Interview 29)

The young offenders to whom we spoke typically perceived themselves as having committed relatively minor offences which had not caused much direct harm. The *overall* police response to their behaviour was therefore seen as disproportionate. The structure of the *cautioning session* itself, however, was perceived as basically fair: offenders valued the chance to put their side of the story, and were glad that their supporters were present. As one explained:

> I don't like the way it was handled by the police. Like they were taking all these DNA tests and everything. I didn't think that was necessary. I didn't know what I was doing was illegal... But today it was definitely fair, yeah...[The police officer] was just really nice all the way through it. (Interview 12)

Offenders quite often conceded that the session had reinforced or deepened their understanding of the multiple harms caused by their behaviour. Whilst finding it difficult to articulate their feelings about whether the cautioning session would make any difference to their relationships with parents or guardians, some of their comments suggested that the process may well have had a reintegrative effect, as in this example:

> It was good that I could find out how [my mum] was feeling, but that's what I expected her to say anyway ... Hearing her say all that like, it was quite upsetting ... [I see what I did as] more serious now ... [because] I didn't know how upset she would be about it, and I didn't know about how in the future I wouldn't be able to go abroad and stuff if it was on my record. (Interview 39)

The cautions we observed may also have had some deterrent effect in that the offenders clearly understood that a record of the caution would be kept and that they now needed to keep out of trouble if they were to avoid prosecution in future. All offenders expressed relief that their contact with the criminal process was at an end, and that they had avoided a court appearance and the stigma of conviction. This was the overriding evaluation of the significance of the caution – that the courtroom had been avoided.

It was clear from our interviews with offenders' parents and guardians (and with the one victim we observed take part in a juvenile caution) that other participants are broadly sympathetic to the way in which the police are using the cautioning process to confront offenders with the harm their actions have caused. These interviewees generally wished, however, to reserve final judgment on the value of the process until enough time had elapsed for them to see whether it had made any difference to the behaviour of the offender.

Our interviews with the cautioning police officers revealed that they were confident about the value of their cautioning model, but not complacent about their use of it – indeed their evaluations of how effective and well-handled each session had been were generally less positive than those of the other participants. We deduced from these interviews, and from our perusal of 600 case files, that the cautioning officers assess whether a particular caution was successful by the extent to which the offender showed visible signs of remorse or shame. Where such signs were perceived to be lacking the notes in the files frequently expressed concern about the likelihood of reoffending. As one would expect, given the strong emphasis on the theory of reintegrative shaming in the Unit's work, the litmus test of success is regarded by the officers as being the impact of this type of caution on recidivism. Due to the exploratory nature of this study we did not attempt ourselves to measure any such impact but we did explore with the staff of the Unit the way in which it was monitoring the apparent effects of the cautioning process.

The impact of restorative cautioning on recidivism

The notion that the Restorative Cautioning Unit has 'slashed'[30] reoffending by those cautioned from 30 to 4 per cent appears to have taken a hold in some influential circles. However, the press reports which quoted these figures left out many important caveats. The 'baseline' 30 per cent figure was taken from a Home Office *nationwide* study of recorded reoffending within five years of a caution for a 'standard list offence'.[31] No accurate record exists of known reoffending following a caution (whether for a 'standard list' offence or not) within the Aylesbury police area prior to the introduction of 'restorative cautioning'. The figures, therefore, are not based on a comparison of like with like. Moreover, the 4 per cent recidivism figure was based on the Aylesbury Unit's own monitoring of 'repeat business'. When its 'clients' committed further offences which were dealt with outside the Aylesbury police area, or which were referred immediately for prosecution within the Aylesbury area (thus by-passing the multi-agency panel), they did not come to the attention of the Unit immediately and many may never do so. Finally, no standard follow-up period was used in calculating the 'reoffending rate'. Whether the caution took place a month or a year ago made no difference – if the Unit had yet to hear of a further offence committed by the individual concerned, the case counted as a 'success'. The upshot is that the reoffending rate as expressed in the national media is almost certain to have considerably overstated the 'success' achieved through restorative cautioning. We simply do not know whether the Aylesbury Unit or any restorative or reintegrative initiative anywhere in the world is achieving any significant reduction in reoffending rates. To obtain reliable evidence on this requires a large-scale longitudinal study, preferably one in which criminal cases are randomly assigned to a 'restorative' or 'traditional' process and in which reoffending is rigorously monitored through a self-report study completed after a standard and sufficient follow-up period. One notable experiment along these lines is underway in Canberra, Australia, and data on reoffending will be available within the next year or so.

Conclusion

It is clear from the above analysis that the shift from degrading cautioning ceremonies to reintegrative shaming sessions is as yet incomplete. There is, however, a strong commitment within Aylesbury to refine and improve its restorative cautioning model in the light of emerging experience and data. With that in mind, we conclude with some reflections about the future development of this model.

There is no reason to think that the Aylesbury model of cautioning will not endure. Its underlying philosophy is certainly in line with that expressed by section 37 of the Crime and Disorder Act 1998 which stipulates that the principal aim of the youth justice system is to prevent offending. The planned replacement (sections 65 and 66) of cautioning with a system of reprimands and final warnings (being piloted for 18 months from September 1998) is also consistent with the deterrent and reintegrative elements of the Aylesbury process.[32]

We believe that it would be wise, however, to place less stress in future on the possible impact of restorative cautioning on reducing reoffending. In our view, the cautioning session should be regarded primarily as an opportunity to allow all those affected by an offence to express their own sense of harm and need for repair in a safe environment, and also as a more accountable, open and discursive form of criminal justice than old-style cautioning.[33] We adopt this position in part because we think that current expectations of what restorative cautioning can achieve are unrealistic and need to be moderated if a media-inspired backlash at some future date is to be avoided. There are good theoretical reasons for believing that cautioning based on the principles of reintegrative shaming will have more of an impact on recidivism than 'old-style' cautioning, but equally good theoretical reasons for doubting that the impact will be spectacular. Even the best designed and implemented programmes for offenders rarely produce reductions in reoffending of more than a dozen percentage points.[34]

But we hold to this position for another reason. In our view the emphasis we saw in Aylesbury on 'promoting behavioural change' was sometimes excessive. Most young offenders do not 'need' the strong deterrent messages communicated in Aylesbury – most will not come to the attention of the police again whatever the content of the cautioning process. Moreover, where harm was exaggerated, or too much remorse expected, the intended additional deterrent effect may have been offset or even outweighed by the sense of unfairness this could engender in offenders.[35] There is evidence that people obey the law (and co-operate with its agents) partly because they acknowledge legal institutions such as the police to be legitimate.[36] Restorative cautioning sessions constitute important encounters between offenders, other members of the public, and the police. If they are perceived to be unfair by those taking part in them, the damage to the legitimacy of the police may be significant. It would be ironic if a cautioning process aimed at reparation resulted in such damage. With that in mind we welcome the emphasis on fair process and proportionality in Thames Valley Police's guidelines for facilitators issued in June 1998. This guidance should help to ensure that practice in Aylesbury and across Thames Valley Police is further shifted away from 'old-style' cautioning.

Notes

1 The practices analysed here are part of a broader Thames Valley Police initiative in restorative justice. From April 1998, all cautions administered by Thames Valley officers are meant to be restorative in character. Whilst the Aylesbury Unit's style of work is not necessarily representative of the Thames Valley Police's restorative cautioning programme, it may be regarded as a prototype of the significant shift in police practice intended by Thames Valley Police headquarters. In the year beginning April 1, 1996 the Unit administered 167 cautions and in the following year 435.

2 Space constraints preclude consideration of the wide variety of theories and practical approaches associated with 'restorative justice'. See further, von Hirsch, A. and Ashworth, A. (1998) *Principled Sentencing*, Oxford, Hart, 2nd edn, Chapter 7.

3 Braithwaite, J. (1989) *Crime, Shame and Reintegration*, Cambridge, Cambridge University Press.

4 See *ibid.*, pp.12–13: 'the distinction is between shaming that leads to stigmatization – to outcasting, to confirmation of a deviant master status – versus shaming that is reintegrative, that shames whilst maintaining bonds of respect or love, that sharply terminates disapproval with forgiveness, instead of amplifying deviance by progressively casting the deviant out.'

5 For example, on October 18, 1997 it was reported in *The Guardian* that 'Thames Valley police ... yesterday claimed they had lowered the numbers of young people reoffending from 30 per cent to 4 per cent'.

6 The larger study, which began in April 1998, is directed by Carolyn Hoyle and Richard Young of the Oxford Centre for Criminological Research, and is funded by the Joseph Rowntree Foundation.

7 Four of the cautions observed were for possessing cannabis, four for criminal damage, two for theft, two for assault, and one each for burglary, cycling on a pavement and possession of an offensive weapon. In the year to March 31, 1997, 69 of the 167 cautions administered were for theft, and nearly all of these were for shoplifting. The next largest categories of offence for which cautions were given were possession of cannabis (14 per cent of the total), and criminal damage and assault (at around 8 per cent each).

8 One offender allowed us to observe but not tape-record his caution. He subsequently agreed to us conducting a tape-recorded interview with him.

9 Victims attend less than half of all cautions administered by the Unit and a high proportion of those who attend are representing large town-centre shops.

10 In two instances, two offenders' supporters were interviewed together, thus making a total of 29 interviews with participants rather than 31.

11 National Standards for Cautioning (Revised), Note 2D, issued as an attachment to Home Office Circular 18/1994, 'The Cautioning of offenders'.

12 For critical discussion of this 'labelling' perspective, and the evidence bearing on its validity, see Braithwaite, *op.cit.*, pp.16–21, and Williams, K. (1997) *Textbook on Criminology*, Blackstone Press, 3rd edn, pp.418–24.

13 Lee, M. (1995) 'Pre-court diversion and youth justice', in Noaks, L. *et al.* (eds) *Contemporary Issues in Criminology*, Cardiff, University of Wales Press.

14 Garfinkel, H. (1956) 'Conditions of successful degradation ceremonies', *American Journal of Sociology*, no.64, p.420.

15 Lee, *op.cit.*, p.320.

16 *ibid.*, p.324.

17 *ibid.*, p.326.

18 Lee's focus was on 'delayed cautions' administered by a senior officer, usually an inspector. She does not discuss the 'instant caution', typically administered quickly by custody sergeants shortly after arrest as an expedient way of disposing of minor cases: see Hoyle, C. and Young, R. (1998) *A Survey of Restorative Cautioning within the Thames Valley*, Oxford, Centre for Criminological Research, p.13. Such cautions are probably more bewildering than degrading for offenders.

19 Nor does she discuss Braithwaite's work in a fuller account of her study of cautioning: Lee, M. (1998) *Youth, Crime and Police Work*, Basingstoke, MacMillan Press.

20 Braithwaite, *op.cit.*, p.101.

21 See Moore, D. with Forsythe, L. (1995) A *New Approach to Juvenile Justice: An Evaluation of Family Conferencing in Wagga Wagga*, A Report to the Criminology Research Council, Wagga Wagga, Centre for Rural Social Research.

22 Braithwaite, J. and Mugford, S. (1994) 'Conditions of successful reintegration ceremonies: dealing with juvenile offenders' *British Journal of Criminology*, no.34, pp.139–71. See also Jackson, S. (1998) 'Family group conferences in youth justice: the issues for implementation in England and Wales', *Howard Journal*, no.37, p.34.

23 Most of those referred are 'first-time' offenders. The Unit's original policy of not carrying out 'repeat' restorative cautions is no longer applied rigidly.

24 At the time of the research, offenders, victims and their respective 'supporters' were asked by letter to attend the session, whereas current practice is for one of the Unit's police officers to explain the cautioning process by telephone or in person.

25 In the other juvenile case the offenders had left home and were leading a near-adult lifestyle. The tone of the session was similar to that of an adult caution, thus helping to account for the officer's relatively low dominance (at 32 per cent).

26 In the remaining taped adult case the offender appeared to be under the influence of cannabis, and the officer, unsurprisingly, did most of the talking (71 per cent).

27 See, in particular, McConville, M., Sanders, A. and Leng, R. (1991) *The Case for the Prosecution*, London, Routledge.

28 A rider should be added that adult offenders were more positive than were juveniles in their evaluations of restorative cautioning.

29 Since we completed our research, the Unit has changed its practice so as to give more information to participants in advance of the cautioning session.

30 *Evening Standard*, 17 October, 1997.

31 The study thus excluded those cautioned for less serious types of summary offence: Dulai, D. and Greenhorn, M. (1995) 'The criminal histories of those cautioned in 1985, 1988 and 1991', *Research Bulletin*, no.37, Home Office Research and Statistics Department, p.75.

32 See the articles by Fionda (1999) *Crim. L.R.* 36 and Dignan (1999) *Crim. L.R.* 48.

33 On the accountability of the cautioning process see Evans, R. (1996) 'Challenging a police caution using judicial review', *Crim. L.R.*, 104.

34 For a recent discussion of this complex issue see P. Goldblatt and C. Lewis (eds), *Reducing Offending, Home Office Research Study 187* (London: Home Office, 1998).

35 For an argument that placing strong expectations on relatively minor offenders to show high levels of remorse may lead to stigmatisation see Vagg, J. (1998) 'Delinquency and shame: data from Hong Kong', 38 *British Journal of Criminology*, 247 at 260.

36 See the important study by Tyler, T. (1990) *Why People Obey the Law*, New Haven, Yale University Press, and the brief discussion in Goldblatt and Lewis (eds), *op.cit.*, p.72.

CHAPTER 9

Restorative Justice and Family Group Conferences in England: Current State and Future Prospects

by Jim Dignan and Peter Marsh

Introduction

The convenient shorthand 'restorative justice' is commonly applied to a wide variety of practices that seek to respond to crime in a more constructive way than conventional forms of punishment (Dignan, 1999, p.48). It is not restricted to a particular approach or programme, but is applicable to any that have the following characteristics: an emphasis on the offender's personal accountability to those harmed by an offence (which may include the community as well as the victim); an inclusive decision-making process that encourages participation by key participants; and the goal of putting right the harm that is caused by an offence (see also Haley, 1996, pp.351–2). Restorative justice approaches vary in the way that these three elements – focus, process and goals – are combined, and it may be helpful to think of a continuum of approaches, from those with a relatively narrow perspective to those in which the perspective is much broader (Dignan and Lowey, 2000).

In this chapter we attempt to chart the recent development of restorative justice in England and will therefore concentrate initially on the current status and progress of family group conferencing there. However, we also wish to assess its future prospects and, for this purpose, will need to take a closer look at recent legislative developments that clearly incorporate some key elements of restorative justice. Although their short-term impact is likely to be restricted to the narrower, more reparative, end of the restorative justice spectrum, we will also consider whether they are also likely to improve the longer-term prospects for conferencing.

We will begin by commenting on the changing implementational context within which family group conferencing initiatives have developed in England. Next we will review progress during the initial phase of development, which preceded the implementation of a major programme of youth justice reforms in 1998 and 1999. We will then assess the opportunities and prospects for the future development of family group conferencing initiatives in the light of these reforms, and will conclude by considering some possible longer-term developments that they might conceivably be associated with in the future.

Conferencing: the changing implementational context

Until recently, England has been a classic example of the 'stand-alone' model for implementing restorative justice reforms (Dignan and Lowey, 2000, p.45). The defining characteristic of this implementational approach is the absence of any statutory authorisation for restorative justice programmes. The projects consequently operate outside of the formal criminal justice system, usually in a fixed term and experimental capacity, and with the aid of small-scale temporary funding. Although there are some short-term advantages associated with this approach, in terms of its flexibility potential in extending the boundaries beyond existing practice limits, these are

Source: Morris, A. and Maxwell, G. (eds) (2001) *Restorative Justice for Juveniles: Conferencing, Mediation and Circles*, Oxford, Hart Publishing, Chapter 5, pp.85–101.

outweighed in the longer term by its very limited impact on mainstream practice. Thus, 'stand-alone' initiatives are nearly always local in character, and have a marginal, if not highly precarious, existence because of their dependence on the support and cooperation of larger, more powerful criminal justice agencies. They tend to be restricted to juvenile first time offenders and minor offences, and even then they often find it difficult to attract a sufficient number of referrals to ensure their longer-term viability. As we shall see, the early experience with family group conferencing in England, at least within the youth justice context, has certainly conformed to this pattern.

Within the 'stand-alone' model, the survival of restorative justice programmes can be slightly tenuous where they are able to secure a good degree of institutional support; one example was the adoption of victim–offender mediation and reparation programmes by juvenile liaison bureaux and police-led cautioning panels in England during the 1980s (Davis *et al.*, 1988; Dignan, 1992). However, implementational problems still abound, particularly when the restorative justice aims and ethos are compromised by rival goals such as the diversion of offenders. There is a parallel development within the sphere of family group conferencing, which managed to secure some institutional support from local authority social services departments within a child welfare context. Even in these circumstances, the viability of restorative justice programmes remains precarious for as long as they continue to operate within a 'stand-alone' context.

Experience in other jurisdictions (most notably New Zealand, but also in parts of Europe) suggests that the implementation of a restorative justice approach is most likely to be successful (though still by no means guaranteed) where it is formally and fully incorporated within the criminal justice system itself: the so-called 'fully integrated' model (Dignan and Lowey, 2000, pp.49–56).

> By establishing restorative justice as a mainstream response that operates at the heart of the criminal justice system, it is much more likely that the problems of marginalisation and subordination that are associated with stand-alone programmes or a partially integrated compromise approach will be avoided.
>
> (Dignan and Lowey, 2000, p.55)

The incorporation of a restorative justice approach within a fully integrated model is likely to depend in turn on three key factors: the enactment and enforcement of an appropriate legislative framework, the creation or nurturing of a receptive professional culture, and the existence or establishment of a supportive institutional setting within which it can flourish.

Before 1997, none of these pre-requisites were in place in England. The 'stand-alone' model was dominant, and restorative justice programmes (including family group conferences) seemed destined to languish on the periphery of the criminal justice system. Since then, however, the implementational context has changed dramatically, with significant developments in relation to all three factors.

First, the legislative framework has been transformed as a result of the Crime and Disorder Act 1998 and the Youth Justice and Criminal Evidence Act 1999, which have begun to implement a radical new youth justice agenda. One important theme within this agenda has been the incorporation of some significant elements of restorative justice as part of the mainstream response to youth offending. Second, a new institutional framework consisting of strategically powerful multi-agency youth offending teams has been established. Third, steps have been taken to foster a more focused and effective professional culture within those teams.

Later in the chapter, we examine the impact that this dramatic change in the implementational context has had on the prospects for restorative justice in general, and for the development of family group conferencing in particular. Before then, however, we will briefly trace the early history of family group conferencing in England, during the era of the 'stand-alone' model.

Developing family group conferences in England: the experience so far

Four of the best-known family group conference projects for young offenders in England are the London-based Victim Offender Conference Service (Liddle, 1999), the Hampshire Youth Justice Family Group Conference Pilot Project (Jackson, 1998), the Sheffield/Kirklees project (Crow and Marsh, 2000), and the Kent intensive support and supervision programme (Gilroy, 1998).

The Victim Offender Conference Service was a pilot project that was initiated by the Inner London Chief Officers' Group and operated briefly in Lambeth and Hackney. The project was aimed at young people (aged 10 to 17), and referrals were made either after a decision to caution had been taken, or after a decision to prosecute, once a guilty plea had been entered. A total of 160 referrals were accepted. However, none of these referrals resulted in a conference, and only a very small minority involved either direct or indirect mediation (4 and 13 per cent respectively). Almost half the cases involved work with only one party, usually the offender. Throughout the project, inter-agency tensions were compounded by entrenched working practices and differences in professional ethos.[1]

The Hampshire project was more typical of recent family group conference developments in that it emanated from the successful implementation of family group conferences within a child welfare context in the same county. The Youth Justice Family Group Conference project was managed by a multi-agency steering group, and made use of co-ordinators who had prior experience convening child welfare conferences. Those eligible for referral were repeat offenders who were deemed unlikely to respond to further cautioning. They were referred to the project (and also cautioned) instead of being prosecuted (or cautioned again). However, the project was slow to develop and encountered a familiar litany of problems. Referrals were slow to materialise, as a result of which the number of completed conferences (12 in the first year) failed to meet even the relatively low target initially adopted. This in turn caused problems for the type of evaluation that had been planned. Professional commitment was also difficult to sustain, and the role of youth justice staff in particular was unclear.[2]

The Sheffield/Kirklees project also experienced developmental problems resulting in a small number of referrals. Nonetheless, the conferences that have been carried out seem to have been well received, with both professionals and families expressing positive views. Victims have come to around half of the conferences, and their views have also been reasonably positive. Despite the small numbers involved (18 in total), the research showed that family group conferences were certainly achievable in the English system, but that considerable development work was still needed. It also showed that some of the lessons from the child welfare projects (considered below) are relevant in this sphere as well.

The Kent scheme targets a group of persistent young offenders who face a custodial sentence. The catchment group is restricted to 15 to 17 year olds (though younger ones may also be eligible), who have been charged or cautioned on three previous occasions in the preceding twelve months, and who have served a custodial or community sentence (JUSTICE, 2000, p.63). The scheme is court-based, and operates in part as an alternative to custody, not court. Intervention in such cases takes place between conviction and sentence. Alternatively, offenders may be referred at the point of release from custody or while an offender is on licence.

The scheme employs a 'family decision-making model' (essentially a family group conference), and the outcome forms part of the pre-sentence report to the court. The project has been evaluated, using a reasonably rigorous methodology based on the use of matched control groups in pilot and non-pilot sites, and also (because of the small numbers involved) a risk of reoffending prediction instrument. An interim evaluation tentatively recorded a 25 per cent reduction in the actual rate of reoffending compared with the predicted rate. However, problems have also been experienced. They include reluctance by victims to participate, and time pressure constraints brought about by tight court schedules that make it difficult for victims to participate in the programme. It has also proved difficult to promote meaningful restorative interventions with a group of offenders whose attitudes towards victims and their offending may often be problematic, and whose risk of reoffending and associated needs often appear to warrant alternative, more therapeutic, forms of intervention.

Within the child welfare field, family group conferences have established a somewhat more secure footing. It has been estimated that around half of the English social services departments may be involved in some way with family group conferences, the great majority of which are concerned with child welfare developments (Challiner *et al.*, 2000). There are unlikely to be more than a handful of social service departments who are currently providing family group conference services in the youth justice area and for many of these, as in the case of Hampshire, it is often an offshoot from their prior involvement with child welfare cases.

Family group conferences that operate in a child welfare setting have a number of advantages compared with the *ad hoc* initiatives that are involved in youth justice cases: notably a greater degree of institutional support and a relatively more secure funding environment. And, because there is no involvement by victims in child welfare conferences, the potentially problematic issue of the conflicting needs of the victim and the offender at the conference does not need to be addressed (Maxwell and Morris, 1993). Moreover, in the child welfare field, there was already a well-established ethic that developing a sense of partnership between professional and service users was a good thing, and likely to be the most effective way of working (Marsh and Fisher, 1992). There was also a good degree of professional freedom, with less possibility of control by other professions, and somewhat less control by courts. Given all of these advantages, and the continuing relatively high profile of family group conferences, it may be surprising that conferencing does not have a higher profile within the child welfare sphere. Why is this?

The evidence from the development of child welfare conferences (Marsh and Crow, 1998) provides substantial reasons why it is likely to be a slow process, requiring a relatively high degree of effort. Working with all of the agencies providing the relevant services has proved crucial to the successful implementation of conferencing within child welfare. All agencies need to agree at least at the level of principle, and all need to examine many aspects of their practice to make sure that obstacles are removed that could stall the family group conference process. Experience shows that discussion alone is rarely enough to convince most staff of the value or practicality of the new approach. It needs a real example or two. But, of course, getting these examples depends on convincing at least some people in discussion. Overall, this is a time consuming and difficult process.

The combination of one or more strongly interested practitioners, with a committed senior manager to support them seems the most powerful force to establish family group conferences. The combination is not that common, and there are many examples of practitioners left to fight policy battles, and of senior managers unable to convince practice staff in the child welfare field. Skilled and trained co-ordinators are needed to carry out the conferences, and this requires some new finance beyond existing services, plus a good degree of project planning. It is, therefore, not at all surprising that in the child welfare field there was generally two years between initial planning meetings and the first conference taking place.

Even with the advantages that accrue from the more supportive institutional environment, it is clear that widespread and rapid adoption of family group conferences is unlikely, and that substantial effort will be required to get them established. As we have seen, there are some powerful positive factors at work, particularly in the child welfare sphere, and we will come to others. But there are also substantial obstacles to be overcome. It is hard to imagine that this could have been achieved, even in the child welfare field, within the conventional 'stand-alone' context that prevailed until 1997 and it is almost inconceivable that it could happen in the youth justice sphere. The question that we will now address is whether the prospects for family group conferences have improved as a result of the move towards implementing at least a partially integrated model of restorative justice after 1997.

Moves to integrate a restorative justice approach within the English criminal justice system: the Crime and Disorder Act

Shortly after coming to power in 1997, the incoming Labour government introduced a radical new agenda for dealing with youth crime (Home Office, 1997), the first part of which was set out in the Crime and Disorder Act, 1998. The main thrust of this new agenda is to promote more effective ways of preventing offending by children and young people, by undertaking early interventions that seek to address known criminogenic factors such as truancy and poor parenting. However, for the first time in England, it also establishes some elements of a restorative justice approach as part of the mainstream response to youth offending.

The measures that have been introduced so far are located very firmly at the narrow end of the restorative justice spectrum, since the emphasis is on making offenders accountable for what they have done by requiring them to undertake some form of reparation for either their victim or the community. In fact, reparation features in a number of new and existing sentencing disposals available to the courts. The first is the reparation order (section 67), which can vary in length up to a maximum of twenty-four hours. This occupies the same place on the sentencing tariff as the conditional discharge[3] and is clearly envisaged as an appropriate entry level penalty for less serious offenders. However, the use of reparation is not confined to less persistent or even less serious offenders, since it can also form part of another new sentencing measure known as the action plan order (section 69). The latter is a short but intensive community sentence that operates higher up the sentencing tariff and is thus aimed at more serious offenders. Moreover, reparation can also be included as a requirement in a supervision order (section 71), which is a measure widely used for more persistent young offenders. The concept of reparation seems to have moved from the margins towards the mainstream, becoming a routine response to a wide range of offences committed by young offenders.

The second important element of a restorative justice approach which the 1998 Act introduces relates to the greater scope for victims' involvement in the sentencing process. The Act stipulates that, before any reparative intervention, of whatever kind, is imposed, the views of the victim should be sought and relayed to the court. Moreover, offenders can only be ordered to make direct reparation to a victim where the latter has consented (which amounts, in effect, to a limited veto). As with the focus of the reforms, the relatively limited scope of the victim's role in the decision-making process confirms that these new restorative justice elements are likely to operate at the narrow end of the spectrum we identified earlier. Nevertheless, compared with their total exclusion from any part in the process for determining outcomes in the past, even these limited changes represent a significant step in a restorative justice direction.

As for the content of the reparative interventions, the 1998 Act is non-prescriptive, but the accompanying guidance (Home Office, 2000a, para. 5.5) stresses that, where possible, any reparation should be made directly to the victim (assuming there is consent). Among the examples cited are letters of apology, meetings or restorative conferences, or several hours per week of practical reparative activity that should, if possible, be related to the nature of the offence. The reference to practical reparative activities suggests a further tendency to operate at the narrow end of the restorative justice spectrum, though the specific reference to mediation meetings and conferences is also consistent with a broader, more participatory and potentially more cathartic type of restorative justice process. We will return to this issue when examining the potential impact of the Act specifically in relation to the future development of family group conferencing.

One final comment on the scope of the 1998 Act is that the range of reparative interventions it introduces is not confined to the post-conviction stage, but may also be available at the pre-trial stage. Under the Act, the traditional system of police cautions is replaced for offenders under the age of 18 by a more structured set of warning measures, known as reprimands and final warnings. Assuming that an offence falls within a formally prescribed gravity range, young offenders may expect to receive a reprimand for a first offence, to be followed respectively by a final warning and then prosecution for second and third offences. Offenders who are given a final warning may also be required to take part in a rehabilitation or change programme, which could also involve some form of reparative activity either for the benefit of the victim or the community. New guidelines, introduced in early 2000, emphasised the benefits of a restorative justice approach. They commended, in particular, the adoption of police-led restorative conferencing of the kind pioneered in certain Australian jurisdictions and adapted for use in an English context by the police force in the Thames Valley (see Chapter 8 by Young and Goold for more information on the operation of restorative conferencing in the Thames Valley).

Taken as a whole, the reparative measures introduced by the Crime and Disorder Act have the potential to incorporate significant elements that are associated with restorative justice as part of the mainstream youth justice system. We will assess the extent to which this potential has been realised later in the chapter. Meanwhile, there is one further aspect of the Crime and Disorder Act that could have an even greater impact in the longer term on the development of restorative justice measures, including family group conferences. This concerns the distinctive new institutional framework created by the Act in order to deliver the new youth justice agenda.

The centrepiece of this new framework involves the creation of a statutory system of strong, multi-agency Youth Offending Teams throughout the country, with effect from 1 June 2000. These Youth Offending Teams or 'YOTs', as they have become known, are staffed by personnel from a range of agencies – social services, police, probation, health services and education – that have never before been required to work so closely together, despite their relevant skills and shared interest in the problem of youth crime (Hine *et al.,* 1999).

Assuming they are adequately resourced, YOTs clearly have the potential to develop into powerful new players in the youth justice arena. From the outset, they have been given a strategic remit to develop a more constructive range of interventions to tackle the problem of youth offending, which includes the battery of restorative justice measures that we have already outlined. YOT staff are also responsible for undertaking consultation with victims, and for ensuring the delivery of the reparative interventions themselves, though they are free to outsource some of this work to specialist external contractors, including those operating in the voluntary and not-for-profit sectors.

The final part of the Act's key developments has been the creation of a powerful new non-departmental public agency, the Youth Justice Board, to monitor the operation of the youth justice system and to support it in pursuing its principal aim by making available substantial sums of money for the purpose of training and the development of good practice (section 41).

A professional restorative justice culture?

So far we have concentrated on the legislative framework that has sought to integrate elements of restorative justice within the mainstream youth justice system, and on changes in the institutional arrangements for delivering such an approach. However, we have also suggested that restorative justice is only likely to become an active part of mainstream youth justice services if there is a receptive professional culture at work within this new institutional set-up. In this section, we will examine the potential for the emergence of a professional restorative justice culture in the light of findings derived from the recently concluded evaluation of the pilot youth justice reform programme (Holdaway *et al.,* 2000).

A culture that is well attuned to restorative justice is likely to involve three main elements. The first and most fundamental is a recognition of the importance of professional work with victims. If this recognition is missing, then motivation will be low and the fulcrum of restorative justice absent. The second is a view that work with offenders needs a clear understanding about the nature, type and impact of the offences committed. Without this, the restorative process will be poorly matched to the harm that has been caused by the crime. The third is a commitment to seeing youth justice work as an integral part of the judicial process, and not as a service add-on to that process. If it is seen as the latter, it will risk over-emphasising offenders' welfare or punishment at the expense of an overall judicial restorative culture.

Work with victims

Historically, youth justice teams in social services have done very little work with victims. Although there has been some finance in recent years to develop victim support services, it is fair to say that most of the staff working in traditional youth justice teams have been directly concerned with offenders, and have rarely had much contact with victims. The picture that is emerging following the introduction of YOTs is a very different one, both in terms of their composition and also, as we have seen, in terms of their remit. Only around half of the professional staff are from social services (which compares with nearly 80 per cent in pre-YOT days), with the others coming from probation, police, education and health. There is now considerably more fertile ground for professional interest in the concerns of the victims. What effect has it had on the practice of the YOTs?

One obvious measure of any change in professional culture with regard to victims is the level of consultation with victims carried out in the pilot YOTs. The provisional findings of the pilot evaluation showed that there is some way to go in this area, given that victims' views are supposed to be routinely canvassed before making any recommendation to the court involving reparation on the part of the offender. In fact, this only happened in around two thirds of the cases involving reparation orders and half of all cases involving action plan orders (and in as few as one in six cases involving final warnings).

A number of factors lay behind this relatively low level of consultation with victims. There was some cultural resistance from longer serving staff; there were poor consultation procedures; and, in particular, there were data protection problems. There was a severe conflict between the rival governmental policy goals of consultation with victims and speeding up the process of justice. These issues will need to be addressed if the measures for consultation with victims are to be successfully implemented, though it is a common finding with restorative justice initiatives that victims' involvement is difficult to secure first time round (Morris *et al.*, 1993).

Work with offenders

The YOTs have also made it more likely that disposal options are well linked to the particularity of offences. The past use of pre-sentence reports continues, providing some of this link, but it is enhanced by the necessity for the YOTs to provide for the court a more detailed link between the disposal and the offence for the new orders. For example, if a reparation order is proposed then the way that the reparation will be undertaken, and how it links to the offence, should be outlined. New-style sentence reports have been introduced for this purpose, since pre-sentence reports would not normally have been used in the past for sentences of this kind. Over time, this will also provide some additional underpinning for the development of a relevant professional culture.

In the meantime, the national evaluation found that while the range of different types of reparative activities varied considerably both between and within the pilot YOTs, much of it undoubtedly fell within the narrow range of the restorative justice spectrum that we identified at the outset. For example, as might be expected in the early days of the YOTs, almost 60 per cent of the reparation orders involved the undertaking of some form of reparation for the benefit of the community, rather than for the benefit of the victims. Nevertheless, some of the reparative work that is being done with offenders, even in the sphere of community reparation, is developing more imaginative and effective ways of conveying the impact of the original offence as part of a restorative process.

Integration of youth justice work and the judicial process

The YOTs are very clearly part of the judicial system in a way in which the old youth justice sections of social services were not. All of their work is clearly focused on offending, and they are an integral part of many developments in youth justice, such as community safety plans. There is no doubt that the new approach emphasises that these professionals are solidly part of the judicial process, and that they should engage in relevant judicial developments. Of course, this needs to be a two-way process. There is a need for a change in the culture of the courts to match the change that is being sought in the youth justice profession. If it is to be achieved, this will necessitate a much greater emphasis on training for magistrates (preferably conducted jointly with YOT staff and other relevant practitioners).

Developing a receptive professional culture

There are now indications that the basis for a receptive professional culture is there. However, the practice development that should accompany this new culture may be difficult to enact in this new area of restorative justice. In social work, there has been a history of the poor and partial understanding of new ideas, and a failure to see the differences with existing practice (Marsh and Fisher, 1992). This problem is not helped by the weak connection between academic research and practice, although there are substantial recent projects, such as the Research in Practice initiative at Dartington and the University of Sheffield, which is attempting to make this connection stronger. The link between academic research and practice may be stronger in the case of the probation service, but there the commitment to victims is relatively vestigial. The professional culture of the police may aid the focus on victims, but their practice development may exhibit similar weaknesses to social work. The work of health and education staff bears little or no professional relation to issues of restorative justice.

Supervision may be the key to the development of a restorative justice culture in these circumstances, and again we have reasons to be cautious about the effectiveness of this with, for example, substantial weaknesses evident in social services' supervision regarding any link between theory and practice (Marsh and Triseliotis, 1996). It will be important for this work that supervision is sophisticated enough to determine whether relevant skills are present but are not used or are absent altogether, as different training strategies are needed for these different circumstances. Such sophistication has been unusual in the past. Perhaps an approach that combines initial and ongoing skills auditing with appropriate supervision, that is backed by routine and thorough monitoring of practice implementation, might offer a useful developmental approach, but it will be a substantial move from current practice.

Lastly, we should note that in the new Youth Offending Teams the professional culture is likely to be extended and enhanced by the development of contracted out services. This is a relatively new initiative in the field of youth justice and regarding the development of restorative justice it could be a mixed blessing. On the one hand, it could provide a vehicle for the theory and practice of restorative justice to spread via the new skills of the outside contractors. This is particularly important given the relatively low reservoir of trained and experienced staff, particularly within traditional criminal justice agencies. On the other hand, it could impede the changes if it allows YOT staff to ignore the issues of restorative justice, seeing them as somewhat esoteric or as simply dealt with by the outside project. The use made of such projects in both practical and strategic development will be crucial.

Overall, the development of a restorative justice culture may be rather similar to the way that research moves into policy and practice: a relatively slow process, first through dissemination, then through some adoption of the ideas, then by practical implementation. Powerful forces are needed for each of these stages to be successful. A sense of realism is, therefore, needed on the part of policy makers, practitioners, academic evaluators and those who commission evaluations, as the switch from a 'stand-alone' to an integrated implementation approach for restorative justice is not something that is likely to be achieved overnight. It is likely to be a much longer term and more organic process. Indeed, the same may be true of the legislative framework itself. Experience elsewhere suggests that the adoption of a restorative justice approach is likely to be an incremental process as, for example, in New Zealand's four-year period between the not wholly successful attempt to establish reparation as a victim-focused sentence in its own right in the Criminal Justice Act of 1985 (Jervis, 1996, p.417; Dignan and Lowey, 2000, p.51) and the introduction of family group conferencing in 1989.

Current developments in Family Group Conferences

So far, as we have seen, there have been relatively few family group conferences carried out within youth justice in England, although there are now a growing number of developments. A potentially major boost to the number of conferences in England occurred in 1999, when the Youth Justice Board, responsible for promoting professional practice in youth justice, set in train a number of development projects. Agencies were asked to tender for work in a variety of areas, one of which was restorative justice. Nine projects with a family group conferences focus were funded. This provides a useful way to examine the way in which family group conferences are being conceptualised within restorative justice developments. We have examined the plans put forward by the projects, and we outline below the focus that they adopted, the way they talked about restorative justice, and the overall aims they set themselves.

Nearly all of the projects described their key objective as reducing offending. Accompanying this, for half of the projects, there was a clear aim to increase victims' satisfaction. Only one talked specifically about repairing the harm done by crime. The language, as we will consider later, was predominantly technocratic around these twin aims of reducing offending and increasing victims' satisfaction. This was in part to be expected given that the documents were tender bids, but there was scope to accompany this with more explicitly restorative aims. Three projects clearly did this and mentioned additional aims, including increasing school attendance, reducing repeat victimisation and increasing community confidence in the justice system.

Specific categories of offenders were identified in the majority of the documents, covering a wide range in all: for example, 'potential persistent offenders', 'first offenders where past interventions have failed [sic]' and 'offenders remanded to care.' Two of the projects linked the work to the new parenting orders available to the courts, where parents of young offenders can be required to attend a specific programme of parenting training. In one case, the family group conference was seen as an alternative to such an order and in the other it was seen as part of such an order.

There were substantial ambitions for the number of family group conferences that were to be held, with three of the projects aiming for over 100 family group conferences in the first year (and one of these talking of up to 250). In half of the projects it was possible to identify the size of the potential target group, and family group conferences were planned for over half of this group in the first year. Ambitions on this scale seem highly optimistic and, in the light of previous experience in developing new projects of this kind, are likely to prove woefully unrealistic.

As noted, the language of the planning documents was predominantly technocratic, outlining work in terms of practice solutions likely to reduce offending and/or increase victims' satisfaction. One of the documents did talk in terms of 'humanising the criminal justice system' and another talked of 'repairing the harm caused by an offence'. Despite these ideas, the language was, overall, distinctly reparative rather than restorative.

The message for restorative justice from these developments is mixed. First, there is clearly interest in the area, with a willingness to move beyond talk to action. Secondly, the recognition of the importance of victims is coming through clearly. But there is little in the way of an underpinning value base in the planning we examined and, given the evidence from other areas, there are over-ambitious hopes for the activities that are proposed, especially in the number of family group conferences in the early years of the projects. Indeed, although it is understandable in view of the 'evidence-led approach' that underpins the current youth justice agenda, there is a risk that an excessive concentration on crime reductivist outcome-based measures may raise unrealistic expectations that could prove very difficult to deliver, particularly when adopted for challenging target groups.

An unfolding restorative justice agenda?

Much valuable progress is now undoubtedly being made in integrating elements of restorative justice as part of the mainstream criminal justice system in England. At the same time, one of us has cautioned previously that there must be grave doubts as to whether the framework that has been established by the Crime and Disorder Act could ever provide a satisfactory basis for the kind of broader, more inclusive and forward-looking strain of restorative justice initiative that we have been considering in this chapter (Dignan, 1999, p.58). Early experience with the YOT pilots, and the first tentative moves to develop family group conferences in England, has confirmed the need for continuing caution. However, we made the point earlier that the process of developing restorative justice is necessarily an incremental one, and one that is unlikely to be accomplished in just one legislative sitting.

It is worth pointing out, therefore, that the next phase in the unfolding youth justice agenda is also now being implemented in England, and that this could help to consolidate the development of broader, more inclusive, and somewhat less overtly reparative strains of restorative justice in the near future. The present government's long-term agenda for reform was spelt out in the White Paper *No More Excuses* (Home Office, 1997, para.9.21), in which it spoke of the need to 'reshape the criminal justice system in England to produce more constructive outcomes with young offenders', and emphasised its commitment to three restorative justice principles: responsibility, restoration and reintegration.

The first part of this legislative programme was accomplished by means of the Crime and Disorder Act. The following year the government enacted the Youth Justice and Criminal Evidence Act 1999 which built on the restorative justice foundations laid by its predecessor. Under this Act, all first time offenders who plead guilty (with the exception of those who are given an absolute discharge or who are sentenced to custody) *must* be referred to a newly created 'youth offender panel' for a specified period. In addition to the mandatory referral provisions, the courts will also have a discretionary power to refer one or more associated offences provided offenders plead guilty to a least one of the offences with which they are charged.

The panels themselves are to be set up by YOTs, and are to comprise three members, one of whom will be from the YOT, while the others will be drawn from a panel of community volunteers. The role of the panel will be to provide a forum away from the formality of the court, in which the young person, the family and, where appropriate, the victim of an offence, will be able to reflect on the offence and its consequences, and to agree a contract that will include reparation for either the victim or the community and a programme of activity that is designed to prevent further offending. A wide range of terms could be included in the agreement which, unlike the reparation order, does not exclude the possibility of financial compensation for victims. It is important to note that where a young offender is referred to the youth offender panel this will constitute the only sentence that may be imposed for the relevant offence(s). Thus, it will not be possible for the court to combine a referral with any other disposal (with the exception of ancillary orders, for example, with regard to costs or compensation).

How might we assess the potential impact of this new measure in restorative justice terms and, in particular, in terms of the three elements we identified at the start of the chapter: focus, process and goals? Perhaps the most significant aspect is the process that is adopted, which is much more inclusive and adopts a conferencing model as the key forum within which decisions are to be taken. Indeed, this switch of decision-making forum, from a court-based judicial model to a community conference model, is potentially one of the most radical aspects of the entire youth justice reform agenda, though not all recent commentators appear to have recognised this. Morris and Gelsthorpe (2000, p.29), for example, state incorrectly that 'youth offender panels do not supplant court proceedings; rather they supplement them and so a key issue will be the extent to which magistrates accede to the recommendations and plans made'. In fact, magistrates have no such power. The panel is responsible for reaching and enforcing any agreements, and only if offenders fail to comply will they be sent back to court.

Secondly, in terms of its focus and goals, there is less emphasis on the offender's accountability towards the immediate victim (though this still does feature) and correspondingly greater emphasis on notions of the restoration and, in particular, of the reintegration of the offender once the matter has been dealt with satisfactorily. This is reflected in the fact that, once a young offender has satisfactorily completed the agreement, the panel (not the court) will discharge the referral order, the effect of which will be to purge the offence, in the sense that it will immediately be regarded as spent for the purposes of the Rehabilitation of Offenders Act 1974. This represents a significant and welcome shift towards a more socially reintegrative approach and away from the conventional open-ended form of stigmatic shaming that has long characterised most retributive forms of punishment.

It is too soon to say how the new procedure will work, and certain aspects (for example, to do with the role of victims and the extent to which they will be encouraged to take part in the panel meetings) are still not entirely certain. Nevertheless, there are grounds for cautious optimism that over time, and provided the reform agenda continues to unfold in the present direction, a somewhat broader and more inclusive form of restorative justice will become an integrated part of the mainstream youth justice system.

Notes

1 After the pilot phase was over, the Victim Offender Conference Service began to deliver reparative interventions to one of the pilot Youth Offending Teams established under the Crime and Disorder Act. These are discussed later.

2 The project continues to operate, however, within the context of the Crime and Disorder Act, and offers conferencing to offenders who are given an action plan order. This is also discussed later.

3 This will no longer be available for most young offenders who have received a 'final warning' within the previous two years.

References

Challiner, V., Brown, L. and Lupton, C. (2000) *A Survey of Family Group Conference Use Across England and Wales*, Portsmouth and Bath, University of Portsmouth Social Services Research and Information Unit and University of Bath Department of Social and Policy Sciences.

Crow, G. and Marsh, P. (2000) *Family Group Conferences in Youth Justice: A Study of Early Work in Two Pilot Projects in Yorkshire*, Sheffield, Sheffield Children and Families Research Group, Department of Sociological Studies, The University of Sheffield, http://www.shef.ac.uk/~fwpg 2000.

Davis, G., Boucherat, J. and Watson, D. (1988) 'Reparation in the service of diversion: the subordination of a good idea', *Howard Journal of Criminal Justice*, no.27, pp.127–62.

Dignan, J. (1992) 'Repairing the damage: can reparation be made to work in the service of diversion?' *British Journal of Criminology*, no.32, pp.453–72.

Dignan, J. (1999) 'The Crime and Disorder Act and the prospects for restorative justice', *Criminal Law Review*, pp.48–60.

Dignan, J. and Lowey, K. (2000) *Restorative Justice Options for Northern Ireland: A Comparative Review,* Belfast, Criminal Justice Review Group.

Gilroy, P. (1998) *The Role of Restoration, Mediation and Family Group Conferencing in the Youth Justice System*, paper presented to a Home Office special conference, 18–20 February.

Haley, J.O. (1996) 'Crime prevention through restorative justice: lessons from Japan', in Galaway, B. and Hudson, J. (eds) *Restorative Justice: International Perspectives*, Monsey, NY, Criminal Justice Press.

Hine, J., Davidson, N., Dignan, J., Hammersley, R. and Holdaway, S. (1999) *Interim Report on Youth Offending Teams*, London, Home Office, http://www.homeoffice.gov.uk/yousys.sheff.html.

Holdaway, S., Davidson, N., Dignan, J., Hammersley, R., Hine, J. and Marsh, P. (2000) *Final Report on Youth Offending Teams*, London, Home Office.

Home Office (1997) *No More Excuses – A New Approach to Tackling Youth Crime in England and Wales*, London, Home Office, cm 3809.

Home Office (2000) *The Crime and Disorder Act Guidance Document: Reparation Order*, London, Home Office, www.homeoffice.gov.uk/cdact/index.html.

Jackson, S. (1998) *Family Justice? An Evaluation of the Hampshire Family Group Conference Project*, Southampton, University of Southampton, Department of Social Work Studies.

Jervis, B. (1996) 'Developing reparation plans through victim offender mediation by New Zealand probation officers', in Galaway, B. and Hudson, J. (eds) *op. cit.*

JUSTICE (2000) *Restoring Justice: New Directions in Domestic and International Law and Practice*, London, Justice.

Liddle, M. (1999) *Evaluation of Victim Offender Conference Service: Final Report*, London, NACRO.

Marsh, P. and Crow, G. (1998) *Family Group Conferences in Child Welfare*, Oxford, Blackwell.

Marsh, P. and Fisher, M. (1992) *Good Intentions: Developing Partnership in Social Services*, York, Joseph Rowntree Foundation.

Marsh, P. and Triseliotis, J. (1996) *Ready to Practise? Social Workers and Probation Officer: Their Training and First Year in Work*, Aldershot, Avebury.

Maxwell, G. and Morris, A. (1993) *Family, Victims and Culture: Youth Justice in New Zealand*, Wellington, Social Policy Agency/ Institute of Criminology, Victoria University.

Morris, A. and Gelsthorpe, L. (2000) 'Something old, something borrowed, something blue, but something new? A new comment on the prospects for restorative justice under the Crime and Disorder Act 1998', *Criminal Law Review*, pp.18–30.

Morris, A., Maxwell, G. and Robertson, J.P. (1993) 'Giving victims a voice: A New Zealand experiment', *The Howard Journal*, vol.32, no.1, pp.304–21.

CHAPTER 10

Young Women Offenders and the Challenge for Restorative Justice

by Christine Alder

Like many discussions of youth policy and juvenile justice, most of the literature thus far on restorative justice in this area assumes a generic rather than a gendered youth population: young women are virtually invisible. The failure to consider gender implies an assumption that the outcomes and the processes will be the same for boys and girls. At this point there is no research that allows examination of this assumption. Nevertheless, a co-ordinator of family conferencing in South Australia has noted that, 'conferencing with young women does raise many ethical, political and social considerations which differ from those which may arise when dealing with other ... youths' (Jan Kitcher in Baines, 1996, p.43).

Some consideration has been given to the appropriateness of the use of conferencing in cases in which women or girls are victims of violence (Stubbs, 1995, 1997; Hudson, 1998). While some of the issues raised in these discussions are pertinent, the focus of this chapter is identification of issues that need to be considered when young women are in conferences as 'offenders' rather than as 'victims'. In this chapter I draw on research on girls' experiences of juvenile justice more generally to suggest that there are issues that need to be acknowledged and addressed if the promises of restorative justice are to hold true for girls. Conferences, while not the only form of restorative justice, are the most widely implemented form in juvenile justice in Australia and therefore are the focus of much of this discussion.

Although it is hard to establish a definitive set of principles which defines 'restorative justice' (Daly and Immarigeon, 1998), some of the more frequently stated objectives present potential improvements over current juvenile justice practice for young women offenders. A first potential benefit is the meaningful involvement of young women offenders in the decision-making process. In relation to programs and policies more broadly, the National Council for Research on Women in the United States (Phillips, 1998) recommends that 'girls' collaboration is solicited in authentic and meaningful ways, through involvement in the design and implementation of programs ...'. Certainly research with young women in the juvenile justice system in Australia indicates that more meaningful involvement in the making of decisions about their lives is of significant concern to girls (Department of Community Services, Victoria, 1992; Alder and Hunter, 1999; Department of Youth and Community Care, 1999).

An indication that conferencing might constitute such an arena for young women in juvenile justice is provided by the observations of those involved in conferencing in Victoria. Drawing on their experiences, Mark Griffith and Sharon Williams suggest that conferencing can be empowering for girls in that it enables them to contribute in more meaningful ways than court procedure in the sentencing plan (Baines, 1996). In research on young women's juvenile justice experiences in South Australia (Alder and Hunter, 1999), only one of the young women

Source: Strang, H. and Braithwaite, J. (eds) (2000) *Restorative Justice: Philosophy to Practice*, Dartmouth, Ashgate, Chapter 7, pp.105–20.

interviewed had been involved in a conference, and she commented:

> Yes my family came to it and all the people that my family are involved in came too, to talk about the stuff that was going to happen and I was able to help decide what was going to happen with me. They didn't just say, well, your going to [detention] for 12 months for property damage. They said 'What do you think should happen?' and I told them what I thought should happen and my mum and that said they think that's fair and I thought that was really good. They respected your opinion like what you thought should happen. And what I said happened, which I thought was really good.

Consistent which this comment, in Adelaide, Jan Kitcher (in Baines, 1996) similarly found that co-ordinators uniformly felt that girls were able to express their feelings in conferences, and in fact observed that they were more eloquent than the boys. An indication of this was the observation that girls were more likely to argue about the outcome.

In their recommendations for programs and services for girls the National Council for Research on Women in the United States (Phillips, 1998) notes further that 'Partnerships among family, schools, community programs, and cultural organisations can provide opportunities for girls, and let them know that they are valued community members'. Potentially, conferencing with young women offenders might provide a mechanism for the involvement of a range of community agencies and services, outside of juvenile justice, in the establishment of new opportunities for these young women.

Young women who have committed a criminal offence find themselves particularly stigmatised in a culture in which being 'bad' is inconsistent with expectations of femininity in a way that it is not necessarily inconsistent with understandings of masculinity for young male offenders. It is perhaps not surprising therefore, that young women in the juvenile justice system are particularly concerned that they are treated with respect and dignity (Alder and Hunter, 1999). The principles of restorative justice which espouse maintenance of the integrity and dignity of the offender are therefore of interest to those of us concerned about the well being of young women in the juvenile justice system.

While the principles of restorative justice hold some promise for young women offenders, I want to turn in the rest of the chapter to consider research on young women in the juvenile justice system which presents a number of concerns and issues that need to be acknowledged and considered. The first concern has to do with community values, expectations and understandings about girlhood and their implications for decision-making in relation to girls' behaviour. A second set of observations relate to girls' experiences of juvenile justice. Finally, there is a growing body of research on the perceived difficulties of working with girls.

Community values and expectations

Traditionally juvenile justice system responses to young women have been significantly influenced by members of the community other than juvenile justice personnel, in particular their family, teachers, social workers, and neighbours (Carrington, 1993; Gelsthorpe, 1986). Consistently, research in the United States, Britain and Australia has shown that decisions in relation to young women taken by all these parties have reflected concerns about girls' sexuality and their independence – their 'passionate and wilful' behaviour (Alder, 1998; Hudson, 1984). As a consequence, research through the 1970s and 1980s showed that young women in juvenile justice were often the subjects of more prolonged and intrusive interventions than boys (Chesney-Lind and Sheldon, 1992).

Although various reforms attempted to address this situation, for example, the deinstitutionalisation of status offenders legislation in the United States, more recent research suggests that in numerous ways the intent of such reforms is being circumvented (see Chesney-Lind and Joe, 1996; Poe-Yamagata and Butts, 1996). It would appear that community expectations in relation to the behaviour of young women and a willingness to use intrusive, coercive forms of control to enforce those expectations, is not easily curbed.

Given the breadth of feminist research documenting the extent to which girls' behaviour is judged, controlled and disciplined informally (Heidensohn, 1985), we cannot assume that informal processing will necessarily be benign or neutral. Noting the extent of the literature on gender bias in courts and legal practice, Bargen and Stubbs (in Baines, 1996) argue we should be wary of assuming that informal processes are any less likely to judge the girls' behaviour according to limited visions of what is appropriate behaviour for girls. Stubbs (in Baines, 1996) notes that alternatives may simply reproduce such practices in the absence of the checks and balances of the formal court system such as public records and the prospect of appeal (Warner, 1994).

Community understandings of gender appropriate behaviour and appropriate response can be expected to affect not only the decision-making process, but also the outcomes of any such decision-making. Restorative justice might be about reintegrating the offender into the community, but it is not always the most welcoming of young women offenders.

People attempting community integration projects for girls have indicated that community attitudes and responses present them with some of their greatest difficulties. In commenting on the early days of Family Group Conferencing in South Australia, a co-ordinator, Jan Kitcher noted that 'different standards of behaviour for girls and boys still exist' and that girls themselves believed that it was 'worse for a girl to commit an offence than a boy' (Kitcher in Baines, 1996). Also in South Australia, the co-ordinator of a community work program, noting the difficulties her program had in placing young women, commented, 'Young women referred with community service orders are often stigmatised in the community as being "very bad" ... there is greater acceptance in the community of offending by young males'. She found that workers needed to undertake more intensive networking to gain relevant and appropriate work opportunities for young women (Althorpe, 1996, p.68).

Community understandings and reactions to them are not trifling matters for young women trying to establish themselves in a community. Negative interactions with those in the community setting in which they have been placed may significantly affect the young woman's successful completion of community based activities. In Queensland girls are twice as likely to be breached for non-compliance with the conditions of a community service order (Beikoff, 1996, p.20). Also, in the United States a higher proportion of girls than boys are institutionalised for justice violations including parole and probation violations (Poe-Yamagata and Butts, 1996).

In summary, what little evidence we have about women serving community based orders suggests that they have difficulty successfully completing such orders. While at this point there is little research to draw upon to help us understand this situation, it does suggest that we have to think carefully about the form and nature of the expectations we place upon young women offenders in the community. It is probably the case that the placement of offending girls in the community will require considerable effort be undertaken to prepare not only the young woman concerned, but also the setting, including others with whom she will be working.

Again it is potentially the case that the very process of conferencing, if it were to involve a range of supportive individuals from the community, could by its very nature begin to address negative community attitudes towards young women offenders. However, unless this issue is first acknowledged, it cannot be addressed and thought will not be given to how community integration can best be accomplished for young women.

Considering girls' experiences

Girls' offending is less accepted by the community and by both their male and female peers, than it is for boys. Thus for girls, their offending challenges their status and value as a 'woman', and thereby has significant negative implications for their sense of identity and self-worth. This has consequences for girls' expectations of others' reactions to them and girls' reactions to others' understandings and expectations of them. The implications of these need to be considered in the development of programs for offending girls.

Shame and self-harm

In part as a consequence of the expectation of strong negative reactions to their behaviour, and also because of a tendency for young women to self-blame, some girls feel guilt and 'shame' about their actions in a way that makes it difficult for them to talk about their offending. Some conferences require not only that the offender talks about their offending, but that they acknowledge 'shame' and contrition. Danny Sandor questions processes that entail young women publicly confronting or acknowledging their guilt, and in particular those processes that intend the young person to experience 'shame'. In relation to conferences, he comments:

> In a culture where shame has been a powerful tool of domestic control over women, this assumed pathway to reintegration has to be questioned. We know for example that self harm rather than violence towards others is a particularly likely response to emotional pain and frustration among young women and any assessment of how conferences work needs to consider this gender difference.
>
> (Sandor in Baines, 1996, p.45)

For some girls, there may be a delicate balance between exhibiting contrition and remorse, and feelings of guilt and self-blame and self-harm. Conferencing systems differ in the degree to which they expect to establish 'shame', or elicit expressions of contrition, as opposed to establishing outcomes. The implications of these differences for girls need to be examined.

Managing their own stories

It is not only their offending that girls may be reluctant to talk about in a conference setting. Managing their own life history, their 'story', is for some girls in juvenile justice an important part of a process of both self-protection and of establishing their independence and their self-sufficiency. This is particularly true for those young women who have had extensive involvement with both the juvenile justice and welfare systems. Girls offending continues to be understood predominantly within a pathological framework. This is evidenced by a preoccupation with girls' past experiences. Young women with more extensive experiences with juvenile justice and welfare become fed up with being asked about very personal issues by a seemingly never-ending stream of workers. Their privacy and their independence are highly valued by these young women and managing their own stories becomes a significant mechanism for asserting both of these. They become very careful about how much and what they tell, to whom and when. Some girls may refuse to access services if they believe they are going to have to tell their story once again, or they refuse to communicate, or they manage the content they do reveal. All of these actions may be understood by others as recalcitrance, 'being difficult', or of reflecting a lack of humility, or of a failure to show remorse.

Again, conferences differ in the significance they give to examination of the offender's personal circumstances and background. The ramifications for girls of these differences warrant investigation.

Establishing trust

A not unrelated issue for some young women in the juvenile justice system is the issue of trust. Who they will talk to and what they will talk with them about is related to the extent to which they believe they can trust a person. Given the backgrounds of many of the young women, they are justifiably cautious about trusting people to understand them or to do the right thing by them. The expectation that a young woman will be forthright and honest when confronted by a group including strangers, no matter how well intentioned, may be unrealistic. The establishment and maintenance of 'trustworthiness' needs to be acknowledged as significant for girls and a key objective of processes involving young women in juvenile justice.

'Girls are harder to work with'

In general those working with delinquent youth find girls more difficult to work with than boys (Baines and Alder, 1996; Kersten, 1990). This is an often heard, but rarely examined, lament among youth workers. The implications of this observation for everyday practice in juvenile justice and related areas require further investigation. Girls are described as 'verbally aggressive', 'hysterical', 'manipulative', 'dishonest' and 'untrusting'. Boys on the other hand, are described as 'honest', 'open', 'less complex' and 'easier to manage'. Workers are also frustrated by their lack of experience and the lack of suitable service options for them to draw upon in addressing girls' problems.

Young women in the juvenile justice system may very well be 'in your face' young women, feisty, and 'difficult'. Some may have had to develop these characteristics in order to survive. Most young women in the 'deep end' of the juvenile justice system are no longer living at home. It takes a good deal of courage to leave home and then to survive as a single young woman forced to live on the margins of our society. Other young women may always have been very assertive, independently minded, and 'wilful' young women. It may well be this 'attitude', unacceptable for girls, that caused them to be labelled as 'trouble' from a very early age by their family, schools, and neighbours. Whatever the precursor, this combination of having been in 'trouble', and their assertiveness, along with an increasing reserve and reluctance to engage with authoritative elders means that people find them 'difficult to work with' and may interpret their behaviour as uncooperative, or lacking the required subservience or contrition.

Concerns regarding sexuality and emotionality run through youth workers' reasons for why they find girls more difficult to work with. Many young women in the juvenile justice system have been, and may be in a situation where they continue to be, physically and sexually abused. Increasing public acknowledgment and awareness of this situation has meant in recent years that it has become one of the generally understood explanations for young women's 'troublesome behaviour'. While on the one hand recognition of this as a problem for some girls is a step forward, on the other, uncertainty surrounding sexual abuse has meant that it has become a catch all explanation for girls' problems.

Few young women readily reveal the full nature and circumstance of their abuse. As a result, even in circumstances in which the girl has not acknowledged it herself, sexual abuse is sometimes presumed to be an underlying factor in her 'troublesome' behaviour. In fact, it has been argued that sexual abuse has become the concept around which the tendency to pathologise girls' behaviour has coalesced in recent years. Baines (1997) considers data suggesting that insinuations of sexual abuse are invoked in ways which pathologise girls' problems, constitute them as a victim and obscure their agency, and limit the range of options considered (see also Haaken, 1994). Sexual abuse thereby becomes another of the 'deficit discourses' (Carrington, 1993) framing responses to female delinquency.

Few people feel comfortable dealing with issues of sexuality, and especially with issues such as abuse which can be related to complex personal problems. To some extent workers can feel intimidated by their inability to deal with the girls' problems when they are understood in these terms. The tendency to define young women's problems in psychological and emotional terms related to sexual abuse, can leave workers feeling as though they as individuals do not have the skills to deal with these sorts of problems. It also defines the range and nature of responses that are considered for addressing the situation of young women.

At the same time, it is nevertheless the case that many young women in the juvenile justice system have been physically and sexually abused, and that many of them have not disclosed this fact, or the name of their abuser, to anyone. One would want to avoid the situation where a conference involved a girl's abuser participating in the determination of her penalty for an alleged offence. As Sandor notes, in such a circumstance, 'Her experience as a victim is then powerfully denied by the perpetrators participation' (Sandor in Baines, 1996, p.45).

There is clearly no easy resolution to this potential, unwanted situation. However, its identification indicates the need for consideration of this potential problem in decisions regarding the composition of conferences. It has been suggested that a practice of having as many carers as possible involved in a conference may be a way of ameliorating or avoiding this situation. The point of this chapter is to indicate the need for identification of the particular situation of young women and issues such as these so that they can be acknowledged, and measures to address them can be identified and evaluated.

Some conferencing models emphasise their role in educating the offender about the inconvenience and pain they have caused the victim. The rhetoric of such models draws clear distinctions between victims and offenders. Recent feminist literature has challenged the form of this dichotomy, noting that women and girls are often both victims and offenders (Gilfus, 1992; Daly and Chesney-Lind, 1988; Maher, 1992). The framing of restorative justice practices such as conferencing in terms of victim awareness strategies becomes questionable when so many girls are themselves victims. Further, as noted above, a problem confronting those working with young women is not that these young women are not aware of the pain that they have caused or that they are not ready to take responsibility or blame for their actions, in fact, the problem is the reverse.

In summary, research in various countries (England, Germany, Canada and the United States) indicates that experienced juvenile justice workers find girls more difficult to work with. The reasons for this are complex and in need of further exploration. Nevertheless, it does suggest that in considering new practices in juvenile justice, the implications of the sex of the offender need to be taken into consideration.

What are the objectives for work with young women in juvenile justice?

The implications of conferencing for young women in the juvenile justice system need to be considered in light of overall objectives of juvenile justice practice with young women offenders. I have argued (Alder, 1993) that key objectives must relate to facilitating and enabling young women: 1) To lead safe, secure and independent lives; and 2) To participate as citizens of their community, that is, to be able to participate and contribute to their community in meaningful ways that provide them with a sense of self-worth.

Essential to this scenario are economic independence by virtue of paid, meaningful employment and suitable long-term living accommodation. When young women in the juvenile justice system are asked about their most pressing needs, they will talk about their desperate need to find economic means of independent survival. Their need to be able to live independent lives, including independence from 'social services', comes through very clearly and strongly in young women's comments (Alder and Hunter, 1999; Department of Community Services, Victoria, 1992).

However, providing young women offenders with educational options, accredited training, vocational planning and employment which leads to a career, have not been a priority of policies and programs for young women. A review of vocational programs and services in Australia in 1995 indicated that very few specifically addressed the needs of young women. If we are serious about assisting young women to move to real independence, to establish legitimate identities, to attain a meaningful role in the community, to have some choices about the direction and form of their lives, we have to look at developing this aspect of our policies for young women in the future.

In 1992, the then Department of Community Services in Victoria developed a young women's policy with overall objectives that I would argue are worthy of further consideration.

> Help young women become independent in ways which recognise the inequalities which have shaped their development as children and young women and have an impact on their ongoing opportunities for independent adulthood.
>
> Ensure safe environments for young women while they achieve greater independence and participation in their communities.
>
> Change those conditions (policies, service distribution, administrative and professional practices) which act to exclude young women from mainstream services and supports.
>
> Provide programs promoting personal and social growth and increasing young women's skills in controlling their experiences and utilising opportunities.

> Ensure that programs are accessible and relevant to the experiences of young women, particularly in terms of their geographic location and the way in which they are provided.
>
> (Department of Community Services, Victoria, 1992, p.1)

The achievement of this goal requires working not only with individual girls. In part workers find girls more difficult to work with because the programs and services available for them to draw upon to meet girls' needs are limited and their efforts are often frustrated. The available options and possibilities for both workers and the young women with whom they work, are structured by broader legislative and policy frameworks that also need to be the targets of change strategies.

At another level, we cannot begin to take on the issues that need to be addressed if we are genuinely concerned with enabling girls to lead independent lives until we challenge longstanding understandings of femininity and what it is to be a young woman. We have tended to understand girlhood in terms of pathology and protection. Our responses to girls have been founded in understandings of girl-as-victim, girl-as-dependent/passive which have evoked coercive restrictive responses to signs of girls' wilfulness and passion. Our responses have consequently been constraining and controlling of girls' efforts at independence, rather than empowering and enabling.

Aspiring to and achieving the sorts of objectives with girls that I have outlined requires directing our efforts at a number of different levels. In considering what restorative justice practices have to offer young women, we need to consider their potential contribution to the achievement of these sorts of objectives. In principle, with the emphasis placed in some restorative justice models on the responsibilities of the community as well as the offender for the resolution of the situation, it is possible to envisage restorative justice practices that could well contribute to the achievement of these objectives. However, the achievement of such objectives for girls will require first and foremost that those framing theories, policies and practices, recognise and consider the situation of young women. Only then will we be able to both implement restorative justice practices sensitive to the needs and interests of girls, and to monitor the processes and outcomes in this light.

Conceptual dilemmas

The situation and experiences of young women in the juvenile justice system raise a number of issues in relation to key concepts of restorative justice that are worthy of further consideration if we are to develop restorative justice practices that address the needs and interests of young women.

The term 'community' is central to the notion of restorative justice, and many other commentators have indicated the complexities of meanings of this term. One aspect of this discussion that is raised for me by the situation of young women, is the need to acknowledge that there is not a single, unified community to which everyone relates or of which everyone is a member. Young women who have left home and have been living 'on the streets' for some time, have often developed a 'community' of their own. Often in order to survive, they have a relatively loose association of peers and others who they look to for protection, shelter, conversation, and advice (Hagan and McCarthy, 1997).

Their 'street' community, if you like, is the one to which they feel closest; it is members from this community that they are more likely to trust. From their perspective, it is the 'community' of their parents, teachers and welfare workers that has harmed them, and continues to harm them. They feel, and in fact, have been ostracised, cast out of that community. A dilemma for young women is the often contradictory expectations of them in these two communities.

To date, in many discussions of restorative justice the use of the term 'community' does not appear to take into account these 'street' communities (as an example of a diversity of communities), but rather refers to restoring 'the' community, of holding offenders accountable to, or making amends to 'the' community. The literature on restorative justice in relation to practice recommendations for juveniles, generally assumes a single community of shared values and commitments from which the young offender is marginalised and has harmed in some way.

'Harm' is a second concept that is often used in statements of restorative justice. In general talk of 'repairing harm' refers to either the harm suffered by the community or the victim. For example, Bazemore (1997, p.195) notes that 'Restorative justice views crime primarily as harm to victims and the justice response should, through restitution, community service, and victim offender dialogue and related processes, seek to repair this harm and actively involve victims and communities'. The situation of young women draws our attention to the fact that we also need to acknowledge and address the 'harm' caused to the offender, perhaps especially by the community. In particular, young women with extensive juvenile justice and/or welfare backgrounds, generally have long experience of being ostracised and stigmatised in a wide variety of both direct and indirect, personal and more general ways by organisations and individuals in the community. If we are interested in 'reintegrating' young women, this will have to be acknowledged and addressed. This requires addressing aspects of the community's actions that cause ongoing 'harm' to young women. 'Repairing the harm' is also a notion that causes some concern when it comes to young women: what does 'repairing' mean? In the case of young women, it is evident that the 'harm' caused to the 'community', that is, parents, teachers, social workers and neighbours, is often not so much the criminality of her actions as it is that her actions contravene dominant understandings of acceptable feminine behaviour. Does repairing the harm in this case, entail reinforcement of the community's traditional expectations of young women? Does this mean that restorative justice is by its very principles, inherently conservative on these dimensions?

On the other hand, is there room for the processes of restorative justice, to repair the harm done to young women by conservative expectations, by challenging traditional expectations and understandings of what it is to be a 'good girl'? Civic republican discourse holds that confronting such forms of domination is a central value of restorative justice. In relation to racist attitudes, Hudson (1998) is hopeful about the 'norm-creating' role of conferences. Drawing on the work of Habermas, Hudson considers whether 'in the exposition of views, the listening to accounts of harm, the attempting to justify prejudice, that more progressive moral consensus can be reached' (Hudson, 1998, p.250). The theoretical foundation for this to occur assumes a situation in which people participate without constraint or oppression, and are power equals or can equally contribute to the discussion (Habermas, 1984, pp.8–42). Achieving this situation is a challenge for conferences and we await the evidence that it can be achieved, especially in situations involving young people as offenders. Whether or not conferences are able to achieve this level of equality has significant implications for the possibilities that restorative justice may, or may not, offer young women.

'Accountability' is a final concept used in some models of restorative justice that has some significance for young women. In general this term is used in relation to holding the young offender accountable for her actions. However, it is not clear that issues of proportionality and equity are necessarily achieved through informal group processes (Warner, 1994). Further, the history of the outcomes of decision-making in relation to young women's troublesome behaviour across a range of organisations including juvenile justice, welfare, mental health, medicine and education (Heidensohn, 1985; Carrington, 1993; Alder, 1998; Chesney-Lind and Joe, 1996), indicates the need for some level of community accountability, or decision-making accountability.

Conclusion

Overall the principles of some restorative justice models suggest potential benefits for young women in the juvenile justice system. Particularly worthy contributions would be the potential for community change and development, and the possibility for respecting young women's contribution to decision-making regarding the most appropriate outcome for their offending behaviour. On the other hand, if young women's needs and interests are to be addressed by restorative justice practice, they have first to be acknowledged. There remain a number of unanswered questions about restorative justice practices in relation to young women offenders. Before we can feel comfortable about the use of restorative justice practices with young women in the juvenile justice system, these questions, and the issues raised in this chapter, need to be acknowledged and addressed. Most urgently, the practices of restorative justice need to be evaluated and monitored in regard to their implications for young women.

References

Alder, C. (1998) 'Passionate and wilful girls', *Women and Criminal Justice*, vol.9, pp.81–101.

Alder, C.M. (1993) 'Programs and services for young women: future directions', in Gerull, S. and Atkinson, L. (eds) *National Conference on Juvenile Justice*, Canberra, Australian Institute of Criminology, pp.305–11.

Alder, C. and Hunter, N. (1999) '"Not worse, just different?" Working with girls in juvenile justice. A Report submitted to the Criminology Research Council, Canberra, Australia', Melbourne, Criminology Department, The University of Melbourne.

Althorpe, G. (1996) 'Young women and community service orders', in Alder, C. and Baines, M. (eds) *'... and when she was bad?' Working with Young Women in Juvenile Justice and Related Areas*, Hobart, National Clearinghouse for Youth Studies, pp.73–9.

Baines, M. (1996) 'Viewpoint on young women and family group conferences', in Alder, C. and Baines, M. (eds) *'... and when she was bad?' Working with Young Women in Juvenile Justice and Related Areas*, Hobart, National Clearinghouse for Youth Studies, pp.41–7.

Baines, M. (1997) 'Mad, bad or angry?', *Youth Studies Australia*, vol.16, pp.19–23.

Baines, M. and Alder, C. (1996) 'Are girls more difficult to work with? Youth workers' perspectives in juvenile justice and related areas', *Crime and Delinquency*, vol.42, pp.467–85.

Beikoff, L. (1996) 'Queensland's juvenile justice system: equity, access and justice for young women', in Alder, C. and Baines, M. (eds) '... *and when she was bad?' Working with Young Women in Juvenile Justice and Related Areas*, Hobart, National Clearinghouse for Youth Studies, pp.15–25.

Carrington, K. (1993) *Offending Girls: Sex, Youth and Justice*, Sydney, Allen and Unwin.

Chesney-Lind, M. and Joe, K.A. (1996) 'Official rhetoric and persistent realities in troublesome behavior: the case of running away', *Journal of Contemporary Criminal Justice*, vol.12, pp.121–50.

Chesney-Lind, M. and Sheldon, R. (1992) 'Girls, delinquency and juvenile justice', Pacific Grove, Ca, Brooks/Cole Publishing.

Daly, K. and Chesney-Lind, M. (1988) 'Feminism and criminology', *Justice Quarterly*, vol.5, pp.497–538.

Daly, K. and Immarigeon, R. (1998) 'The past, present and future of restorative justice: some critical reflections', *Contemporary Justice Review*, vol.1, pp.21–45.

Department of Community Services, Victoria (1992) *Becoming Stronger. An Action Plan for Young Women*, Melbourne, Victoria, Community Services.

Department of Youth and Community Care (1999) *What About the Girls? Young Women's Perceptions of Juvenile Justice Programs and Services*, Brisbane, Department of Youth and Community Care.

Gelsthorpe, L. (1986) 'Towards a sceptical look at sexism', *International Journal of the Sociology of Law*, vol.14, pp.125–53.

Gilfus, M.E. (1992) 'From victims to survivors to offenders: women's routes of entry and immersion into street life', *Women and Criminal Justice*, vol.4, pp.63–89.

Haaken, J. (1994) 'Sexual abuse, recovered memory and therapeutic practices', *Social Text*, vol.40, pp.115–45.

Habermas, J. (1984) *The Theory of Communicative Action, Vol.1. Reason and Rationalisation of Society*, London, Heinemann Educational Books.

Hagan, J. and McCarthy, B. (1997) *Mean Streets: Youth Crime and Homelessness*, New York, Cambridge University Press.

Heidensohn, F. (1985) *Women and Crime*, New York, New York University Free Press.

Hudson, B. (1984) 'Femininity and adolescence', in McRobbie, A. and Nava, M. (eds) *Gender and Generation*, London, Macmillan, pp.31–54.

Hudson, B. (1998) 'Restorative justice: the challenge of sexual and racial violence', *Journal of Law and Society*, vol.25, pp.237–56.

Kersten, J. (1990) 'A gender-specific look at patterns of violence in juvenile institutions: or are girls really more "difficult to handle"', *International Journal of the Sociology of Law*, vol.18, pp.473–93.

Maher, L. (1992) 'Reconstructing the female criminal: women and crack cocaine', *University of Southern California Review of Law and Women's Studies*, vol.2, pp.131–54.

Phillips, L. (1998) *The Girls Report. What We Know and Need to Know about Growing up Female*, New York, The National Council on Research on Women.

Poe-Yamagata, E. and Butts, J.A. (1996) *Female Offenders in the Juvenile Justice System. Statistics Summary*, Pittsburgh, PA, National Centre for Juvenile Justice.

Stubbs, J. (1995) 'Communitarian conferencing and violence against women: a cautionary note', in Valverde, M., MacLeod, L. and Johnson, K. (eds) *Wife Assault and the Canadian Criminal Justice System: Issues and Policies*, Toronto, Centre of Criminology, University of Toronto, pp.260–89.

Stubbs, J. (1997) 'Shame, defiance and violence against women: a critical analysis of "communitarian" conferencing', in Cook, S. and Bessant, J. (eds) *Women's Encounters with Violence: Australian Experiences*, Thousand Oaks, CA, Sage, pp.109–26.

Warner, K. (1994) 'The rights of the offender in family conferences', in Alder, C. and Wundersitz, J. (eds) *Family Conferences and Juvenile Justice*, Canberra, Australian Institute of Criminology, pp.141–53.

CHAPTER 11

Re-visioning Men's Violence against Female Partners

by Allison Morris and Loraine Gelsthorpe

> Re-vision – the act of looking back, of seeing with fresh eyes … is for women … an act of survival
>
> (Rich, 1979)

There is still considerable debate about the value of the criminal justice system in affecting men's violence against their female partners. Many of the law reforms introduced in the 1980s and early 1990s – specifically mandatory arrest, prosecution and imprisonment in their various guises – seem to have failed to increase women's safety. A number of writers have suggested that this is because the criminal justice system does not and cannot challenge the patriarchal structures which both underlie and sanction men's violence against their female partners (see, for example, Smart, 1989, 1995; Snider, 1998; Morris, 1993). Other writers continue to promote a law enforcement response and suggest that the reasons for its failure lie in practical difficulties and that stricter enforcement, controls on discretion and so on would make a difference (see, for example, Hanmer, 1989; Edwards, 1989 and most recently, Kelly, 1999).

Intriguingly, feminist writers can be found on both sides of this argument and, further, those feminist writers who continue to argue for increased criminalisation and penalisation are directly at odds with feminist or pro-feminist writers who have argued that feminist values have the potential to transform the criminal justice and penal systems and to provide a more 'caring' vision of justice (see, for example, Heidensohn, 1986; Daly, 1989).[1] In addition, in recent years, some writers have made connections between the ethic of care and the principles and practices of restorative justice as a way of transforming and re-visioning conventional justice processes (Masters and Smith, 1998).[2] However, violence by men against their female partners is often excluded from these debates as being inappropriate for restorative processes and practices. This article tries to come to grips with these conflicts and tensions. It reviews what has been achieved through criminal justice routes for women experiencing violence at the hands of their partners by raising a number of questions and then explores an alternative, or additional, way in which this violence might be addressed.

Has law reform reduced men's violence against their female partners?

The difficulty with trying to answer this question is that it is impossible to know precisely the 'true' level of men's violence against their female partners. We know that the number of arrests is a poor indication of the extent of this violence and that changes in these may result from changes in reporting and recording practices rather than increases or decreases in offending.[3] Awareness of the inadequacy of these statistics led to the use of other sources of data, particularly victim surveys in trying to obtain a more accurate picture (for example, the British Crime Survey [Mirrlees-Black, 1995]). However, conventional victim surveys do not produce reliable estimates either[4] and increases in prevalence rates over time are usually explained by an increased willingness to report such incidents and by improvements in research methodology.[5] Surveys which have focused generally on the extent of violence against women may also not provide a reliable estimate

Source: *The Howard Journal* (2000) vol.39, no.4, pp.412–28.

of the extent of men's violence against their partners.[6] Surveys which specifically explore violence by partners, including current partners, are arguably better able to capture the extent of this violence and certainly these surveys produce higher estimates of this violence though the extent to which these are 'real' differences or methodological constructs again remains unclear (Morris, 1998).[7] Overall, then, we have to conclude that there is no evidence to suggest that prevalence rates have declined since the 1980s and 1990s – for the reasons outlined earlier, they are more likely to have increased.[8]

Do women want to rely on the criminal justice system?

Research shows that only a few of the women who experience violence at the hands of their male partners rely on the law, police or courts to deal with it, at least in the first instance (see, for example, Gelles and Straus, 1988; Morris, 1997; Mirrlees-Black, 1999).[9] Some women may 'accept' this violence and see it as simply part of 'ordinary' life (Bush and Hood-Williams, 1995). Almost all have to overcome a reluctance to take action; their preference seems to be to turn first to friends or family, and then to general practitioners, lawyers and other 'helping' agencies as much as to the police.[10]

When women do call the police, they do so for many reasons which may or may not include wanting their partner arrested. In Hoyle's (1998) sample of 33 victims, for example, only a third wanted their partner arrested and many of these women did not want the police to proceed further: they wanted immediate protection but not necessarily prosecution. Indeed, in Hoyle's view, some victims judged interventions as successful even though they did not result in a prosecution and whether or not their partner was arrested was unrelated to women's level of satisfaction with the police. In the victim's terms, therefore, this decision not to proceed further with a prosecution was a rational choice. It may be 'for the sake of the children', for instance, or it may be because she is still 'in love' with her partner, because she wants the relationship to 'work', because she has nowhere else to go, because she has no money, or because she is afraid of her partner and knows that the violence will continue irrespective of police action. Moreover, even Kelly (1999, p.113), whose recent research clearly had at its base a pro-arrest stance, concluded that women who called the police 'wanted some form of action'. There is no clear evidence that what women wanted was arrest and prosecution.[11]

Whatever the reason – and whether we as outsiders agree with it or not – if a woman does not want her partner arrested, prosecuted or imprisoned, it is arguable that she should be listened to. For us, as outsiders, to dictate otherwise in order that we might fulfil some assumed greater goal – for example, the penalisation of all violent men – is to increase the powerlessness of this woman. To do so in the name of 'women's interests' or 'feminism' seems to us even more problematic. After reviewing the now extensive literature on arrest, Buzawa and Buzawa (1996, p.161) concluded that it imposed 'unacceptable costs' on victims. Indeed, Hoyle (1998, p.229) suggests on the basis of her research findings that pro-arrest and pro-prosecution policies could do more harm than good. In any event, it is unlikely that the criminal justice system will be able to intervene effectively against a woman's express wishes. There is some evidence from the United States that women stopped calling the police when they lost any say about the prosecution of their partner (Buzawa and Buzawa, 1996).[12] Ford (1991) made a point which is also relevant here. He described women's use of the criminal justice system as a resource which they could use to increase their relative power and as a way of managing the violence they experienced. He advocated against, therefore, any policies which might 'inadvertently disempower victims' (p.329).

Do the police arrest violent men when called?

Although police policy on violence in relationships in most Western jurisdictions specifies offenders should be arrested except in exceptional circumstances, research suggests that the police do not always follow this policy (see, for example, Edwards, 1989; Stanko, 1989,

1995; Grace, 1995; Hoyle, 1998; Kelly, 1999). For example, Kelly (1999) quotes arrest figures (for periods between 1993 to 1995) of only 13% for Greater Manchester, of 18% for Northumbria and of 24% for West Yorkshire. In the two Home Office pilot areas (funded from 1992 to 1995) in which Kelly's research was based, the arrest rate was only 19% and 12%. Even where there were visible injuries and the offender was present, the arrest rate was only 45%.[13] And, more recently, Hanmer *et al.* (1999) quote a figure of 27% for one division of West Yorkshire (Killingbeck) for 1997 – a reduction over the 1996 figure.[14]

There are various reasons for this difference between police policy and practice: policies are permissive; they can be manipulated; they can be followed to the letter but not in spirit; and they can be ignored, resisted or broken (for a discussion, see Hoyle, 1998, pp.12–13). But importantly in this context, Hoyle (1998, p.181) suggests that a key factor for the failure of the police to arrest or for the crown prosecution service to prosecute was the victim's preferences.[15] We dealt with the implications of this earlier.

Does penalisation or rehabilitation work?

Given what we have said in the above two sections, it is apparent, in the main, that men who are violent towards their partners are not held accountable for their actions and that the criminalisation and penalisation of this violence touches only a minority of violent men. Conversely, it can be argued that the penalisation of violent men may brutalise them further and thus may make them behave more violently or oppressively towards women (Carlen, 1992). Research also suggests that arrest in fact increases the level of violence in some men (see, for example, Sherman, 1992). Hudson (1998) further makes explicit the likelihood that increased criminalisation and penalisation has impacted primarily on the poor and the marginalised and that this penalisation is more likely to reinforce than to change sexist attitudes. Moreover, there is very little evidence to suggest either generally with respect to criminal behaviour or specifically with respect to violence against women that increased penalties deter many offenders (see, for example, von Hirsch *et al.*, 1999; Sherman, 1992) or that rehabilitative sanctions 'work' (see, for example, Gendreau and Andrews, 1990; Edleson and Syers, 1990). It is true that more recently there has been some evidence that programmes make a difference (Dobash *et al.*, 1996;[16] Scourfield and Dobash, 1999; Davis and Taylor, 1999), but many programmes dealing with men's violence towards their partners do not take men on court orders and it remains to be seen whether or not men who voluntarily attend such programmes have even higher 'success' rates. Certainly, at a general level the evidence suggests that the effectiveness of interventions is increased when offenders become involved voluntarily (McGuire, 1995; McIvor, 1992; McLaren, 1992).

A different direction: towards restorative justice

The above research findings, taken together, indicate to us the need to fundamentally rethink how better to respond to women who are experiencing violence in relationships, especially when much of this violence is within current relationships (Mirrlees-Black, 1999; Morris, 1997) and given women's apparent reluctance to invoke criminal justice processes and sanctions. As noted earlier, at least some of these women do not wish to end their relationship for a range of emotional, financial or cultural reasons (Carbonatto, 1998). Hoyle (1998, pp.221ff) recently suggested an integrated approach incorporating both the civil and criminal law to create 'family justice', but there is no reason to suppose that this combination would serve women any better than the individual components. She also refers (at page 222) to specialist courts which exist in some American and Canadian cities and which deal only with family violence cases (Clark *et al.*, 1996). And indeed, the first of these in England has recently been established in Leeds (BBC News Online, 1999). However, there does not seem to have been any systematic evaluation of these and they continue to rely on conventional criminal justice practices.

Our preference is to explore the possibilities

of restorative justice.[17] Research in New Zealand has shown that, through restorative processes, offenders can be held accountable for their offending in meaningful ways; that the voices of victims can be heard; that victims can feel better as a result of their participation; and that outcomes which address both victims' and offenders' needs or interests can be reached (Maxwell and Morris, 1993). Maxwell and Morris (1999) and Maxwell *et al.* (1999) have also found that restorative processes can reduce reoffending. Conventional criminal justice processes and practices cannot make these claims.

The principal difference between restorative justice and traditional criminal justice processes is that restorative justice stresses the inclusion of the key parties to the offence – in particular, the victim, the offender and their friends and families – in decision-making processes and reaching outcomes and thus envisages them coming together to resolve collectively how to deal with that offence, its consequences and implications for the future. Thus, within the context of men's violence against their partners, a meeting would take place between all those with an 'interest' in the offence and its aftermath (the victim, the offender, possibly their children, their families, their friends and any significant others the parties wish to be present) aided by a facilitator. The expectation would be that the offender would acknowledge his responsibility for the violence and that all the participants would be involved in a search for a way of ensuring the violence is not repeated. This might involve the man agreeing to live elsewhere for a while or to join a drug or alcohol programme or a programme specifically focused on preventing men's violence. A safety plan for the woman and her children would usually also be developed – for example, the provision of a personal alarm for the woman, agreement to ring the police or some nominated others if the violence seemed likely to recur or agreement to leave the relationship if the violence was repeated. These agreements could be monitored by all members of the meeting or nominated individuals. Some, if not all, of these actions might be possible within the criminal justice system. But there are clear differences in emphasis: the parties want them to happen, they are not coerced; and the support systems commonly relied on by women have been brought into play more forcefully so that the violence is no longer 'private' or 'personal'.

There are a number of claims which have to be addressed in seeking to advocate restorative responses to men's violence against women. In the next section, we explore some of these and attempt to answer them.

Claim 1: Restorative justice perpetuates power imbalances

The principal argument against the use of restorative justice in men's violence against women is that the power imbalance in violent relationships is too entrenched for restorative processes to 'work' (see, for example, Martin, 1996; Stubbs, 1997). These relationships are said to be characterised by dominance (by the abuser) and submission (by the abused) and, consequently, it is argued that women are unlikely to be able to assert their needs or wishes.[18]

No-one could deny the power of men's violence against their partners, including the power of threats and emotional abuse. These are controlling behaviours. However, power imbalances can be addressed by ensuring procedural fairness, by supporting the less powerful, and by challenging the powerful. Thus restorative processes could provide a forum in which the victim can make clear to the offender and, importantly, to their friends and families the effects of the violence on her. Friends and families can also provide a supportive basis for that voice to be heard or, if appropriate, may speak for the woman, more powerfully than any prosecutor in a criminal court. A reasonable expectation for facilitators of restorative justice processes is that they should create an environment which ensures that women do participate, by whichever way is necessary. Examples cited by Braithwaite and Daly (1994) include mobilising the support of men who are anti-violence or women with experience in highlighting the effects of violence against women. They also refer to the fact that in some Maori tribes an accused male abuser would have no right to speak and that statements would have to be made on his behalf.

Claim 2: Restorative justice removes men's responsibility

Linked to power imbalances is the claim that violent men commonly reject responsibility for their violence and place responsibility for it onto women, minimise the consequences of their violence, blame women for 'provoking' them and so on (see, for example, Liebrich *et al.*, 1995; Dobash and Dobash, 1992). Because of this, it is believed that restorative processes would be powerless to challenge men's attitudes and behaviour. Stubbs (1997), for example, argues that setting up restorative processes 'holds no guarantee that women will feel empowered to speak about their experiences, their fears for the future, and their wishes concerning the sanction' (p.123).

In restorative processes, however, the abuser is expected to accept responsibility for the abuse and men's techniques of neutralisation can be challenged. Violent men may be unable to 'hear' their female partners, but they are likely to find it more difficult not to hear the voices of concern from their friends, their parents, their partner's parents, their siblings and so on. Of course, Stubbs (1997, p.123) is right that a single restorative meeting of however many supporters will not be able to effectively challenge 'structural inequality and deeply held misogynist views'. But that is hardly a reason for abandoning the very different principles and practices of restorative justice and passing the matter over to a criminal justice system which itself is deeply embedded in structural inequality and misogynist views (Edwards, 1996; Smart, 1989). And, of course, Stubbs is also right when she points to contrition and apology – key elements in restorative processes – being part of the cycle of violence (Walker, 1979) – the lull before the storm. The difference in restorative processes is the 'public' nature of that contrition and apology and the shared monitoring of subsequent events to ensure that it is 'real'.

Claim 3: Restorative justice decriminalises men's violence

Another main argument for rejecting alternative processes is that men's violence against their partners must be recognised for what it is: criminal behaviour. As such, criminal justice responses are required and nothing should be done which might be viewed as minimising the seriousness of this violence. Critics tend to see restorative processes as decriminalising men's violence against their partners and as returning it to the status of a 'private' matter.

The use of restorative processes, however, does not signify the decriminalisation of men's violence against their partners. The criminal law remains as a signifier and denouncer, but the belief within restorative processes is that the abuser's family and friends are by far the more potent agents to achieve this objective of denunciation. Research has found that there is some community support for the belief that it is 'okay' to hit women in some circumstances. Liebrich *et al.* (1995), for example, found that about one in five men held this view in 11 out of 20 scenarios. But this means that four in five did not and restorative processes are a way of mobilising this censure. Of course, we are not anticipating that large social or geographical communities can be mobilised in this way (even if they could be defined with some precision). Our references to 'community' here mean specific members of a woman's small social network, neighbourhood or family with whom she maintains contact – her 'personal community' so to speak.[19]

Arguably, by challenging men's violence in the presence of the abuser's family and friends the message of denunciation is loud and clear for those who matter most to the offender. In this way, restorative processes also have the potential to challenge community norms and values about men's violence against their partners. In Hudson's (1998) words, restorative justice 'can ... not only perform the norm-affirming expressive role of adversarial criminal justice; it can perform an additional norm creating role' (p.250). There is also nothing in a restorative justice approach which prevents the police from arresting violent men or which prevents them and other agencies from educating the public that men's violence against their partners is wrong. And, of course, the availability of restorative processes does not prevent women who prefer to use the criminal justice system from doing so. In addition, the criminal justice system can be used as part of an escalation of responses (on the lines proposed by Braithwaite and Daly, 1994).

There is one other matter which needs to be dealt with here. Kelly (1999, p.ix) asserts that 'victims of domestic violence think domestic violence should be responded to as a crime'. There are three points to make. First, this strong statement is made on the basis of a questionnaire with a response rate of 28% and it is clear that few of those who responded were still living with their violent partners. Second, and related to this latter point, in our experience, women still living in violent relationships rarely 'see' that violence as crime (Morris, 1997); this is a common criticism of the ability of victim surveys to uncover the extent of men's violence against their partners. Third, even if Kelly's statement is valid at a general level, it does not lead automatically and exclusively to the promotion of a law enforcement response. Other crimes are now being diverted if the circumstances are appropriate and, in some areas, restorative conferences (such as those organised by the Thames Valley Police) are being held for a range of crimes (Young and Goold, 1999).

Claim 4: Restorative justice mediates men's violence

Critics of restorative justice seem to see it as the same as mediation or conflict resolution and, therefore, as open to the same concerns. They are not. Indeed, there are few examples of offending or victimisation in which it would be appropriate to advocate mediation. For example, if someone takes your umbrella, unless there is a conflict about its ownership, there is no basis for negotiation or bargaining over who owns it and who has stolen it. This lack of bargaining or negotiation is even more explicit in restorative responses to violence against women by their partners. There may be two quite separate views on 'what happened', but in restorative processes the victim's perspective is central and the meeting can only proceed on the basis of the offender's acceptance of responsibility.

Martin (1996) cites as an example of mediation practice an agreement in which the victim agreed to comply with the abuser's rules of behaviour (for example, to have her partner's dinner ready at a particular time) in return for his agreement not to batter her. But this is not in accord with restorative principles: violence is not negotiable and freedom from violence could never be conditional. Martin (1996) also quotes findings from Maxwell and Morris's (1993) research on family group conferencing that about a quarter of the victims felt worse as a result of the conference. But, in the main, this was the result of poor practice and ignores the fact that about 60% of victims felt better as a result of the process.[20] Women with experience of court processes have also often expressed their dissatisfaction with these (Shapland *et al.*, 1985).

Claim 5: Restorative justice encourages women to remain in violent relationships

An implicit or underlying assumption when parties seek legal remedies is that where there was a relationship, it has broken down, and contact is not desired. This is not necessarily so when men are violent towards their current partners. A principal argument presented in support of the use of restorative processes with respect to men's violence against their partners is that many women for a range of reasons wish to remain in or return to relationships which others would see as abusive (see, for example, Carbonatto, 1995).[21] What restorative processes envisage is allowing women to make choices about their futures from a range of options.

The diversity of the nature of men's violence against their female partners and of women's responses to it is an indication of the need for a range of responses rather than a primary or sole reliance on criminal justice responses. This speaks to the importance of allowing women to make the choices which best suit them rather than allowing professionals to decide for them.[22]

Indeed, one way of addressing the power imbalances referred to earlier is to provide women with these choices. Some critics seem unwilling to accept that women who have experienced violence can effectively make choices for themselves because they have to have been involved in a relationship founded on power and control. But transferring this power and control to the State (often in reality male professionals) does little to address women's concerns.

Claim 6: Restorative justice reduces women's safety

The first part of this article doubted whether or not the criminal justice system could increase women's safety. In our view, friends and families are far better placed than professionals to prevent the recurrence of violence and to play a role in monitoring the safety plan. Restorative justice processes directly involve them, in contrast to the exclusion intrinsic to criminal justice interventions. This 'opening up' of knowledge and awareness is especially important when one of the possible outcomes of the restorative meeting is the separation or the continued separation of the parties since it is widely recognised that women are more 'at risk' after leaving their violent partners (Morley and Mullender, 1994).[23] Criminal justice interventions can do little to prevent this. Families and friends maybe can, because they can arrange networks of support and surveillance where necessary. Knowledge empowers them to act as well as the woman.

Claim 7: Restorative justice encourages vigilantism

Restorative justice is sometimes equated with community or popular justice which is, in turn, equated with vigilantism.[24] It is true that community justice can be repressive, retributive, hierarchical and patriarchal. But these values are fundamentally at odds with the defining values of restorative justice and cannot, therefore, be part of it. That is why also we believe that 'community' involvement in restorative processes needs to be defined quite narrowly and to exclude the attendance of 'representative' members of geographical or social communities. Also, if there were concerns about communities taking over this process for non-restorative purposes, checks could be introduced – for example, courts could provide some oversight of restorative justice outcomes for the purposes of ensuring that the outcomes are in accordance with restorative justice values. Finally, of course, vigilantism does not require the introduction of restorative processes to emerge. Abrahams (1998) provides many examples of vigilantism from modern day Britain (and elsewhere) which seem rather to have been reactions against the failings of conventional criminal justice processes and sanctions. The spectre of vigilantism in debates on restorative justice, therefore, is perhaps something of a red herring.

Claim 8: Restorative justice lacks legitimacy

Tyler (1990) found that citizens treated with respect by the police, listened to by them and so on were likely to see the law as fair; conversely, when they were treated without respect and were not listened to the law was seen as unfair. He distinguished between 'process control' and 'outcome control' and concluded that 'having a say' (that is, process control) was more important than determining the outcome of the decision. Tyler's research, however, was based in a context in which decisions were made by third parties (judges). To this extent, his conclusions may not be relevant for restorative conferencing which is premised on consensual decision making. The same point can be made with respect to the elements subsequently identified by Paternoster *et al.* (1997) as providing legitimacy. These include: representation (playing a part in decision making), consistency, impartiality, accuracy (the competency of the legal authority), correctability (the scope for appeal) and ethicality (treating people with respect and dignity).

Restorative justice embodies some of these principles – particularly with regard to respect for victims and offenders. However, it does not meet others since they relate primarily to expectations of the 'legal authority'. To our minds, however, this is not problematic because this notion of legitimacy is derived principally from conventional justice values. Restorative justice involves somewhat different values and its legitimacy must derive from these. Important elements, therefore, in providing the legitimacy of restorative justice are the inclusion of the key parties, increased understanding of the offence, and its consequences and respect.

Conclusion

Family violence has a particular set of underlying characteristics: the existence of a prior relationship between the parties; the fact that the parties have lived together and may wish to continue to live together; the likelihood of repeat victimisation; the context of emotional abuse and ongoing power imbalances in the relationship; the victim's fear of the offender; the secrecy of the violence; the isolation of the victim; and the offender's minimising of the seriousness of the violence. Although some see these as requiring criminal justice solutions, in our view, they equally justify a restorative justice approach. Moreover, it can be argued that, because many women do not seem to wish to use conventional criminal justice processes, these processes themselves perpetuate many of these characteristics. Women's unwillingness to call the police, for example, keeps the violence secret and may allow men both to continue to minimise and to repeat their violence.

We are not, of course, saying that the criminal justice system has no place at all in dealing with men's violence towards their female partners. The criminal law and criminal sanctions play an important declaratory and denunciatory role. And there will be many times when women want their partners arrested or where it is necessary to prevent further assaults, as with other offences. But the criminal justice system does not serve women who have experienced violence at the hands of their male partners particularly well. Few violent men are reported to the police by their partners and, despite the existence of pro-arrest policies and the expectation that violent offenders will be arrested and imprisoned except in exceptional circumstances, many men escape both criminalisation and penalisation and, even when they do not, there is little evidence to show that these approaches 'work'. This is hardly a surprising conclusion. The criminal justice system has not been particularly successful in controlling crime and so why should we expect any more with respect to violence against women?

There is some support from women themselves for a different approach. This article has advocated moving in a new direction: towards restorative justice. There is increasing reliance on co-ordinated responses to crime and violence against women is no exception (Kelly, 1999; Clark *et al.*, 1996; Hague and Malos, 1996; Hague *et al.*, 1996). Whilst these may be positive developments in themselves, they could be strengthened by moving outside the criminal justice system. Restorative justice processes increase women's choices, provide women not only with the support of family and friends, but also with a voice, and, through this, may increase women's safety.[25] By offering constructive rather than penal solutions, restorative processes may also be opted for at an earlier stage in women's experience of violence. The Women's Aid network is premised on principles of empowerment for women. Restorative justice could be a powerful tool in this.

Notes

1. They discuss differences in the perceptions of justice from a care as opposed to a retributive perspective and portray these as 'female' and 'male' respectively. The female perspective emphasises needs, motives and relationships; retributive punishment and deterrence are not viewed as consistent with the ethic of care.

2. For more information on restorative justice, see Braithwaite (1989); Walgrave (1998); van Ness (1997); van Ness and Strong (1997); Zehr (1990); Consedine (1995); Consedine and Bowen (1999).

3. Criminal statistics in England and Wales do not distinguish violence against women by men. Other jurisdictions do – for example, in New Zealand, there is a specific offence

called 'male assaults female'. This, however, includes all such assaults and is not restricted to offences where there is a relationship between the parties. Similarly, some states in the United States record 'domestic violence' offences but these can include child as well as adult victims.

4 There are a number of reasons for this: for example, these surveys are set within definitions of crime and violence against women within relationships but matters are not necessarily viewed by participants in these terms; participants may be too afraid to disclose incidents to interviewers, especially but not only where the abuser is present in the household at the time; or participants may feel too embarrassed to disclose the offence.

5 The number of incidents of domestic violence reported in the 1995 British Crime Survey was more than three times higher than in 1981, but this was probably affected by the change in method of data collection from face-to-face interview to participants' private use of laptop computers. Some methodological problems remain, however; see Mirrlees-Black (1999).

6 By having first explored violent crime by strangers, these surveys may have shaped women's responses to the extent of violence they experienced at the hands of their partners. Examples of this kind of survey are the Australian Bureau of Statistics (1997) and Johnson and Sacco (1995).

7 Taken together, however, although these (and other) surveys vary considerably in their estimates of prevalence of men's violence against their female partners, we can suggest that probably somewhere between one in three and one in five women have experienced some level of violence at the hands of their current partner at least once during their relationship and that around one in ten have experienced at least one act of physical or sexual abuse in the previous twelve months. See Mirrlees-Black (1999, p.89) for a table summarising the findings of six surveys relating to five countries.

8 Sometimes, the reduction of repeat calls to the police from the same woman has been taken as an indicator of the reduction of violence (Kelly, 1999; Hanmer *et al.*, 1999), but it is not this clear cut; it could equally mean that the woman did not view the previous intervention as meeting her needs or wishes (Hoyle, 1998; Buzawa and Buzawa, 1996). Lloyd *et al.*, (1994) specifically mention the likelihood of an increase in the number of calls to the police if police responses are seen as more effective.

9 In Moms's 1997 sample, for example, only 11% of the women who disclosed any level of physical violence, said that they had ever asked the police to come to their home to deal with their partner's violence. The comparable figures in Mirrlees-Black (1999) were 9% for 'intermittent' victims (women who reported being assaulted 'once or twice') and 22% for chronic victims (women who reported being assaulted three or more times). Gelles and Straus (1988) estimate that only 14% of American women who experience 'severe' violence ever contact the police.

10 The ESRC Violence Research Programme (1998) quotes three studies on this point. The proportion of women experiencing violence who contacted GPs ranged from 14% to 22%, the proportion contacting lawyers ranged from 12% to 22% and the proportion contacting the police ranged from 15% to 24%.

11 Kelly's data are difficult to interpret because of definitional elisions. For example, on page 52 it is said that the women wanted the offender 'arrested/removed'. These are different types of actions. Similarly, on page 53, it is said that women wanted 'assertive action, including arrest', but there is no indication of whether or not assertive action always included arrest.

12 Women also have recourse to a number of civil remedies through injunctions. There have been numerous criticisms of these, especially around their lack of enforcement (see Morley and Mullender, 1994 and Edwards, 1996 for details). It is hard to make comparisons over the years because of

changes in the legislation, but in 1998 there were around 37,500 non-molestation orders and around 20,000 occupation orders. The issue for us here is the extent to which women actually use these orders. Less than half the orders had the power of arrest attached and there were very few applications for warrants of arrest (Lord Chancellor's Department, 1999). Changes in legal aid provision may affect the number of applications for orders. It is estimated that violence is a feature in as many as a third of divorces in England and Wales (Hester *et al.*, 1996).

13 Arrest does not automatically result in prosecution though contrast those jurisdictions with 'no plea' (that is, no plea bargaining) and 'no drop' (that is, mandatory prosecution policies with respect to violence against women). In Kelly's (1999) research, only 20 cases were able to be tracked through to prosecution. Only two of these men were given prison sentences. Nine were bound over to keep the peace and five were conditionally discharged. It seems unlikely that these sentences did much to increase women's safety. Provision was introduced in the Police and Criminal Evidence Act 1984 to make wives competent and compellable witnesses against partners where the offence involved an assault on the wife by the accused to encourage (and make easier) prosecution in these cases but the provisions are not widely used for both pragmatic and humanitarian reasons (for more information, see Cretney and Davis, 1997).

14 A recent American study (Feder, 1999) found a similarly low figure – 20% – in the area investigated and Feder cites this (at page 63) as somewhat higher than was found in other American studies other than one jurisdiction which had a mandatory arrest policy. Even there, the figure quoted is 22%.

15 Other researchers put a different interpretation on the failure of the police to arrest. Kelly (1999, p.ix), for example, suggests it is related rather to value judgments about 'victim worthiness', and assessments that the incident is a 'one off' or that the victim is likely to withdraw the complaint. However, Kelly also notes (1999, pp.29–30) that what victims wanted from the crisis counsellors in the Domestic Violence Matters pilot was the space to talk about the abuse and to obtain advice rather than to talk about their partner's arrest or prosecution or about leaving their partner.

16 For example, men who participated in two men's programmes (CHANGE and the Lothian Domestic Violence Probation project) as a condition of probation showed reductions in their violence and associated controlling behaviour some twelve months after the programmes compared with men given prison, probation or fines/admonishments. The difficulty with generalising from such findings is that the men were not randomly allocated to the outcomes (those on the programmes were first assessed as suitable for the programmes) nor were the samples adequately matched. The controls were much younger and had much higher levels of unemployment: both factors likely to affect reoffending rates. The programme men were then compared with the other men, irrespective of their very different sanctions. Samples were small: there were 51 men involved in the two programmes and the 'control' group was 71. The differences in 'reoffending' also appeared only when the men's self-report data (obtained through postal questionnaires) were used and not on the basis of police or court data. And the recontact rate at the twelve-month point was only 53% for programme men and 49% for the 'control' group men. It is at least possible that involvement in the programmes influenced admission rates and that those who could not be contacted had higher 'reoffending' rates. The programme men's partners also reported lower 'reoffending' rates and had higher recontact rates (60% and 57% respectively), but this has to be read within the context of the above critical points. We are not suggesting here that the programmes did not have a positive effect; the issue is the extent to which one can generalise from the findings.

17 Examples of 'pure' restorative justice in practice are difficult to find, but family group conferences (Maxwell and Morris, 1993) and community panel adult pre-trial diversion programmes (Maxwell *et al*., 1999) certainly get close to restorative ideals. We do not include victim–offender mediation programmes as examples of restorative justice. Dignan and Cavadino (1996) distinguish restorative conferencing (an example, in their terms, of a communication model of justice) from mediation (an example, in their terms, of a reparation model of justice) on the basis of four characteristics: the delegation of powers from the state to members of the community; the convening of a meeting to which supporters of victims and offenders are invited as a mechanism for arriving at a negotiated community response; the empowerment of the offender and his or her family through formulating a plan which is acceptable to the other participants; and monitoring of those plans.

18 As an aside, it is worth noting that the power imbalances associated with childhood and adulthood have not been seen as a problem in the same way in the increasing use of restorative processes and practices for young offenders. One could also, of course, suggest that there is always a power imbalance between offenders and victims as offenders have 'taken' from victims, but restorative justice processes and practices routinely work towards removing this imbalance.

19 Some women, especially those who are abused may be isolated generally and specifically from their families. In these cases it might be possible to involve lay advocates (such as refuge workers) to support the women through the process. Equally, there may be situations where 'local communities' or families tolerate violence; here too lay advocates could play a useful role.

20 The other victims felt neutral about the process.

21 For example, two-thirds of the women interviewed by Carbonatto (1998) who had contact with the police as a result of their partner's violence towards them wanted the relationship with their partner to continue despite the violence. Mirrlees-Black (1999) also reports that more than two-thirds of the 'chronic female victims in the British Crime Survey were living with their partner at the time of the last assault and a quarter of them were still living with their partners at the time of the survey interview. Almost 60% of the chronic victims assaulted in the last year also reported that they were living with their partners at that time; 56% were still living with their partners at the time of the survey interview.

22 An example of professionals rather than women deciding is reflected in the policy in Ontario, Canada, of mandatory charging. Kelly (1999, p.3) describes this as having the 'added advantage' of the police taking pro-active responsibility for law enforcement. She also notes that police are expected to lay the charges, not on the basis of victims' wishes, but on the basis of the behaviour complained about.

23 Surveys consistently show that higher levels of violence by partners are reported by women no longer living in that relationship (see, for example, Morris, 1997). Separated women may be more willing to report violence by partners and violence may have been a factor in the decision to leave, but it is likely also that violence escalates around and after separation.

24 Von Hirsch and Ashworth (1998, p.303) certainly justify conventional justice practices on the grounds that they displace vigilantism and prevent people from taking the law into their own hands.

25 The police in some areas already recognise the role which friends, neighbours and family can play in their introduction of 'cocoon watches'. Here the police request the help and support of these various individuals in protecting the victim by calling the police if the violence seems likely to recur.

References

Abrahams, R. (1998) *Vigilant Citizens*, Cambridge, Polity Press.

Australian Bureau of Statistics (1997) *Women's Safety Australia 1996*, Canberra, Australian Bureau of Statistics.

BBC News Online (1999) 'Court tackles domestic violence', 2 June, http://news.bbc.co.uk/.

Braithwaite, J. (1989) *Crime, Stigma and Reintegration*, Cambridge, Cambridge University Press.

Braithwaite, J. and Daly, K. (1994) 'Masculinities and communitarian control', in Newburn, T. and Stanko, E. (eds) *Just Boys Doing Business*, London, Routledge.

Bush, T. and Hood-Williams, J. (1995) 'Domestic violence in a London housing estate', *Home Office Research Bulletin*, no.37, pp.11–18.

Buzawa, E. and Buzawa, C. (eds) (1996) *Domestic Violence: The Criminal Justice Response*, Thousand Oaks, CA, Sage.

Carbonatto, H. (1995) *Expanding Intervention Options for Spousal Abuse: The Use of Restorative Justice* (Occasional Papers in Criminology New Series: no.4), Wellington, New Zealand, Institute of Criminology, Victoria University of Wellington.

Carbonatto, H. (1998) 'The criminal justice response to domestic violence in New Zealand', *Criminology Aotearoa/New Zealand*, a newsletter from the Institute of Criminology, Victoria University of Wellington, no.10, pp.7–8.

Carlen, P. (1992) 'Criminal women and criminal justice: the limits to, and potential of, feminist and left realist perspectives', in Matthews, R. and Young, J. (eds) *Realist Criminology*, London, Sage.

Clark, S., Burt, M., Schulte, M. and Maguire, K. (1996) 'Co-ordinated community responses to domestic violence in six communities: beyond the justice system', http://aspe.os.dhhs.gov/hsp/cyp/domvilnz.htm.

Consedine, J. (1995) *Restorative Justice: Healing the Effects of Crime*, Lyttelton, Ploughshares Publications.

Consedine, J. and Bowen, H. (1999) *Restorative Justice: Contemporary Themes and Practice*, Lyttelton, Ploughshares Publications.

Cretney, A. and Davis, G. (1997) 'The significance of compellability in the prosecution of domestic assault', *British Journal of Criminology*, vol.37, pp.75–89.

Daly, K. (1989) 'Criminal justice ideologies and practices in different voices: some feminist questions about justice', *International Journal of Sociology of Law*, vol.17, pp.1–18.

Davis, R. and Taylor, B. (1999) 'Does batterer treatment reduce the violence? A synthesis of the literature', *Women and Criminal Justice*, vol.10, pp.69–93.

Dignan, J. and Cavadino, M. (1996) 'Towards a framework for conceptualising and evaluating models of criminal justice from a victim's perspective', *International Review of Victimology*, vol.4, pp.153–82.

Dobash, R.E. and Dobash, R.P. (1992) *Women, Violence and Social Change*, London, Routledge.

Dobash, R., Dobash, R., Cavanagh, K. and Lewis, R. (1996) *Research Evaluation of Programmes for Violent Men*, Edinburgh, The Scottish Office Central Research Unit.

Edleson, J. and Syers, M. (1990) 'Relative effectiveness of group treatments for men who batter', *Social Work Research and Abstracts*, vol.26, no.2, pp.10–17.

Edwards, S. (1989) *Policing Domestic Violence*, London, Sage.

Edwards, S. (1996) *Sex and Gender in the Legal Process*, London, Blackstone Press.

ESRC Violence Research Programme (1998) *Taking Stock: What do we Know About Violence?*, Uxbridge, Brunel University.

Feder, L. (1999) 'Policing handling of domestic violence calls: an overview and further investigation', *Women and Criminal Justice*, vol.10, pp.49–68.

Ford, D. (1991) 'Prosecution as a victim power resource: a note on empowering women in violent conjugal relationships', *Law and Society Review*, vol.25, no.2, pp.313–34.

Gelles, R. and Straus, M. (1988) *Intimate Violence: The Causes and Consequences of Abuse in the American Family*, Beverly Hills, CA, Sage.

Gendreau, P. and Andrews, D. (1990) 'Tertiary prevention: what the meta-analysis of the offender treatment literature tells us about "what works"', *Canadian Journal of Criminology*, vol.32, pp.173–84.

Grace, S. (1995) *Policing Domestic Violence in the 1990s*, Home Office Research Study no.139, London, Home Office.

Hague, G. and Malos, E. (1996) *Tackling Domestic Violence: A Guide to Developing Multi-Agency Initiatives*, Bristol, The Policy Press.

Hague, G., Malos, E. and Dear, W. (1996) *Multi-agency Work and Domestic Violence: A National Study of Inter-agency Initiatives*, Bristol, The Policy Press.

Hanmer, J. (1989) 'Women and policing in Britain', in J. Hanmer, J. Radford and E. Stanko (eds) *Women, Policing and Male Violence*, London, Routledge and Kegan Paul.

Hanmer, J., Griffiths, S. and Jerwood, D. (1999) *Arresting Evidence: Domestic Violence and Repeat Victimisation*, Police Research Series Paper 104, London, Home Office.

Heidensohn, F. (1986) 'Models of justice: Portia or Persephone? Some thoughts on equality, fairness and gender in the field of criminal justice', *International Journal of the Sociology of Law*, vol.14, pp.287–98.

Hester, M., Pearson, C. and Radford, L. (1996) *A National Survey of Court Welfare and Voluntary Sector Mediation Practices*, Bristol, The Policy Press.

Hoyle, C. (1998) *Negotiating Domestic Violence: Police, Criminal Justice and Victims,* Oxford, Oxford University Press.

Hudson, B. (1998) 'Restorative justice: the challenge of sexual and racial violence', *Journal of Law and Society*, vol.25, pp.237–56.

Johnson, H. and Sacco, V. (1995) 'Researching violence against women: Statistics Canada national survey', *Canadian Journal of Criminology*, July, pp.281–304.

Kelly, L. (1999) *Domestic Violence Matters: An Evaluation of a Development Project*, Home Office Research Study no.193, London, Home Office.

Liebrich, J., Paulin, J. and Ransom, R. (1995) *Hitting Home: Men Speak About Abuse of Women Partners*, Wellington, Department of Justice.

Lloyd, S., Farrell, G. and Pease, K. (1994) *Preventing Repeated Domestic Violence: A Demonstration Project on Merseyside*, Police Research Group Crime Prevention Unit Series, Paper 49, London, Home Office.

Lord Chancellor's Department (1999) *Judicial Statistics: England and Wales*, Cm. 4371.

Martin, P. (1996) 'Restorative justice – a family violence perspective', *Social Policy Journal of New Zealand*, vol.6, pp.56–68.

Masters, G. and Smith, D. (1998) 'Portia and Persephone revisited: thinking about feeling criminal justice', *Theoretical Criminology*, vol.2, pp.5–27.

Maxwell, G.M. and Morris, A. (1993) *Families, Victims and Culture: Youth Justice in New Zealand*, Wellington, New Zealand, Social Policy Agency and Institute of Criminology, Victoria University of Wellington.

Maxwell, G.M., Morris, A. and Anderson, T. (1999) *Community Panel Adult Pre-trial Diversion*, Wellington, New Zealand, Crime Prevention Unit.

Maxwell, G.M. and Morris, A. (1999) *Understanding Reoffending*, Wellington, New Zealand, Institute of Criminology, Victoria University of Wellington.

McGuire, J. (1995) *What Works: Reducing Offending?*, Chichester, John Wiley.

McIvor, G. (1992) *Reducing Reoffending: What Works Now?*, Wellington, New Zealand, Department of Justice.

McLaren, K. (1992) *Sentenced to Serve?*, Aldershot, Gower.

Mirrlees-Black, C. (1995) 'Estimating the extent of domestic violence: findings from the 1992 British Crime Survey', Research Bulletin no.3, London, Home Office Research and Statistics Directorate.

Mirrlees-Black, C. (1999) *Domestic Violence: Findings from a New British Crime Survey Self-Completion Questionnaire*, Home Office Research Study no.192, London, Home Office.

Morley, R. and Mullender, A. (1994) *Preventing Domestic Violence to Women*, Police Research Group Crime Prevention Unit Series, Paper 48, London, Home Office.

Morris, A. (1993) *Law Reform Initiatives on Violence against Women: Successes and Pitfalls*, Occasional Papers in Criminology New Series, no.4, Wellington, New Zealand, Institute of Criminology, Victoria University of Wellington.

Morris, A. (1997) 'The prevalence in New Zealand of violence against women by their current partners', *Australia and New Zealand Journal of Criminology*, vol.31, no.3, pp.267–86.

Morris, A. (1998) *Women's Safety Survey 1996*, Wellington, New Zealand, Ministry of Justice.

Paternoster, R., Backman, R., Brame, R. and Sherman, L. (1997) 'Do fair procedures matter? The effect of procedural justice on spousal assault', *Law and Society Review*, vol.31, pp.163–204.

Scourfield, J. and Dobash, R. (1999) 'Programmes for violent men: recent developments in the UK', *Howard Journal*, vol.38, pp.128–43.

Shapland, J., Willmore, J. and Duff, P. (1985) *Victims and the Criminal Justice System*, Aldershot, Gower.

Sherman, L. (1992) *Policing Domestic Violence*, New York, The Free Press.

Smart, C. (1989) *Feminism and the Power of Law*, London, Routledge.

Smart, C. (1995) *Law, Crime and Sexuality: Essays in Feminism*, London, Sage.

Snider, L. (1998) 'Towards safer societies: punishment, masculinities and violence against women', *British Journal of Criminology*, vol.38, pp.1–39.

Stanko, E. (1989) 'Missing the mark? Policing battering', in Hanmer, J., Radford, J. and Stanko, E. (eds) *Women, Policing and Male Violence*, London, Routledge and Kegan Paul.

Stanko, E. (1995) 'Policing domestic violence', *Australian and New Zealand Journal of Criminology (Special Supplementary Issue)*, vol.31, p.44.

Stubbs, J. (1997) 'Shame, defiance and violence against women', in Cook, S. and Bessant, J. (eds) *Women's Encounters with Violence: Australian Experiences*, London, Sage.

Tyler, T. (1990) *Why People Obey the Law*, New Haven, CT, Yale University Press.

van Ness, D. (1997) 'Perspectives on achieving satisfying justice: values and principles of restorative justice', *The ICCA Journal of Community Corrections*, vol.8, no.1, pp.7–12.

van Ness, D. and Strong, K.H. (1997) *Restorative Justice*, Cincinatti, OH, Anderson Publishing.

von Hirsch, A. and Ashworth, A. (eds) (1998) *Principled Sentencing: Reading on Theory and Policy*, 2nd edn, Oxford, Hart.

von Hirsch, A., Bottoms, A.E., Burney, E. and Wikstrom, P.O. (1999) *Criminal Deterrence and Sentencing Severity*, Oxford, Hart.

Walgrave, L. (1998) *Restorative Justice for Juveniles: Potentialities, Risks and Problems for Research* (a selection of papers presented at the International Conference, Leuven, 1997), Belgium, Leuven University Press.

Walker, L. (1979) *The Battered Woman*, New York, Harper and Row.

Young, R. and Goold, B. (1999) 'Restorative police cautioning in Aylesbury: from degrading to reintegrative shaming ceremonies', *Criminal Law Review*, February, pp.126–38.

Zehr, H. (1990) *Changing Lenses: A New Focus for Crime and Justice*, Scottsdale, PA, Herald Press.

CHAPTER 12

Suite Justice or Sweet Charity? Some Explorations of Shaming and Incapacitating Business Fraudsters

by Michael Levi

Introduction

White-collar crime in general and frauds committed by 'respectable' individuals in particular have always presented difficulties both for the *explanation* of sentencing (in particular, issues of socio-economic bias) and for the *normative* aspects of what is the most appropriate form of sentencing (fairness). In one of the few interview-based studies of sentencing white-collar criminals, Wheeler *et al.* (1988) discuss 'the paradox of leniency and severity' whereby (as I summarize) US federal judges wavered between (a) accepting that there was little or no point in sentencing offenders to jail who were professionally ruined anyway, (b) satisfying the general public by tough retribution and (c) expressing their own moral revulsion at offending by those who have the capacity to behave honestly but who choose not to do so.[1] Their work, together with my own analysis of sentencing cases and discussions with English judges, suggest that judges commonly assume a serious loss of social and economic standing in the community arising from conviction or even prosecution per se. In short, for elites, 'the process is the punishment' (Levi, 1993; von Hirsch and Wasik, 1997). For example, conviction can lead to formal professional disqualification for accountants, lawyers, senior bankers and anyone directly selling financial services. Disbarment may even follow acquittal, if breaches of regulatory rules are demonstrated. These professional sanctions are imposed in order to protect the depositing and investing general public, consumers of professional services[2] and also to protect the image of the professions. So whether or not shame or its more negativistic, socially excluding close cousin, stigma *actually* occur, some sorts of meaningful sanctions – social and/or professional – are assumed by sentencers to take place arising from or independent of the criminal process. Professional consequences of this kind, like the more informal sanctions, vary between nation states and occupational cultures, often in quite subtle ways.

This article examines the evidence for the existence and impact of shaming on white-collar offenders, and discusses whether what happens and/or is intended to happen is reintegrative shaming or exclusionary stigma. Braithwaite (1989 *et seq.*) and, in a different way, Elias (1982) have focused academic and political attention upon the shaming process, both (a) as an explanation for variations in crime rates and (b) as a normative approach to crime control, which should partly replace imprisonment and other severe formal sanctions. Braithwaite argues that society's emphasis on punishment as desirable in itself and its assumption that punishment leads to reformation constitute a mistake both of principle and practical judgement. Instead, he argues, societies like Japan that shame offenders and then (supposedly) reintegrate them into normal life are better able to control deviance without wasting money and human capital on pointless punishment. He does not claim that such reintegration is easy, and one might expect shaming to work best with those who are already well integrated into law-conforming groups and therefore fear loss of esteem from their peers

Source: *Punishment and Society*, vol.4, no.2, pp.147–63.

and feel the need to atone for past conduct: people, in other words, who have some grace from which to fall. In relation to fraud and corporate crime, evidence of the effects of either punishment or shaming is poor compared with street and household crime, since measures of commercial offending and victimization are less well established. However, Braithwaite plausibly argues that large corporations are concerned about their reputations and commit fewer health and safety and other violations than do marginal firms that tend to be less concerned about complying with standards. Because he is more concerned about behavioural change than about moral deserts, the question of whether corporations – which have 'no body to kick, no soul to damn' – are appropriate objects of deserved punishment is by-passed in favour of pragmatic concerns about 'what works'. Braithwaite's focus on improving behavioural standards in major corporations leads him to neglect frauds committed by individuals and corporations that do not intend to continue in business or whose offending is essential to their economic viability. This omission is significant because the costs and benefits of 'reputation' for these marginal firms differ substantially from those of large multinational corporations, who devote considerable resources to reputation maintenance. We might also question whether and under what plausible monitoring conditions we should allow *every* shamed business person or professional to be reintegrated into their 'trade' as well as into 'society'. Might there not be some businesses for which stigma and exclusion are appropriate sanctions?

Shaming and fraud: the context

In this article, the focus is upon fraud rather than the wider area of corporate malefaction (for which, see Fisse and Braithwaite, 1983, 1993; Slapper *et al.*, 1999). In principle, one might expect shame to be applied most strongly to those who are seen as having the ability to behave honestly (*noblesse oblige*) and to those offences that are viewed most seriously. These are also areas in which emotionally it is most difficult to avoid a preference for retribution rather than forgiveness. Both the people and the activities that fall within the category of 'fraud' are heterogeneous, ranging from blue-collar credit card fraudsters to elite insider dealers, and from fraud against the poor and elderly to fraud against wealthy institutions. Furthermore, analyses of the impact of shame should incorporate wider reference groups to which the offender belonged at the time of the offending and at the time at which sanctions were applied, as well as the narrower relationship between the offender and the victim.

Reference group attitudes are affected by the shift towards more impersonal dealings in an increasingly globalized market society. Though it is true that 'the financial City' remains a place in which repeat players interact rather than being a virtual network of strangers, the level of mutual integration and dependency has lessened to varying degrees.[3] In a highly mobile, anomic culture (Friedrichs, 1996; Passas, 1999), individual traders and their managers are focused more on this year's performance-related bonus than on next year's, not least because many are unlikely to be around to face the consequences of the risks that they take. (Though of course retribution via criminal or regulatory sanctions may follow eventually.) Nevertheless, my unpublished interviews in the UK suggest that many traders are avid readers of the professional trade and broadsheet press (such as the *Financial Times* and *Wall Street Journal*) so they can be expected to be aware of any formal sanctions imposed on their peers and the basis for those sanctions. In relation to the more technical forms of market abuse, however, such concerns are more likely to reflect classic 'rational actor' deterrence models than be internalized views about the wrongfulness of the behaviour.

What factors would one predict would influence the effectiveness of shaming? One element would be sub-cultural and national variation. Victimization and business perception surveys conducted for Transparency International (TI, 2001) indicate substantial variations in general levels of corruption and consumer fraud within and between first- and third-world countries (Levi and Pithouse, forthcoming; www.gwdg.de). Conceptions of the 'normality' of commercial criminal behaviours can thus be expected to differ, with business people in Finland or New Zealand (at the moral end of the TI business perceptions index) finding bribery of foreign public officials far less normal or acceptable than their counterparts in China, Nigeria and Russia (at the low end of the index). In addition to personal values and cultural norms, expectations of whether people in their social group will learn about their offences and what their reactions will be are also salient. This is not a function solely of the denunciatory intentions of the prosecutors[4] or sentencers but also of how any such publicity is 'read' by the potential offender's reference group.[5] 'Abused' tycoons or corporations are not passive victims of the media, for they are often able to employ PR staff to produce more positive readings of how they have behaved. They do this partly for their egos and partly because public scandal is usually regarded as bad for business (Levi and Pithouse, forthcoming). When successful, this media 'spin' reduces the *need* to atone in order to be reintegrated – though of course they may also have to satisfy regulators whatever the views of their friends and colleagues. Whatever the general perceptions of the seriousness of a particular crime, some potential offenders will always be able to regard their offending as belonging to the lower range of harmful or even harmless actions.[6]

Braithwaite and others who write about 'degradation rituals' set great store by the symbolic communication between offenders, victims and the relevant publics. Here, some white-collar offenders may benefit from public ambivalence. There have been heated media debates about events such as the Queen Mother shaking hands at a Covent Garden opera fund-raising party with Guinness convict Gerald Ronson while he was on parole;[7] the rapid move of the Guinness offenders to open prisons; the home leave and outside working conditions of imprisoned white-collar offenders; and the 18 months jail sentence imposed on former Conservative Cabinet Minister Jonathan Aitken, convicted of perjury in 1999.[8] These debates usually revolve around the amount of deserved punishment rather than the needs of reintegration and whether the offender has atoned enough. Those who defraud 'widows and orphans' are treated as irredeemable by the media and public figures, their hedonistic lifestyles aggravating the harms they have caused victims (Levi and Pithouse, forthcoming). Those who manufacture defective cars or tyres but fail to respond to actual warnings are often viewed as very serious offenders, but there is no real evidence about how credible the public finds their protestations of guilt or shame.[9]

In countries such as Japan, senior executives 'accept responsibility' and resign for acts such as unsecured 'lending' of hundreds of thousands of pounds – or, in more sophisticated cases such as Japan Airlines in 1998, allegedly grossly overpaying for the supply of plants on contract that were not in fact supplied – to *Sokaiya* (organized criminals) in return for not disrupting or asking awkward questions at Annual General Meetings.[10] They lose some prestige and direct power, and arguably this constitutes reintegrative shaming. But there is no evidence that such sanctions and acceptance of responsibility have any effect on *corporate* behaviour,[11] however helpful they may be in terms of preventing individual white-collar recidivism.[12] Thus, when the Chairmen of Nomura Securities and other 'blue-chip' Japanese financial institutions step aside and are re-engaged merely 'in an advisory capacity', just as when they become Prime Minister years *after* resigning as Finance Minister following a criminal political funding scandal (as did Prime Minister Hashimoto), does this suggest a conflict between the needs of reintegrative shaming and the need for corporate deterrence? Several suicides also ensued, including the head of the Bank of Japan's investigative group in 1998 and a senior investigator for the Financial Supervision Agency in 1999, who presumably found the process of dealing with their colleagues in such an adversarial way too much – too shameful? – to bear, even if they were to be reintegrated afterwards.[13] Like the UK scandal of the mid-1990s that revealed systematic misleading of the public by private pensions salespeople, the Japanese business scandals illustrate the difficulties of shaming when particular forms of criminality or discreditable behaviour are widespread. In an organizational context, unless there is admissible evidence to the contrary, senior staff usually claim that they had no or insufficient knowledge of the activities of their subordinates, so their shame applies to neglect of supervisory duties rather than to malefaction. Nonetheless, though it may be impossible to determine until *after* the fact whether shaming is going to be *re*integrative or *dis*integrative – a serious problem for the explanatory power of his model – Braithwaite (1989) has plausibly argued that reintegrative shaming is the key to successful crime control. (A neo-Durkheimian might counter that some shaming might be effective as a general deterrent precisely because it is disintegrative and exclusionary, generating a tension between 'what works' for general prevention and 'what does not work' for the prevention of recidivism.)

Conditions of shaming in contemporary societies

Levi and Suddle (1989) examined the lack of control and the absence of shaming for tax evasion in Pakistan, arguing that elites were almost entirely impervious to general social sentiments and that the media were largely uncritical of whoever occupied power in government until after they fell.[14] Braithwaite responded (personal communication) rightly that he never wrote or even implied that white-collar criminals were *in fact regularly* shamed or formally sanctioned along the lines of his model. He pointed out that he did not want to omit this category from his analysis, and there was some evidence from case studies that corporations misbehaved less after they received bad publicity. But if the issue is one of remedial effectiveness rather than simple retribution, it might be fruitful to return to this theme in both a national and an international context.

First, let us examine the conditions of successful degradation ceremonies, where one means by 'success' the kind of normative restoration that Braithwaite describes, rather than the social mortification portrayed by Garfinkel. These appear to me to be the following:

(1) shaming must be applied against an act or set of acts, rather than against a person or an institution (since the latter would be a form of essentialism and stigma);

(2) the conduct must be seen as negative by the offender's reference groups;

(3) shaming must result in behavioural change on the part of the offender (and also by those onlookers influenced by viewing the shaming ritual);

(4) the shamed persons must be reintegrated back into 'society', putting past mis-deeds behind them.

Stages 1 and 2: the application of shaming and its interpretation by significant others

Some forms of criminal behaviour are less visible than others to victims, criminal investigators and the media: this applies also to categories of fraud, with the frauds of the poor being more readily detected as well as more likely to be prosecuted (Nelken, 1997; Croall, 2001). The more stringent the libel laws and the more that the media are controlled by 'big-business' and/or politicians, the less the impetus on the authorities to act against those frauds and corporate crimes that implicate elites as suspects. However, this does not affect those frauds *not* committed by elites and ironically, one can use the word 'sleaze' with relative impunity[15] in the UK. Levi and Pithouse (forthcoming) have shown how dependent most of the media are upon official actions of one sort or another to give journalists a peg on which to hang the investigation so that they do not look 'punitive' or excessively risky in the eyes of their cautious editors and programme producers. (These official actions need not amount to a criminal prosecution, they may be administrative measures such as disciplinary tribunals, liquidations or director disqualifications.) This varies by culture and legal system, but given the economic pressure on the media in many parts of the world, and active censorship and quiescence in others, only a conscious decision by editors and proprietors is going to give journalists the time and the paper/programme space for any extended proactive or even reactive investigative work.

Globalization has a special influence here. Scanning and on-line electronic newsgathering have made collation and distribution of corporate news much easier when investigators can identify corporate ownership linkages. On the one hand, globalization extends reputational risk to geographical areas over which the company may have little control; on the other, as Union Carbide's experience after the explosion of toxic gas at Bhopal showed, shaming and media publicity in one country may not reach other countries and may not persist if they do. And, as the recent BCCI and Bank of New York scandals suggest, the suspects may have no need to feel or display shame because their reference groups may view the charges as politically motivated – in these cases, by anti-Islamic and anti-Russian sentiments respectively. There are no examples where financial services firms other than the Bank of Credit and Commerce International (which was closed down in 1991) have been shamed globally by fraud allegations, and the evidence on the non-regulatory effects of money-laundering scandals is not clear.[16] There are many examples however where corporate behaviour has been altered by shaming, for example dumping oil machinery at sea (Blankenburg, 2000) and child labour exploitation in the third world (see also Fisse and Braithwaite, 1993). Such corporate shaming can be risky: allegations by the UK television documentary *World in Action* that Marks & Spencer knowingly or recklessly deceived consumers into believing that shirts made abroad were 'made in England' led to a successful libel action and huge damages for reputational loss. But except in the sense that these shamed corporate actions were originally intended to increase profitability, these are not financial crimes and are only distantly related to fraud.

In practice, the level of shame or stigma applied is *related* to the 'nature' of the victims, but not in any obvious or ideological way. Usually, the greater the perceived harm, the more vulnerable the perceived victim, the greater the negative publicity. Shaming may take place in the media, or merely in the social or occupational reference groups in which the offender lives. It may take place as the result of moral entrepreneurial activity by investigators and/or prosecutors, operating individually or as part of policy strategy. Thus, encouraged by the Labour government, the UK Environment Agency placed on the Internet its '1999 Hall of Shame', including a 'League table based on amount of fines during 1998', complete with graphic Top Five Polluters, headed by ICI (www.environment-agency.gov.uk).[17] People and occupations differ in the scale of their reference groups: politicians have large ones, though politicians can sometimes deflect shame by representing themselves as the victim of an establishment conspiracy. To paraphrase Nelken and Levi (1996), it is not just Italians who usually take it for granted that *prosecution* is simply the surface manifestation of personal or political *persecution*. In contrast, the reference group for derivatives traders may be quite small except where the financial scandal has the sort of massive and far-reaching consequences that brought down Barings Bank.[18]

Frauds against the Inland Revenue or against large corporations, or that involve quasi-victimless crimes such as insider trading, may be more or less tolerated, though only professional criminals are likely to view them positively (see Levi and Sherwin, 1995). On the other hand, the embezzlement of small sums from a charity collection may generate national or even international obloquy. The relationship between size of fraud and social exclusion is not consistent.

The cases that the media pick up in order to 'tickle the public' (Engel, 1996) usually contain traumatized personal or institutional victims, evil offenders and/or people who are already famous. Often the important benefit for white-collar 'offenders' of being shamed only in a restricted professional group is that their children are less likely to be humiliated at their private school because their father (or much more rarely in practice, their mother) has appeared as a scoundrel on the TV News, and the offender or his/her partner is less likely to be snubbed in the local store. Appearance in a negative light in a trade paper can of course be devastating professionally: the difference is that it does not cover all the facets of daily routines.

Stigma: the dark side of shaming

Shame can unintentionally turn into stigma when some of those shamed are inappropriate targets: everyone working with an anathematized institution gets 'tarred with the same brush'. This is true also of the *employees* of the Bank of Credit and Commerce International itself, at least in the West, so devastating was the BCCI's 'master status' as the 'Bank of Cocaine [or Crooks] and Conmen International' that staff found it very difficult to obtain re-employment in the financial services sector. They were seen as being ethically tainted (*Malik and Mahmoud 41 Bank of Credit and Commerce International* [1998] AC 20). By July 1998, ex-employee claims for stigma and misrepresentation totalled over $500 million, while employee loans outstanding totalled £42 million (including rolled up high interest). Stigma can even apply to citizens of a whole country, such as Nigerians who are widely assumed by the banking community in the West to be fraudsters unless demonstrated otherwise. Attempts by Nigerians to counter this stigma include the placing of advertisements in UK and US newspapers telling the public not to invest in 'advance fee frauds' with which Nigerians have been associated (Levi and Pithouse, forthcoming).

In response to an anonymous general questionnaire about their reactions to a series of fraud issues, a very large proportion of UK executives of Times 1000 largest companies – 88 per cent in 1994 – stated in surveys conducted with Ernst & Young (Levi and Sherwin, 1995) that they would refuse to do business with people convicted of fraud, though they were more tolerant of those convicted of tax fraud. A substantial majority state consistently in successive surveys that they would also avoid *socially* those convicted of fraud against other people and investors: indeed, over one-third stated that they would avoid them even if they were merely *suspected* of such frauds. But the *effects* of this depend on how much potential fraudsters *care* about such reactions and on what they *expect* such reactions to be. The issue of time also has to be taken into account: hostile publicity may be intense for a few weeks but if they tough it out, the media usually will soon lose interest. Moreover, if the shamed is charming and/or is useful to others in business or politics then s/he may re-emerge into 'respectable society'.[19]

American economists Karpoff and Lott observe that 'the reputational cost of corporate fraud is large and constitutes most of the cost incurred by firms accused or convicted of fraud' (1993, pp.758–9). Their work does not involve any sophisticated model of how large organizations work, but they appear to be correct in asserting that

(1) there are indeed reputational effects partly independent of formal sanctions;[20] and
(2) we should be wary about the imposition of more punishment than is needed to regulate the activity 'sensibly'.

For them, as perhaps for Braithwaite, fairness vis-à-vis penalties in *non*-white-collar crime cases, and the concern to satisfy small investors and the general public that the authorities are combating 'unjust enrichment', are largely irrelevant. Shares can plummet after negative publicity in the media – here, a change in top management or a strengthening of non-executive directors may achieve rebirth of investor and media confidence – but it is hard to disentangle the pure reputational effects from expected financial and legal losses (as well as the diversion of executives' time) from sanctions imposed by regulators or in the courts.[21] If it were not for internationalization of share markets, one might expect larger price falls in high-regulatory penalty countries like the USA than in low-penalty ones such as the UK used to be. Inasmuch as manipulations are intended to conceal poor economic and/or technical performance (for example, new pharmaceuticals), exposure and executive changes following scandal may at best merely return the firm to its expected true economic value.

Both for retributive reasons and in relation to reintegrative shaming, it is important to appreciate that cross-culturally, in smaller-scale societies where informal sanctions are widely communicated and are likely to be effective both in harming people's social standing and in incapacitating them from future misconduct, *informal* punishment may have *more* (and formal punishment correspondingly less) marginal effect than it does in more anonymous societies. One might think of differences between the impact of admonition for securities violations in Sri Lanka, Tokyo, London and New York respectively. Nevertheless, Japanese traders who have lost money may be no more able than traders of any other nationality to resist the temptation to try to 'win it back' by further trading, despite the increased risk for their firm (e.g. Daiwa and Sumitomo during the 1990s). To have failed at all may lead to shame, and the risk of increased shame for the trader, if detected, may not save the company from devastation. Nor will shame act as a deterrent in circumstances where the trader is confident that he will be able to repay the losses without detection, as many reckless traders convince themselves they can.

The morally neutralizing effect of money may give shamed persons (or rather, persons who are stigmatized by traditional elites) the capacity to elude the socially restrictive effects of shame or stigma while living in some luxury. They may not wish to be reintegrated if this means giving back the money. From the 1970s onwards, British criminal exiles enjoyed the warmer climate of Spain and the companionship of fellow professionals, alongside the expanded legitimate and illegitimate business opportunities this presented. Continued freedom from official intervention may depend on the failure of harmonization of mutual criminal legal assistance (of which corruption is but one cause). Whether being pardoned by President Clinton and in theory allowed out of comfortable exile in Switzerland counts as reintegrative shaming for Marc Rich is a moot point. There is no evidence that he either displayed atonement for his wrong or was castigated by his reference group of wealthy international business people or indeed by Israeli government officials, to whom he provided various forms of assistance. Whether assisting charities counts as atonement is difficult, as it involves subjective inferences of motives. Rich did engage in numerous charitable activities, but so too did 'junk bond guru' Mike Milken, who was refused a pardon, perhaps because of organized pressure from groups who wanted to see him punished. Whatever the World Bank and 'western values' of 'good governance' might recommend, my own interviews with some third-world elites suggest that they believe that they are *entitled* to use their positions for private gain and that their citizens and peers would despise and distrust them if they did not do so.

Caught between the Scylla of cultural imperialism and the Charybdis of moral relativism, the conceptualization of what shaming might be expected to achieve nonetheless remains obscure. Is it primarily social pressure to impact on social prestige? If so, this social prestige has to matter to the individual or corporation concerned, in a way that produces some psychodynamic effect analogous to guilt, but which is injected situationally from the outside rather than from the internalized super ego. How can we know when someone has expiated their past and become trustworthy again? This is particularly difficult in the case of professional fraudsters. Fraud is not the only area in which issues arise about manipulation of victims and observers, but people who commit frauds are more practised than most at it.

Whatever the case, part of the effect of shaming depends on how much the particular business wants to continue operating. *Ex hypothesi*, the following tentative propositions may be made:

(1) Career fraudsters are unlikely to find it easy to change from the inside as a result of attempts to make them ashamed of what they have done.

(2) Those who turn to fraud when their businesses are about to go bust may not care about the *prospect* of shame, for they are focused narrowly on 'staying alive' or 'saving a few pennies for my wife and children'.[22] This does not mean that they will not care when confronted afterwards, but these retrospective regrets do not ensure that they would not do the same again if put in a similar situation.

(3) The people who care most about being shamed are (a) those respectables whose social lives are embedded and who are sufficiently distanced from their business situation to appreciate the impact that exposure for fraud might have upon their social standing (though the proper comparator would be the standing that they would have if they did *not* defraud, which

might be lower than their present standing); and (b) those who fear that they may be excluded economically from markets. In both cases, however, this looks closer to fear of stigma – i.e. deterrence through social conformity – than to moral conversion to law-obedience. Such fears, for example, are doubtless what is propelling activity by the UK pensions industry, whose corporations fear exclusion from lucrative new markets.

The capacity to boost shame in contemporary societies is limited by the mild reactions of business and political elites, though ironically, this is balanced by the ease of reintegration that arises from that mildness. By contrast, in societies where public office is seen as an opportunity for extortion and embezzlement, and the public is cynical about their leadership, what extra shame is conveyed by public exposure compared with public prejudice? Thus, the domestic impact of scandals involving ex-Presidents Bokassa, Duvalier, Estrada, Marcos and Suharto; ex-Pakistan Prime Ministers Bhutto and Sharif; and ex-Italian Prime Ministers Berlusconi and Andreotti – to name but a few – may be modest unless accompanied by criminal sanctions and asset recovery.

'Shame' is a subjective emotional state of considerable complexity. There is a sense in which without social hypocrisy, the possibility of shaming is much reduced, so entrepreneurial, 'greed is good' societies have less possibility of shaming than Japan or than Catholic societies such as Italy. Moreover, over the long term, one may hypothesize diminishing marginal returns to shaming: as in the Italian *mani pulite* corruption investigations, if everyone is believed to be guilty, no-one can readily be shamed. Hence, the rise of former Prime Minister Berlusconi who was elected once again in the 2001 Italian elections in spite of previous convictions for corruption.[23] Although the heterogeneous construct 'society' is one audience that witnesses punishment, the range of offenders and the social milieux of offenders constitute other audiences which may take a different view of sanction severity. To know this, one must know what *they* value and about whom, if anyone, *they* care. Directors of troubled rail services in the UK probably would prefer not to be termed 'fat cats' and to be more respected than they are, but the extent to which those condemnations have changed their behaviour rather than their styles of presentation of self remains unknown.

Stage 3: The offenders' behaviour must change in response

The problem is that the Braithwaite formula – which borrows from Fisse and Braithwaite (1983) on the impact of publicity – takes it for granted that the aim of the corporation is to continue trading. But many people who commit frauds against individuals (with or without the use of a company as a tool for fraud) or *against* corporations and government have no intention of continuing in the same firm or job. To understand fully the possibilities of reintegrative shaming (or any other mode of sanctioning) one needs a more complex typology of the relevant victim–offender relationships and of the situational elements of fraud.

Given that fraudsters can change their identities without undue difficulty, and can use 'front persons' to act for them in business, our knowledge of the social and economic consequences of shaming is limited. The media review the reappearance of collapsed stars and arguably, the fact that they are required to use 'front people' is evidence of impact: but it is *not* evidence of behavioural change in their commercial behaviour, only of their efforts at avoidance of exposure. And bad publicity may lead to loss of credibility in the true identity anyway. On the other hand, although disqualifying someone from being a company director – a common sanction independent of prosecution in the UK, but unknown in the USA – is not a conscious exercise in shaming but in incapacitation, an unknown number of those disqualified probably change their identities and trade satisfactorily or else stop trading when they become insolvent.[24] Such discipline *may* be the effect of shaming, but there is no evidence of the effects of being confronted with their recklessly bad behaviour. As for professional fraudsters who may be shamed or just stigmatized, few criminal careers studies have been conducted and none have examined the particular effect of shame on future business activities (Weisburd and Waring, 2001).

Stage 4: Reintegration into society

How can we tell whether or not the commercial leopard has changed his spots? When should people be given another chance, and should their chance – for example, the chance to be a director of a pensions company or a bank – be unrestricted once they have been shamed and have (apparently) accepted that they have done wrong? What counts as sufficient evidence of reformation? This is a special case of the general dangerousness debate. We might base our decision partly on the level of harm that might arise if our generosity turned out to be misplaced. If, for example, banks wish to lend large sums of money to someone such as the late Robert Maxwell – very publicly condemned in a Department of Trade and Industry report of 1970 as someone 'unfit to be a director of a public company' and who took £400 million from company pension funds before his death at sea on his huge yacht in 1991 – or to some of the US Savings & Loans fraudsters, then that may be regarded as a matter for them and for their shareholders. Some people in the sports entertainment business have been reintegrated after shaming and after disqualification as company directors or conviction, but this – especially boxing – is an arena in which people's pasts can glamorize rather than stigmatize.[25] But to allow such a person control over *company* pensions when he would almost certainly not have been licensed by regulators to deal in financial services is a trusting approach to reintegration that might generate reasonable controversy. Reintegration into society is one thing: reintegration into the trusted elite economy is another. But how does one show that one is trustworthy once the trust has gone?

Having sketched out these considerations, let us turn now to the issue of globalization. Economic crime does offer more realistic prospects of globalized crime opportunities than do most other 'garden-variety' crimes, but given that the victims may be in countries other than those in which the frauds or the money-laundering or the corporate crimes occur, we know little of how locals react to what are in effect 'crimes against strangers'. If the criminal behaviour generates local jobs and stimulates the local economy, this is a difficult context in which to generate shame. Furthermore, both the crimes and the victims may have been located elsewhere, and fraudsters have the option of living in other countries, where they can forge a new identity for themselves. This was not a situation readily envisaged in the original Braithwaite formulation. Much of the policy focus of international corporate crime regulation has been upon incapacitation rather than reintegrative shaming. But anyone who doubts what business sentiment about appropriate conduct *can* do should examine the cancellation of well-paid speech invitations to President Clinton by Swiss and other international banks following the scandal surrounding his pardon of sanctions-busting, tax exile Marc Rich. Clinton has no obvious opportunity to atone, since he is no longer President and thus cannot deny or grant pardons any more. But it is unlikely that a confession – true or false – that he knew Rich's very friendly ex-wife was going to donate a large sum to his Presidential library would lead to his being reinvited to the banks.

Another area where shaming tactics may be questioned has been in relation to the (at best reckless) 'mis-selling' of unsuitable private pension schemes by UK insurers to thousands of savers. The Prudential was reprimanded by the lead regulator 'for failure to exercise the due skill, care and diligence required by us in its pensions review', for the firm had over one-third of the uncompensated serious cases. A spokesperson for 'the Pru' showed his low estimation of commercial and reputational risk when commenting: 'It is not our share of the problem. It is our share of a statistic' (*Daily Telegraph,* 22 October 1997). However, by the end of the year, this complacency had changed, as the political and economic pressure was stepped up. The strong condemnation of the firm by the newly formed Financial Services Authority for its 'deep-seated and long-standing failure of management [and] failure to address and remedy defects previously identified' was the lead item in the business sections of all the broadsheets and in the influential (for middle-class/lower middle-class investors who might well purchase 'Pru' products) tabloid papers such as the *Daily Mail* – 'Regulator runs out of patience with the Pru' and *The Express* – 'Watchdog mauls men from Pru' (all 17 December 1997). The Prudential's Chief Executive subsequently took personal charge of the reforms, signifying its altered salience within the corporate culture. But until this public humiliation, he felt able to continue with his 'trust me personally' television adverts to save with the Prudential, despite about 60,000 urgent cases not being dealt with and criticisms in Parliament. The corporate response (from this and several other insurers) was that from 2001, direct salespeople no longer visited people at home but were replaced by telemarketers in call centres: conversations are recorded and more easily monitored, creating greater discipline. So it looks as if shaming was effective. However, my interviews with policy staff suggest that the principal reason for corporate policy changes was not so much the bad publicity and fines but the fear of exclusion from lucrative new government-inspired markets.

The important of honorific titles awarded by the British monarch (on the advice of the government) may act to create discipline among some business people who know that usually, a bad commercial reputation will stop their title from being awarded. But the reactions of the public towards, say, selling officially condemned meat to consumers are also important, and these populist factors may determine the allocation of police resources and thus the amount of publicity for the 'offender'. Fear of stigma and fear of economic loss are intertwined in such a case. But there is no evidence that many people will refuse to book their cruises with Royal Caribbean because that company was heavily fined in the US for repeated dumping of untreated waste at sea. If more people did reject the cruise line, this might create greater shareholder pressure on management to comply

Concluding remarks

Shaming arguably is a process which relies for its effectiveness upon people being 'centred' and embedded deeply in a network of social relations. There may be scope for inducing conscience by making offenders more aware of the effects that their behaviour has on others: but the individuals most susceptible to shame may be those with limited social and geographical mobility. Thus the salaried managerial classes may be easier to shame than are the super-rich or professional confidence tricksters. But salaried professionals form the traditional white-collar group whose numbers and power are on the wane in financial services compared with high-bonus dealers and salespeople. For firms that wish to continue doing business – as contrasted with (1) intentional 'scams' and (2) businesses that are defrauding or cutting corners on regulatory compliance in order to stay afloat – the threat of stopping firms from doing new business is likely to be more effective than shaming as a technique of control. These comments do not mean that Braithwaite's *normative* model is wrong or that shaming policies are not worth pursuing. They rather emphasize the difficulties of getting to what communitarians and others might regard as the socially interdependent ideal within a relatively pathogenic and individuated, mobile global culture in which, very largely, *pecunia non olet*: money has no smell.

Notes

1 However – unacknowledged by the authors – this dilemma applies to only a modest proportion of those sentenced for fraud/crimes of the middle classes, in the American Federal and in other courts, most of whom are blue-collar and/or professional criminals rather than criminal professionals. See Weisburd *et al.* (1991); Levi and Pithouse (forthcoming).

2 Allegations of impropriety can lead to incapacitation even where there are no prosecutions. Thus, Mohammed al Fayed could not be prevented from buying Harrods store, but criticism of his conduct and

character in a government report on the purchase of Harrods was sufficient to stop him becoming a Director of Harrods *Bank*. Nick Leeson, who brought down Barings Bank, was prohibited from selling financial services in the UK because he failed to declare a bad debt judgement against him of less than £1,000.

3 My interviews (unpublished) indicate that Japan and Switzerland remain more culturally homogeneous and interdependent than the English-speaking centres, but anywhere, it is harder to trade successfully if one is viewed as crooked. Clarke (1986, 1999) writes about the decline in self-regulation, though the empirical evidence for integrity before liberalization is weaker than he suggests. An excellent retrospection may be found in Augar (2000).

4 My interviews with tax and social security investigators and lawyers make it clear that publicity is an important part of the motivation, since it brings in extra declared income from others (in the case of the Revenue) or, more speculatively in the case of social security, is believed to lead to a reduction in claims.

5 Clearly, this is relevant only to those in a position to defraud. This includes most professionals as well as many people in clerical jobs in financial institutions or salaries departments, so potential offenders constitute an extensive set of people, depending on which sorts of fraud one is reviewing.

6 The explanation of individual variations in techniques of neutralization (Sykes and Matza, 1957) is beyond the scope of this article and this author's knowledge.

7 In essence, this was a case in which personal and business friends of the Guinness Chief Executive were offered large guaranteed profits in order to enable Guinness to succeed in its share bid to take over Distillers. Four people were convicted in 1990. The Court of Appeal concluded in 2001 that the Human Rights Act 1998 did not apply retrospectively. The European Court of Human Rights ruled that requiring suspects to answer regulators' questions and using those answers in a subsequent criminal trial, though allowed by the laws of England, constituted a violation of their human rights.

8 Though the length or brevity of that sentence almost certainly reflected the judge's belief that Aitken would suffer severe social as well as economic damage from conviction: shame here would be used to limit retribution, though there was little evidence from Aitken's behaviour that he had felt any need to atone for lying to his Cabinet colleagues, to the public and to the court about his whereabouts when in fact accepting hospitality from an Arab middleman in the Paris Ritz (Aitken, 2000).

9 In addition to the well-known work on the Ford Pinto (Cullen *et al*., 1987) – though it is seldom stressed that whatever their seriousness rankings for the conduct in the abstract, the jury acquitted the executives – the much higher than average accidents caused by Bridgestone tyres on Ford Explorer cars would be worthy of examination, receiving enormous media publicity in the USA and causing huge job losses for Bridgestone and the resignation of its Japanese Chairman.

10 In 1997, after the scandal in which all major securities firms in Japan were exposed as having made illegal payments to a corporate racketeer, 60 top executives resigned from their roles to enable the new management to have a fresh start.

11 Though one might find difficulty in working out what would count as evidence in terms of practical access. Here, the victimization measurement issue is important.

12 To the extent that offences were committed 'for the company' or 'for the Party', future offending opportunities would have been low anyway if they were dismissed.

13 These Japanese cases are good illustrations, as were the UK Guinness prosecutions of 1988–92, of executives and civil servants being caught out by changes in the political and legal environment that criminalize de facto behaviour which allegedly was fairly commonplace.

14 This sociopathy appears to have been amply confirmed if there is substance in civil and criminal allegations against subsequent Prime Ministers – Benazir Bhutto and Nawaz Sharif – who have both been accused of plundering national assets and taking bribes for awarding contracts. Bhutto has been convicted (with her husband) of corruption and at the time of writing has not returned to Pakistan.

15 An excellent example is the way that the current Treasurer of the Conservative Party, tax exile Michael Ashcroft, found himself in the middle of a sleaze campaign in July 1999, including leaked Foreign Office and US Drug Enforcement Administration memos. If he had been accused explicitly of fraud or money-laundering or tax evasion, his libel lawyers would have been rubbing their hands with glee. His action for libel against *The Times* was settled before trial.

16 Measures against laundering have changed dramatically around the world in response to scandal and political pressure, culminating in the Wolfsberg Agreement in 2000 between the world's top banks to develop a higher *global* standard for themselves than that required by law.

17 Due to lack of media interest (allegedly), this has now been dropped, but multiple prosecutions and fines are still listed.

18 The effectiveness of Nick Leeson's claim of being scapegoated led to almost as much shaming of his social superiors at Barings as he may have experienced himself. Indeed, he became a sympathetic figure in the film *Rogue Trader*, based on his autobiography, and was generally feted on his release from Singaporean prison in 1999, earning a lucrative career as a business speaker, though many of the fees went back to the bank's creditors.

19 Though in a non-fraud context, the dangers of adopting too permissive a line on past behaviour may be seen in the humiliation of the Conservative Party following revelations in November 1999 that their candidate for Mayor of London, Lord Jeffrey Archer, had generated a false alibi for a libel action some 13 years previously. In 2001 he was jailed for four years after being found guilty of perjury and perverting the course of justice.

20 My media analysis offers no consistent pattern, but 'normal' media publicity tends to get stronger when the media are criticizing the lightness of sentences, thus creating or reinforcing the sort of disparity between actual and perceived sentencing practices noted by Hough and Roberts (1999). There are no clear comparators in the white-collar crime arena, but unpublished survey work done by me suggests that expectations of sentences are lower than those believed by senior management to be *deserved*, though this does not tell us whether these expectations are actually higher or lower than those imposed. Media campaigns may be either tougher or more lenient in white-collar cases, but sentences at either extreme do tend to generate publicity, even though small fines for companies in non-controversial cases are unlikely to be newsworthy. For a good general analysis of what are termed 'event studies' see Rao and Hamilton (1996) and Frooman (1997).

21 A good example is the fall in Microsoft's share prices subsequent to the US court's ruling in November 1999 that it had behaved oppressively and was guilty of anti-trust behaviour. It seems plausible that this was affected more by expected commercial impact than by moral judgements. Indeed, to the extent that previous high share prices benefited from the oppressive behaviour, it represents a simple market adjustment based on what one might opprobriously call 'the capacity to plunder'.

22 Though there are likely to be personality and cognitive dimensions in reaction to failing business conditions here.

23 Silvio Berlusconi stated to a journalist: 'Today I'm the number one man in the country … There is nobody in Italy whom the public trusts more … Most people know that if the richest man in Italy wants to govern the country, it is not because he wants to get wealthier but because he wants the complete confidence, the affection … of the people' (*Financial Times*, 16 October 2000).

24 On the assumption that if they go badly 'bust' again, their original identities will be discovered. This is not necessarily the case. According to Experian credit information services, in 1999, 212,028 directors (6.66 per cent total director pop.) are 'serial failures' (two or more previous failures); 0.085 per cent of all current directors – eight in 10,000 – had more than 10 failures each. (See, further, Levi and Pithouse, forthcoming.)

25 Illustrations include Roger Levitt, convicted of misleading the regulators. Promoter Keith Warren was not prosecuted for fraud but was disqualified as a director, but this is not viewed seriously by his peers. It is not clear how convicted UK fraudsters such as Levitt and former Guinness Chairman/Chief Executive Saunders were able to enter the United States and to work legitimately, given their criminal convictions, especially in Saunders' case as someone having served a term of imprisonment recently. However, companies often get general executive clearance.

References

Aitken, J. (2000) *Pride and Perjury*, London, HarperCollins.

Augar, P. (2000) *The Death of Gentlemanly Capitalism*, London, Penguin.

Blankenburg, E. (2000) 'Multinational firms as agents of civic virtues', in Karstedt, S and Bussman, Kai-D. (eds) *Social Dynamics of Crime and its Control*, Oxford, Hart Publishing, pp.133–42.

Braithwaite, J. (1989) *Crime, Shame, and Reintegration*, Cambridge, Cambridge University Press.

Clarke, M. (1986) *Regulating the City*, Milton Keynes, Open University Press.

Clarke, M. (1999) *Regulation: Social Control of Business between Law and Politics*, London, Macmillan.

Croall, H. (2001) *Understanding White-Collar Crime*, Buckingham, Open University Press.

Cullen, F., Maakestad, W. and Cavender, G. (1987) *Corporate Crime Under Attack*, Cincinnati, OH, Anderson Publishing.

Elias, N. (1982) *State, Formation and Civilization: The Civilizing Process*, Oxford, Blackwell.

Engel, M. (1996) *Tickling the Public: 100 Years of Popular Press*, London, Gollancz.

Fisse, B. and Braithwaite, J. (1983) *The Impact of Publicity on Corporate Offenders*, Albany, NY, State University of New York Press.

Fisse, B. and Braithwaite, J. (1993) *Corporations, Crime, and Accountability*, Cambridge, Cambridge University Press.

Friedrichs, D. (1996) *Trusted Criminals*, Belmont, CA, Wadsworth.

Frooman, J. (1997) 'Socially irresponsible and illegal behavior and shareholder wealth: A meta-analysis of event studies', *Business and Society*, vol.36, p.221.

Hough, M. and Roberts, J. (1999) 'Sentencing trends in Britain: Public knowledge and public opinion', *Punishment and Society*, vol.1, no.1, pp.11–26.

Karpoff, J. and Lott, J. (1993) 'The reputational penalty firms bear from committing criminal fraud', *Journal of Law and Economics*, vol.36, pp.757–802.

Levi, M. (1993) *The Investigation Prosecution and Trial of Serious Fraud*, Royal Commission on Criminal Justice Research Study No.14, London, HMSO.

Levi, M. and Pithouse, A. (forthcoming) *White-Collar Crime and its Victims*, Oxford, Clarendon Press.

Levi, M. and Sherwin, D. (1995) *Fraud: The Unmanaged Risk*, London, Ernst & Young.

Levi, M. and Suddle, M. S. (1989) 'White-collar crime, shamelessness, and disintegration: The control of tax evasion in Pakistan', *Journal of Law and Society*, vol.16, no.4, pp.489–505.

Nelken, D. (1997) 'White-collar crime', in M. Maguire, R. Morgan and R. Reiner (eds) *Oxford Handbook of Criminology*, Oxford, Oxford University Press, pp.891–924.

Nelken, D. and Levi, M. (1996) 'The corruption of politics and the politics of corruption: An overview', *Journal of Law and Society*, vol.23, no.1, pp.1–17.

Passas, N. (1999) 'Globalization, criminogenic asymmetries and economic crime', *European Journal of Law Reform*, vol.1, no.4, pp.399–423.

Rao, S. and Hamilton III, J.B. (1996) 'The effect of published reports of unethical conduct on stock prices', *Journal of Business Ethics*, vol.15, pp.13–21.

Slapper, G., Tombs, S. and Mansfield, M. (1999) *Corporate Crime*, London, Longman.

Sykes, G. and Matza, D. (1957) 'Techniques of neutralization: A theory of delinquency', *American Sociological Review*, vol.22, pp.664–70.

Transparency International (2001) *Global Corruption Report 2001*, Berlin, TI.

Von Hirsch, A. and Wasik, M. (1997) 'Civil sanctions attending disqualifications: A suggested conceptual framework', *Cambridge Law Journal*, vol.56, no.3, pp.599–626.

Weisburd, D., Waring, E. and Chayer, E. (1995) 'Specific deterrence in a sample of offenders convicted of white-collar crimes', *Criminology*, vol.33, no.4, pp.587–607.

Weisburd, D., Wheeler, S., Waring, E. and Bode, N. (1991) *Crimes of the Middle Classes: White-Collar Offenders in the Federal Courts*, New Haven, CT, Yale University Press.

Weisburd, D. and Waring, E. (2001) *White Collar Crime and Criminal Careers*, Cambridge, Cambridge University Press.

Wheeler, S., Mann, K. and Sarat, A. (1988) *Sitting in Judgement: The Sentencing of White-Collar Criminals*, New Haven, CT, Yale University Press.

Part Three

Contesting Restorative Justice

CHAPTER 13

Restorative Justice and Social Justice

by John Braithwaite

Restorative values

Restorative justice is now a global social movement advocating transformation of the criminal justice system. There is no criminal justice system that it has yet actually transformed, but there are few it has not touched. Few have played a more important role in the new social movement for a restorative justice system than the Canadian criminal justice system.[1]

Part of this movement stems from a greater openness in Canada to learning from the wisdom of Indigenous people about justice, a greater openness than we see in my own country or in the United States, for example. In particular, Canadian senior judges listen more to the wisdom of First Nations Peoples than judges in other countries, and show more judicial leadership toward restorative justice alternatives. In his 1997 Culliton Lecture, Chief Justice Bayda suggested changes in law school curricula to include 'extensive classes in restorative justice and in sentencing.'[2] Justice Bayda found it 'a rather exciting thought' that there might be '[t]housands of law students across the country thinking and talking about innovative ways to involve the community in the healing of the breaches in relationships caused by an offender's offense'.[3]

Healing relationships, as opposed to balancing hurt with hurt, is one core value of restorative justice.[4] So is community deliberation: putting the problem in the centre of the circle rather than putting the criminal at the centre of the criminal justice system.[5] Whatever a retributive system deems as the right punishment for the criminal will usually be the wrong solution to the problem. Non-domination also merits consideration as a core value of restorative justice – ensuring that all voices in the circle are heard and that none are silenced by domination.

What Philip Pettit refers to as the republican value of freedom as non-domination leads to the key process requirement of restorative justice.[6] For justice to be restorative, it must involve a process where all key stakeholders have an opportunity to be heard with respect to their views of the consequences of a crime and what is to be done to restore victims, offenders, and communities in the aftermath of the crime.

If freedom as non-domination is a value of restorative justice, it leads to the existence of a strong connection between restorative justice and social justice. This connection is the topic of my lecture.

Three hypotheses about the relationship between restorative justice and social justice

There are reasons for taking seriously three competing hypotheses:

A Restorative justice is unimportant to struggles for social justice.

B Restorative justice risks the worsening of social injustice.

C Restorative justice can be an important strategy for advancing social justice.

We consider these hypotheses in turn.

A Restorative justice is unimportant to struggles for social justice

This is what I used to think. Social justice requires restructuring the economy, confronting unemployment, land rights for Indigenous peoples, equal employment opportunities for women and other categories of people subject

Source: *Saskatchewan Law Review*, vol.63, no.1, pp.185–94.

to discrimination, more effective regulation of corporate power, a different kind of tax system, greater equity at the International Monetary Fund and the World Trade Organization, and a fairer education system. Any kind of reform to the criminal justice system does not seem central to achieving any of these social objectives.

B Restorative justice risks the worsening of social justice

Some critics accuse restorative justice, at least in some of its manifestations, as being 'orientalism'.[7] According to Harry Blagg: 'Justice systems have a tendency to generate and reflect mono-culturalist narratives. ... Orientalist discourses are, primarily, powerful acts of representation that permit Western/European cultures to contain, homogenize and consume 'other' cultures'.[8] In the New Zealand Maori context, for example, to interpret the 1989 reforms to juvenile justice in New Zealand as a shift to 'restorative justice' is to frame a local struggle over decolonization and justice of much wider significance into the narrowing discourse of a global, Western-led social movement. The deeper significance of the legal struggles between Maori and Pakeha cultures is whether Maori people are able to do their own justice in ways that connect to their meaning systems, not whether they are enabled to do 'restorative justice'.

On the other hand, the meaning of restorative justice might be culturally plural – creating spaces where Indigenous peoples (and other minority cultures) can do their own justice in ways that make sense to them. This would be a shift from the univocal 'consistent' justice of extant Western systems. Sounds simple. But, of course, this is a complex and difficult prescription in contexts where there is an offender from one culture and a victim from another.

Even when restorative justice is read in a way that maximizes cultural plurality, tensions remain between restorative justice and social justice for Indigenous people. Imagine, for example, that research on restorative justice processes reveals the procedures that best ensure that non-Western cultures – be they Vietnamese, African, or Cree – are given space to transact justice in ways that have the most meaning to them. In response, we require restorative justice facilitators to undertake training courses in how to assure this plurality. But do we then forbid Indigenous elders, who have not been so certified as trained restorative justice facilitators, from presiding over Indigenous justice processes? I think we should not. To do so would be to privilege our restorative justice aspirations over more important social justice aspirations of Indigenous peoples seeking empowerment (Blagg's caution). To some degree, however, these tensions are unavoidable. Most readers who would agree with this position would not want to persist with it in the context of the rape of an Asian or African woman by a First Nations man, or even perhaps the rape of a First Nations woman by a man from another culture who does not wish to submit to the justice of the elders. Once colonialism, slavery, and immigration has ruptured the lives of Indigenous peoples, all forms of justice, including the most plural forms of restorative justice, serve as a threat to social justice for First Nations.

There is no inevitability in the proposition that disempowering state courts in favour of empowering the people will advance social justice. Peoples' Courts and Bang Jiao programs in China have quite often empowered officials of a totalitarian political party rather than the people. Even when the people have been empowered, we have seen tyrannies of the majority oppress homosexual minorities in Cuban Peoples' Courts. Indeed, there have been cases where Indigenous elders empowered by restorative justice programs have used that power as males to protect male friends who have abused Indigenous women. In the far north of Australia, I once confronted the dilemma of Aboriginal elders who wanted to deploy restorative justice conferences in order to compel young girls to marry the men the elders told them to marry. Their prescription was not without the good intent of restoring civility to communities where traditional responsibilities to control young men rested not with their parents but with the father of the girl promised to marry them.

In Rwanda, genocide appeared as an upshot of unaccountable power over on-the-spot justice being returned to leaders of a disenfranchised group suffering a terrible colonial legacy.

While there can be no social justice without empowerment for peoples who have suffered dreadful colonial histories, that empowerment can itself worsen social injustices for others. Hence, both restorative justice that crushes Indigenous empowerment (as in Bragg's analysis) and Indigenous empowerment that crushes social justice are complex post-colonial possibilities.

The most forceful critique of restorative justice has been a feminist one. Whatever the limitations of adversarial legalism, a battered woman with a lawyer standing beside her against a batterer and his lawyer is a more equal contest than one-on-one mediation between victim and offender. The question is whether a meeting of two communities of care where both victim and offender are surrounded by supporters involves more or less an imbalance of power. A feminist perspective asserts that one of the accomplishments of the women's movement since the 1970s was to have violence against women and children treated as a crime.[9] The worry about restorative justice is that by not taking such crimes to court, restorative justice might fail to treat these crimes seriously.[10] Worse, restorative justice might return family violence to being a private matter rather than a social problem whose dimensions are profoundly public.

Restorative justice advocates reply that court processing of family violence cases actually tends to foster a culture of denial, while restorative justice fosters a culture of apology. Apology, when communicated with ritual seriousness, is actually the most powerful cultural device for taking a problem seriously, while denial is a cultural device for dismissing it. Gale Burford and Joan Pennell's sophisticated research on family group conferences for domestic violence in Newfoundland is persuasive that family violence was reduced by their interventions.[11] This is the best piece of research done on the topic and it is of significance that one of its authors, Joan Pennell, came out of a background of distinguished contributions to the women's shelter movement in Canada.

Another Canadian contribution that changed the international debate was Hollow Water. Healing circles in this Manitoba First Nation community began to deal with what many first considered an epidemic of alcohol abuse.[12] As citizens sat in these circles discussing the problems of individual cases, they realized that there was a deeper underlying problem: they lived in a community that was sweeping the sexual abuse of children under the carpet. By setting up a complex set of healing circles to help one individual victim and offender after another, it was eventually discovered that a majority of Hollow Water citizens were at some time in their lives victims of sexual abuse. Forty-eight adults out of a community of six hundred formally admitted to criminal responsibility for sexually abusing children, forty-six as a result of participating in healing circles, and only two as a result of being referred to a court of law for failing to do so.[13] Because there have only been two known cases of reoffending,[14] Rupert Ross claims that the healing circles have been a success. Tragically, however, there has been no genuinely systematic outcome evaluation of Hollow Water.

What is more important than the crime prevention outcome of Hollow Water is its crime detection outcome. When and where has the traditional criminal process succeeded in uncovering anything approaching forty-eight admissions of criminal responsibility for sexual abuse of children in a community of just six hundred? Before reading about Hollow Water, I had always said that the traditional criminal trial process is superior to restorative justice processes for getting to the truth of what happened. Restorative justice processes were only likely to be superior to traditional Western criminal process when there was a clear admission of guilt. The significance of Hollow Water is that it throws that position into doubt.

What we have learned from Pennell and Burford, and from Hollow Water, is that the initial feminist assumption, that restorative justice would be a threat to social justice for women, may sometimes be in error – not always in error, but sometimes in error. This innovative Canadian work shows that restorative justice has potential as a tool for advancing social justice for women and children who suffer at the hands of violent men. Let us now turn to explore this potential more systematically.

C Restorative justice can be an important strategy for advancing social justice

We have already said that restorative justice can and should empower all communities of care for victims and offenders – Indigenous and non-Indigenous. It is possible to design restorative justice so as to not shift power over Indigenous people from the hands of white judges to the hands of the police who are not accountable to judges. It is possible for dialogue to occur between Indigenous elders and experts who have had experience with cross-cultural restorative justice, each learning lessons from the other. I have seen a conference where a trained state restorative justice coordinator handed the facilitation of the conference over to an Indigenous elder, taking a back seat to the process, intervening only when voices were unjustly silenced by the elder. Even when voices are unjustly silenced by an elder (a circumstance I have not seen), the state coordinator can still intervene in a respectful and deferential way: 'Uncle Frank, some of the members of the group sound like they want to hear what Mary has to say and I would like to hear her story myself.'

Our experience of restorative justice programs in Australia is that they have been quite successful in empowering women's voices in the justice process. Kathy Daly reports that this has been the experience so far in her extensive observations, from a feminist theoretical frame, of conferences in South Australia.[15] Mothers are often the most eloquent communicators at restorative justice conferences. Sometimes they even speak of the violence they suffer at the hands of their sons, a matter on which they never want to testify in court. The empowerment of young people has been accomplished less often: the young are often silenced by 'a room full of adults'.[16]

In Australia, we have been disappointed by the proportion of juvenile conferences where the offender is an Aboriginal young person – only 11 per cent of the young offenders in the Canberra program, which is scarcely better than the percentage of court cases that are Aboriginal (10 per cent).[17] To date, we have failed to use restorative justice to reduce Aboriginal imprisonment rates in Australia. This has been the biggest disappointment for me in the way restorative justice has developed in Australia.

In Canada, I think you have done better. Programs like the John Howard initiative in Manitoba show the way. In that program, First Nations offenders are a priority and the program is targeted at the deep end – cases where the prosecutor is already recommending at least six months of prison time. This is the kind of program that, if big enough, could put a dent in imprisonment rates for Indigenous people.

The best restorative justice conferences help young offenders who have dropped out of, or have been excluded from, school, to return to their education. They also help unemployed offenders find jobs. But these accomplishments are rare. Even if they became common, it is hard to imagine that restorative justice could make a major positive contribution to reducing the injustice of joblessness.

It may be important to think of restorative justice in terms of avoiding harm rather than in terms of doing good. The evidence is persuasive that a criminal record is a significant cause of unemployment.[18] It is even more evident that the criminal justice system is a major part of the social injustice that Black peoples suffer in nations such as Australia and the United States. In the United States, the prison system is the most important labour market program for young Black men. For example, there are more young Black men in the prison system than in the higher education system. In Australia, the prison system is a major cause of suicide in the Aboriginal community. It is also a major cause of rape and drug addiction, both of which disproportionately afflict the poor. The spread of AIDS is another concern. We also have an epidemic of Hepatitis C in Australian prisons.[19] In Russia, up to 50 per cent of the prison population are infected with tuberculosis bacillus – a legacy of overcrowding.[20]

A pathbreaking report produced this year by Anne Stringer shows that imprisonment is also a major cause and effect of debt among poor people irrespective of their race.[21] Among one hundred and twenty-one Queensland prisoners, 80 per cent had some debt when they went into prison. Drug use, rather than investment in housing, was the most prevalent cause of that debt. Forty-nine per cent said that they had committed a crime to repay a debt. Imprisonment cut them off from a variety of means of sorting out these debts, leaving their families vulnerable to repossession and other assaults on their circumstances. Inequalities grounded in the indebtedness of poor families to finance companies are greatly worsened by imprisonment.

The most important way restorative justice may be able to reduce social injustice involves reducing the impact of imprisonment as a cause of the unequal burdens of unemployment, debt with extortionate interest burdens, suicide, rape, AIDS, Hepatitis C, and potentially most important, the epidemic of multiple-drug-resistant tuberculosis. Although presently worst in Asia and Eastern Europe, the threat of tuberculosis in Canada is real, thanks in part to overcrowded American prisons. There is not much evidence yet that restorative justice realizes this potential. Early results from the Re-Integrative Shaming Experiments (RISE) in Canberra are not consistent on this, but there is some encouragement:

> Juvenile Property (Security) offenders who were treated in court significantly more often reported that they had experienced financial pressures in the preceding year and that they had had 'serious troubles or problems with people who were close to you'. Youth Violence offenders who had been to court significantly more often said that they had changed jobs during the preceding year, while Drunk Driving offenders who had been to court significantly more often had dropped out of full time study or been fired or laid off from a job in that period.[22]

In other words, offenders randomly assigned to a restorative justice conference rather than a court case as a result of their crime were, in some respects, less likely to suffer adverse life events such as being fired in the two years after their apprehension.

Finally, I have argued that the empirical experience of corporate restorative justice in the finance, nuclear, coal mining, and nursing home industries suggests that it offers an approach to attacking the criminal abuses of corporate power that can be so important to understanding the advantaging of the rich over the poor.[23] In some cases, such as the major frauds against Aboriginal consumers by Australian insurance companies in the early 1990s, the restorative process can engage even prime ministers with the need for structural change in the regulation of an industry. My colleagues and I in the Australian National University Centre for Tax System Integrity are hoping to develop restorative strategies for tax compliance that might turn around some of the stupendous advantaging of the rich over the poor in this arena.

Conclusion

I have rejected our first hypothesis that 'restorative justice is unimportant to struggles for social justice'. Restorative justice involves both serious risk of worsening social injustice and real potential to reduce it. So far neither possibility has been realized in any major way because restorative justice has made marginal inroads into the criminal justice system. Which possibility will be realized depends considerably on the centrality of non-domination as a restorative justice value: specifically, whether non-domination prevails to ensure the maximum plurality of contesting voices are heard concerning both process and outcome.

Restorative justice has the potential to lift some of the silencing of the voices of dominated groups such as First Nations people, women, and children suffering abuse. If it succeeds in this, the Canadian work of Pennell and Burford, and Hollow Water, is a basis for optimism that restorative justice can reduce violence and sexual abuse against women and children. Further, our Australian work suggests that there is potential for reducing criminal abuse of corporate power. But we must be careful that it does not subvert some of the protections that courts occasionally afford to such victims of injustice. This is a policy design challenge we can rise to.

Restorative justice has the potential to reduce the prevalence of school expulsion, unemployment, imprisonment, and the effects of imprisonment – suicide, drug addiction, disease, and physical abuse – among the poor.

Criminal offenders and victims who are caught up in the criminal justice system have a lot in common. For example, they are more likely to be poor than non-victims and non-offenders.[24] A restorative justice strategy that succeeds in empowering both victims and offenders therefore empowers those, on both sides, who are disproportionately powerless. If both victims and offenders get some restoration out of a restorative justice process, that has progressive rather than regressive implications for social justice. Conversely, a retributive justice system that responds to the hurt of one side by inflicting hurt on the other side is regressive in its distributive impact. It adds to the hurt in the world in a way in which those burdens of hurt fall more heavily on the poor. This is more pointedly true when a vicious spiral is triggered by retributive values – where criminals want to hurt victims again and victims want to hurt criminals back[25] – as hurt endlessly begets more hurt. Whereas the poor are the greatest losers from our present propensity to institutionalize hurt begetting hurt, it could be that the poor will be the greatest beneficiaries of a world where help begets help and grace begets grace.[26]

Notes

1 See Canada, Law Commission of Canada, 'From restorative justice to transformative justice' (discussion paper), online: http://www.lcc.gc.ca/en/forum/rj/paper.html (last modified: 1 October 1999); K. Roach, *Due Process and Victims' Rights: the New Law and Politics of Criminal Justice* (Toronto, University of Toronto Press, 1999).

2 Bayda, E.D. (1996) 'The theory and practice of sentencing: are they on the same wavelength?', *Sask. L. Rev.*, no.60, p.317 at 331.

3 *Ibid.*

4 See Zehr, H. (1990) *Changing Lenses: A New Focus for Crime and Justice* (Waterloo, Herald Press).

5 Melton, A.P. (1995) 'Indigenous justice systems and tribal society', *Judicature*, no.79, p.126.

6 Braithwaite, J. (1997) *Republicanism: A Theory of Freedom and Government* (Oxford, Oxford University Press); Braithwaite, J. and Pettit, P. (1990) *Not Just Deserts: A Republican Theory of Criminal Justice* (Oxford, Oxford University Press).

7 Said, E.W. (1995) *Orientalism: Western Conceptions of the Orient* (London, Penguin).

8 Blagg, H. (1997) 'A just measure of shame? Aboriginal youth and conferencing in Australia', no.37, *Brit.J.Criminology*, p.481 at 482–3.

9 See for example Dobash, R.E. and Dobash, R.P. (1979) *Violence Against Wives: A Case Against the Patriarchy* (New York, Free Press).

10 See Stubbs, J. (1995) '"Communitarian" conferencing and violence against women: a cautionary note', in Valverde, M., MacLeod, L. and Johnson, J. (eds), *Wife Assault and the Canadian Criminal Justice System* (Toronto, Centre of Criminology, University of Toronto), p.260.

11 Burford, G. and Pennell, J. (1996) 'Family group decision making: outcome report volume I' (St John's, Memorial University, 1998); J. Pennell and G. Burford, 'Attending to context: family group decision making in Canada', in J. Hudson *et al.* (eds), *Family Group Conferences: Perspectives on Policy and Practice* (Annandale, NSW, The Federation Press) p.206; J. Pennell and G. Burford, 'Family group decision making: outcome report Volume II' (St John's Memorial University, 1997).

12 Bushie, B. (1999) 'Community holistic circle healing: a community approach', in Wachtel, T. (ed.) *Building Strong Partnerships for Restorative Practices* (Burlington, VT, Vermont Department of Corrections), p.59.

13 Ross, R. (1996), *Returning to the Teachings: Exploring Aboriginal Justice* (London, Penguin Books) at 29–48. See also Aboriginal Peoples Collection, *Community Holistic Circle Healing: Hollow Water First Nation* by T. Lajeunesse (1993) (Ottawa, Supply and Services Canada).

14 Ross, *supra* note 13 at p.36.

15 'Diversionary conferences in Australia: a reply to the optimists and skeptics' (Paper presented at American Society of Criminology Annual Meeting, 20–23 November, 1996).

16 Haines, K. (1998) 'Some principled objections to a restorative justice approach to working with juvenile offenders', in L. Walgrave (ed.) *Restorative Justice for Juveniles: Potentialities, Risks and Problems for Research* (Leuven, Leuven University Press) 93 at 99.

17 This 10 per cent figure is from 1995 Children's Court appearances in Canberra. This is the most recent data Heather Strang has been able to extract. My appreciation to Heather Strang for providing this information.

18 Hagan, J. (1991) 'Destiny and drift: subcultural preferences, status attainments, and the risks and rewards of youth', 56, *Am. Soc. Rev.*, p.567.

19 Parliament of NSW, Standing Committee on Social Issues, 'Hepatitis C: the neglected epidemic' (1998). Survey estimates range from 33–60 per cent for males and 66–80 per cent for female prisoners with Hepatitis C in New South Wales prisons. *Ibid.* at 69–70.

20 Lee, K. (1999) 'Globalization, communicable disease and equity: a look back and forth' (International Roundtable on 'Responses to Globalization: Rethinking equity in health', Geneva, 12–14 July).

21 Stringer, A. (1999) *The Findings of the Prison and Debt Project* (Brisbane, Prisoners' Legal Service).

22 H. Strang *et al.* (1999) *Experiments in Restorative Policing: A Progress Report* (Canberra, Australian National University) at 95.

23 Braithwaite, J. (1999) 'Restorative justice: assessing optimistic and pessimistic accounts' in M. Tonry (ed.) *Crime and Justice: A Review of Research*, vol.25 (Chicago, The University of Chicago) p.1.

24 Hindelang, M.J., Gottfredson, M.R. and Garofalo, J. (1978) *Victims of Personal Crime: An Empirical Foundation for a Theory of Personal Victimization* (Cambridge, MA, Ballinger); J. Braithwaite and D. Biles (1984) 'Victims and offenders: The Australian experience', in R. Block (ed.) *Victimization and Fear of Crime: World Perspectives* (Washington, DC, US Department of Justice) p.3.

25 Heather Strang's data from Canberra finds victims randomly assigned to restorative justice conferences are significantly less likely to say they would harm their offender if they had the chance (6 per cent) than victims randomly assigned to court (21 per cent). See H. Strang, forthcoming PhD dissertation.

26 I think I am indebted to Howard Zehr for all this begetting talk from a lecture I heard him give in New Zealand. Or perhaps, I am indebted to the Bible. Or perhaps, we both are!

CHAPTER 14

Is Restorative Justice the Way Forward for Criminal Justice?

by Andrew Ashworth

What is restorative justice?

This is probably too large and unspecific a question to have a clear answer. Vessels of widely differing shapes, sizes, and modes of propulsion sail under this particular flag, not least because RJ (as it tends to be called) is to some extent a practice-led movement. One of the leading lights in the English RJ movement, Tony Marshall, offers this as a commonly accepted definition of RJ:

> Restorative Justice is a process whereby parties with a stake in a specific offence collectively resolve how to deal with the aftermath of the offence and its implications for the future.[1]

For this purpose, the stakeholders are assumed to be the victim, the offender, and the community. What is to be restored? That international trail-blazer in RJ theory and practice, John Braithwaite, gives the following answer: 'whatever dimensions of restoration matter to the victims, offenders and communities affected by crime'.[2] No less significant are the values promoted by RJ: Braithwaite lists 'healing, moral learning, community participation and community caring, respectful dialogue, forgiveness, responsibility, apology, and making amends'.[3] Lawyers and professionals should not be dominant in the dialogue: the voices of victim, offender and community representatives must be the loudest. Indeed, process is central to RJ, and in particular two elements in that process – that offenders should be expected to speak about their offences, and that victims are encouraged to speak about the offences too. The keynotes are empowerment, dialogue, negotiation, and agreement. The fairness of outcomes appears to be measured by the satisfaction of the stakeholders in each case, and not by comparison with the outcomes of like cases. If that is correct, there appears to be no objective standard of fairness or justice by which the outcomes of RJ processes are to be measured (such as the equal treatment of similarly situated offenders, which is associated with the principle of proportionality), but rather a deference to the subjective satisfaction of victims, their families, and the community.

As we shall see below, the principles of RJ are being used in a variety of initiatives, including mediation, sentencing circles, and conferences. Much as advocates of RJ emphasize the all-round fairness of its processes for dealing with the aftermath of offences, many of them also insist on the wider objectives of the RJ movement. Thus Marshall states that the primary objectives of RJ are:

- to attend fully to victims' needs – material, financial, emotional and social (including those personally close to the victim who may be similarly affected)
- to prevent re-offending by re-integrating offenders into the community
- to enable offenders to assume active responsibility for their actions
- to recreate a working community that supports the rehabilitation of offenders and victims and is active in preventing crime
- to provide a means of avoiding escalation of legal justice and the associated costs and delays.[4]

These are wide-ranging objectives which, even if we pass over the sweeping use of the term 'community', might be thought to establish some very high expectations.[5] At the very least,

Source: Current Legal Problems 2001, vol.54, pp.347–76.

objectives of this kind raise pertinent questions about the ambit of RJ approaches. Braithwaite promotes the widespread use of RJ for conflict resolution throughout social, regulatory, family, and criminal spheres, but he is frank in suggesting that a sort of conventional criminal justice system needs to be retained to deal with cases where either offender or victim refuse to take part in an RJ process, or where either of them exercises a veto on the outcome, or where the offender is a recalcitrant recidivist or the offence is very grave.[6] We return to these questions below.

What is not RJ

Although the history of criminal justice initiatives is strewn with failures, RJ sounds to be such a good thing in so many directions that it is not surprising that some people are keen to associate their initiatives with the 'restorative' cachet. We will have something to say about this below, when commenting on the present government's policies, but for the moment let us focus on what might loosely be called the 'victim movement'.

It is well known that in the final quarter of the last century there were developments in many legal systems which attempted to give greater protection to victims' rights. In England and Wales we saw (for example) the introduction of the compensation order as an order which courts must consider making in all cases of loss or damage, death, or injury; the expansion of Victim Support to offer practical help and support to the victims of crime; the efforts in 1976 and in 1999 to give greater protection to rape complainants from questions about their private life, and the Youth Justice and Criminal Evidence Act 1999, went further in trying to protect victims and other vulnerable witnesses; and the experiments in providing victim statements to prosecutors and courts. Positive and welcome as most of these initiatives are, they concern victims' rights and not RJ. They are attempts to remedy deficiencies in the existing (adversarial) system for the administration of criminal justice, rather than parts of a movement towards a different kind of conflict resolution.

We might also note another strand of policy, which is the tendency of politicians and others to claim that longer prison sentences serve the interests and wishes of victims. This should be set against the ample Home Office evidence that many members of the public are ill informed about existing sentencing levels, and that most victims are less interested in severe sentencing than in compensation and constructive sentences.[7] Politicians who 'play the victim card' in discussions about sentencing must be viewed with suspicion; certainly they and their concerns cannot be allied to RJ.

However, in one respect arguments about victims' rights and RJ flow together. Both lines of argument make the case for greater victim involvement in the sentencing process. In RJ it is axiomatic that the victim should have the right to attend a conference or circle and to participate in a dialogue with the offender – not simply to ensure that an apology and appropriate reparation is promised, but more broadly to gain an understanding of the crime and its motivation and to regain a feeling of security and respect. In what we might term conventional criminal justice systems, many countries have begun to allow the victim to make a victim impact statement to the court, or even to make a statement to the court about sentencing. Without going into detail, it is clear that both sets of initiatives start from the premise that the victim has a right to be involved in the process whereby her or his offender is sentenced. We will refer to (indeed, criticize) this argument below; it is important at this stage to recognize that the argument is not exclusive to RJ, and is shared by the wider victim movement.

What are the forms of RJ initiatives?

It is now time to summarize some of the forms that RJ initiatives have taken in different parts of the world and different settings. I shall be selective, in the knowledge that fuller surveys may be consulted elsewhere.[8] Brief reference can be made to five different RJ formats:

i) *Victim-Offender Mediation*: since the 1980s both in the United Kingdom and in the United States there have been some schemes enabling victims and their offenders to be brought together in the presence of a mediator. Some of them are instead of formal court processes, others occur before or after formal court processes. The aims are very much as stated earlier – to allow the victim to tell the offender about the effects of the offence, and to hear the offender's explanation; to secure an apology by the offender and perhaps a promise of reparation.[9]

ii) *Family Group Conferences*: the most influential model of conferencing is that introduced in New Zealand in 1989 for young offenders. To the basic elements of mediation the FGC adds not only the victim's family and the offender's family but also one or more community representatives.[10] Versions of this model are also in operation in Australia, where every state has a legislative framework for restorative conferences. Most states have rejected the notion of police-led conferences, but the Australian Capital Territory (where the RISE experiment is being carried out) has police-led conferences, which extend to such crimes as drunk driving and assault by adults.[11] In most systems the outcome of the conference is subject to approval by a court.

iii) *Sentencing Circles*: forms of sentencing circle emerged in Canada during the 1980s. They have some similarity with conferences, in that the victim's family, the offender's family, and community representatives are present. However, the community emphasis seems to be somewhat greater, and many circles are chaired by a judicial officer. As with conferences, the aim is not only to secure a dialogue and agreement between victim and offender, but to enable the reintegration of both offender and victim into the community.[12]

iv) *Restorative Cautioning*: in the late 1990s the Thames Valley Police began a scheme for restorative cautioning which is now fully established and spreading to other police areas.[13] These are police-led conferences, which aim to involve the victim and the offender, and to elicit an apology and perhaps an offer of reparation, as well as giving the parties the opportunity for a dialogue about the offence.

v) *Regulatory RJ*: in his writings Braithwaite describes a number of ways in which RJ has been used in regulatory settings, often as a result of research and initiatives in which he has been involved.[14] In essence, efforts to bring about dialogue between interested parties (usually both those who are being regulated and their customers) have tended to result in enhanced compliance with requirements, and certainly a higher degree of compliance than that achieved by occasional prosecutions.

These five variations on practical RJ can be seen to reflect, to a greater or lesser degree, the core principles set out in the first section above. The essence of RJ is that it is voluntary, and therefore it is usual for both victim and offender to have not only the right to opt out of RJ (and into formal court processes) but also to veto the outcome of the conference or circle (in which case formal processes would resume). There are differences of emphasis among the five formats, and there is much scope for debating the roles of the victim and of community representatives, whether the police should be involved as centrally as they are in some forms of RJ, and whether there should be a facilitator or judge whose approval of the agreement is necessary.

Those and other arguments of principle will be taken up below. To many proponents of RJ they are less important than the claim that RJ has more desirable consequences than 'conventional' criminal justice processes. These consequences are said to extend to victims, offenders, and the wider community, and are often phrased as claims of superior 'effectiveness'. The evidence for them is also considered below.

Forms of RJ in England and Wales

For many years there have been scattered mediation schemes in England and Wales. Martin Wright in 1996 referred to the existence of seven mediation schemes for juveniles and twelve for all ages.[15] The number of referrals is low, and the schemes vary in the stage of the process at which mediation is considered – sometimes before or instead of court proceedings, sometimes afterwards. Since 1998 the Thames Valley Police has been developing restorative cautioning, as mentioned above, which is a form of diversion from prosecution.

Various ideas labelled as 'restorative justice' are being promoted as part of the response to youth offending. The Crime and Disorder Act 1998 abolished cautioning for young offenders in favour of a new system of reprimands and (for second or more serious offences) final warnings. According to the White Paper:

> When a Final Warning is given, this will usually be followed by a community intervention programme, involving the offender and his or her family to address the cause of the offending and so reduce the risk of further crime.[16]

Reference is made to the Thames Valley restorative cautioning scheme and to the Northamptonshire Diversion Scheme[17] as desirable models for interventions after a final warning. It is anticipated that Youth Offending Teams (YOTs) will devise local schemes of intervention along these lines. A second piece of legislation, the Youth Justice and Criminal Evidence Act 1999, contemplates restorative elements in more serious cases: where a young offender who has not previously been convicted pleads guilty in court, the youth court must make a referral order. This has the effect of referring the offender to a YOT, which is required to establish a youth offender panel for the offender with a view to deciding on the responses appropriate in this case and drawing up a 'youth offender contract'.[18] It is contemplated that a version of Family Group Conferences [FGC] (similar to the New Zealand model described above) will be developed for some such cases. Thus, the Youth Justice Board's guidance proposes that restorative processes should be used to tackle the causes of offending and to strengthen 'protective factors':

> FGCs are intended to produce tailor-made plans that will directly support young offenders, and tackle specific risk factors. For those young offenders assessed as being a high risk, FGCs should be considered as an effective way to produce the content of Action Plan Orders, and Youth Offender Panel contracts. FGCs seek to work with families, encouraging them to be creative in designing solutions and interventions that they will support, significantly increasing the likelihood that they will be successful.[19]

It is not envisaged that versions of family group conferencing will be used in large numbers of cases: the document points out that 'FGCs are resource intensive' and that in New Zealand they are used in only 20 per cent of youth cases.[20] Both victims and offenders will be given a choice whether to participate in any form of RJ, but it is contemplated that some FGCs will go ahead without the victim,[21] and the mediation need not involve face-to-face contact between victim and offender.[22] In cases where a prosecution has been brought, there will be issues of timing to be resolved: youth courts are being urged to deal with cases as soon as possible, whereas FGCs take time to set up, prepare, and conduct. Although the logistics are not absolutely clear, the guidance suggests that in 'fast-tracked' cases, 'restorative processes should best be attempted once an order has been made, which should include the potential for restorative work if desired by the victim(s)'.[23]

It thus appears that the new processes which are labelled 'restorative' may be invoked either instead of prosecution, or when a court makes a referral order, or after the youth court has sentenced the offender. Where a conference-style approach is taken, it is not just the victim and offender and their families who will be involved. A full statement of RJ, as we saw in the first section above, includes the restoration of the community among its objectives. The Youth Justice Board's document shows a clear preference for various agencies being involved in FGCs, and suggests that 'FGCs are most effective when facilitated by persons completely independent of any agency'[24] – although where that leaves police-led conferencing is not explained. It appears that there is to be no representative of 'the community' as such in the RJ initiatives that are being promoted. In the diversion cases, such as those following a final warning, it is perhaps assumed that no great community interest is involved, or that the police will safeguard it. Where there is a referral order or some other involvement of a YOT it seems that professionals will dominate, as in Scottish children's hearings, and it is perhaps assumed that the YOT will ensure that community interests are upheld. This is one of the many opaque areas about which questions will be raised in the next two sections.

Before concluding this brief discussion of the new initiatives, it is worth reflecting on the extent to which the label 'restorative' is properly applied to them. Allison Morris and Loraine Gelsthorpe have argued strongly that the new practices distort the fundamental elements of RJ. Most poignantly, any mediation or conferencing that takes place as part of the 'community intervention programme' which accompanies a final warning for a young offender must be viewed in its context:

> the whole tenor of the legislation suggests 'no negotiation' and 'no excuses' ... What distinguishes this scheme from a restorative justice perspective is that the power and control will remain with the professionals, and will not be transferred to the key parties to the offence – the offenders, victims and their families.[25]

The same applies where conferences are used as part of the process of producing young offender 'contracts' under referral orders. Not only is there an element of coercion deriving from the underlying court order, but also the processes are likely to be dominated by professionals from the relevant agencies.[26] Although in law the offender does have the power not to consent to the proposed contract, the element of 'consent' will often betoken a fairly small amount of free will, in that the young offender may believe that to walk away from the conference may result in the court taking an adverse view of him.

As for reparation orders, they are claimed to be restorative but it seems that the victim's views on reparation will be conveyed to the court rather than given in person, and that the victim may not have the opportunity to meet the offender – two desiderata, so far as RJ is concerned.[27] These remarks on conferences and reparation orders are surely sufficient to raise the question whether the use of the language of RJ by the Government and the Youth Justice Board is entirely faithful to its principles.

Some constitutional objections to RJ

One of the features of RJ processes is that they aim to take the determination of the response to an offender out of the hands of 'the State' (in the shape of formal court processes) and to place it in the hands of others such as the victim and family, the offender and family, and representatives of 'the community' or at least its agencies. Some of the reasons for doing so have been mentioned above, but is it right in principle to take the administration of criminal justice out of the hands of the state? What do we mean when we refer to the public interest in preventing or prosecuting crime? What is the significance of the phrase 'a crime against society'?

The idea seems to be that, when it is decided to make certain conduct a crime rather than simply a civil wrong, this implies that it should not be merely a matter for the victim whether some action is taken against the malefactor; and even that there is a public interest in ensuring that people who commit such wrongs are liable to punishment, not merely to civil suit. Thus Antony Duff argues for a category 'of "public" wrongs that are properly condemned and dealt with as wrongs by the community as a whole',[28] and he illustrates this with crimes of 'domestic' violence:

> But whatever else is unclear about the rights and wrongs of a domestic dispute ... such violence should surely *not* be seen as a matter for negotiation or compromise. It should be condemned by the whole community as an unqualified wrong; and this is done by defining and prosecuting it as a crime.[29]

These are not propositions with which an RJ advocate would necessarily disagree. But the next step in my argument is: that it is the responsibility of the State to ensure that there is order and law-abidance in society, so that citizens are not at the mercy of ruffians, thieves, terrorists, etc. The political theory, briefly, is that citizens agree to obey laws in return for protection of their vital interests, though keeping their right of self-defence for occasions of emergency when state protection is unavailable. In practical terms this is the justification for maintaining a police force, a system of public prosecutions, the courts, and other aspects of the criminal justice system. There is also a justification for the state taking over the administration of criminal justice from victims and other individuals, so as to avoid the social instability that would result if people had to 'take the law into their own hands' in responding to offences, thereby preventing vigilantism.[30] Thus, Duff regards it as obvious 'that the state owes it to its citizens to protect them from crime' through the criminal law and its administration.[31]

> If a community is, through the legal organs of the state, to take seriously the public wrong done to a citizen, it must not only sympathize with the victim but also censure the offender. It owes it to the victim, whose wrong it shares, and to the offender as a member of the normative community, to try to get the offender to recognize the wrong and to make a suitable apology for it.[32]

None of this is to rule out the delegation of this function by the state (in whole or in part) to others, either by moving it down to the level of the local community[33] or by elements of privatization. But on either view the principle is that this power ought to belong to the state in modern industrialized societies, and it is for the state to decide whether or not to delegate.

In many political systems the application of this principle is attended by various unwanted effects, which there is insufficient effort to eradicate. Thus, Kent Roach writes of disadvantaged groups having to 'rely on the criminal sanction's false promise of security and equality'[34] and argues that the state's responsibility for protecting citizens should be viewed in the wider context of public health, and therefore tackled as one element in a social programme to improve the conditions of life of groups who are disproportionately victimized and are not in a position to buy private security or health care.[35] This important corrective serves as a reminder of the limitations of the criminal justice system, but it does not detract from (and may even enhance) the importance of ensuring public control over the administration of justice.

Insofar as the state controls the sentencing process, and does so 'in the public interest', there is an argument that it ought to do so consistently. That is, it owes it to offenders to exercise its power to the same extent in similar cases. The function of deciding on sentence is that of the judiciary, within the legal framework, and the courts should operate on principle and transparently. There is an important distinction between judges responding in a principled manner to relevant factual differences between cases, and judges or other tribunals passing sentence on the basis of their own pet theories or preferences. It is the latter that is contrary to the rule of law. As John Gardner has argued, one of the implications of acting according to the 'rule of law' is that 'questions of how people are to be treated relative to one another always come to the fore at the point of its application'. This is not to rule out mitigation or mercy in sentencing, but to assert that 'what falls to be mitigated is none other than the sentence which is, in the court's [judgment], required by justice'.[36] This reasoning lies at the heart of one objection to RJ (and to various victims' rights initiatives): the response to offending should not be influenced by preference of the particular victim, but should be decided by reference to publicly debated and democratically determined policies that show respect for the human rights of victims and defendants.

It is the hallmark of many RJ approaches that they draw into criminal justice both victims and the wider community. David Garland is among those who have argued for the delegation of sentencing powers to communities: to 'authorities intermediate between the State and the individual'.[37] He does this for reasons similar to those of RJ theorists – that the closer the adjudicators and enforcers are to the offender, the more likely they are to be effective in achieving the desired changes in behaviour (perhaps partly because their legitimacy is more likely to impress itself on the offender).

One consequence of thus empowering 'communities'[38] might be to sacrifice the 'rule of law' values which, it was argued, ought to be attached to state criminal justice. If different communities can adopt separate standards, the result is likely to be a form of 'justice by geography' or 'postcode lottery'. Is it right for the state, or for a body exercising authority delegated by the state, to use its coercive powers differently against each of two people, one of whom commits an offence in one locality and another with an exactly similar background who commits a similar offence in a different locality? It is no argument to point to the existence of local magistracy, local police forces, and so on, because that raises the same questions of fairness. In principle, justice should be administered in a consistent manner so that individuals do not find themselves subject to variable standards in different locations. There may be merit in allowing local responses to peculiar local problems, but if the rule of law is to be upheld any such variations should be kept within proper bounds; and any 'local problems' justification should be scrutinized to check that it is not a camouflage for particular local views on appropriate responses to law-breaking. This is not to overlook the problem of determining what should be the relevant political unit, particularly where there is a devolved system of government.

Another question of principle concerns the goal of 'community restoration'. Many RJ theorists, among others, regard community service orders as the paradigm of community restoration.[39] Restoration is often said to require reintegration, but the practical implications of that concept are no clearer. Without raising questions about other possibilities, there remains the question of quantum: by what criteria is the amount of community restoration to be calculated? I have found very little indication of an answer from RJ theorists here. This is largely because it remains uncertain what 'restoration of the community' means in real terms. The restoration is plainly symbolic, and therefore it seems necessary to devise a scale of 'wrongs to the community' and to match it with a register of degrees of community restoration. Desert theorists have attempted to develop proportionality theory so as to cope with these inevitable questions about quantum,[40] but I see no such endeavour among RJ theorists.

The issue of 'community restoration' raises a further institutional question, concerning impartiality. It is one thing for critics of conventional criminal justice systems to argue that those systems fail to sentence 'objectively', despite their aspirations, because they fail to get away from class bias, or even from race bias and gender bias. It is quite another thing to devise a system that would avoid problems of bias, or of informal hierarchies growing up, or of local power structures tending to dominate.[41] Indeed, even if one can agree about the relevant 'community' for RJ purposes, there remains a whole raft of questions about constitution, definition, and representation.[42] Advocates of community justice stress the importance of inclusion rather than exclusion, and there are examples of circles and RJ conferences that appear to avoid these difficulties. But if RJ is to be put forward as a major approach to criminal justice, taking a wide range of cases in urban settings, these doubts and dangers have to be taken seriously.[43]

A related question concerns the role of the police. There are considerable variations across the world in the forms of RJ processes, in terms of the involvement of police, social workers, or judicial officers, and in terms of the role of facilitator or the possession of a veto over the outcome. Braithwaite asks 'whether there is something wrong in principle with the police facilitating a conference. Does it make the police investigator, prosecutor, judge and jury?'[44] He never answers the question of principle which he rightly raises, but instead goes on to ask whether police culture might benefit from involvement in RJ initiatives and to assert that pragmatically it is a good thing if anyone is willing to take on the onerous responsibility of facilitation, so long as the dangers are recognized and managed. However, I submit that the question of principle must be answered, even if pragmatism tempts us away from it. The question is not one that can be answered immediately, because it is first necessary to reflect on the function and standing of conferences and circles. Are they sentencing processes, or at least some kind of legal/political equivalent? If that is the correct characterization, then there ought to be some control by an 'independent and impartial' person,[45] and it is clear that the police cannot fulfil that requirement because of their investigative and (in England and Wales) prosecutorial roles.

A judicial officer would meet the requirement, and it is possible that a social or community worker might also do so. But perhaps circles and conferences are not sentencing processes or an equivalent, and should be seen instead as voluntary alternatives to formal sentencing. One might point to the victim's veto and offender's veto as evidence that this is not a sentencing process, which should in principle have a non-optional outcome. On this basis, it does not much matter who is involved in facilitating circles and conferences, since the formal criminal justice system stands behind them in case of disagreement or complaint. If an offender or a victim does not like the police role, the answer is simply to use the veto and push the case back into the formal system.[46]

I infer from Braithwaite's treatment of the issue that he does not regard the vetoes as a satisfactory counter-weight to police facilitation.[47] His republican ideal is that most conferencing should take place in the community without the disputes being referred to the police at all. His preferred approach in a non-republican system is to guard against any 'institutional domination' of circles or conferences, a danger courted if the police have the central role of facilitation. I do not believe that this hesitancy is based solely on empirical worries about undue influence by the police. I suspect that the issue of principle, or 'separation of powers', comes into it. If so, I fully agree. That is also one reason why I have reservations about the Thames Valley Restorative Cautioning scheme, which is by definition police-dominated. It is true that it 'merely' replaces formal cautioning, which was police-dominated, but I have opposed that for the same reasons. It is also true that a defendant or offender can opt for formal criminal justice processes instead of restorative cautioning; but, as suggested earlier, the 'option' is hardly a free one if the taking of it is perceived as likely to reflect adversely on the offender. In principle such a system with dispositive powers should involve a quasi-judicial body such as public prosecutors, not a chiefly investigative body such as the police. This is the position with the so-called 'fiscal fines' levied by procurators fiscal on minor offenders in Scotland.[48]

Some rights-based objections to RJ

It is common for advocates of RJ to insist that all parties 'with a stake in the offence' ought to participate in the disposition of the case, through a circle, conference, etc. The assumption, then, is that the victim certainly has 'a stake', and so the discussion tends to focus on others. But we should not move so quickly. Nils Christie's assertion that the 'conflict' in some sense 'belongs' to the victim[49] has become a modern orthodoxy among RJ supporters and some others.[50] The doctrine has ancient roots,[51] although growing awareness of the existence of secondary victimization increases the complexity of the issues.[52] The politico-historical argument is that most modern legal systems exclude the victim so as to bolster their own power. Originally the state wanted to take over criminal proceedings from victims as an assertion of power, and also to raise revenue, and what now passes for 'normal' is simply a usurpation which has no claim to be the natural order.

My concern is not to trifle with the rather romantic interpretation of criminal justice in early history[53] but rather to raise three points of principle: the principle of independence and impartiality, the principle of proportionality, and the principle of compensation for wrongs. The first point is that Article 6.1 of the European Convention on Human Rights declares that everyone has a right to a fair hearing 'by an independent and impartial tribunal'. Insofar as a victim plays a part in determining the disposition of a criminal case, the tribunal is not 'independent'. The victim's voice also detracts from the impartiality of the proceedings:[54] that voice is not a judicial or quasi-judicial one, nor can it be expected to be informed by the available range of sentences and principles for the disposition of criminal cases. All of this suggests that a conference or circle fails to meet the basic standards of a fair hearing. Most RJ supporters will be unimpressed with this, because the argument simply assumes that what has become conventional in modern criminal justice systems is absolutely right. That may be criticized as historically flawed and theoretically question-begging. But the issue of principle must be confronted. Impartiality and independence ought to be basic standards of the criminal process, particularly the trial and sentencing, and the involvement of the victim in decision-making which places a burden on the offender seems to be incompatible with those standards.

No doubt my argument will be attacked on the ground that the claimed 'impartiality' and 'objectivity' are so impersonal and detached as to demonstrate exactly what is wrong with conventional systems, and why they fail. But that raises further questions about the shortcomings of the adversarial trial and the (rather one-sided) sentencing process in England and Wales, questions which need to be debated fully rather than simply tacked onto the present debate. We should not assume that it would be impossible to make changes to the trial and sentencing processes which would ensure a fuller opportunity for the victim to confront the offender with the effects of the crime, even though this would be a radical step. Some might wish to avoid these implications by means of the side-stepping manoeuvre considered above, characterizing circles and conferences as alternatives to sentencing rather than as sentencing processes, and therefore not bound by the same principles. But I doubt whether this would be any more satisfying here than it was in relation to the police.

My second point of principle concerns proportionality. A political system that respects the rule of law and regards citizens as rational, choosing beings ought to insist that sentences should bear a relationship to the seriousness of offences. To desert theorists this is axiomatic: punishment should in principle be proportionate to the offence(s) committed, unless an extremely strong argument for creating a class of exceptional cases can be sustained.[55] The government has also expressed some commitment to this principle.[56] The proportionality principle generates an expectation of consistency: similar offenders and offences should result in similar sentences. It should also function as a protection against discrimination, by attempting to rule out certain factors from sentencing calculations. I am not so naïve as to imagine that any actual sentencing system operationalizes this ideal; but one surely would not discard an ideal of justice on the ground that, because the world is imperfect, there are always difficulties in achieving it.

The principle of proportionality goes against victim involvement in sentencing decisions because the views of victims may vary, and few would expect victim involvement to result in proportionate sentencing.[57] Some victims will be forgiving, others will be vindictive; some will be interested in new forms of sentence, others will not; some shops will have one policy in relation to thieves, others may have a different policy. If victim satisfaction is one of the aims of circles and conferences, then proportionate sentencing is unlikely to form part of this.

Two replies may be anticipated. One is that it is victims' views of proportionality that are important, not someone else's, and so again I am skewing the criterion towards a conventional notion of justice and away from a victim-centred conception. A reply to this is that the execution of sentences depends to a large extent on the presence (foreground or background) of state coercion. Therefore the issue is one of the exercise of state power over individuals, and 'rule of law' principles ought to apply. This requires a consistent and coherent principle of proportionality, not one that varies according to the wishes of the individual victim. A second reply is to recall Braithwaite's reference to 'guaranteeing offenders against punishment beyond a maximum'.[58] There is a range of possible proportionality theories: modern desert theory requires the sentence to be proportionate to the seriousness of the offence,[59] whereas various forms of limiting retributivism recognize looser boundaries. Michael Tonry, for example, argues against the 'strong proportionality' of desert theorists and in favour of 'upper limits' set in accordance with a less precise notion of proportionality.[60] It remains unclear whether Braithwaite's 'guarantee' incorporates as much of proportionality theory as Tonry seems prepared to accept, or whether it imposes less demanding constraints. We simply do not know. Nor do we know where many other RJ advocates stand in relation to the 'deep end' of sentencing.

There is a range of possible extensions of proportionality: that no sentence should be disproportionate, clearly disproportionate, wholly disproportionate, etc. I remain uneasy about this part of Braithwaite's theory: at least Tonry's adaptation of proportionality theory puts parsimony distinctly in the foreground, whereas Braithwaite's 'guarantee' comes amid dark phrases about the use of deterrence and incapacitation when RJ fails or is thought inappropriate.[61]

My third point of principle is the most direct of all in its target. What I want to argue is that the victim's legitimate interest is in compensation from the offender, and not in the punishment of the offender. I will not weary this readership with discussions of the distinction between punishment and compensation, but it is worth pointing out that the comments of victims and their families on court sentences often betray some confusion about the distinction. When a court fines an offender £300 for careless driving in a case where death resulted (although there was no conviction for the more serious offence of causing death by dangerous driving) newspapers often report comments such as 'my son's life has been valued at just £300'. The sentence is not intended as a valuation of the life, but as a measure of the offender's culpability (and, perhaps, financial means). Compensation is something different, and victims certainly have a right to compensation from the offender.[62] The dispute is whether the victim's legitimate interest goes beyond reparation or compensation (and the right to victim services and support, and to proper protection from further harm) and extends to the question of punishment. I would not suggest that the victim has no legitimate interest in the disposition of the offender in his or her case, but I would suggest that the victim's interest is no greater than yours or mine. The victim's interest is as a citizen, as one of many citizens who make up the community or State. In democratic theory all citizens have a right to vote at elections and sometimes on other occasions, and to petition their elected representatives about issues affecting them. If I am an ardent advocate of RJ or of indeterminate imprisonment for repeat offenders, I can petition my elected representative about it. Just because a person commits an offence against me, however, that does not privilege my voice above that of the court (acting 'in the public interest') in the matter of punishment. A justification for this lies in social contract reasoning, along the lines that the State may be said to undertake the duty of administering justice and protecting citizens in return for citizens giving up their right to self-help (except in cases of urgency) in the case of better social order. But this really adds little to the substance of the earlier argument in favour of transparency and consistency in the use of coercion by the State when punishing citizens as offenders.

This third point is not opposed by all those who advocate a version of RJ. Thus Michael Cavadino and James Dignan draw a strong distinction between the victim's right to reparation and the public interest in responding to the offence.[63] In their view it is right to empower victims to participate in the process which determines what reparation is to be made by the offender, and reparation to the offender should be the major element of the response. In serious cases some additional response (punishment) may be considered necessary, and they insist on a form of limiting retributivism in which proportionality sets upper and lower boundaries for the burdens placed on offenders (and also serves as a default setting for cases where a conference or circle proves impossible or inappropriate). It is a matter of regret that few RJ theorists refer to Cavadino and Dignan's work on the interfaces between RJ and desert theory. Their endeavour is to preserve some key values of restorative justice, whilst insisting on limits to the burdens that may be placed on offenders and to the proper ambit of victims' views. Cavadino and Dignan rightly regard the distinction between compensation and punishment as crucial; they also regard victim involvement as a value to be enhanced where appropriate. I see problems of principle in allowing a statement from the victim to inform sentencing (as distinct from reparation).[64] I do not think the recent proposals from the Council of the European Union necessarily cast doubt on this distinction.[65] Edna Erez claims that 'providing victims with a voice has therapeutic advantages', and enhances proportionality in sentencing.[66] But if one accepts that the victim's voice should not be determinative, then raising expectations in this way may prove cruel and disillusioning.[67]

Some critics will claim that, in pressing these three principled arguments against recognizing a role for the victim in sentencing, I have aligned myself with conventional notions of criminal justice which fail to show proper respect for victims. I think there is an important distinction to be made here. The modern trial process, in England and elsewhere, does fail to show proper respect for victims. No doubt victims are treated with greater respect at conferences and circles (although it should be noted that the true comparison there is with sentencing procedures in the conventional system, not with trials.)[68] I have welcomed recent reforms in England designed to improve respect for victims in trials, although I remain critical of much of the ethos of the English criminal trial.[69] There is much to be done to ensure that victims who give evidence are valued as citizens, not treated as prosecution fodder, and the recent European Union proposals are right to emphasize this.[70] But the present debate is about the sentencing or disposal stage of the process, and in my view the role of the victim ought to be severely limited. There are certainly good arguments for enhancing the prosecutor's role at the sentencing stage,[71] although in practice it would be important to tread cautiously until English prosecutors had sufficient knowledge and experience to deal with this role fairly.

Before leaving the issue of victims' rights, a few words must be said about victims' responsibilities. There is ample evidence about the suffering of victims of crime, and about the ways in which the legal process can sometimes add to that suffering. It is therefore important to ensure that the criminal justice system avoids placing on victims any additional burdens with respect to participation in sentencing or in other responses to offending, such as conferences.[72] Participation must be voluntary, and provision must be made to ensure that, in those cases where the victim does not wish to become involved, there is no disadvantage to the offender.

Some doubts about the effectiveness of RJ

The response of some RJ supporters to my institutional and rights-based objections may be that, even if they are not devoid of substance, the real belief of RJ is that it is more effective, and surely we all want greater effectiveness in criminal justice. If that is the response, then I am unwilling to concede any ground to it. Arguments of principle cannot be easily overridden. Moreover, I have doubts about the claims of superior effectiveness for RJ, and those are concerned with wider doubts about the preventive potential of social reactions to offending.

Let us focus on the claims of some supporters of RJ that it is successful and effective on several fronts. The Youth Justice Board certainly makes a wild claim of this kind:

> Restorative practice clearly contributes to the objective of preventing offending. Recent research has established that participation in VOM alone is likely to reduce re-offending by 32% among young offenders.[73]

This wild claim is compounded by the statement, at the end of a discussion of restorative conferencing in New Zealand and in the Thames Valley, that 'there is now a great deal of evidence illustrating this process to be as effective as VOM'.[74] Unless the infelicitous use of the word 'illustrating' is intended to convey some qualification, it is extraordinary that this claim is not supported by reference to any of the alleged evidence.

Why do I describe these claims as wild? After all, one might expect that the combination of the (presumably deterrent, or remorse-inducing) effect of the victim confronting the offender with the consequences of the offence, with the support and understanding for both victim and offender that is said to be characteristic of RJ, would have significant effects. The problem is that much of the evidence fails to achieve the standards which ought to be expected if assertions of superior effectiveness are to be made. Even leaving aside the formidable problems of relying on recorded reconvictions,[75] a reconviction study ought to be constructed so as to ensure that the particular form of disposal (be it VOM, FGC, or whatever) is compared with one or more alternative forms of disposal, by means of randomized or matched samples of offenders, with sufficiently large numbers to ensure statistical significance. Thus even that doyen of RJ, John Braithwaite, does not believe that we yet have robust evidence to justify claims of superior efficacy for RJ processes, concluding that 'statistical power, randomization, and control have mostly been weak to very weak in this research'.[76] The Youth Justice Board (committed to 'evidence-led' policies) and several others are deluding themselves if they believe that robust evidence now exists.

Before it is thought that I am urging rejection of RJ initiatives, let me attempt to reposition the debate. I do not believe it is necessary to claim superior efficacy for RJ. It would surely be sufficient if we could establish that it fares no worse, in terms of reconvictions, than other forms of intervention. In general, comparative reconviction studies seem to suggest that, once key variables are taken into account, most forms of sentence and intervention have roughly similar results, and the previous record of the offender is a more powerful predictor of reconviction than the type of disposal.[77] My own preference would be not to focus on claims about preventing reoffending, and to continue with experiments whilst gathering evidence on all fronts. Surely the primary claim made for RJ must be that it can bring other desired improvements, particularly in victim satisfaction.

To its credit, the Youth Justice Board does re-assert, from time to time, that the introduction of RJ is not just for the benefit of offenders:

> It is important that the FGC is not perceived as only being held to provide support for the offender, but is also being convened to hold the young offender accountable to the victim. The FGC should be a forum through which things may be put right with the victim either through communication, reparation or both.[78]

Thus the Board states that one of the greatest benefits of mediation (VOM) to victims is in terms of 'returning a sense of control and peace and alleviating their fears of revictimisation'.[79] There is varying international evidence of victim satisfaction: Braithwaite's review shows that victims tend to be less satisfied than offenders with many of the outcomes of conferences, but nonetheless that victims who agree to be involved in RJ processes are more satisfied than those whose cases go to court.[80] Daly's assessment of her evidence from South Australia is, as always, both measured and pointed:

> About 30 to 50 per cent of conferences in the SAJJ project seemed to succeed in repairing the harm and in victims feeling more positive toward offenders. Such success needs to be balanced against a core of about 15 to 20 per cent of offenders who held negative views toward the conference and felt it was a waste of time, and about 40 per cent of victims who continued to feel negative toward those who victimised them. Overall the 'real story' of restorative justice has many positives and much to commend it, but the evidence is mixed. Conferencing, or any other new justice practice, is not nirvana and ought not to be sold in those terms.[81]

I believe there has been considerable over-selling of RJ in England and Wales. The Home Office and the Youth Justice Board are hoping that their initiatives will be successful in two directions at once, in improving victim satisfaction and in reducing reoffending. This is compatible with the 'holistic' claims made by many RJ advocates and practitioners,[82] as part of their argument that one of the many drawbacks of 'conventional' criminal justice systems is that they fail to bring together all the affected parties for a dialogue which can have beneficial effects all round. The two major problems with the current programme are that exaggerated claims about effectiveness have been made, and that in any event many of the initiatives labelled as RJ will take place in such a changed youth justice system that findings from RJ projects elsewhere will not be readily transferable.

It would be wrong to close this brief discussion of effectiveness without recalling one other difficulty of applying the concept to criminal justice interventions. Whether the system is predominantly 'conventional' or contains large elements of RJ, its effects on people's social behaviour are likely to be small unless other aspects of the social and political system are pulling in the same direction. Thus, as Braithwaite recognizes:

> the most fundamental things we must do to control crime and improve the lot of victims are not reforms to the justice system. They are reforms about liberty, equality, and community in more structural and developmental senses.[83]

He draws attention to 'the need to engage with other forms of social movement politics beside the social movement for restorative justice', and refers to the need 'to tackle unemployment, homelessness, educational disadvantage, sexism, racism and the like'.[84] These are criminological commonplaces which Braithwaite rightly restates in his assessment of RJ. Unfortunately they tend not to be mentioned by many of those advocating RJ in England and Wales.

Carrying RJ forwards

My conclusion is that RJ is being over-sold by many of its advocates in this country. 'Evangelism' best describes the excesses of some of those who portray it as a successful approach which can be widely used for the settlement of disputes both in criminal justice and in society at large. This heady optimism is bolstered by a romantic view of history, and by the device of 'story-telling' which offers details of a few spectacular successes of RJ rather than undertaking the demanding task of a full social and criminological evaluation.[85] If RJ is to be promoted on the basis of its effectiveness, we need proper evidence of this, not to mention a frank appreciation of the limitations of the available evidence. There should be no concealing the fact that the initiatives in the youth justice system are different in significant respects from conferencing, circles, and mediation in many other countries – so much so that there is some doubt whether they should be described as RJ at all.[86] Nor should there be any overlooking of the differences in structure and purpose between the English youth justice system and that of other countries. For example, the New Zealand system is underpinned by a philosophy of diversion,[87] and in New South Wales there is a statutory requirement that any measure taken in respect of a young offender should be the 'least restrictive alternative'.[88] The English system of reprimands and warnings is intended to have little flexibility, and the powers of courts to grant discharges are curtailed, all in order to demonstrate the toughness of the new system.

The problem of assessing the effectiveness of RJ runs even deeper. Section 37 of the Crime and Disorder Act 1998 states that the principal aim of the youth justice system shall be to prevent offending, but that is too broad an aim, and it fails to deal with questions of priority in relation to other aims such as the efficient use of resources and proper respect for victims. Thus there is an obvious conflict between the 'fast-tracking' of cases against young defendants and the preparation required for proper RJ processes. As mentioned above,[89] the Youth Justice Board is concerned that conferences should not be used too much because they are expensive; yet if they really are as effective as the Board's literature proclaims, this seems rather short-sighted. And where do victims of crime come in all of this? The Board mentions them from time to time, but it is not clear whether their interests form part of the rationale for the new approach to youth justice. In view of all this confusion, therefore, it is impossible to identify coherent criteria of effectiveness: victim satisfaction, or the reconviction rates of offenders, or economic efficiency? What if we obtain reliable comparative or randomized research which shows greater effects in one direction than the other?

I set out above what I believe to be at least four major objections of principle to Braithwaite's theoretical framework for RJ: that the state should retain responsibility for the administration of criminal justice; that the determination of the disposal of criminal cases should be effected by an independent and impartial tribunal; that the principles applied by such a tribunal should be consistent with the rule of the law, and that disposals ought always to be proportionate to the seriousness of the offence(s); and that victims have a legitimate interest in reparation or compensation from the offender but not in the making of any wider orders or sentences.

No doubt many RJ advocates will be unimpressed by those objections, and even by the questions raised about the effectiveness of RJ, because they still believe that the kinds of process that RJ promotes have distinct social merits. Empowering those who have become victims of crime is a benefit; holding round-table discussions which involve negotiation may increase the legitimacy of the outcome; allowing individuals to play a significant part, rather than professionals (particularly lawyers), may increase both satisfaction and legitimacy; involving members of the community in both the response to the offence and the reintegration of the offender may contribute to social inclusion; and so on. These are worthwhile goals, and they emphasize the value of fair processes as well as outcomes.[90] A significant element of the impetus behind RJ lies in a dissatisfaction with formal court hearings and with lawyers: Christie's argument against the 'stealing of the conflict' was a deprecation of the way in which lawyers and other professionals have replaced individuals in the resolution of disputes, to the extent that the vast majority of words spoken in formal processes are those of lawyers. One of the key features of conferences and circles is that this predominance is reversed,[91] with lawyers acting only as advisers at the periphery. Thus the RJ movement has affinities with the increasing popularity of alternative dispute resolution in other fields.[92] However, the human rights of individuals must be safeguarded in these developments: increased informality should not lead to disrespect for rights. The precepts of the International Convention on the Rights of the Child must be honoured in any youth justice system, and that makes it particularly worrying that the government wishes to keep legal advisers out of conferences and youth offender panels.[93] More generally, ways must be found of allowing the parties to enter directly into dialogue whilst ensuring that defendants have ready access to legal advice in order to safeguard their rights.

Nobody with detailed knowledge of our criminal justice system, in particular the sentencing system, could take such pride in its present form as to be unwilling to consider alternatives. The remedies for this require deep social reforms, which cannot be discussed here. Different approaches must be tried, and RJ, with its emphasis on dialogue, apology, and making amends, is one of them. I believe it is well worth continuing to explore the possibilities of RJ, but that it should be taken forward within a firm legislative framework with clear aims, with enthusiasm but without exaggerated claims, with respect for rights, and within the bounds of proportionality. There should be the possibility of involving victims in procedures which deal with reparation and compensation, on the Cavadino and Dignan model, but not with the wider sentencing function. Those procedures should be carefully monitored and assessed in the context of England and Wales, looking at the effects on victims and at questions of differential access to justice (would more conferences be held for some types of offender than for others?) rather than focusing on reconvictions. By all means let us celebrate the new range of possibilities brought by RJ, but not by making claims that are so exaggerated that the criminal justice system is judged to have failed yet again.

Notes

1 Marshall, T.F. (1999) *Restorative Justice: an Overview*, London, p.5.

2 Braithwaite, J. (1999) 'Restorative justice: assessing optimistic and pessimistic accounts', in *Crime and Justice: a Review of Research*, vol.25, Chicago, p.6.

3 *Ibid.*

4 Marshall, n.1, above, p.6.

5 For similarly high expectations, see Wright, M. (1996) *Justice for Victims and Offenders: a Restorative Response to Crime* (Winchester), and M. Wright (1999) *Restoring Respect for Justice: a Symposium* (Winchester).

6 Braithwaite, n.2, above, pp.28, 97. Note, however, that the background system preferred by Braithwaite involves a pyramid of enforcement strategies which relies on types of deterrent and incapacitative measure: *ibid.*, pp.61–5.

7 Successive sweeps of the British Crime Survey tend to confirm this: see particularly Hough, M. and Roberts, J. (1998) *Attitudes to Punishment: Findings from the British Crime Survey*, Home Office Research Study 179 (London); and Mattinson, J. and Mirrlees-Black, C. (2000) *Attitudes to Crime and Criminal Justice: Findings from the 1998 British Crime Survey*, Home Office Research Study 200 (London).

8 Useful sources are Wright, n.6 above, esp. ch. 6; Braithwaite, n.2 above; Marshall, n.1 above; Daly, K. and Immarigeon, R. (1998) 'The past, present and future of restorative justice',1, *Contemporary Justice Review* 21; JUSTICE (2000), *Restoring Youth Justice: New Directions in Domestic and International Law and Practice* (London).

9 See particularly Marshall, n.1 above, p.11.

10 For a recent assessment, see Morris, A. and Maxwell, G. (2000) 'The practice of family group conferences in New Zealand: assessing the place, potential and pitfalls of restorative justice', in Crawford, A. and Goodey, J. (eds) *Integrating a Victim Perspective within Criminal Justice* (Aldershot).

11 A full evaluation is awaited, but for some discussion see Braithwaite, n.2 above, pp.63–5.

12 See Stuart, B. (1996) *Building Community Justice Partnerships: Community Peace-making Circles* (Ottawa).

13 See Young, R. 'Integrating a multi-victim perspective into criminal justice through restorative justice conferences', in Crawford and Goodey, n.10 above.

14 For references see Braithwaite, n.2 above, esp. pp.9–15.

15 Wright, n.6 above, 168; JUSTICE, n.8 above, pp.55–8.

16 Home Office (1997) 'No more excuses: a new approach to tackling youth crime in England and Wales', Cm. 3809 (London) para. 5.12.

17 Cf. Dignan, J. (1992) 'Repairing the damage: can reparation be made to work in the service of diversion?' 32, *BJ Crim*, 453; JUSTICE, n.8 above, pp.57–8 and 62.

18 For fuller details, see Ball, C. (2000) 'The Youth Justice and Criminal Evidence Act 1999: a significant move towards restorative justice, or a recipe for unintended consequences?', *Crim. LR*, p.211.

19 Taken from para. 3.11 of the policy document at www.youth-justice-board.gov.uk/policy/restorative.html; hereinafter cited as Youth Justice Board.

20 *Ibid*., para. 6.11; cf. Ball, n.20 above, p.217, on the questions raised by the fact that 70–80 per cent of cases in New Zealand and Scotland are dealt with outside conferences and panels. JUSTICE, n.8 above, p.28 also gives details of the proportions of cases dealt with by different methods in New Zealand.

21 *Ibid*., para. 4.3.

22 As is the case in existing mediation schemes: *ibid*., para. 2.3.

23 *Ibid*., para. 3.9.

24 *Ibid*., para. 6.14.

25 Morris, A. and Gelsthorpe, L. (2000) 'Something old, something borrowed, something blue, but something new? A comment on the prospects for restorative justice under the Crime and Disorder Act 1998', *Crim. LR* , pp.18, 27.

26 *Ibid*., p.26; see also Ball, n.18 above, p.217.

27 Morris and Gelsthorpe, n.25 above, p.28; JUSTICE, n.8 above, p.70.

28 Duff, R.A. (2000) *Punishment, Communication and Community* (New York), p.62.

29 *Ibid*.

30 MacCormick, N. and Garland, D. (1998) 'Sovereign states and vengeful victims: the problem of the right to punish' in A. Ashworth and M. Wasik (eds) *Fundamentals of Sentencing Theory* (Oxford), pp.22, 27.

31 Duff, n.28 above, p.112.

32 *Ibid*., p.114.

33 MacCormick and Garland, n.27 above, p.27.

34 Roach, K. (1999) *Due Process and Victims' Rights* (Toronto), p.117.

35 *Ibid*., p.261.

36 Gardner, J. 'Crime: in proportion and in perspective', in Ashworth and Wasik, n.27 above, pp.36–7.

37 MacCormick and Garland, n.27 above, p.27.

38 It should be noted that Maxwell and Morris, two leading RJ advocates, regard the involvement of community members as being 'at odds with the principles underlying conferencing' and oppose it: Maxwell and Morris, above, n.10 above, p.215.

39 E.g. Zedner, L. (1994) 'Reparation and retribution: are they reconcilable?' 57, *MLR*, 228; L. Walgrave (1995) 'Restorative justice for juveniles', 34, *Howard JCJ*, p.228; Duff, n.25 above, pp.99–106.

40 See esp. von Hirsch, A. and Jareborg, N. (1991) 'Gauging criminal harm: a living standard analysis' 11, *Oxford JLS,* 1, developed by Ashworth, n.33 above, ch.4.

41 See Lacey, N. (1996) 'Community in legal theory: idea, ideal or ideology?' 15, *Studies in Law, Politics and Society*, p.105.

42 See Crawford, A. (1997) *The Local Governance of Crime* (Oxford); and Crawford, A. 'Salient themes towards a victim perspective and the limitations of restorative justice', in Crawford and Goodey, n.10 above, pp.290–1.

43 See Braithwaite, n.2 above, p.84 for a questionable claim; cf. *ibid*., p.38 for greater realism. JUSTICE, n.8 above, pp.32–3, describe how the New Zealand system has been far more successful in the small city of Wellington than in the large conurbation of Auckland.

44 *Ibid*., p.99.

45 As required by Article 6 of the European Convention on Human Rights: see n.54 below, and accompanying text.

46 This is the way in which the European Court of Human Rights has dealt with complaints about fines levied by prosecutors or 'administrative fines' in other European countries: so long as the offender has the right not to accept the fine and instead to go to court, there is no breach of Article 6 (*Le Compte, van Leuven and de Meyere* v. *Belgium* A. 43, 1981).

47 Braithwaite, n.2 above, pp.98–101.

48 See Duff, P. and Meechan, K. (1992) 'The prosecutor fine', *Crim. LR*, p.22.

49 Christie, N. (1977) 'Conflicts as property', 17 *BJ Crim*., p.1.

50 E.g. Morris and Maxwell, n.10 above, who write (p. 207) of 'returning the offence to those most affected by it and encouraging them to determine appropriate responses to it.'

51 See Braithwaite, n.2 above, pp.1–2, for a summary and references.

52 E.g. Morgan, J. and Zedner, L. (1992), *Child Victims* (Oxford).

53 Kathleen Daly does this to good effect in her 'Restorative justice: the real story' (unpublished conference paper, September 2000), commenting that such histories 'slide over practices that the modern "civilised" Western mind would object to, such as a variety of harsh physical (bodily) punishments and banishment'.

54 See *McCourt* v. *United Kingdom* (1993) p.15 EHRR CD 110, for some acceptance of this proposition by the European Commission on Human Rights. Compare the Council of the European Union, Draft Framework Decision on the standing of victims in criminal procedure (Brussels, 26 June 2000).

55 von Hirsch, A. (1993) *Censure and Sanctions* (Oxford), ch.2.

56 Cf. Home Office (1998), *Crime and Disorder Act 1998: Youth Justice* (London) para. 17.1 on proportionality and consistency.

57 For the claim that it does, based on aggregative data, see Erez, E. (1999) 'Who's afraid of the big, bad victim? Victim impact statements as empowerment and enhancement of justice', *Crim. LR*, p.545.

58 Braithwaite, above, n.2 above, 105; the context almost suggests that he is referring only to statutory maximum sentences, and not to any case-specific notion of proportionality. If so, this would be a poor guarantee in many modern systems, which have broadly defined offences with high maxima.

59 von Hirsch, A. (1993) *Censure and Sanctions* (Oxford), esp. ch.2.

60 Tonry, M. (1994) 'Proportionality, parsimony and interchangeability of punishments', in Duff, A., Marshall, S., Dobash, R.E. and Dobash, R.P. (eds) *Penal Theory and Practice* (Manchester).

61 Braithwaite recognizes that RJ needs to be reinforced by a background system, which he describes in terms of an 'enforcement pyramid' which has RJ at its base, forms of deterrence as the next line of defence, and then incapacitation as the final resort (Braithwaite, n.2 above, pp.61–4). Elsewhere he and his co-author Philip Pettit have stated that, in pursuit of the goal of 'community reassurance', courts should take account of 'how common that offence has become in the community' and 'how far the offender is capable of re-offending again'. The relationship of this kind of sentencing to the claimed proportionality guarantee remains opaque: see the debate in von Hirsch, A. and Ashworth, A. (eds) (1998) *Principled Sentencing: Readings in Theory and Policy* (Oxford) pp.317–36.

62 See e.g. Ashworth, A. (1986) 'Punishment and compensation: state, victim and offender', *Oxford JLS*, pp.6, 86.

63 Cavadino, M. and Dignan, J. (1997) 'Reparation, retribution and rights', *International Review of Victimology*, pp.4, 233.

64 Ashworth, A. (1993), 'Victim impact statements and sentencing', *Crim. LR*, p.498.

65 In Article 6 of the recent draft it is stated: 'Each Member State shall provide a real and appropriate role for victims in its criminal justice system and shall maximise the involvement of victims in criminal procedure to the extent allowed by its legal system' (Council of the European Union, n.52 above). The closing words seem to deprive the Article of much force, and the arguments underlying the provision are not clear. Cf. JUSTICE (1998) *Victims in Criminal Justice* (London) ch.4.

66 Erez, n.54 above, p.555.

67 Sanders, A., Hoyle, C., Morgan, R. and Cape, E. (2001) 'Victim statements: don't work, can't work', *Crim. LR*, p.447.

68 Cf. Braithwaite, n.2 above, pp.41–2 with 101–3.

69 Ashworth, A. (1998) 'Victims' rights, defendants' rights, and criminal procedure', in Crawford and Goodey, n.10 above; M. Blake and A. Ashworth 'Some ethnical problems in prosecuting and defending criminal cases', *Crim. LR*, p.16.

70 Council of the European Union, n.54 above, Articles 2 and 8.

71 Ashworth, A. (1979) 'Prosecution and procedure in criminal justice', *Crim. LR*, p.480; Zellick, G. (1979) 'The role of prosecuting counsel in sentencing', *Crim. LR*, p.493.

72 Reeves, H. and Mulley, K. 'The new status of victims in the UK: opportunities and threats', in Crawford and Goodey, n.10 above, p.130.

73 *Ibid.*, para. 3.4. The reference is to Nugent *et al.*, 'Participation in victim-offender mediation and re-offense: successful replications?'. Cf. Strang 'Restorative justice programmes in Australia', www.aic.gove.au/rjustice, esp. p.38.

74 Youth Justice Board, n.19 above, para. 2.9.

75 Lloyd, C., Mair, G. and Hough, M. (1994) *Explaining Reconviction Rates: A Critical Analysis*, Home Office Research Study 136, London.

76 Braithwaite, n.2 above, p.30. He does comment that his survey of over 30 studies fails to reveal any evidence of increased recidivism. In fact, one of the studies he discusses did show a higher rate of recidivism in conferenced cases (the Bethlehem project in Pennsylvania, where property cases but not violence cases fell into this category). The finding was not statistically significant, but neither were those of several other studies.

77 Lloyd, Mair and Hough, above, n.73 above, p.51 and *passim*.

78 Youth Justice Board, n.19 above, para. 2.15; see also para. 3.3.

79 *Ibid.*, para. 2.4. Earlier, in para. 1.8, the Board claims that 'it has now been established that, for victims, participation reduces fears of revictimisation by approximately 50 per cent.' No source for this claim is indicated, but see Marshall, n.1 above, p.18, for an interpretation of some such evidence.

80 Braithwaite, n.2 above, pp.21–3.

81 Daly, n.53 above, p.25.

82 E.g. Marshall, n.1 above; C. Pollard (2000) 'Victims and the criminal justice system: a new vision', *Crim. LR,* p.5.

83 Braithwaite, n.2 above, p.105.

84 *Ibid.*, p.93.

85 For a recent example of this genre see Pollard, n.76 above.

86 E.g. Morris and Gelsthorpe, n.25 above.

87 JUSTICE, n.8 above, p.28.

88 *Ibid.*, p.40.

89 See p.145 above.

90 Tyler, T. (1990) *Why People Obey the Law* (New Haven)

91 Cf. however, the finding that in the early police-led conferences in Thames Valley the police facilitators were fairly dominant: R. Young and B. Goold (1999) 'Restorative police cautioning in Aylesbury: from degrading to reintegrative shaming ceremonies?', *Crim. LR,* pp.126, 131.

92 See Freeman, M.D.A. (ed.) (1995) *Alternative Dispute Resolution* (Aldershot).

93 See Ball, n.18 above, 221; JUSTICE, n.54 above, p.75.

CHAPTER 15

Thinking Critically about Restorative Justice

by Chris Cunneen

> All stories are haunted by the ghosts of stories they might have been.
>
> Salman Rushdie, *Shame*, Picador, London, 1984, p.116

Introduction

This chapter is presented as a sympathetic critique of restorative justice. It is both the critical story of the restorative justice discourse that *is*, as well as a contemplation of the restorative justice that might be. The restorative justice movement as a radical social movement needs to be continually and deeply reflexive about the nature of the theories used to ground restorative justice principles, as well as the way in which restorative justice practices are developing.

I do not believe there is anything inherent to restorative justice that will automatically prevent it from being used alongside repressive crime-control strategies. Indeed, there are already many examples of such a coalition of criminal justice strategies in place. However, what attracts me to restorative justice is its potential as a critique of existing systems and as a promise of alternative practices that are more just in responding to criminal offending. Much of this paper will concentrate on a critique of restorative justice, but underpinning this discussion is a view of the possibilities for a critical and reflexive restorative justice practice.

Critical perspectives on restorative justice have emerged from a number of avenues. For the purposes of this discussion, these arguments may be grouped as neo-marxist, postmodernist, feminist, postcolonial and liberal. These five perspectives are broad and provide a way of structuring the discussion within this chapter. Not surprisingly, there are often intersections and overlaps. These critiques cover various points relating to the role of the state and its agencies, concepts of globalization and community, relations of class, 'race', ethnicity and gender, and questions about the rule of law, legal principles and appropriate process. Fundamental to these critiques are questions of power and resistance and modes of punishment within neo-liberal regimes.

I will deal with what I consider to be the essential elements of the critique within these five perspectives, perhaps more determinedly from a perspective informed by postcolonial critiques because that has been a major concern of my recent writing (Cunneen, 1997, 2001a, 2001b, 2002a). I have centred these critiques on a number of issues: the state; globalization; community; gender; human rights and indigenous rights; and the rule of law. The chapter concludes with a discussion of evaluations of existing restorative justice practices and possible future directions.

The state

Some of the core critiques of restorative justice revolve around its relationship with the state. There is a concern that the claims of restorative justice embody both a profound naïvety about the nature of politics and a sanguine view of state power. As White (1994, p.187) argues, restorative justice accepts at face value the liberal democratic notion that the state is somehow neutral and above sectional interests, that it operates for the 'common good', and that it is an impartial and independent arbiter of conflicts.

A neo-marxist perspective would assert that there is not enough recognition by restorative

Source: Specially commissioned for this volume.

justice proponents of the move over the last two decades from a social state to a repressive state. The withdrawal of the state from responsibility in areas of health, education and welfare, and the shift towards privatization have all had profound effects on the role of the state in crime control. Similarly, the class-based impact of unemployment and marginalization, particularly among young people, poses very real problems for restorative justice practice – especially if that practice is built on a concept of individualized responsibility for crime and restoration. What the neo-marxist critique demands is that restorative justice respond seriously to these broader social and economic issues and that it be able to deal constructively with the various 'hidden injuries' of class, including alienation from school and work, homelessness, drug abuse and marginalization.

A further point of critique revolves around the failure to understand the complexity of the relationship between colonized peoples and colonial/postcolonial states. There is often an assumption in restorative justice that this relationship is not problematic; the state is seen as representative and legitimate. In regard to indigenous peoples in settler states, there is little acknowledgement that if a restorative programme is initiated and controlled by the state it may be viewed with suspicion. There is no reason to believe that a state-sponsored restorative justice programme will necessarily be seen as legitimate: it may well be viewed as another imposed form of control which undermines existing indigenous modes of governance. In this context, it is worth noting that restorative justice has been formulated in Australia and New Zealand in specifically defined conferencing programmes and is a state-controlled activity.

Policing

A major issue stemming from the relationship between restorative justice and the state has been the question of policing and criminalization. This problem relates to the role of police in restorative justice processes, as well as the broader issue of criminalization. In many jurisdictions the police exercise significant discretionary powers over restorative justice programmes. Police determine access to conferencing programmes, and play a key role in the operation of the conferencing process and the agreements that are reached there.

The centrality of the police to the process is especially problematic given concerns about the inappropriate exercise of police discretion, the dominance of police or other professionals over other conference participants and the lack of police accountability (White, 1994, Cunneen, 1997). The expanded police role in restorative justice programmes has led to procedural concerns over the significant extension of police powers at various stages of the decision-making process. In most jurisdictions the extended role of the police has not been accompanied by any greater accountability or control over police decision-making (Blagg, 1997).

Indigenous, 'racial' and ethnic minorities may have good reason to be sceptical that police can be viewed as independent arbiters in the process of restorative justice. When police utilize discretionary powers, there is the danger that minority youth will receive adverse or more punitive decisions – that they will be classified as 'unsuitable' for restorative justice. There is indeed some evidence in Australia that this discrimination occurs. My own research has shown that Aboriginal young people are *less* likely than non-Aboriginal youth to be referred by police to youth conferences and are more likely to be referred to court (Cunneen, 2001a, pp.132–43).

The role of police in restorative justice processes also raises questions about police legitimacy. The effectiveness of a police role in restorative justice programmes is tied to respect for police and their authority. It assumes that policing is consensual. The likelihood of whether a sense of legitimacy and respect for police is apparent will be determined by a range of factors including class and 'race', as well as the specific histories of the relationship between police and particular groups. Whether police authority is seen as legitimate or not will have direct consequences for the success or failure of restorative justice programmes.

Police respect and authority will also be affected by the use of discretion. Findlay (1993, p.32) has noted that, 'If police discretion becomes consistently perceived by the public as unworthy of respect rather than as ensuring it, then ... the legitimacy of police authority for the exercise of discretion will be undermined'. This relationship between respect, authority and the use of restorative justice has resonance in understanding how police are likely to be perceived by minority groups who have a history of poor relations with them. For minority groups, the symbolic role of police may be one of racism and harassment. Thus, the role of police in a restorative justice programme must confront the particular relationships with minority communities – a relationship structured through colonial and postcolonial processes.

There is also a concern that restorative justice processes need to be able to critique inappropriate and 'racist' policing and broader processes of criminalization effectively. Police, and more generally, the criminal have a determining role in actually constituting social groups as threats and in reproducing a society built on racialized boundaries. In Keith's (1993, p.193) terms, 'the process of criminalization itself now constitutes a significant racializing discourse'. If restorative justice lacks the ability to critique, for example, increases in police powers, public order interventions over minor offences or the discriminatory use of stop and searches, then it is nothing more than another regulatory device used in the service of power.

Punishment

Daly and Immarigeon (1998) note that discussion of restorative justice reaches into long-standing debates about the nature and purpose of punishment, and about the relationship between the citizen, state and community. They also question whether restorative justice is indeed contrary to retributivist or rehabilitation models of justice or whether it can combine elements of these approaches. In addition, it is also worth noting that restorative justice programmes have been introduced within a framework that places greater emphasis on individual responsibility, deterrence and incapacitation (Cunneen, 1997). In effect, there may be elements of restorative justice, retribution, just deserts, rehabilitation and incapacitation all operating within a particular jurisdiction at any one time.

Discussions of postmodern penality are useful in contextualizing the place of restorative justice in contemporary fields of punishment. Pratt (2000), for example, has discussed the resurfacing of premodern penal approaches such as the use of public shaming. He also notes the development of other phenomena that would seem out of place within a modern penal framework – including boot camps, curfews and the abandonment of proportionality (2000, pp.131–3). O'Malley (1999) has discussed the 'bewildering array' of developments in penal policy including policies based on discipline, punishment, enterprise, incapacitation, restitution and reintegration – policies which are mutually incoherent and contradictory. However, much of the discussion around a postmodern penality has centred on the movement of penal regimes towards the prediction of risk: the development of 'techniques for identifying, classifying and managing groups assorted by dangerousness' (Feeley and Simon, 1994, p.173).

The emphasis on actuarialism (the prediction of risk) and policies of incapacitation are not contradictory with the way restorative justice practices have developed; rather, they can be seen as complementary strategies put in place within single systems of justice. Indeed, risk assessment becomes a fundamental tactic in dividing populations between those who benefit from restorative justice practices and those who are channelled into more punitive processes of incapacitation such as 'three strikes' and mandatory imprisonment.

We can see these processes operating more clearly in the context of a greater *bifurcation* of existing justice systems. For example, in Australia, conferencing models have been introduced in a context where juvenile justice systems are increasingly responding to two categories of offenders: those defined as 'minor' and those who are seen as serious and/or repeat offenders. Minor offenders benefit from various diversionary programmes such as conferencing schemes. Serious and repeat offenders, on the other hand, are classified as ineligible for diversionary programmes and are dealt with more punitively through sentencing regimes that are more akin to adult models.

Some form of conferencing operates in all Australian jurisdictions, and, along with New Zealand, Australia is regularly held as an example of restorative justice programmes in action. During the late 1990s and early 2000, however, the Australian government was criticized by no less than four United Nations human rights monitoring bodies for possible breaches of a range of international human rights conventions. All criticisms were partly based on the operation of 'three strikes' mandatory sentencing legislation for juveniles in the Northern Territory and Western Australia, and in particular their effect on indigenous young people (Cunneen, 2002b). These same jurisdictions simultaneously had conferencing programmes operating.

There is as a result an important theoretical issue in how we conceptualize restorative justice within the complex of approaches being used to deal with young people. State-run restorative justice programmes need to be seen within the totality of policing and criminal justice strategies. These strategies increasingly involve retribution and incapacitation. O'Malley's (1999, pp.185–6) argument is that these different approaches are united under the competing strands of neo-conservatism and neo-liberalism of the New Right. Neo-conservatism is socially authoritarian and rests on punitive disciplinary approaches. In contrast, neo-liberalism privileges the market and individualism for achieving social order and it emphasizes managerialism in its approach to criminal justice policy. The outcome is a range of inconsistencies in punishment from programmes that hark back to a nostalgic past (emphasizing either discipline or 'shaming') while others stress individual responsibility (just deserts and incapacitation).

Reparations for state harm

Another avenue that needs to be considered when discussing the state is the potential role of restorative justice in dealing with matters of state crime and the gross violation of human rights. There is only the space in this chapter to refer a growing literature that considers the importance of reparations for historical injustices and the potential links between reparations and restorative justice.[1] Internationally, there has been growing acceptance that governments should acknowledge and make reparations to the victims of human rights abuses, as well as a widespread acceptance of the principle of reparations. The notion of reparations has significant potential overlap with the goals of restorative justice.

Globalization

Globalization has the effect of imparting *preferred* models of capitalist development, modernization and urbanization (Findlay, 1999). In this context, globalization increasingly demands particular forms of capital accumulation, as well as associated social and legal relations both within and between nation states. At first glance this may seem irrelevant to the localized claims of restorative justice.

Nonetheless, discussions around globalization should alert us to the need to situate the growing interest in restorative justice within the shifting boundaries of relations within and between the First and Third World. This is particularly the case when much restorative justice talk presents itself as an alternative narrative on justice, as something outside the justice paradigms of retribution, deterrence and rehabilitation, and as a form of resolving disputes which is 'non-Western'. Little attention has been paid to whether restorative justice can be seen as much as a globalizing force as traditional western legal forms. The potential to overrun local custom and law is as real with restorative justice as it is with other models built on retributivism or rehabilitation (Cunneen, 2002a). The risk is that restricted and particularized notions of restorative justice will become part of a globalizing tendency that restricts local justice mechanisms in areas where there is a demand to 'modernize' (Findlay, 1999; Zellerer and Cunneen, 2001, p.251).

Community

A core concept underpinning restorative justice has been the concept of 'community'. 'Community', however, is not a natural set of relations between individuals nor a natural social process lying at the foundation of civil society. Communities are always constructed on the broad terrain of history and politics. Radical critiques provide a multi-layered understanding of the problematic relationship between community and state. Basic to this understanding is a concern that the notion of community presents a harmonious view of social and political relations and masks conflict, power, difference, inequality and potentially exploitative social and economic relations.

The postmodernist critique of restorative justice has centred on the implicit consensual notions of civil society and community. Pavlich (2001, p.3) argues that 'community' is also fundamentally about *exclusion*: 'The promise of community's free and uncoerced collective association is offset by a tendency to shore up limits, fortify a given identity, and rely on exclusion to secure self-preservation'. Such a vision of community is only a short step away from the 'gated' community of the wealthy excluding the poor; the community of interest generated by power and prestige. 'Community' can easily spill over into class, cultural and racial purity, xenophobia and racism. Indeed, globalizing processes can add to 'spatial segregation, separation and exclusion' (Bauman, 1998, p.3). The problem here is that restorative justice can become what it opposes: a practice which closes, limits and excludes individuals, rather than reintegrating them.

Another point of departure in radical critique is to question the claim that restorative justice provides an avenue for community to take back from the state the ownership of the problem of crime. From feminist perspectives the problem has been that the state has never adequately criminalized crimes of violence against women. To the extent that we can discuss 'community' in this context we may well find that 'community' reflects the patriarchal relations which provide for the acceptance of violence against women. Rather than providing a barrier and safeguard against offending, it may provide social and cultural legitimation for violence.

From a postcolonial perspective, colonial policies were directly responsible for constructing community in the interests of the colonizers. For example, many indigenous communities arose directly as a result of colonial government policies of forced relocations. From another perspective, 'racial' and minority ethnic communities within First World metropoles are specifically created under conditions determined by neo- and post-colonial relations. History and contemporary politics have shaped these communities. What then does 'community' mean for minority people in these situations and how does it influence relations with the police, the criminal justice system and the state more generally? Importantly, where does restorative justice fit within these relations and processes?

Neo-marxist and governmentality critiques of neo-liberalism also identify the current tendencies towards the responsibilization of individuals, families and communities and the preference towards 'governing at a distance'. This critique also has implications for our understanding of the popularity of 'community' within contemporary crime control strategies.

According to O'Malley (1996), state programmes and policies that allow 'government at a distance' have been attractive and have included 'community-based' indigenous processes. He discusses specifically the involvement of indigenous forms of control where they are seen as complementary to the broader aims of government. The attempt is usually made to appropriate certain aspects of indigenous forms of governance and to ignore others. I will return to this point below.

Gender

Feminist critiques of restorative justice emphasize the lack of understanding of gendered power relations and nature of crimes against women. Feminist arguments have been particularly important in relation to the problems of applying restorative justice practices to domestic violence. The starting-point in this critique is that domestic violence is a particular type of crime and that the fundamental priority of any type of intervention must be to ensure the physical protection for victims (usually women and children) (Stubbs, 1997, 2002).

An important part of the question of applying restorative justice practices to domestic violence is that the nature of domestic violence is specific. The violence is not a discrete act between two individuals who are unknown to each other. Rather, the violence may be part of a number of gendered strategies of control including various forms of behavioural and coercive tactics. It may be part of a patterned cycle of behaviour which includes contrition. Furthermore, there are social and cultural dimensions that give meaning and authorization to the violence and constrain women's options in response (Stubbs, 2002, p.45).

These complexities include women's relationship with their children and the fact that women may seek assistance from the criminal justice system, including police, after a long process of violence. The issue of how gendered power imbalances can be addressed in restorative justice practices is of fundamental concern to feminists. We cannot assume that actors marshalled together for a restorative justice conference or circle will be capable of reflecting on the necessary support for victims who are in a structurally disadvantaged position. Indeed, the basic premise of restorative justice, that the harm between victim and offender is to be repaired, must be questioned as a outcome sought by women seeking intervention, support and protection against violence (Stubbs, 2002, p.51).

It is also fundamental to recognize the diversity of different experiences of women which are differentiated along various lines including class and 'race'/ethnicity. For example, it is important to remember that colonial processes were profoundly gendered in their design and have resulted in 'deep colonising effects' (Rose, 1996). One result of these multi-dimensional effects has been the valorization of men's knowledge over women's. Western legal traditions continue to have an impact on gender relations in indigenous societies and may treat men's knowledge as universal and women's knowledge as particular and sectional; women's knowledge may be excluded because it is defined as 'partial' .

In terms of restorative justice, such changes have had and continue to have an impact in the area of criminal law and domestic violence. The long-term gendered effect of colonization has not been well understood and there is often inadequate attention paid to the voices of indigenous women (Zellerer and Cunneen, 2001). The realignment of gender interests influences the ability of indigenous and minority women to develop and utilize restorative justice mechanisms. It seems that there is still little understanding of the complexity of the way gendered patterns of knowledge and culture have shifted with the external interference of colonial political and legal power. There is no a *à priori* reason to assume that restorative justice practices will privilege or indeed give a voice to minority women.

Other issues of importance include how restorative justice practices will respond to different groups of women who experience differing levels of violence. In Australia, for example, the homicide rate for indigenous women is ten times that of other women, and other evidence suggests considerably higher rates of domestic violence. Other minority women also have variable rates: for example, Filipino women's homicide rate is five times the general rate for other women in Australia (Cunneen and Stubbs, 2002). These differences reflect directly the gendered outcomes of colonial and postcolonial conditions.

Human rights and indigenous rights

In discussing 'race', ethnicity and restorative justice, it is important to recognize that proponents of restorative justice have drawn on justice processes among colonized peoples, particularly indigenous peoples in Australia, New Zealand, Canada and the United States. Indeed, restorative justice often lays claim to a pre-modern indigenous authenticity as part of its search for a 'myth of origin' (Daly, 2000). Often the claims that link restorative justice practices to indigenous peoples are trivializing and patronizing. They disavow the complex effects of colonial policies which have, at various times, sought to exterminate, assimilate, 'civilize', and Christianize Aboriginal peoples through warfare, the establishment of reservations, the denial of basic citizenship rights, the forced removal of children and their forced education in residential schools, the banning of cultural and spiritual practices, and the imposition of an alien criminal justice system. They also disavow the complexity and variations in indigenous dispute-resolution mechanisms (Zellerer and Cunneen, 2001, pp.246–7).

A central component of the indigenous critique of restorative justice has been that indigenous rights have been ignored, in particular the right to self-determination. The best place to begin to understand the emerging human rights norms which reflect the aspirations of indigenous peoples is in the United Nations draft *Declaration on the Rights of Indigenous Peoples.* This declaration contains a number of basic principles, including self-determination, which have a direct impact on how restorative justice programmes that are respectful of indigenous rights might develop.

The draft declaration affirms 'the right of Indigenous people to control matters affecting them'. Article 3 describes the right of self-determination as involving the free choice of political status and the freedom to pursue economic, social and cultural development. Article 4 provides that 'Indigenous peoples have the right to maintain and strengthen their distinct political, economic, social and cultural characteristics, *as well as their legal systems*' (emphasis added). Article 31 sets out the extent of governing powers of indigenous peoples, which include the right to autonomy, or self-government in matters relating to their internal and local affairs. Taken together, it is clear that the declaration provides the basis for indigenous people to maintain cultural integrity and exercise jurisdiction over various justice matters, if they so choose (Coulter, 1995).

While indigenous people have been highly critical of the impact of colonial and neo-colonial criminal justice systems on indigenous communities (Cunneen, 2001a), a question rarely asked is whether the vision of justice for restorative advocates and indigenous peoples is the same. There is rarely any discussion of the similarities and differences between restorative and indigenous justice. There is often either an explicit or implicit assumption that they are one and the same, falling under the umbrella concept of restorative justice (Zellerer and Cunneen, 2001, p.248). Often a brief reference is made to the fact that some restorative initiatives, such as family group conferencing in New Zealand and circle sentencing in Canada, were derived from indigenous practices of resolving conflict. Little critical discussion about the nature of the contemporary relationship between the process and indigenous political aspirations for self-determination, however, typically follows such observations (Blagg, 1997; Cunneen, 1997; Tauri, 1998).

There are assumptions that underpin the restorative justice project which need to be made explicit. In particular, there is a lack of recognition of cultural difference and as a result these differences may not be adequately dealt with within restorative justice processes. Firstly, there is an assumption that indigenous and restorative justice processes for resolving conflicts are homologous. This is not necessarily true and may reflect a failure to understand the complexity in indigenous dispute resolution. Many restorative approaches focus on bringing the parties together to confront and resolve the problem through the use of a neutral mediator. There are a variety of sanctions, however, used by indigenous peoples – for instance, temporary or permanent exile, withdrawal from and separation within the community, and restitution by kin. Many of the sanctions are based on *avoidance* – rather than confrontation between offender and victim (Blagg, 1997; Cunneen, 1997).

While there are processes and sanctions that a restorative model uses that may be deemed culturally inappropriate by indigenous peoples, conversely, there may be aspects of indigenous justice that are not adopted by restorative justice. There is a tendency to romanticize indigenous dispute resolution and avoid any mention of the use of physical punishments or processes that elaborately separate the offender from the victim through mechanisms of social avoidance or banishment (Zellerer and Cunneen, 2001, p.250).

A further assumption is that indigenous peoples will experience the restorative process in a similar way to non-indigenous peoples. There is ample evidence of the difficulties and disadvantages indigenous people face in the formal legal process (Cunneen, 1997). These derive partly from cultural and communicative (verbal and non-verbal) differences, and the difficulties faced in the formal legal system may also be experienced in restorative programmes – particularly where the dominant players in the process are traditional figures of non-indigenous authority (such as police, welfare, juvenile justice, and so on).

The power imbalance in processes of restorative justice may also reflect the wider power imbalances embedded in neo- and post-colonial states. We cannot assume that the discriminatory treatment of indigenous and other 'racial' and minority ethnic groups by the criminal justice system will disappear with the development of restorative justice practices, particularly if state agencies continue to play a central role in the administration of these processes. Indeed, a key argument against the way restorative justice programmes have been introduced is that there has been a lack of negotiation and consultation with indigenous and minority communities; that specific procedural processes have been imposed which do not effectively alter power relations; that there remains an inappropriate use of police; and a fear that existing discriminatory police practices may be entrenched.

Where consultation with indigenous communities has occurred, there has been insufficient regard paid to indigenous views (Kelly and Oxley, 1999). As a result, the model of conferencing (which has a legislative foundation in most states of Australia and compels a particular form to the interaction between offender and victim) has been imposed on indigenous communities without consideration of indigenous cultural values, and without consideration of how communities might wish to develop their own approaches to the issue (Blagg, 1997; Cunneen, 1997; National Inquiry into the Separation of Aboriginal and Torres Strait Islander Children from Their Families, 1997). There is no statutory obligation to consider cultural issues. There are no legal provisions for indigenous organizations and communities to make decisions about whether their children would be best served by attending a conference, or indeed any other form of justice intervention. In other words, the right of indigenous self-determination is ignored.

It was noted above that one result of restorative justice has been a greater bifurcation of existing responses in juvenile justice. There is substantial evidence in Australia that indigenous young people are discriminated against by police in their decisions to utilize diversionary options (Luke and Cunneen, 1995). The end result is that bifurcation tends to split along increasingly racialized boundaries, with youth from minority groups receiving more punitive outcomes. The Australian example suggests that the entrenchment of unequal and racialized outcomes in the criminal justice system may in fact be exacerbated by restorative justice programmes (Cunneen, 2001a, pp.132–43).

Liberal critique, rule of law and legal process

A consistent voice of disquiet over aspects of the operation of restorative justice programmes has come from youth activists and lawyers. Criticisms tend to revolve around what might be broadly characterized as liberal arguments about the rule of law. They include concerns over abuse of due process; absence of procedural rights and protections; excessive, disproportionate or inconsistent outcomes and so forth (see for example Warner, 1994, pp.142–6). These concerns include the potential undermining of young people's rights at the investigatory, adjudicatory and sentencing stages of the criminal justice system.

At the investigatory stage the lack of independent legal advice, pressures to admit an offence to obtain the benefit of a diversionary alternative to court and the avoidance of a criminal record, and the lack of testing of the legality of police searches, questioning and evidence-gathering may all be compromised. Furthermore, the pressure to admit an offence means that issues relating to *mens rea* and legal defences are not considered by the court.

Related to these points is the concern that the outcome from a restorative justice programme may be more punitive than might be expected if the normal sentencing principles of consistency, proportionality and frugality were applied. There is also potential to ignore the basic human rights principles relating to children and young people: the primacy of the best interests of the child and rehabilitation when making sentencing and other decisions affecting children and young people.

At a more theoretical level there has been a question of whether the imbalance of power between participants in restorative justice programmes can be effectively neutralized. This issue was raised above in terms of gender and 'race'/ethnicity, however, there are several other possible axes of power imbalances including age, professional or lay status, and offender/victim status. Can a genuine consensus can be achieved in the face of such an imbalance? Part of this issue can be dealt with as an empirical question in terms of whether victims and offenders feel 'satisfied' with the process (I discuss this further below).

Another concern is that the establishment of conferencing and other restorative justice procedures introduces the potential for net-widening. In particular, young people may become subject to conferencing procedures for behaviour that would have previously been regarded as too trivial to warrant official intervention (Polk, 1994, pp.133–5). Whether this emerges as a problem in particular jurisdictions will to some extent depend on the specific legislative and policy framework within which the restorative justice procedures operate. For example, legislative criteria determining use, and checks and balances over referral and other official decision-making may act to minimize the potential problem. In New South Wales the Young Offenders Act 1997 provides the legislative framework for conferencing. The Act sets out a hierarchy of interventions for dealing with juveniles, starting from police warnings to police cautions, to youth justice conferences. Legislative criteria including offence type and seriousness, and prior offending determine eligibility to various stages of intervention. However, it should be noted that even in jurisdictions where restorative justice programmes have a legislative base these issues may not be addressed adequately.[2]

The Australian Law Reform Commission (1997) has recommended that national standards for juvenile justice should provide best-practice guidelines for family group conferencing. Standards should include the following:

- The desirability of diversionary schemes being administered by someone independent of law-enforcement bodies, such as a judicial officer, youth worker or community-based lawyer.
- The need to monitor penalties agreed to in conferences to ensure that they are not significantly more punitive than those a court would impose as appropriate to the offence.
- The need to ensure that young people do not get a criminal record as a result of participating in conferencing.
- The need to monitor conferencing proceedings to ensure that they do not operate in a manner that is oppressive or intimidating to the young person.
- The child's access to legal advice prior to agreeing to participate in a conference.
- Whether it is preferable for schemes to have a legislative basis so that the process is more accountable and less *ad hoc*.
- The need to monitor the overall effect of conferencing schemes to ensure they do not draw greater numbers of young people into the criminal justice system or escalate children's degree of involvement with the system.

(Australian Law Reform Commission, 1997, p.482)

Finally, it is recognized that conferencing is both a resource- and labour-intensive option, and it may be an inefficient use of resources, particularly if it is applied to minor offenders who are unlikely to reoffend (Coumarelos and Weatherburn, 1995). One way of answering this question is through measures of effectiveness. Do restorative justice programmes decrease the likelihood of reoffending compared to other types of interventions?

Pragmatism and evidence-based approaches

There have been numerous evaluations of restorative justice programmes in New Zealand, Australia, the United Kingdom, Europe and North America. A summary of the research can be found in Strang (2001) and Luke and Lind (2002). It is not the purpose of this chapter to review this literature. However, the evaluations do caste some light on the questions of legal process and the rule of law.

The Re-Integrative Shaming Experiments (RISE) evaluation in Canberra found that offenders reported greater procedural justice (defined as being treated fairly and with respect) in conferences than in court; offenders reported higher levels of restorative justice (defined as the opportunity to repair the harm they had caused) in conferences than in court; and offenders' respect for the police and law was higher in conferences than court. Victims' sense of restorative justice was also higher for those who went to conferences rather than to court (Daley and Hayes, 2001, p.5). South Australian research found that conferences received 'high marks' by police, coordinators, victims and offenders on measures of procedural justice, including being treated fairly and with respect, and having a voice in the process. However, there appeared to be limits on offenders' interests to repair the harm and on victims' capacities to see offenders in a positive light (Daley and Hayes, 2001, p.5).

Evaluations have given mixed results in terms of the effect of restorative justice on recidivism, although on balance evaluations tend to show either no difference or one favourably inclined towards restorative justice programmes. Luke and Lind (2002, pp.2–3) have summarized the research as follows. In Victoria (Australia) there was no significant difference in reoffending when compared to a matched probation group. In South Australia and New Zealand both evaluations showed that lower rates of recidivism were found when the young person showed remorse and agreed with the conference outcome. The RISE evaluation in Canberra found a range of results for different types of offenders – very little difference for young property offenders, a 6 per cent increase in recidivism for drink-driving adults and a 38 per cent decrease for young violent offenders. Luke and Lind's (2002) research in New South Wales found that the young people appearing before youth justice conferences for property and violent crime had a lower reoffending rate than similar young people appearing before the courts. The difference was between 24 and 28 per cent.

In North America results have been mixed, although there are more positive results with violent offenders. Meta-analyses in both Canada and the USA support some reduction in recidivism for restorative-justice participants compared to those appearing in conventional courts. European studies tend to a consensus that that offending rates are no worse for restorative justice compared to court and there is some evidence of lower re-offending rates for restorative justice participants (Luke and Lind, 2002).

The evaluation literature casts light on the question of whether 'restorative justice works'. However, the results of this literature, which are generally positive, should not be isolated from broader issues of rights, power and equity. For example, restorative justice programmes might prove positive from a technocratic view, but still fail to ensure equitable or just outcomes for particular groups of people. Conversely, we might support some restorative justice programmes from a human rights perspective (for example, because they comply with the Convention on the Rights of the Child), although in terms of measurable outcomes such as recidivism they rate much the same as traditional court-based forms of intervention.

Conclusion

This chapter has sought to outline some of the key issues that have emerged in critiques of restorative justice. Finding answers to these criticisms is an important part of developing restorative justice practice and theory in a way that is sensitive to issues of social justice and political transformation. It is important to recognize that many progressive political activists, in the youth justice field and among minority and indigenous-rights groups, see conferencing and other forms of restorative justice as a preferable policy alternative to more punitive criminal justice approaches. The issue is whether restorative justice can actually live up to their expectations.

Many of the problems that have been identified can be summarized in a few questions. Firstly, how do people experience the restorative justice process? Subjectivity and identity go to the heart of restorative justice. There are often assumptions made that all individuals will experience the restorative justice process in a certain way irrespective of their gender, class, 'race', ethnicity, or age. Restorative justice narratives have tended to construct subjectivity as a unified field of either offenders or victims, with little attention paid to the profound difficulties that underpin these classifications.

'Victim' and 'offender' are often understood as uncomplicated and homogenous categories of self. There are no ontological complexities and the assumption is that we all subjectively experience these categories in identical or, at least, similar ways. Related to this point are the difficulties associated with 'shaming' processes. Can we be so sure whether any shaming that might take place is either disintegrative or reintegrative?

Secondly, is the vision for reform or change the same between restorative justice proponents and other social movements? For example, there are issues as to whether feminist interests in the protection of women, or indigenous interests in promoting self-determination, or anti-'racist' organizations in reforming the criminal justice system or neo-marxist interests in social justice coalesce with restorative justice aims. The compatibility of these interests is not always as self-evident as some restorative justice discourses would appear to indicate. Perhaps part of the problem is the lack of clear definitions or theories of justice underpinning much of the restorative justice literature.

Closely related to the second question is whether the difficulties and disadvantages particular groups face in the formal legal process are resolved by the restorative justice process. Will the racism, sexism and class-based interests and biases of the criminal justice system be removed, modified or left untouched by restorative justice? Indeed, will greater bifurcation of justice systems serve to compound existing oppressions?

Harry Blagg (1998) has discussed the need to open up and imagine new pathways and meeting places between indigenous people and the institutions of the colonizer. He refers to this as the 'liminal spaces' where dialogue can be generated, where hybridity and cultural difference can be accepted. There are lessons here about the need for genuine dialogue that certainly go beyond indigenous people to include other possibilities of justice for 'racial' and minority ethnic groups, young people and women. To this extent restorative justice might pose an unrealized promise that still has considerable opportunity for development. That development, however, depends on the establishment of a critical reflexivity about the relationship of restorative justice to other forms of power.

Notes

1. See Cunneen (2001b) and the Special Issue of the *Third World Legal Studies Journal*, 2000/2001 edition.
2. See Strang (2001) for an overview of the legislation in Australia.

References

Australian Law Reform Commission (1997) *Seen and Heard: Priority for Young People in the Legal Process*, Canberra, Australian Government Printing Service.

Bauman, Z. (1998) *Globalization. The Human Consequences*, New York, Columbia University Press.

Blagg, H. (1997) 'A just measure of shame', *British Journal of Criminology*, vol.37, no.4.

Blagg, H. (1998) 'Restorative visions and restorative justice practices: conferencing, ceremony and reconciliation in Australia', *Current Issues in Criminal Justice*, vol.10, no.1, July.

Blagg, H. (2002) 'Aboriginal youth and restorative justice: critical notes from the frontier', in Morris, A. and Maxwell, G. (eds) *Restorative Justice for Juveniles*, Portland, Hart Publishing.

Coulter, R. (1995) 'The Draft UN Declaration on the Rights of Indigenous Peoples: What is it? What does it mean?', *Netherlands Quarterly of Human Rights*, vol.13, no.2.

Coumarelos, C. and Weatherburn, D. (1995) 'Targeting intervention strategies to reduce juvenile recidivism', *Australian & New Zealand Journal of Criminology*, vol.28, no.1, pp.54–72.

Cunneen, C. (1997) 'Community conferencing and the fiction of Indigenous control', *Australia and New Zealand Journal of Criminology*, vol.30, no.3, pp.292–311.

Cunneen, C. (2001a) *Conflict, Politics and Crime*, Sydney, Allen and Unwin.

Cunneen, C. (2001b) 'Reparations and restorative justice: responding to the gross violation of human rights', in Strang, H. and Braithwaite, J. (eds) *Restorative Justice and Civil Society*, Cambridge, Cambridge University Press.

Cunneen, C. (2002a) 'Restorative justice and the politics of decolonisation', in Weitekamp, E. and Kerner, H.-J. (eds) *Restorative Justice: Theoretical Foundations*, Uffculme, Willan Publishing.

Cunneen, C. (2002b) 'Mandatory sentencing and human rights', *Current Issues in Criminal Justice*, vol.13, no.3, pp.322–7.

Cunneen, C. and Stubbs, J. (2002) 'Migration, political economy and violence against women: the post immigration experiences of Filipino women in Australia', in Freilich, J.D., Newman, G., Shoham, S.G. and Addad, M. (eds) *Migration, Culture, Conflict and Crime*, Aldershot, Ashgate.

Daly, K. (2000) 'Restorative justice: the real story', paper presented to the Scottish Criminology Conference, Edinburgh, 21–22 September.

Daly, K. and Hayes, H. (2001) 'Restorative justice and conferencing in Australia', *Trends and Issues*, no.186, Canberra, Australian Institute of Criminology.

Daly, K. and Immarigeon, R. (1998) 'The past, present and future of restorative justice: some critical reflections', *Contemporary Justice Review*, vol.1, no.1, pp.21–45.

Feeley, M. and Simon, J. (1994) 'Actuarial justice: the emerging new criminal law', in Nelken, D. (ed.) *The Futures of Criminology*, London, Sage.

Findlay, M. (1993) 'Police, authority, respect and shaming', *Current Issues in Criminal Justice*, vol.5, no.1, pp.29–41.

Findlay, M. (1999) *The Globalisation of Crime. Understanding Transitional Relationships in Context*, Cambridge, Cambridge University Press.

Keith, M. (1993) 'From punishment to discipline', in Cross, M. and Keith, M. (eds) *Racism, the City and the State*, London, Routledge.

Kelly, L. and Oxley, E. (1999) 'A dingo in sheep's clothing?', *Indigenous Law Bulletin*, vol.4, no.18.

Luke, G. and Cunneen, C. (1995) *Aboriginal Over-Representation and Discretionary Decisions in the NSW Juvenile Justice System*, Sydney, Juvenile Justice Advisory Council of NSW.

Luke, G. and Lind, B. (2002) 'Reducing juvenile crime: conferencing versus court', *Crime and Justice Bulletin*, no.69, Sydney, New South Wales Bureau of Crime Statistics and Research.

National Inquiry into the Separation of Aboriginal and Torres Strait Islander Children from Their Families (1997) *Bringing Them Home*, Canberra, Australian Government Printing Service.

O'Malley, P. (1996) 'Indigenous governance', *Economy and Society*, vol.25, no.3, August, pp.310–26.

O'Malley, P. (1999) 'Volatile and contradictory punishments', *Theoretical Criminology*, vol.3, no.2, May, pp.175–96.

Pavlich, G. (2001) 'The force of community', in Strang, H. and Braithwaite, J. (eds) *Restorative Justice and Civil Society*, Cambridge, Cambridge University Press.

Polk, K. (1994) 'Family conferencing: theoretical and evaluative concerns', in Alder, C. and Wundersitz, J. (eds) *Family Conferencing and Juvenile Justice: The Way Forward or Misplaced Optimism?*, Canberra, Australian Institute of Criminology.

Pratt, J. (2000) 'The return of the Wheelbarrow Men', *British Journal of Criminology*, vol.40, pp.127–45.

Rose, D. Bird (1996) 'Land rights and deep colonising: the erasure of women', *Aboriginal Law Bulletin*, vol.3, no.85, pp.6–14.

Strang, H. (2001) *Restorative Justice Programmes in Australia*, A Report to the Criminology Research Council, Canberra, Australian Institute of Criminology.

Stubbs, J. (1997) 'Shame, defiance and violence against women: a critical analysis of "communitarian" conferencing', in Bessant, J. and Cook, S. (eds) *Violence Against Women: An Australian Perspective*, Thousand Oaks, CA, Sage.

Stubbs, J. (2002) 'Domestic violence and women's safety: feminist challenges to restorative justice', in Strang, H. and Braithwaite, J. (eds) *Restorative Justice and Family Violence*, Cambridge, Cambridge University Press.

Tuari, J. (1998) 'Family group conferencing: a case study of the indigenisation of New Zealand's justice system', *Current Issues in Criminal Justice*, vol.10, no.2, pp.168–82.

Warner, K. (1994) 'Family group conferences and the rights of offenders', in Alder, C. and Wundersitz, J. (eds) *op. cit.*

White, R. (1994) 'Shaming and reintegrative strategies: individuals, state power and social interests', in Alder, C. and Wundersitz, J. (eds) *op. cit.*

Zellerer, E. and Cunneen, C. (2001) 'Restorative justice, indigenous justice and human rights', in Bazemore, G. and Schiff, M. (eds) *Restorative Community Justice: Repairing Harm and Transforming Communities*, Cincinnati, Anderson Press.

CHAPTER 16

Restorative Justice: the Real Story

by Kathleen Daly

Introduction

Much has been written in recent years that damns and sings the praises of restorative justice. In contrast to the voluminous critical and advocacy literatures, there is a thin empirical record of what is happening on the ground.[1] My aim in this article is to present the 'real story' of restorative justice, one that reflects what has been learned from research on youth justice conferencing[2] in Australia and New Zealand. I am being mostly, although not entirely, ironic in proposing to tell the real story of restorative justice. There are many stories and no real one. I shall recount what I have learned on my journey in the field, which began in the early 1990s (Braithwaite and Daly, 1994) and intensified in 1995 when I moved to Australia to work with restorative justice researchers at the Australian National University and to initiate my own program of research.

It has taken me some time to make sense of the idea of restorative justice. Initially, my questions centred on what was happening in the youth justice conference process. What were victims, offenders and their supporters saying to each other? How did they relate to one another? What did the professionals (the co-ordinators and police) think was going on? Did the critiques of conferencing, especially from feminist and indigenous perspectives, have merit? I began to observe conferences in 1995; since then, I have observed close to 60 of them; and as part of a major project on conferencing in South Australia, members of my research group and I observed 89 youth justice conferences and interviewed over 170 young people (offenders) and victims associated with them, in 1998 and again, in 1999 (Daly *et al.*, 1998; Daly, 2001b).

The more I observed conference processes and listened to those involved in them, attended sessions on restorative justice in professional meetings and read about restorative justice, the more perplexed I became. I discovered that there was a substantial gap between what I was learning from my research in the field and what the advocates and critics were saying about restorative justice. This moves me to tell the real story, and I do so by analysing four myths that feature in advocates' stories and claims:

(1) Restorative justice is the opposite of retributive justice.

(2) Restorative justice uses indigenous justice practices and was the dominant form of pre-modern justice.

(3) Restorative justice is a 'care' (or feminine) response to crime in comparison to a 'justice' (or masculine) response.

(4) Restorative justice can be expected to produce major changes in people.

Although I focus on advocates' claims, there can be as much distortion by the critics, as well. Moreover, there are debates among the advocates on the meaning and practice of restorative justice; thus, my characterization of the advocacy position is meant to show its general emphasis, not to suggest uniformity.

I use the concept of myth in two ways. First, myth can be understood simply as a partial truth, a distorted characterization that requires correction by historical or contemporary evidence. Second, myth can be understood as a special form of narrative. Following Engel (1993, pp.790–2), myth 'refers not to fantasy or fiction but to a "true story" ... which is sacred, exemplary, significant.' 'The "truth" of myth differs from the

Source: *Punishment and Society* (2002) vol.4, no.1, pp.55–79.

"truth" of historical or scientific accounts.' Engel suggests that myths 'differ from other forms of storytelling' in that they 'deal with origins, with birth, with beginnings ... with how something ... began to *be*'. He discovers in his analysis of the 'origin stories' of parents of children with disabilities that they 'perceive the world in terms of a set of oppositions that originate in the diagnosis of their child' (1993, p.821). A recurring origin story is that the professional (a doctor) is wrong about the initial diagnosis, and 'the parent's insights have ultimately triumphed over those of the professional' (1993, p.821). As such, when parents retell their stories, 'the triumphant ending will be achieved again'. 'The very act of retelling is a way to ensure that ... values and outcomes in the myth will triumph over pain, opposition, and disorder.' Engel says that this sense of triumph reveals the 'affirmative, creative power of myth', where myth 'abolishes time' and 'the work of myth [transcends adversity]' (1993, pp.823–4).

When I began this article, I used the concept of myth as partial truth, a foil against which I could write a more authoritative story. But in analysing the myths, I began to see them in a different light, in Engel's terms, as origin stories that 'encode a set of oppositions' (1993, p.822). While I shall spend more analytical time telling the real story of restorative justice, using myth as partial truth, I also offer a sympathetic reading of advocates' true story of restorative justice by viewing myth as a creative device to transcend adversity. I end by reflecting on whether the political future of restorative justice is better secured by telling the real story or the mythical true story.

The problem of definition

Restorative justice is not easily defined because it encompasses a variety of practices at different stages of the criminal process, including *diversion* from court prosecution, actions taken *in parallel* with court decisions and meetings between victims and offenders *at any stage* of the criminal process (for example, arrest, pre-sentencing and prison release). For virtually all legal contexts involving individual criminal matters, restorative justice processes have only been applied to those offenders who have *admitted* to an offence; as such, it deals with the penalty phase of the criminal process for admitted offenders, not the fact-finding phase. Restorative justice is used not only in adult and juvenile criminal matters, but also in a range of civil matters, including family welfare and child protection, and disputes in schools and workplace settings. Increasingly, one finds the term associated with the resolution of broader political conflicts such as the reconstruction of post-apartheid South Africa (South African Truth and Reconciliation Commission, 1998: Christodoulidis, 2000 for more critical appraisal), post-genocide Rwanda (Drumbl, 2000) and post-sectarian Northern Ireland (Dignan, 2000, pp.12–13).

Given the extraordinarily diverse meanings of the term and the contexts in which it has been applied, it is important for analytical purposes to bound the term to a particular context and set of practices. In this article, I discuss its use in the response to individual crime (as compared to broader political conflict); and in reviewing what is known about restorative justice practices, I focus on studies of youth justice conferencing in Australia and New Zealand, giving particular emphasis to my research in South Australia. Even with a narrowed focus on responses to individual crime, there remain problems of definition. One reason is that because *the idea* of restorative justice has proved enormously popular with governments, the term is now applied after the fact to programmes and policies that have been in place for some time, or it is used to describe reputedly new policing and correctional policies (e.g. La Prairie, 1999 for Canada; Crawford, 2001 for England and Wales). Until careful empirical work is carried out, we cannot be certain what is going on or the degree to which any of these newer or repackaged practices could be considered 'restorative'.

There is great concern among restorative justice advocates to distinguish practices that are near and far from the restorative ideal, and there is debate over how to draw the line on a continuum of practices. One definition, proposed by Marshall, is that restorative justice is 'a process whereby all the parties with a stake in a particular offence come together to resolve collectively how to deal with the aftermath of the offence and its implications for the future'

(1996, p.37). This definition, which McCold (2000, p.358) associates with the 'Purist' model of restorative justice, has been criticized by other restorative justice advocates who say that the definition is too narrow because it includes only face-to-face meetings, it emphasizes process over the primary goal of repairing a harm and actions to repair the harm may need to include coercive responses (Walgrave, 2000, p.418). These latter advocates call for a 'Maximalist' model, where restorative justice is defined as 'every action that is primarily oriented towards doing justice by repairing the harm that has been caused by crime' (Bazemore and Walgrave, 1999, p.48). In this debate, advocates are considering the uses of restorative justice in youth justice cases only; and yet we continue to see debate and uncertainty over the optimal size of the restorative justice 'tent' and which practices should be included in it.

McCold (2000, p.401) constructed a Venn Diagram to distinguish practices that he considers to be fully, mostly or only partly restorative. He suggests that fully restorative practices occur at the intersection of the three circles of 'victim reparation', 'offender responsibility' and 'communities of care reconciliation'. At that intersection are practices such as peace circles, sentencing circles and conferences of various types. Outside the intersection are practices he defines as mostly restorative (e.g. truth and reconciliation commissions, victim–offender mediation) or only partly restorative (reparation boards, youth aid panels, victim reparation). The three circles relate to the three major 'stakeholders' in the aftermath of a crime: victims, offenders and 'communities' (which include victims' and offenders' family members and friends, affected neighbourhoods and the broader society). Using McCold's diagram, the research reviewed here are of practices associated with a 'fully restorative' model, although as McCold points out (and I concur), this is no guarantee that actual practices are 'restorative'.

A selected review of the many lists of 'core elements' of restorative justice (e.g. Zehr, 1995, pp.211–12; Nova Scotia Department of Justice, 1998, pp.1–2; Dignan, 2000, pp.4–7; McCold, 2000, pp.364–72, pp.399–406, to name a few) shows these common elements: an emphasis on the role and experience of victims in the criminal process; involvement of all the relevant parties (including the victim, offender and their supporters) to discuss the offence, its impact and what should be done to 'repair the harm'; and decision making carried out by both lay and legal actors. While definitions and lists of core elements of restorative justice vary, all display a remarkable uniformity in defining restorative justice by reference to what it is *not*, and this is called *retributive justice*.

Myths about restorative justice

Myth 1. Restorative justice is the opposite of retributive justice

When one first dips into the restorative justice literature, the first thing one 'learns' is that restorative justice differs sharply from retributive justice. It is said that:

(1) restorative justice focuses on *repairing the harm* caused by crime, whereas retributive justice focuses on *punishing an offence*;

(2) restorative justice is characterized by *dialogue and negotiation* among the parties, whereas retributive justice is characterized by *adversarial relations* among the parties; and

(3) restorative justice assumes that community members or organizations take a more active role, whereas for retributive justice, 'the community' is represented by the state.

Most striking is that all the elements associated with restorative justice are *good*, whereas all those associated with retributive justice are *bad*. The retributive–restorative oppositional contrast is not only made by restorative justice advocates, but increasingly one finds it canonized in criminology and juvenile justice textbooks. The question arises, is it right?

On empirical and normative grounds, I suggest that in characterizing justice aims and practices, it is neither accurate nor defensible. While I am not alone in taking this position (see Barton, 2000; Miller and Blackler, 2000; Duff, 2001), it is currently held by a small number of us in the field. Despite advocates' well-meaning intentions, the contrast is a highly misleading simplification, which is used to sell the superiority of restorative justice and its set of justice products. To make the sales pitch simple, definite boundaries need to be marked between the *good* (restorative) and the *bad* (retributive) justice, to which one might add the *ugly* (rehabilitative) justice. Advocates seem to assume that an ideal justice system should be of one type only, that it should be pure and not contaminated by or mixed with others.[3] Before demonstrating the problems with this position, I give a sympathetic reading of what I think advocates are trying to say.

Mead's (1917–18) 'The psychology of punitive justice' (as reprinted in Melossi, 1998, pp.33–60) contrasts two methods of responding to crime. One he termed 'the attitude of hostility toward the lawbreaker' (p.48), which 'brings with it the attitudes of retribution, repression, and exclusion' (pp.47–8) and which sees a lawbreaker as 'enemy'. The other, exemplified in the (then) emerging juvenile court, is the 'reconstructive attitude' (p.55), which tries to 'understand the causes of social and individual breakdown, to mend … the defective situation', to determine responsibility 'not to place punishment but to obtain future results' (p.52). Most restorative justice advocates see the justice world through this Meadian lens; they reject the 'attitude of hostility toward the lawbreaker', do not wish to view him or her as 'enemy', and desire an alternative kind of justice. On that score, I concur, as no doubt many other researchers and observers of justice system practices would. However, the 'attitude of hostility' is a caricature of criminal justice, which over the last century and a half has wavered between desires to 'treat' some and 'punish' others, and which surely cannot be encapsulated in the one term, 'retributive justice'. By framing justice aims (or principles) and practices in oppositional terms, restorative justice advocates not only do a disservice to history, they also give a restricted view of the present. They assume that restorative justice *practices* should exclude elements of retribution; and in rejecting an 'attitude of hostility', they assume that retribution as a justice *principle* must also be rejected.

When observing conferences, I discovered that participants engaged in a flexible incorporation of *multiple* justice aims, which included:

(1) some elements of retributive justice (that is, censure for past offences);

(2) some elements of rehabilitative justice (for example, by asking, what shall we do to encourage future law-abiding behaviour?); and

(3) some elements of restorative justice (for example, by asking, how can the offender make up for what he or she did to the victim?).

When reporting these findings, one colleague said, 'yes, this is a problem' (Walgrave, personal communication). This speaker's concern was that as restorative justice was being incorporated into the regular justice system, it would turn out to be a set of 'simple techniques', rather than an 'ideal of justice … in an ideal of society' (Walgrave, 1995, pp.240, 245) and that its core values would be lost. Another said (paraphrasing), 'retribution may well be present now in conferences, but you wouldn't want to make the argument that it *should be* present' (Braithwaite, personal communication).

These comments provoked me to consider the relationship between restorative and retributive justice, and the role of punishment in restorative justice, in normative terms. Distilling from other articles (e.g. Daly and Immarigeon, 1998, pp.32–5; Daly, 2000a, 2000b) and arguments by Duff (1992, 1996, 2001), Hampton (1992, 1998), Zedner (1994) and Barton (2000), I have come to see that apparently contrary principles of retribution and reparation should be viewed as dependent on one another. Retributive censure should ideally occur before reparative gestures (or a victim's interest or movement to negotiate these) are possible in an ethical or psychological sense. Both censure and reparation may be experienced as 'punishment' by offenders (even if this is not the intent of decision-makers), and both censure and reparation need to occur before a victim or community can 'reintegrate' an offender into the community. These complex and contingent interactions are expressed in varied ways and should not be viewed as having to follow any one fixed sequence. Moreover, one cannot assume that subsequent actions, such as the victim's forgiving the offender or a reconciliation of a victim and offender (or others), should occur. This may take a long time or never occur. In the advocacy literature, however, I find that there is too quick a move to 'repair the harm', 'heal those injured by crime' or to 'reintegrate offenders', passing over a crucial phase of 'holding offenders accountable', which is the retributive part of the process.

A major block in communicating ideas about the relationship of retributive to restorative justice is that there is great variability in how people understand and use key terms such as punishment, retribution and punitiveness. Some argue that incarceration and fines are punishments because they are *intended deprivations*, whereas probation or a reparative measure such as doing work for a crime victim are not punishment because they are *intended to be constructive* (Wright, 1991). Others define punishment more broadly to include anything that is unpleasant, a burden or an imposition of some sort; the intentions of the decision-maker are less significant (Davis, 1992; Duff, 1992, 2001). Some use retribution to describe a *justification* for punishment (i.e. intended to be in proportion to the harm caused), whereas others use it to describe a *form* of punishment (i.e. intended to be of a type that is harsh or painful).[4] On proportionality, restorative justice advocates take different positions: some (e.g. Braithwaite and Pettit, 1990) eschew retributivism, favouring instead a free-ranging consequentialist justification and highly individualized responses, while others wish to limit restorative justice responses to desert-based, proportionate criteria (Van Ness, 1993; Walgrave and Aertsen, 1996). For the form of punishment, some use retribution in a neutral way to refer to a censuring of harms (e.g. Duff, 1996), whereas most use the term to connote a punitive response, which is associated with emotions of revenge or intentions to inflict pain on wrong-doers (Wright, 1991). The term *punitive* is rarely defined, no doubt because everyone seems to know what it means. Precisely because this term is used in a commonsensical way by everyone in the field (not just restorative justice scholars), there is confusion over its meaning. Would we say, for example, that any criminal justice sanction is by definition 'punitive', but sanctions can vary across a continuum of greater to lesser punitiveness? Or, would we say that some sanctions are non-punitive and that restorative justice processes aim to maximize the application of non-punitive sanctions? I will not attempt to adjudicate the many competing claims about punishment, retribution and punitiveness. The sources of antagonism lie not only in varied *definitions*, but also the different *images* these definitions conjure in people's heads about justice relations and practices. However, one way to gain some clarity is to conceptualize punishment, retribution and punitive (and their 'non' counterparts) as separate dimensions, each having its own continuum of meaning, rather than to conflate them, as now typically occurs in the literature.

Because the terms 'retributive justice' and 'restorative justice' have such strong meanings and referents, and are used largely by advocates (and others) as metaphors for the bad and the good justice, perhaps they should be jettisoned in analysing current and future justice practices. Instead, we might refer to 'older' and 'newer' modern justice forms. These terms do not provide a content to justice principles or practices, but they do offer a way to depict developments in the justice field with an eye to recent history and with an appreciation that any 'new' justice practices will have many bits of the 'old' in them.[5] The terms also permit description and explanation of a larger phenomenon, that is, of a profound transformation of justice forms and practices now occurring in most developed societies in the West, and certainly the English-speaking ones of which I am aware. Restorative justice is only a part of that transformation.

By the *old justice*, I refer to modern practices of courthouse justice, which permit no interaction between victim and offender, where legal actors and other experts do the talking and make decisions and whose (stated) aim is to punish, or at times, reform an offender. By the *new justice*,[6] I refer to a variety of recent practices, which normally bring victims and offenders (and others) together in a process in which both lay and legal actors make decisions, and whose (stated) aim is to repair the harm for victims, offenders and perhaps other members of 'the community' in ways that matter to them. (While the stated aim of either justice form may be to 'punish the crime' or to 'repair the harm', we should expect to see mixed justice aims in participants' justice talk and practices.[7]) New justice practices are one of several developments in a larger justice field, which also includes the 'new penology' (Feeley and Simon, 1992) and 'unthinkable punishment policies' (Tonry, 1999). The field is fragmented and moving in contradictory directions (Garland, 1996; Crawford, 1997; O'Malley, 1999; Pratt, 2000).

Myth 2. Restorative justice uses indigenous justice practices and was the dominant form of pre-modern justice

A common theme in the restorative justice literature is that this reputedly new justice form is 'really not new' (Consedine, 1995, p.12). As Consedine puts it:

> Biblical justice was restorative. So too was justice in most indigenous cultures. In pre-colonial New Zealand, Maori had a fully integrated system of restorative justice ... It was the traditional philosophy of Pacific nations such as Tonga, Fiji and Samoa ... In pre-Norman Ireland, restorative justice was interwoven ... with the fabric of daily life ...
>
> (1995, p.12)

Braithwaite argues that restorative justice is 'ground[ed] in traditions of justice from the ancient Arab, Greek, and Roman civilisations that accepted a restorative approach even to homicide' (1999, p.1). He continues with a large sweep of human history, citing the 'public assemblies ... of the Germanic people', 'Indian Hindu [traditions in] 6000–2000 B.C.' and 'ancient Buddhist, Taoist, and Confucian traditions...'; and he concludes that *'restorative justice has been the dominant model of criminal justice throughout most of human history for all the world's peoples*' (1999, p.1, my emphasis). What an extraordinary claim!

Linked with the claim that restorative justice has been the dominant form of criminal justice throughout human history is the claim that present-day indigenous justice practices fall within the restorative justice rubric. Thus, for example, Consedine says:

> A new paradigm of justice is operating [in New Zealand], which is very traditional in its philosophy, yet revolutionary in its effects. A restorative philosophy of justice has replaced a retributive one. Ironically, 150 years after the traditional Maori restorative praxis was abolished in Aotearoa, youth justice policy is once again operating from the same philosophy.
>
> (1995, p.99).

Reverence for and romanticization of an indigenous past slide over practices that the modern 'civilized' western mind would object to, such as a variety of harsh physical (bodily) punishments and banishment. At the same time, the modern western mind may not be able to grasp how certain 'harsh punishments' have been sensible within the terms of a particular culture.

Weitekamp combines 'ancient forms' of justice practice (as restorative) and indigenous groups' current practices (as restorative) when he says that:

> Some of the new ... programs are in fact very old ... [A]ncient forms of restorative justice have been used in [non-state] societies and by early forms of humankind. [F]amily group conferences [and] ... circle hearings [have been used] by indigenous people such as the Aboriginals, the Inuit, and the native Indians of North and South America ... It is kind of ironic that we have at [the turn of this century] to go back to methods and forms of conflict resolution which were practiced some millennia ago by our ancestors ...
>
> (1999, p.93)

I confess to a limited knowledge of justice practices and systems throughout the history of humankind. What I know is confined mainly to the past three centuries and to developments in the United States and several other countries. Thus, in addressing this myth, I do so from a position of ignorance in knowing only a small portion of history. Upon reflection, however, my lack of historical knowledge may not matter. All that is required is the realization that advocates do not intend to write *authoritative histories* of justice. Rather, they are constructing origin myths about restorative justice. If the first form of human justice was restorative justice, then advocates can claim a need to recover it from a history of 'takeover' by state-sponsored retributive justice. *And*, by identifying current indigenous practice as restorative justice, advocates can claim a need to recover these practices from a history of 'takeover' by white colonial powers that instituted retributive justice. Thus, the history of justice practices is rewritten by advocates not only to authorize restorative justice as the *first* human form of justice, but also to argue that it is congenial with modern-day indigenous and, as we shall see in Myth 3, feminist social movements for justice.

In the restorative justice field, most commentators focus specifically (and narrowly) on changes that occurred over a 400-year period (8th to 11th centuries) in England (and some European countries), where a system of largely kin-based dispute settlement gave way to a court system, in which feudal lords retained a portion of property forfeited by an offender. In England, this loose system was centralized and consolidated during the century following the Norman Invasion in 1066, as the development of state (crown) law depended on the collection of revenues collected by judges for the king. For restorative justice advocates, the transformation of disputes as offences between individuals to offences against the state is one element that marked the end of pre-modern forms of restorative justice. A second element is the decline in compensation to the victim for the losses from a crime (Weitekamp, 1999).

Advocates' constructions of the history of restorative justice, that is, the origin myth that a superior justice form prevailed before the imposition of retributive justice, is linked to their desire to maintain a strong oppositional contrast between retributive and restorative justice. That is to say, the origin myth and oppositional contrast are both required in telling the true story of restorative justice. I do not see bad faith at work here. Rather, advocates are trying to move an idea into the political and policy arena, and this may necessitate having to utilize a simple contrast of the good and the bad justice, along with an origin myth of how it all came to be.

What does concern me is that the specific histories and practices of justice in pre-modern societies are smoothed over and lumped together as one justice form. Is it appropriate to refer to all of these justice practices as 'restorative'? No, I think not. What do these justice practices in fact have in common? What is gained, and more importantly, what is lost by this homogenizing move? Efforts to write histories of restorative justice, where a pre-modern past is romantically (and selectively) invoked to justify a current justice practice, are not only in error, but also unwittingly reinscribe an ethnocentrism their authors wish to avoid. As Blagg (1997) and Cain (2000) point out, there has been an orientalist appropriation of indigenous justice practices, largely in the service of strengthening advocates' positions.

A common, albeit erroneous, claim is that the modern idea of conferencing 'has its direct roots in Maori culture' (Shearing, 2001, p.218, note 5; see also Consedine, 1995). The real story is that conferencing emerged in the 1980s, in the context of Maori political challenges to white New Zealanders and to their welfare and criminal justice systems. Investing decision-making practices with Maori cultural values meant that family groups (whanau) should have a greater say in what happens, that venues should be culturally appropriate and that processes should accommodate a mix of culturally appropriate practices. New Zealand's minority group population includes not only the Maori but also Pacific Island Polynesians. Therefore, with the introduction of conferencing, came awareness of the need to incorporate different elements of 'cultural appropriateness' into the conference process. But the devising of a (white, bureaucratic) justice practice that is *flexible and accommodating* towards cultural differences does not mean that conferencing *is* an indigenous justice practice. Maxwell and Morris, who know the New Zealand situation well, are clear on this point:

> A distinction must be drawn between a system, which attempts to re-establish the indigenous model of pre-European times, and a system of

> justice, which is culturally appropriate. The New Zealand system is an attempt to establish the latter, not to replicate the former. As such, it seeks to incorporate many of the features apparent in whanau decision-making processes and seen in meetings on marae today, but it also contains elements quite alien to indigenous models.
>
> (1993, p.4)

Conferencing is better understood as a fragmented justice form: it splices white, bureaucratic forms of justice with elements of informal justice that may include non-white (or non-western) values or methods of judgement, with all the attendant dangers of such 'spliced justice' (Pavlich, 1996; Blagg, 1997, 1998; Daly, 1998; Findlay, 2000). With the flexibility of informal justice, practitioners, advocates and members of minority groups may see the potential for introducing culturally sensible and responsive forms of justice. But to say that conferencing *is* an indigenous justice practice (or 'has its roots in indigenous justice') is to re-engage a white-centred view of the world. As Blagg asks rhetorically, 'Are we once again creaming off the cultural value of people simply to suit our own nostalgia in this age of pessimism and melancholia?' (1998, p.12). A good deal of the advocacy literature is of this ilk: white-centred, creaming off and homogenizing of cultural difference and specificity.

Myth 3. Restorative justice is a 'care' (or feminine) response to crime in comparison to a 'justice' (or masculine) response

Myths 2 and 3 have a similar oppositional logic, but play with different dichotomies. Figure 1 shows the terms that are often linked to restorative and retributive justice. Note the power inversion, essential to the origin myth of restorative justice, where the subordinated or marginalized groups (pre-modern, indigenous, eastern and feminine) are aligned with the more superior justice form.

Many readers will be familiar with the 'care' and 'justice' dichotomy. It was put forward by Gilligan in her popular book, *In a Different Voice* (1982). For about a decade, it seemed that most feminist legal theory articles were organized around the 'different voice' versus 'male dominance' perspectives of Gilligan (1987) and MacKinnon (1987), respectively. In criminology, Heidensohn (1986) and Harris (1987) attempted to apply the care/justice dichotomy to the criminal justice system. Care responses to crime are depicted as personalized and as based on a concrete and active morality, whereas justice responses are depicted as depersonalized, based on rights and rules and a universalizing and abstract morality. Care responses are associated with the different (female) voice, and these are distinguished from justice responses, which are associated with the general (if male) voice. In her early work, Gilligan argued that both voices should have equal importance in moral reasoning, but women's voices were misheard or judged as morally inferior to men's. A critical literature developed rapidly, and Gilligan began to reformulate and clarify her argument. She recognized that 'care' responses in a 'justice' framework left 'the basic assumptions of a justice framework intact … and that as a moral perspective, care [was] less well elaborated' (Gilligan, 1987, p.24). At the time, the elements that Gilligan associated with a care response to crime were contextual and relational reasoning, and individualized responses made by decision-makers who were not detached from the conflict (or crime). In 1989, I came into the debate, arguing that we should challenge the association of justice and care reasoning with male/masculine and female/feminine voices, respectively (Daly, 1989). I suggested that this gender-linked association was not accurate empirically, and I argued that it would be misleading to think that an alternative to men's forms of criminal law and justice practices could be found by adding women's voice or reconstituting the system along the lines of an

Restorative justice	*Retributive justice*
Pre-modern	Modern
Indigenous (informal)	State (formal)
Feminine (care)	Masculine (justice)
Eastern (Japan)	Western (US)
Superior justice	Inferior justice

Figure 1 Terms linked to restorative and retributive justice

ethic of care. I viewed the care/justice dichotomy as recapitulating centuries long debates in modern western criminology and legal philosophy over the aims and purposes of punishment, e.g. deterrence and retribution or rehabilitation, and uniform or individualized responses. Further, I noted that although the dichotomy depicted different ideological emphases in the response to crime since the 19th century, the relational and concrete reasoning that Gilligan associated with the female voice was how in fact the criminal law is interpreted and applied. It *is* the voice of criminal justice practices. The problem, then, was not that the female voice was absent in criminal court practices, but rather that certain relations were presupposed, maintained and reproduced. Feminist analyses of law and criminal justice centre on the androcentric (some would argue, phallocentric) character of these relations for what comes to be understood as 'crime', for the meanings of 'consent', and for punishment (for cogent reviews, see Smart, 1989, 1992; Coombs, 1995). While feminist scholars continue to emphasize the need to bring women's experiences and 'voices' into the criminological and legal frame, this is not the same thing as arguing that there is a universal 'female voice' in moral reasoning. During the late 1980s and 1990s, feminist arguments moved decisively beyond dichotomous and essentialist readings of sex/gender in analysing relations of power and 'difference' in law and justice. Gilligan's different voice construct, though novel and important at the time, has been superseded by more complex and contingent analyses of ethics and morality.

But the different voice is back, and unfortunately, the authors who are using it seem totally unaware of key shifts in feminist thinking. We see now that the 'ethic of care' (Persephone) is pitched as the alternative to retributive justice (Portia). One example is a recent article by Masters and Smith (1998), who attempt to demonstrate that Persephone, the voice of caring, is evident in a variety of restorative responses to crime. Their arguments confuse, however, because they argue that Persephone is 'informed by an ethic of care as well as an ethic of justice' (1998, p.11). And towards the end of the article, they say 'we cannot do without Portia (ethic of justice), but neither can we do without Persephone' (1998, p.21). Thus, it is not clear whether, within the terms of their argument, Persephone stands for the feminine or includes both the masculine and feminine, or whether we need both Portia and Persephone. They apparently agree with all three positions. They also see little difference between a 'feminine' and a 'feminist approach', terms that they use interchangeably. In general, they normally credit 'relational justice as a distinctly feminine approach to crime and conflict' (1998, p.13). They say that 'reintegrative shaming can be considered a feminine (or Persephone) theory' and that there is a 'fit between reintegrative shaming practice and the *feminist* ethic of care' (1998, p.13, my italics since the authors have shifted from a feminine ethic to a feminist ethic). Towards the end of the article, they make the astonishing claim, one that I suspect my colleague John Braithwaite would find difficult to accept, that 'reintegrative shaming is perhaps the first feminist criminological theory'. They argue this is so because the 'practice of reintegrative shaming can be interpreted as being grounded in a feminine, rather than a masculine understanding of the social world' (1998, p.20).

There is a lot to unpick here, and I shall not go point by point. Nor do I wish to undermine the spirit of the article since the authors' intentions are laudable, in particular, their desire to define a more progressive way to respond to crime. My concern is that using simple gender dichotomies, or any dichotomies for that matter, to describe principles and practices of justice will always fail us, will always lead to great disappointment.[8] Traditional courthouse justice works with the abstraction of criminal law, but must deal with the messy world of people's lives, and hence, must deal with context and relations. 'Care' responses to some offenders can re-victimize some victims; they may be helpful in *some cases* or for *some offenders* or for *some victims* or they may also be oppressive and unjust for other offenders and victims. Likewise, with so-called 'justice' responses. The set of terms lined up along the 'male/masculine' and 'female/feminine' poles is long and varied: some terms are about process, others with modes of response (e.g. repair the harm) and still others, with ways of thinking about culpability for the harm.

I am struck by the frequency with which people use dichotomies such as the male and female voice, retributive and restorative justice or West and East, to depict justice principles and practices. Such dichotomies are also used to construct normative positions about justice, where it is assumed (I think wrongly) that the sensibility of one side of the dualism necessarily excludes (or is antithetical to) the sensibility of the other. Increasingly, scholars are coming to see the value of theorizing justice in hybrid terms, of seeing connections and contingent relations between apparent oppositions (see, for example, Zedner, 1994; Bottoms, 1998; Hudson, 1998; Daly, 2000a; Duff, 2001).

Like the advocates promoting Myth 2, those promoting Myth 3 want to emphasize the importance of identifying a different response to crime than the one currently in use. I am certainly on the side of that aspiration. However, I cannot agree with the terms in which the position has been argued and sold to academic audiences and wider publics. There is a loss of credibility when analyses do not move beyond oppositional justice metaphors, when claims are imprecise and when extraordinary tales of repair and goodwill are assumed to be typical of the restorative justice experience.

Myth 4. Restorative justice can be expected to produce major changes in people

I have said that attention needs to be given to the reality on the ground, to what is actually happening in, and resulting from, practices that fall within the rubric of restorative justice. There are several levels to describe and analyse what is going on: first, what occurs in the justice practice itself; second, the relationship between this and broader system effects; and third, how restorative justice is located in the broader politics of crime control. I focus on the first level and present two forms of evidence: (1) stories of dramatic transformations or moving accounts of reconciliation; and (2) aggregated information across a larger number of cases, drawing from research on conference observations and interviews with participants.

Several reviewers of this article took issue with Myth 4, saying that 'advocates are less likely to claim changes in people' or that 'there is no real evidence that restorative justice of itself can be expected to produce major changes in people'. Although I am open to empirical inquiry, my reading of the advocacy literature from the United States, Canada, Australia and New Zealand suggests that Myth 4 is prevalent. It is exemplified by advocates' stories of how people are transformed or by their general assertions of the benefits of restorative justice. For example, McCold reports that 'facilitators of restorative processes regularly observe a personal and social transformation occur during the course of the process' (2000, p.359) and 'we now have a growing body of research on programs that everyone agrees are truly restorative, clearly demonstrating their remarkable success at healing and conciliation' (2000, p.363). McCold gives no citations to the research literature. While 'personal and social transformation' undoubtedly occurs some of the time, and is likely to be rare in a courtroom proceeding, advocates lead us to think that it is typical in a restorative justice process. This is accomplished by telling a moving story, which is then used to stand as a generalization.

Stories of restorative justice

Consedine opens his book by excerpting from a 1993 New Zealand news story:

> The families of two South Auckland boys killed by a car welcomed the accused driver yesterday with open arms and forgiveness. The young man, who gave himself up to the police yesterday morning, apologised to the families and was ceremonially reunited with the Tongan and Samoan communities at a special service last night.
>
> ... The 20-year old Samoan visited the Tongan families after his court appearance to apologise for the deaths of the two children in Mangere. The Tongan and Samoan communities of Mangere later gathered at the Tongan Methodist Church in a service of reconciliation. The young man sat at the feast table flanked by the mothers of the dead boys.
>
> (Consedine, 1995, p.9)

Consedine says that this case provides:

> ample evidence of the power that healing and forgiveness can play in our daily lives … The grieving Tongan and Samoan communities simply embraced the young driver … and forgave him. His deep shame, his fear, his sorrow, his alienation from the community was resolved.
>
> (1995, p.162)

Another example comes from Umbreit (1994, p.1). His book opens with the story of Linda and Bob Jackson, whose house was broken into; they subsequently met with the offender as part of the offender's sentence disposition. The offender, Allan, 'felt better after the mediation … he was able to make amends to the Jacksons'. Moreover, 'Linda and Bob felt less vulnerable, were able to sleep better and received payment for their losses. All parties were able to put this event behind them'. Later in the book, Umbreit (1994, pp.197–202) offers another case study of a second couple, Bob and Anne, after their house was burglarized a second time. He summarizes the outcome this way:

> Bob, Anne, and Jim [the offender] felt the mediation process and outcome was fair. All were very satisfied with participation in the program. Rather than playing passive roles … [they] actively participated in 'making things right'. During a subsequent conversation with Bob, he commented that 'this was the first time (after several victimizations) that I ever felt any sense of fairness. The courts always ignored me before. They didn't care about my concerns. And Jim isn't such a bad kid after all, was he?' Jim also indicated that he felt better after the mediation and more aware of the impact the burglary had on Bob and Anne.
>
> (Umbreit, 1994, p.202)

Lastly, there is the fable of Sam, an adolescent offender who attended a diversionary conference, which was first related by Braithwaite (1996) and retold by Shearing (2001, pp.214–15). Braithwaite says that his story is a 'composite of several Sams I have seen' (1996, p.9); thus, while he admits that it is not a real story of Sam, it is said to show the 'essential features … of restorative justice' (Shearing, 2001, p.214). This is something like a building contractor saying to a potential home buyer, 'this is a composite of the house I can build for you; it's not the real house, but it's like many houses I have sold to happy buyers over the years'. What the composite gives and what the building contractor offers us is a *vision of the possible*, of the perfect house. Whether the house can ever be built is less important than imagining its possibility and its perfection. This is the cornerstone of the true story of restorative justice, like many proposed justice innovations of the past.

Sam's story, as told by Braithwaite, is longer than I give here, and thus, I leave out emotional details that make any story compelling. Sam, who is homeless and says his parents abused him, has no one who really cares about him except his older sister, his former hockey coach at school and his Uncle George. These people attend the conference, along with the elderly female victim and her daughter. Sam says he knocked over the victim and took her purse because he needed the money. His significant others rebuke him for doing this, but also remember that he had a good side before he started getting into trouble. The victim and daughter describe the effects of the robbery, but Sam does not seem to be affected. After his apparent callous response to the victim, Sam's sister cries, and during a break, she reveals that she too had been abused by their parents. When the conference reconvenes, Sam's sister speaks directly to Sam, and without mentioning details, says she understands what Sam went through. The victim appreciates what is being said and begins to cry. Sam's callous exterior begins to crumble. He says he wants to do something for the victim, but does not know what he can do without a home or job. His sister offers her place for him to stay, and the coach says he can offer him some work. At the end of the conference, the victim hugs Sam and tearfully says good luck, Sam apologizes again and Uncle George says he will continue to help Sam and his sister when needed.

Many questions arise in reading stories like these. *How often* do expressions of kindness and understanding, of movement towards repair and goodwill, actually occur? What are the typical 'effects' on participants? Is the perfect house of restorative justice ever built? Another kind of evidence aggregated data across a larger number of cases, can provide some answers.

Statistical aggregates of restorative justice

Here are some highlights of what has been learned from research on youth justice conferences in Australia and New Zealand.[9] Official data show that about 85 to 90 percent of conferences resulted in agreed outcomes, and 80 percent of young people completed their agreements. From New Zealand research in the early 1990s (Maxwell and Morris, 1993), conferences appeared to be largely offender-centred events. In 51 percent of the 146 cases where a victim was identified, the victim attended the conference (1993, p.118). Of all the victims interviewed who attended a conference (sometimes there were multiple victims), 25 percent said they felt worse as a result of the conference (1993, p.119). Negative feelings were linked to being dissatisfied with the conference outcome, which was judged to be too lenient towards the offender. Of all those interviewed (offenders, their supporters and victims) victims were the least satisfied with the outcome of the family conference; 49 percent said they were satisfied (1993, p.120) compared with 84 percent of young people and 85 percent of parents (1993, p.115). Maxwell and Morris report that 'monitoring of [conference] outcomes was generally poor' (1993, p.123), and while they could not give precise percentages, it appeared that 'few [victims] had been informed of the eventual success or otherwise of the outcome' and that this 'was a source of considerable anger for them' (1993, p.123). Elsewhere, Maxwell and Morris report that 'the new system remains largely unresponsive to cultural differences' (1996, pp.95–6) in handling Maori cases, which they argue is a consequence, in part, of too few resources.

The most robust finding across all the studies in the region (see review in Daly, 2001a) is that conferences receive very high marks along dimensions of procedural justice, that is, victims and offenders view the process and the outcomes as fair. In the Re-Integrative Shaming Experiments (RISE) in Canberra, admitted offenders were randomly assigned to court and conference. Strang *et al.* (1999) have reported results from the RISE project on their website by showing many pages of percentages for each variable for each of the four offences in the experiment (violent, property, shoplifting and drink-driving). They have summarized this mass of numbers in a set of comparative statements without attaching their claims to percentages. Here is what they report. Compared to those offenders who went to court, those going to conferences have higher levels of procedural justice, higher levels of restorative justice and an increased respect for the police and law. Compared to victims whose cases went to court, conference victims have higher levels of recovery from the offence. Conference victims also had high levels of procedural justice, but they could not be compared to court victims, who rarely attended court proceedings. These summary statements are the tip of the RISE iceberg. In a detailed analysis of the RISE website results, Kurki (2001) finds offence-based differences in the court and conference experiences of RISE participants, and she notes that RISE researchers' reports of claimed court and conference differences are not uniform across offence types.

Like other studies, the South Australia Juvenile Justice (SAJJ) Research on Conferencing Project finds very high levels of procedural justice registered by offenders and victims at conferences. To items such as, were you treated fairly, were you treated with respect, did you have a say in the agreement, among others, 80 to 95 percent of victims and offenders said that they were treated fairly and had a say. In light of the procedural justice literature (Tyler, 1990; Tyler *et al.*, 1997), these findings are important. Procedural justice scholars argue that when citizens perceive a legal process as fair, when they are listened to and treated with respect, there is an affirmation of the legitimacy of the legal order.

Compared to the high levels of perceived procedural justice, the SAJJ project finds relatively less evidence of restorativeness. The measures of restorativeness tapped the degree to which offenders and victims recognized the other and were affected by the other; they focused on the degree to which there was positive movement between the offender and victim and their supporters during the conference (the SAJJ measures are more concrete and relational measures of restorativeness than those used in RISE). Whereas very high proportions of victims and offenders (80 to 95 percent) said that the process was fair (among other variables tapping procedural justice), 'restorativeness' was evident in 30 to 50 percent of conferences (depending on the item), and solidly in no more than about one-third. Thus, in this jurisdiction where conferences are used routinely,[10] fairness can more easily be achieved than restorativeness. As but one example, from the interviews we learned that from the victims' perspectives, less than 30 percent of offenders were perceived as making genuine apologies, but from the offenders' perspectives, close to 60 percent said their apology was genuine.

The SAJJ results lead me to think that young people (offenders) and victims orient themselves to a conference and what they hope to achieve in it in ways different than the advocacy literature imagines. The stance of empathy and openness to 'the other', the expectation of being able to speak and reflect on one's actions and the presence of new justice norms (or language) emphasizing repair – all of these are novel cultural elements for most participants. Young people appear to be as, if not more, interested in *repairing their own reputations* than in repairing the harm to victims. Among the most important things that the victims hoped would occur at the conference was for the offender to hear how the offence affected them, but half the offenders told us that the victim's story had no effect or only a little effect on them.

How often, then, does the exceptional or 'nirvana' story of repair and goodwill occur? I devised a measure that combined the SAJJ observer's judgement of the degree to which a conference 'ended on a high, a positive note of repair and good will' with one that rated the conference on a five-point scale from poor to exceptional. While the first tapped the degree to which there was movement between victims, offenders and their supporters towards each other, the second tapped a more general feeling about the conference dynamics and how well the conference was managed by the co-ordinator. With this combined measure, 10 percent of conferences were rated very highly, another 40 percent, good; and the rest, a mixed, fair or poor rating. If conferencing is used routinely (not just in a select set of cases), I suspect that the story of Sam and Uncle George will be infrequent; it may happen 10 percent of the time, if that.

Assessing the 'effects' of conferences on participants is complex because such effects change over time and, for victims, they are contingent on whether offenders come through on promises made, as we learned from research in New Zealand. I present findings on victims' sense of having recovered from the offence and on young people's re-offending in the post-conference period. In the Year 2 (1999) interviews with victims, over 60 percent said they had 'fully recovered' from the offence, that it was 'all behind' them. Their recovery was more likely when offenders completed the agreement than when they did not, but recovery was influenced by a mixture of elements: the conference process, support from family and friends, the passage of time and personal resources such as their own resilience. The SAJJ project finds that conferences *can* have positive effects on reducing victims' anger towards and fear of offenders. Drawing from the victim interviews in 1998 and 1999, over 75 percent of victims felt angry towards the offender before the conference, but this dropped to 44 percent after the conference and was 39 percent a year later. Close to 40 percent of victims were frightened of the offender before the conference, but this dropped to 25 percent after the conference and was 18 percent a year later. Therefore, for victims, meeting offenders in the conference setting can have beneficial results.

The conference effect everyone asks about is, does it reduce reoffending? Proof (or disproof) of reductions in reoffending from conferences (compared *not only to court*, but to other interventions such as formal caution, other diversion approaches or no legal action at all) will not be available for a long time, if ever. The honest answer to the reoffending question is 'we'll probably never know' because the amounts of money would be exorbitant and research methods using experimental designs judged too risky in an ethical and political sense.

To date, there have been three studies of conferencing and reoffending in Australia and New Zealand, one of which compares reoffending for a sample of offenders randomly assigned to conference and court and two that explore whether reoffending can be linked to things that occur in conferences.[11] The RISE project finds that for one of four major offence categories studied (violent offences compared to drink-driving, property offences, shoplifting), those offenders who were assigned to a conference had a significantly reduced rate of reoffending than those who were assigned to court (Sherman *et al.*, 2000).

As others have said (Abel, 1982, p.278; Levrant *et al.*, 1999, pp.17–22), there is a great faith placed on the conference process to change young offenders, when the conditions of their day-to-day lives, which may be conducive to getting into trouble, may not change at all. The SAJJ project asked if there were things that occurred in conferences that could predict reoffending, over and above those variables known to be conducive to lawbreaking (and its detection): past offending and social marginality (Hayes and Daly, 2001). In a regression analysis with a simultaneous inclusion of variables, we found that over and above the young person's race-ethnicity (Aboriginal or non-Aboriginal), sex, whether s/he offended prior to the offence that led to the SAJJ conference and a measure of the young person's mobility and marginality, there were two conference elements associated with reoffending. When young people were observed to be mostly or fully remorseful and when outcomes were achieved by genuine consensus, they were less likely to reoffend during an 8- to 12-month period after the conference. These results are remarkably similar to those of Maxwell and Morris (2000) in their study of reoffending in New Zealand. They found that what happens in conferences (e.g. a young person's expressions of remorse and agreeing [or not] with the outcome, among other variables) could distinguish those young people who were and were not 'persistently reconvicted' during a six and a half-year follow-up period.

The real or the true story?

Advocates want to tell a particular kind of story, the mythical true story of restorative justice. This story asks people to develop their 'caring' sides and to 'resist tyranny with compassion' (Braithwaite, 1999, p.2). It suggests that amidst adversity, there is great potential 'for doing good' for self and others (Braithwaite, 1999, p.2, paraphrasing Eckel, 1997). It rewrites the history of justice practices by celebrating a return to pre-modern forms, and it re-colonizes indigenous practices by identifying them as exemplars of restorative justice. The true story offers some hope, not only for a better way to do justice, but also for strengthening mechanisms of informal social control, and, consequently, to minimize reliance on formal social control, the machinery and institutions of criminal justice.

In order to sell the idea of restorative justice to a wide audience, advocates have painted a dichotomous, oppositional picture of different justice forms, with restorative justice trumping retributive justice as the superior one. There is a certain appeal to this framing of justice: it offers two choices, and it tells us which side is right. With this framing, who could possibly be on the side of retribution and retributive justice? Only the bad guys, of course. When we move from the metaphors and slogans to the hard work of establishing the philosophical, legal and organizational bases of this idea, and of documenting what actually occurs in these practices, the true story fails us. It lets us down because simple oppositional dualisms are inadequate in depicting criminal justice, even an ideal justice system. With respect to youth justice conferencing, extraordinary tales of repair and goodwill may occur, but we should not expect them to occur as frequently as the advocates would have us think.

The real story of restorative justice is a more qualified one. Empirical evidence of conferencing in Australia and New Zealand suggests that very high proportions of people find the process fair; on many measures of procedural justice, it succeeds. However, I am finding from the SAJJ project that it is relatively more difficult for victims and offenders to find common ground and to hear each other's stories, or for offenders to give sincere apologies and victims to understand that apologies are sincere. There appear to be limits on 'repairing the harm' for offenders and victims, in part because the idea is novel and unfamiliar for most ordinary citizens. For youthful lawbreakers, the limits also inhere in the salience of *any* legal process or adult exhortations to 'stay out of trouble', and the problems that adolescents may have in 'recognizing the other', an empathetic orientation that is assumed to be central to a restorative process. For victims, the limits reside in the capacity to be generous to lawbreakers and to see lawbreakers as capable of change. A variety of observational and interview items from the SAJJ project suggests that a minority of conferences have the necessary raw material for restorativeness to occur. (One needs to be careful in generalizing: the frequency of restorativeness would depend greatly on whether a jurisdiction uses conferences selectively or routinely and what kinds of cases are in the sample, that is, the mix of violence and property, the degree of seriousness and victim–offender relations.) Overall, the real story of restorative justice has many positives and has much to commend, but the evidence is mixed. Conferencing, or any new justice practice, is not nirvana and ought not to be sold in those terms.

In the political arena, telling the mythical true story of restorative justice may be an effective means of reforming parts of the justice system. It may inspire legislatures to pass new laws and it may provide openings to experiment with alternative justice forms. All of this can be a good thing. Perhaps, in fact, the politics of selling justice ideas may *require* people to tell mythical true stories. The real story attends to the murk and constraints of justice organizations, of people's experiences as offenders and victims and their capacities and desires to 'repair the harm'. It reveals a picture that is less sharp-edged and more equivocal. My reading of the evidence is that face-to-face encounters between victims and offenders and their supporters *is* a practice worth maintaining, and perhaps enlarging, although we should not expect it to deliver strong stories of repair and goodwill most of the time. If we want to avoid the cycle of optimism and pessimism (Matthews, 1988) that so often attaches to any justice innovation, then we should be courageous and tell the real story of restorative justice. But, in telling the real story, there is some risk that a promising, fledgling idea will meet a premature death.

Acknowledgements

This article is revised from a plenary address given to the Scottish Criminology Conference, Edinburgh, 21–2 September 2000. My thanks to the conference organizers, Lesley McAra and David J. Smith, for the invitation; and to Emilios Christodoulidis, Neil Hutton, Ian Loader, Richard Sparks and the anonymous reviewers for their comments on earlier versions.

Notes

1 Indicative examples of advocates are Umbreit (1994), Consedine (1995), Zehr (1995), Van Ness and Strong (1997), Bazemore and Walgrave (1999) and Braithwaite (1999). Among the sceptics and critics are Ashworth (1993), Pavlich (1996), Blagg (1997), Hudson (1998), Levrant *et al.* (1999) and Delgado (2000). Because the modern idea of restorative justice is new, publications reporting findings from research are few. Among them are contributors in collections edited by Hudson *et al.* (1996), Crawford and Goodey (2000), Bazemore and Schiff (2001) and Morris and Maxwell (2001).

2 Conferences are meetings where an admitted offender(s), his/her supporters, a victim(s), his/her supporters and relevant other people come together to discuss the offence, its impact and what sanction (or reparation) is appropriate. The conference, which is run by a co-ordinator and attended by a police officer, is typically used as diversion from court prosecution, but it may also be used to give pre-sentencing advice to judges and magistrates. Police-run diversionary conferencing is highly atypical of Australian and New Zealand conferencing, whereas it

is more typical in UK and North American practices. See Bargen (1996), Hudson *et al.* (1996) and Daly and Hayes (2001) for overviews of jurisdiction variation in Australia and New Zealand.

3 Even when calling for the need to 'blend restorative, reparative, and transformative justice ... with the prosecution of paradigmatic violations of human rights', Drumbl (2000, p.296) is unable to avoid using the term 'retributive' to refer to responses that should be reserved for the few.

4 Drawing from Cottingham's (1979) analysis of retribution's many meanings, restorative justice advocates tend to use retributivism to mean 'repayment' (to which they add a punitive kick) whereas desert theorists, such as von Hirsch (1993), use retributivism to mean 'deserved' and would argue for decoupling retribution from punitiveness.

5 It is important to emphasize that new justice practices have not been applied to the fact-finding stage of the criminal process; they are used almost exclusively for the penalty phase. Some comparative claims about restorative justice practices (e.g. they are not adversarial when retributive justice is) are misleading in that restorative justice attends only to the penalty phase when negotiation is possible. No one has yet sketched a restorative justice process for those who do not admit to an offence.

6 I became aware of the term *new justice* from La Prairie's (1999) analysis of developments in Canada. She defines new justice initiatives as representing a 'shift away from a justice discourse of punitiveness and punishment toward one of reconciliation, healing, repair, atonement, and reintegration' (1999, p.147), and she sees such developments as part of a new emphasis on 'community' and 'partnership' as analysed by Crawford (1997). There may be better terms than the 'old' and 'new justice' (e.g. Hudson, 2001, suggests 'established criminal justice' for the old justice), but my general point is that the retributive/restorative couplet has produced, and continues to produce, significant conceptual confusion in the field.

7 Restorative justice advocates speak of the *harm* not of the *crime*, and in doing so, they elide a crucial distinction between a civil and criminal harm, the latter involving both a *harm* and a *wrong* (Duff, 2001).

8 In response to this point, one reader said there had to be some way to theorize varied justice forms (both in an empirical and normative sense), and thus, the disappointment I speak of reflects a disenchantment with the theoretical enterprise to adequately reflect particularity and variation in the empirical social world. This is a long-standing problem in the sociological field. What troubles me, however, is the construction of theoretical terms in the justice field, which use dualisms in adversarial and oppositional relation to one another.

9 The major research studies in the region are Maxwell and Morris (1993) for New Zealand, Strang *et al.* (1999) for the ACT and the RISE project and the results reported here for the SAJJ project in South Australia. See Daly (2001a) for a review of these and other studies. Space limitations preclude a detailed review of the methods and results of each study.

10 It is important to distinguish jurisdictions like South Australia, New South Wales and New Zealand, where conferences are routinely used, from other jurisdictions (like Victoria and Queensland), where conferences are used selectively and in a relatively few number of cases (although Queensland practices are undergoing change as of April 2001). When conferences are used routinely, we should not expect to see 'restorativeness' emerging most of the time.

11 Space limitations preclude a review of the definitions and methods used in the reoffending studies; rather general findings are summarized.

References

Abel, R.L. (1982) 'The contradictions of informal justice', in Abel, R.L. (ed.) *The Politics of Informal Justice*, New York, Academic Press, vol.1, pp.267–320.

Ashworth, A. (1993) 'Some doubts about restorative justice', *Criminal Law Forum*, vol.4, no.2, pp.277–99.

Bargen, J. (1996) 'Kids, cops, courts, conferencing and children's rights: A note on perspectives', *Australian Journal of Human Rights*, vol.2, no.2, pp.209–28.

Barton, C. (2000) 'Empowerment and retribution in criminal justice', in Strang, H. and Braithwaite, J. (eds) *Restorative Justice: Philosophy to Practice*, pp.55–76, Aldershot, Ashgate/ Dartmouth.

Bazemore, G. and Schiff, M. (eds) (2001) *Restorative Community Justice*, Cincinnati, OH, Anderson Publishing.

Bazemore, G. and Walgrave, L. (1999) 'Restorative juvenile justice: In search of fundamentals and an outline for systemic reform', in Bazemore and Walgrave, L. (eds) *Restorative Juvenile Justice: Repairing the Harm of Youth Crime*, Monsey, NY, Criminal Justice Press, pp.45–74.

Blagg, H. (1997) 'A just measure of shame? Aboriginal youth and conferencing in Australia', *British Journal of Criminology*, vol.37, no.4, pp.481–501.

Blagg, H. (1998) 'Restorative visions and restorative justice practices: Conferencing, ceremony and reconciliation in Australia', *Current Issues in Criminal Justice*, vol.10, no.1, pp.5–14.

Bottoms, A.E. (1998) 'Five puzzles in von Hirsch's theory of punishment', in Ashworth, A. and Wasik, M. (eds) *Fundamentals of Sentencing Theory: Essays in Honour of Andrew von Hirsch*, Oxford, Clarendon Press, pp.53–100.

Braithwaite, J. (1996) 'Restorative justice and a better future', Dorothy J. Killam, Memorial Lecture, reprinted in *Dalhousie Review*, vol.76, no.1, pp.9–32.

Braithwaite, J. (1999) 'Restorative justice: Assessing optimistic and pessimistic accounts', in Tonry, M. (ed.) *Crime and Justice: A Review of Research*, Chicago, IL, University of Chicago Press, vol.25, pp.1–127.

Braithwaite, J. and Daly, K. (1994) 'Masculinities, violence and communitarian control', in Newburn, T. and Stanko, E.A. (eds) *Just Boys doing Business?*, New York, Routledge, pp.189–213.

Braithwaite, J. and Pettit, P. (1990) *Not Just Deserts: A Republican Theory of Criminal Justice*, New York, Oxford.

Cain, M. (2000) 'Orientalism, occidentalism and the sociology of crime', *British Journal of Criminology*, vol.40, no.2, pp.239–60.

Christodoulidis, E. (2000) 'Truth and reconciliation as risks', *Social & Legal Studies*, vol.9, no.2, pp.179–204.

Consedine, J. (1995) *Restorative Justice: Healing the Effects of Crime*, Lyttelton, New Zealand, Ploughshares Publications.

Coombs, M. (1995) 'Putting women first', *Michigan Law Review*, vol.93, no.6, pp.686–712.

Cottingham, J. (1979) 'Varieties of retribution', *Philosophical Quarterly*, vol.29, pp.238–46.

Crawford, A. (1997) *The Local Governance of Crime: Appeals to Community and Partnerships*, Oxford, Clarendon Press.

Crawford, A. (2001) 'The prospects for restorative youth justice in England and Wales: A tale of two acts', in McEvoy, K. and Newburn, T. (eds) *Criminology and Conflict Resolution*, London, Macmillan.

Crawford, A. and Goodey, J. (eds) (2000) *Integrating a Victim Perspective within Criminal Justice*, Aldershot, Ashgate/Dartmouth.

Daly, K. (1989) 'Criminal justice ideologies and practices in different voices: Some feminist questions about justice', *International Journal of the Sociology of Law*, vol.17, no.1, pp.1–18

Daly, K. (1998) 'Restorative justice: Moving past the caricatures', paper presented to Seminar on Restorative Justice, Institute of Criminology, University of Sydney Law School, Sydney, April, Available at: http://www.gu.edu.au/school/ccj/kdaly.html.

Daly, K. (2000a) 'Revisiting the relationship between retributive and restorative justice', in Strang, H. and Braithwaite, J. (eds) *Restorative Justice: Philosophy to Practice*, Aldershot, Ashgate/Dartmouth, pp.33–54.

Daly, K. (2000b) 'Sexual assault and restorative justice', paper presented to Restorative Justice and Family Violence Conference, Australian National University, Canberra, July, Available at: http://www.gu.edu.au/school.ccj/kdaly.html.

Daly, K. (2001a) 'Conferencing in Australia and New Zealand: Variations, research findings, and prospects', in Morris, A. and Maxwell, G. (eds) *Restorative Justice for Juveniles: Conferencing, Mediation and Circles*, Oxford, Hart Publishing, pp.59–89. Available at http://www.gu.edu.au/school/ccj/kdaly.html.

Daly, K. (2001b) *South Australia Juvenile Justice (SAJJ) Research on Conferencing, Technical Report No. 2: Research Instruments in Year 2 (1999) and Background Notes*, Brisbane, Queensland, School of Criminology and Criminal Justice, Griffith University, Available at: http://www.aic.gov.au/rjustice/sajj/index.html.

Daly, K. and Hayes, H. (2001) 'Restorative justice and conferencing in Australia', in *Trends & Issues in Crime and Criminal Justice No. 186*, Canberra, Australian Institute of Criminology. Available at: http://www.aic.gov.au/publications/tandi/tandi186.html.

Daly, K. and Immarigeon, R. (1998) 'The past, present, and future of restorative justice: Some critical reflections', *Contemporary Justice Review*, vol.1, no.1, pp.21–45.

Daly, K., Venables, M., McKenna, M., Mumford, L. and Christie-Johnston, J. (1998) *South Australia Juvenile Justice (SAJJ) Research on Conferencing, Technical Report No. 1: Project Overview and Research Instruments (Year 1)*, Brisbane, Queensland, School of Criminology and Criminal Justice, Griffith University, Available at: http://www.aic.gov.au/rjustice/sajj/index.html.

Davis, G. (1992) *Making Amends: Mediation and Reparation in Criminal Justice*, London, Routledge.

Delgado, R. (2000) 'Prosecuting violence: A colloquy on race, community, and justice', *Standford Law Review*, vol.52, pp.751–74.

Dignan, J. (2000) *Restorative Justice Options for Northern Ireland: A Comparative Review*, Belfast, The Stationery Office Bookshop.

Drumbl, M.A. (2000) 'Retributive justice and the Rwandan genocide', *Punishment & Society*, vol.2, no.3, pp.287–308.

Duff, R.A. (1992) 'Alternatives to punishment – or alternative punishments?', in Cragg, W. (ed.) *Retributivism and its Critics*, Stuttgart, Franz Steiner, pp.44–68.

Duff, R.A. (1996) 'Penal communications: Recent work in the philosophy of punishment', in Tonry, M. (ed.) *Crime and Justice: A Review of Research*, Chicago, IL, University of Chicago Press, vol.20, pp.1–97.

Duff, R.A. (2001) 'Restoration and retribution', paper presented to Cambridge Seminar on Restorative Justice, Toronto, May.

Engel, D. (1993) 'Origin myths: Narratives of authority, resistance, disability, and law', *Law & Society Review*, vol.27, no.4, pp.785–826.

Feeley, M. and Simon, J. (1992) 'The new penology: Notes on the emerging strategy of corrections and its implications', *Criminology*, vol.30, no.4, pp.449–74.

Findlay, M. (2000) 'Decolonising restoration and justice in transitional cultures', in Strang, H. and Braithwaite, J. (eds) *Restorative Justice: Philosophy to Practice*, Aldershot, Ashgate/Dartmouth, pp.185–201.

Garland, D. (1996) 'The limits of the sovereign state', *British Journal of Criminology*, vol.36, no.4, pp.445–71.

Gilligan, C. (1982) *In a Different Voice*, Cambridge, MA, Harvard University Press.

Gilligan, C. (1987) 'Moral orientation and moral development', in Kittay, E. and Meyers, D. (eds) *Women and Moral Theory*, Totowa, NJ, Rowman & Littlefield, pp.19–33.

Hampton, J. (1992) 'Correcting harms versus righting wrongs: The goal of retribution', *UCLA Law Review*, vol.39, pp.1659–702.

Hampton, J. (1998) 'Punishment, feminism, and political identity: A case study in the expressive meaning of the law', *Canadian Journal of Law and Jurisprudence*, vol.11, no.1, pp.23–45.

Harris, M. Kay (1987) 'Moving into the new millennium: Toward a feminist vision of justice', *The Prison Journal*, vol.67, no.2, pp.27–38.

Hayes, H. and Daly, K. (2001) 'Family conferencing in South Australia and re-offending: Preliminary results from the SAJJ project', paper presented to Australian and New Zealand Society of Criminology Conference, Melbourne, February. Available at: http://www.gu.edu.au/school/ccj/kdaly.html.

Heidensohn, F. (1986) 'Models of justice: Portia or Persephone? Some thoughts on equality, fairness and gender in the field of criminal justice', *International Journal of the Sociology of Law*, vol.14, nos 3–4, pp.287–98.

Hudson, B. (1998) 'Restorative justice: The challenge of sexual and racial violence', *Journal of Law and Society*, vol.25, no.2, pp.237–56.

Hudson, B. (2001) 'Victims and offenders', paper presented to Cambridge Seminar on Restorative Justice, Toronto, May.

Hudson, J., Morris, A., Maxwell, G. and Galaway, B. (eds) (1996) *Family Group Conferences: Perspectives on Policy and Practice*, Monsey, NY, Willow Tree Press.

Kurki, L. (2001) 'Evaluation of restorative justice practices', paper presented to Cambridge Seminar on Restorative Justice, Toronto, May.

La Prairie, C. (1999) 'Some reflections on new criminal justice policies in Canada: Restorative justice, alternative measures and conditional sentences', *Australian and New Zealand Journal of Criminology*, vol.32, no.2, pp.139–52.

Levrant, S., Cullen, F.T., Fulton, B. and Wozniak, J.F. (1999) 'Reconsidering restorative justice: The corruption of benevolence revisited?', *Crime & Delinquency*, vol.45, no.1, pp.3–27.

McCold, P. (2000) 'Toward a holistic vision of restorative juvenile justice: A reply to the maximalist model', *Contemporary Justice Review*, vol.3, no.4, pp.357–414.

MacKinnon, C. (1987) *Feminism Unmodified*, Cambridge, MA, Harvard University Press.

Marshall, T. (1996) 'The evolution of restorative justice in Britain', *European Journal of Criminal Policy and Research*, vol.4, no.4, pp.21–43.

Masters, G. and Smith, D. (1998) 'Portia and Persephone revisited: Thinking about feeling in criminal justice', *Theoretical Criminology*, vol.2, no.1, pp.5–27.

Matthews, R. (1988) 'Reassessing informal justice', in Matthews, R. (ed.) *Informal Justice?*, pp.1–24. Newbury Park, CA, Sage.

Maxwell, G. and Morris, A. (1993) *Family, Victims and Culture: Youth Justice in New Zealand*, Wellington, Social Policy Agency and the Institute of Criminology, Victoria University of Wellington.

Maxwell, G. and Morris, A. (1996) 'Research on family group conferences with young offenders in New Zealand', in Hudson, J., Morris, A., Maxwell, G. and Galaway, B. (eds) *Family Group Conferences: Perspectives on Policy & Practice*, pp.88–110, Monsey, NY, Willow Tree Press.

Maxwell, G. and Morris, A. (2000) 'Restorative justice and reoffending', in Strang, H. and Braithwaite, J. (eds) *Restorative Justice: Philosophy to Practice*, pp.93–103, Aldershot, Ashgate/Dartmouth.

Mead, G.H. (1917–18) 'The psychology of punitive justice', *The American Journal of Sociology*, vol.23, pp.577–602.

Melossi, D. (ed.) (1998) *The Sociology of Punishment: Socio-Structural Perspectives*, Aldershot, Ashgate/Dartmouth.

Miller, S. and Blackler, J. (2000) 'Restorative justice: Retribution, confession and shame', in Strang, H. and Braithwaite, J. (eds) *Restorative Justice: Philosophy to Practice*, Aldershot, Ashgate/Dartmouth, pp.77–91.

Morris, A. and Maxwell, G. (eds) (2001) *Restorative Justice for Juveniles: Conferencing, Mediation and Circles*, Oxford, Hart Publishing.

Nova Scotia Department of Justice (1998) *Restorative Justice: A Program for Nova Scotia*, Halifax, Department of Justice.

O'Malley, P. (1999) 'Volatile and contradictory punishment', *Theoretical Criminology*, vol.3, no.2, pp.175–96.

Pavlich, G.C. (1996) *Justice Fragmented: Mediating Community Disputes under Post-Modern Conditions*, New York, Routledge.

Pratt, J. (2000) 'The return of the Wheelbarrow men; or, The arrival of postmodern penality?', *British Journal of Criminology*, vol.40, no.1, pp.127–45.

Shearing, C. (2001) 'Punishment and the changing face of the governance', *Punishment & Society*, vol.3, no.2, pp.203–20.

Sherman, L.W., Strang, H. and Woods, D.J. (2000) *Recidivism Patterns in the Canberra Reintegrative Shaming Experiments (RISE).* Canberra, Centre for Restorative Justice, Australian National University. Available at: http://www.aic.gov.au/rjustice/rise/recidivism/index.html.

Smart, C. (1989) *Feminism and the Power of Law*, London, Routledge.

Smart, C. (1992) 'The woman of legal discourse', *Social & Legal Studies*, vol.1, no.1, pp.29–44.

South African Truth and Reconciliation Commission (1998) *The Report of the Truth and Reconciliation Commission*, Available at: http://www.org.za/truth/report.

Strang, H., Sherman, L.W., Barnes, G.C. and Braithwaite, J. (1999) *Experiments in Restorative Policing: A Progress Report to the National Police Research Unit on the Canberra Reintegrative Shaming Experiments (RISE)*, Canberra, Centre for Restorative Justice, Australian National University. Available at: http://www.aic.gov.au/rjustice/rise/index.html.

Tonry, M. (1999) 'Rethinking unthinkable punishment policies in America', *UCLA Law Review*, vol.46, no.4, pp.1751–91.

Tyler, T.R. (1990) *Why People Obey the Law*, New Haven, CT, Yale University Press.

Tyler, T.R., Boeckmann, R.J., Smith, H.J. and Huo, Y.J. (1997) *Social Justice in a Diverse Society*, Boulder, CO, Westview Press.

Umbreit, M. (1994) *Victim Meets Offender: The Impact of Restorative Justice and Mediation*, Monsey, NY, Criminal Justice Press.

Van Ness, D. (1993) 'New wine and old wineskins: Four challenges of restorative justice', *Criminal Law Forum*, vol.4, no.2, pp.251–76.

Van Ness, D. and Strong, K. (1997) *Restoring Justice*, Cincinnati, OH, Anderson Publishing.

Von Hirsch, A. (1993) *Censure and Sanctions*, New York, Oxford University Press.

Walgrave, L. (1995) 'Restorative justice for juveniles: Just a technique or a fully fledged alternative?', *The Howard Journal*, vol.34, no.3, pp.228–49.

Walgrave, L. (2000) 'How pure can a maximalist approach to restorative justice remain? Or can a purist model of restorative justice become maximalist?', *Contemporary Justice Review*, vol.3, no.4, pp.415–32.

Walgrave, L. and Aertsen, I. (1996) 'Reintegrative shaming and restorative justice: Interchangeable, complementary or different?', *European Journal on Criminal Policy and Research*, vol.4, no.4, pp.67–85.

Weitekamp, E. (1999) 'The history of restorative justice', in Bazemore, G. and Walgrave, L. (eds) *Restorative Juvenile Justice: Repairing the Harm of Youth Crime*, Monsey, NY, Criminal Justice Press, pp.75–102.

Wright, M. (1991) *Justice for Victims and Offenders*, Philadelphia, PA, Open University Press.

Zedner, L. (1994) 'Reparation and retribution: Are they reconcilable?', *Modern Law Review*, vol.57, March, pp.228–50.

Zehr, H. (1995) 'Justice paradigm shift? Values and vision in the reform process', *Mediation Quarterly*, vol.12, no.3, pp.207–16.

CHAPTER 17

Community Justice: Transforming Communities through Restorative Justice?

by Adam Crawford and Todd R. Clear

In this chapter, we discuss the feasibility of underlying assumptions of 'community' and 'restorative' justice. These justice paradigms, often used interchangeably, are thought to embody a different conception of public safety that: (1) is delivered through a local or neighbourhood level operational focus, (2) seeks to involve and empower ordinary citizens, (3) relies upon 'private' and 'parochial' forms of social control, and (4) operates within a problem-solving approach to social issues. Our discussion of their underlying assumptions leads us to pose a number of critical questions and concerns regarding the role and place of 'community' within restorative justice and its potential implications for theory and practice. This leads us to consider the transformative potential and limitations of restorative justice within broader notions of crime prevention, community safety, and social policy. We begin with an attempt to distinguish community and restorative justice concepts.

Community justice and restorative justice in contrast

In recent usage, these two concepts have become blurred, but there are important distinctions between them. There are good reasons why this is so. Restorative justice advocates and community justice advocates tend to use similar language, begin with a similar critique of the current justice system, and seek similar outcomes of restoration. Nevertheless, a useful distinction may be drawn between restorative and community justice, one that is nuanced and conceptual and (as we shall discuss later) poses distinct issues for reformers interested in either agenda.[2]

At the risk of oversimplifying, restorative justice defines the problem of justice as lying within the processes and outcomes attached to 'cases' of crime. In this regard, it is much like a traditional justice model, though it distinguishes itself from established justice processes and outcomes in important ways. Procedurally, restorative justice opens doors to effective participation of those who are normally denied a voice in traditional criminal justice: offenders, victims, their families, and neighbors. It defines successful outcomes in terms of the experiences of these people to whom the doors have been opened. It is radical in the sense that it is suspicious of credentialed professionals, distrustful of formal procedures, and embracing of a creative range of potential in solutions (as opposed to a list of presumptive sanctions). As a reform, though, restorative justice is profoundly traditional in the location of its efforts. It works at the level of particular criminal cases, seeking to alter how they are handled and how they are resolved. When the case is satisfactorily concluded, restorative justice may be seen as having achieved its objectives.

Community justice, by contrast, sets its focus on a different level. It is concerned with, for want of a better phrase, 'what it is like for a person to live and work in this place' (see Clear and Karp, 1999). Criminal cases matter, but they matter because of the way crime affects community life in locations that are typically smaller than legal jurisdictions: neighborhoods, rather than cities. Whatever is done about the handling of criminal cases in these locations is justified on the basis of how the strategy in question (as opposed to other alternative strategies) affects what it is like to be in that place. Community justice may be seen as having a more radical reform orientation

Source: in Bazemore, G. and Schift, M. (eds) (2001) *Restorative Community Justice*, Cincinnati, Anderson Publishing, pp.127–49.

than restorative justice. It holds its advocates accountable not only for the handling of cases but for the nature of a collective experience. It embraces a much wider array of strategies including crime prevention schemes that fall well outside the restorative justice domain.

The melding of these ideas has been relatively recent. Earlier forms of restorative justice in the northeastern United States came out of a vision on the part of Mennonites and other religious groups of an inclusive, interpersonal, and problem-solving alternative to the traditional adversarial system of justice (Van Ness and Strong, 1997; Zehr, 1990). Outside the United States (and later in the southwestern United States), indigenous traditions served as models for reformers who sought to replace what they saw as sterile – and even bankrupt – formal justice processes with hopeful, participatory, and sympathetic alternatives. Most notable among these have been family group and community conferences, community mediation, and sentencing and 'healing' circles (Hudson *et al.*, 1996; Morris and Maxwell, 2000; LaPrairie, 1995; Stuart, 1996). Collectively, these developments involve meetings at which all those with a stake in the resolution of the issues surrounding a crime are brought together in the presence of a facilitator to discuss the harm the offense caused and how it might be repaired.

Outside of the New Zealand experience of family group conferences for young offenders as institutionalized at the heart of youth justice by the Children, Young Persons and Their Families Act 1989, the practice of restorative justice has tended to occupy peripheral positions at the margins of criminal justice. Nevertheless, the ideas that inform restorative justice have had considerable (and increasing) impact upon public policy debates,[1] as well as research-based notions about how we might reconstruct and rethink criminal justice in the future. As such, restorative justice came to constitute 'the emerging social movement for criminal justice reform in the 1990s' (Braithwaite, 1998, p.324).

If restorative justice finds its emotional roots in religious-like exhortations to do good for fellow humans, community justice's emotional roots are located in a faith of civic life, a belief in the importance of 'collective efficacy' (Sampson *et al.*, 1997) or 'capacity for self-regulation' (Bursik and Grasmick, 1992). While restorative justice is about cases, community justice is about places.

This conceptual distinction shows why the two ideas can be integrated in the minds of so many reformers: restorative justice is often seen as an important way to promote community justice. Likewise, when community justice initiatives aim to improve quality of life for victims, offenders, families, and neighbors who happen to live in a place of high crime, then restorative justice case outcomes may be an important part of the overall approach. However, restorative justice is not the only way to try to bring about the improvement in community life that is sought through community justice. Such disparate ideas as 'zero-tolerance policing,' community courts, Neighborhood Watch, and police–probation partnerships can be promoted under the community justice banner, because they have as their central justification the improvement of community life *in particular places where crime has damaged community life.*

Finally, this distinction clarifies the questions one would entertain in constructing an evaluation of programs associated with the two different ideas. A restorative justice program 'works' when key constituents experience a restorative process and end up feeling restored by it. Community justice programs 'work' when the quality of life in a given place improves.

Common themes in restorative and community justice

While these two visions of justice may be distinguished from one another, they also share certain underlying themes. Practical expressions of both restorative and community justice seek to recognize that crime is more than an offense against the state. They aim to consider the impact on victims and others involved, be they family, kinship, friends, or members of broader networks of interdependencies. They also endeavor to explore how communities can assist in the processes of restoration and conflict resolution. Implicitly, they seek to curtail and limit the role of criminal justice professionals, preferring to empower victims and offenders, as well as other family or kinship members, citizens, and community and voluntary groups or associations as partners in the justice process. These 'significant others' are the 'stakeholders' of a revised vision of justice, which is about recognizing and bringing into play, through their active involvement, a broader conceptualization of the stakeholders in the process of dispute processing and resolution. In this sense, Braithwaite has described this alternative view of justice as 'deliberative justice,' in contrast to the 'professional justice of lawyers':

> it is about people deliberating over the consequences of crimes, and how to deal with them and prevent their recurrence ... Thus restorative justice restores the deliberative control of justice by citizens.
>
> (1998, p.329)

In essence, community and restorative justice embody both a critique of existing formal legal procedures and practices (what we might call a 'negative attraction') and a quest to revive some notion of community, mutuality, or civic trust (a 'positive attraction'). Crime, after all, 'is the most emotionally compelling symbol of lost community' (Abel, 1995, p.118). Consequently, the quest to revitalize the community fabric constitutes a powerful force in the appeal of both community justice and restorative justice, as they envision this as both a means to an end (the prevention of crime) and as an end in itself (community identified as the home of the ideal of genuine human identity, connectedness, and reciprocity).

Both of these negative and positive appeals have different resonances within differing societies, as they are refracted through divergent legal traditions, institutional apparatuses, and cultural context. Moreover, the rise of non-traditional justice expresses itself through, and coincides with, a rearticulation of the relationship between the state and civil society in which the nation-state, and hence the apparatus of criminal justice, appears to be confronting the dual pressures of globalization and localization. As a consequence, the contemporary 'monopolistic' and 'sovereign' state is increasingly forced to confront its own limitations with regard to its ability to guarantee public order and safety. New challenges now confront the tasks of policing and crime control, the pre-eminent and central symbols of state sovereignty, while economic pressures from one side collide with claims for greater cultural plurality from another side. Pluralization and fragmentation, in turn, have questioned traditional claims to universal security within a nation's boundaries. Increasingly, modern states find themselves able only to deliver punishment rather than security. In this context, governments have sought to experiment with, and explore, alternative means of crime control that aim to responsibilize individuals, families, groups, and communities as 'partners against crime' in a new 'corporate' approach (Crawford, 1994). This heralds a fundamental rearticulation of individual and group responsibilities and professional 'expertise,' as well as traditional notions of state paternalism and monopoly of control – all of which seep into, and affect debates about, community and restorative justice in relation to established modes of state justice.

The community and restorative justice movements have managed to draw support from diverse interests with often conflicting motivations. Particular initiatives have met with enthusiasm from divergent quarters, across the political spectrum, and within professional and community groups. The divergent nature of the interests and groups promoting these reforms in traditional justice has resulted in initiatives often meaning different things to different people. On one level, this has allowed the movement to gain support from diverse sources and to fit into the prevailing political rhetoric at given moments. However, it also means that specific initiatives can be (and have been) pulled in different, and often competing, directions as they attempt to meet multiple aims and objectives and satisfy the divergent demands of the different constituencies. In attempting (or claiming) to 'do too much,' the danger is that community and restorative justice initiatives can end up falling short on a number of fronts.

Questions regarding restorative justice

The involvement of different stakeholders beyond the individual offender and direct victim is justified by restorative justice commentators on a number of levels. First, some commentators have preferred to extend and expand the notion of 'victim' to include those indirectly affected by victimization, such that 'it is more fruitful to theorize crime as typically affecting multiple victims in a range of ways' (Young, 2000, p.227). In this way, 'significant others' are seen as having suffered indirectly either through their relationship with the primary victim or because of the disruption caused to communal peace and order by the offense. A common aim, then, is to draw extended family and community members into the process of finding resolutions and redress to crimes. The idea is to assemble actors with the closest relations and social interdependencies to the principal parties in dispute, most notably with a view to bringing together those people with the best chance of persuading the offender of the irresponsibility of a criminal act (Braithwaite and Mugford, 1994, p.142).

This has led some restorative justice commentators to include the local 'community' more broadly as having a stake in the resolution of the conflict and, hence, as a party in restorative responses to offending. The involvement of the parties in the process of disputing through restorative justice is seen by proponents to be an essential element of community membership (Wright, 1991, pp.76–7). For some, the community has a stake as an affected party. For others, the community is seen as a resource for the resolution of disputes and victim/offender reintegration. Still others see dispute resolution as a fundamentally communal activity requiring community input. As such, in some of the restorative justice literature, 'the community' is drawn upon to constitute the role of the 'third party' – as mediator or facilitator – in place of the state.

Finally, restorative justice presupposes that community involvement *per se* in the decision-making process in response to offending assists in the building or reconstruction of community institutions and that, as such, it has the capacity to engender fundamental change in communities. Hence, restorative justice both draws upon, and simultaneously seeks to reinvigorate, a sense of community. Consequently, the response to crime is an activity that is conducted both on behalf of the community and that reflects a community's moral sensibilities. Conflict processing is, therefore, a highly *communal* act. It strengthens and reaffirms communal bonds. It represents not only a 'potential for activity, for participation' but also allows the parties 'opportunities for norm-clarification' (Christie, 1977, pp.7–8). Hence, it is argued that the process of restorative justice – through party participation in conflict negotiation – is itself socially constructive. Resolving a conflict between parties is instrumental to the construction of shared values and commitment among the local community of residents. Consequently, restorative justice mechanisms are believed to empower the parties and the wider community through a heightened form of communication.

As a consequence, it is argued, community conferences and family group conferences go beyond some of the limitations of traditional victim–offender mediation because of the involvement of participants from the wider community with whom the parties have a 'relationship of genuine care.' Firstly, it opens up what can otherwise be a private process (Braithwaite and Daly, 1994, pp.206–7). Secondly, in doing so, it can limit the power that mediation accords to professional mediators. Thus, the power of mediators is curbed and the process is open to greater scrutiny. Thirdly, it confirms accountability upon those citizens who have concern for victims and offenders. 'In contrast to mediation, conferences are designed to encourage community dialogue' (Braithwaite and Daly, 1994, p.207). Finally, it addresses the potentially unequal bargaining power of the parties by incorporating extended members.

For some commentators, the strengthening of the community bonds that restorative justice mechanisms facilitate is itself crime-preventive. Implicit in this understanding is the idea that strong communities (and, hence, a strong moral order) act to prevent crime. Echoing social disorganization theories of crime, a lack of informal control is associated with criminality; such disputes are seen as arising where 'normal' community controls have broken down.

However, restorative justice immediately raises questions about legitimacy, as it reconfigures the notion of the 'public interest' through its appeal to a wider notion of stakeholders and to more localized normative orderings that rely upon private and parochial forms of social control. Ideally, the normative order should emerge from the extended parties themselves rather than being imposed from above. However, this tends to presuppose an unproblematic consensus without addressing the question of what the moral community *is*. The restorative justice response tends to assume organic wholeness of a given collectivity, one that accords little space for (or acknowledgement of) intra-community conflict and diversity of value systems. Will victims and offenders always belong to the same moral community? Some restorative justice initiatives explicitly attempt to recognize and accommodate the cultural needs of specific parties or even the cultural differences between victims and offenders. This may extend to the selection criteria of the third party or other parties to the dispute and/or its location and format. However, this recognition of multicultural heterogeneity raises a number of normative, as well as practical, dilemmas. For example, which cultural identities (ascriptions of difference) are sufficiently appropriate or worthy to be acknowledged and accommodated within the process of 'representation' or structure of negotiation? How inclusive can such a moral community be before it loses its capacity to induce compliance and encourage conformity?

Perversely perhaps, the expanded notion of 'stakeholder' in restorative justice can serve to dilute the centrality of the primary parties: the victim and the offender. It can hand power to unrepresentative community members, service providers, and paraprofessionals (potentially with their own interests to serve) that coalesce around restorative justice programs, be they the new 'experts' in techniques of reintegrative shaming, conference facilitation, or mediation. Some of the primary lessons from the experiments in 'informal justice' in the 1980s were that programs established in the name of community mediation soon became increasingly formalized and professionalized, often under external pressures (Merry and Milner, 1993). The somewhat pessimistic conclusion reached by Yngvesson in relation to the San Francisco Community Boards was that community empowerment may be possible only for a privileged 'internal community' of volunteers rather than the external 'community neighbors' (1993, p.381).

Before rushing to be inclusive by expanding the notion of 'stakeholders' to incorporate ever-greater numbers of people, restorative justice needs to problematize, and ask fundamental questions about, the notion of stakeholder. Is a stakeholder in restorative justice someone who either provides, uses, or benefits from a service, or has relevant expert or local knowledge? If so, what does stakeholding entail? Is it merely an appeal to greater inclusiveness and mutual responsibility? Or is it that people 'own' disputes such that they should determine outcomes themselves? How far should the involvement of stakeholders be taken in terms of decisionmaking or decision-taking? And finally, what is meant by the *co-production* of stakeholders in restorative justice?

Nevertheless, the identification of different stakeholders raises some important issues with regard to how success (or failure) is to be measured. It forces a reappraisal of the traditional question of 'what works?' and introduces new variables into the measurement, posing a tiered series of questions concerning: 'what works, for whom, and under what conditions?' As such, restorative justice should cause governments, practitioners, and researchers to rethink the process of evaluation and to broaden the notions of success and failure to include the views and experiences of other stakeholders whose voice is all-too-often silenced. Hence, the impact of restorative justice upon victims and the local community may be as important for proponents of restorative justice as its impact upon offenders.

Restoring or transforming communities?

For some commentators, the consequences of the community justice and restorative justice movements for communities are more important than the consequences of offenders. This is suggested by Judge Barry Stuart with regard to 'healing' circles in North America:

> The principal value of Community Sentencing Circles cannot be measured by what happens to offenders, but rather by what happens to communities. In reinforcing and building a sense of community, Circle Sentencing improves the capacity of communities to heal individuals and families and ultimately to prevent crime.
>
> (Stuart, 1994, pp.18–19)

It is argued that the reinvigoration of community through restorative justice mechanisms facilitates strong bonds of social control. Strong communities can speak to us in moral voices. They allow 'the policing *by* communities rather than the policing *of* communities' (Strang, 1995, p.217).

However, by necessity, alternative justice processes presuppose an existing degree of informal control upon which mutuality, reciprocity, and commitment can be reformed. As Braithwaite notes, informal control processes (such as reintegrative shaming), which some community conferences seek to engender, are more conducive to – and more effective when drawing upon – communitarian cultures (Braithwaite, 1989, p.100). The paradox is that in urban, individualistic, and anonymous cultures, such as these that prevail in most Western towns and cities, informal control mechanisms such as shaming lack potency. The appeal to revive or transform community has arisen at exactly the moment when it appears most absent. In some senses, for some, this paradox provides the basis for the attraction of restorative and community justice.

However, the conception of community extends beyond locality (with its spatial or geographic communities) and embraces a multiplicity of groups and networks to which, it is believed, we all belong (Strang, 1994, p.16). This conception of community, which is argued to be more in keeping with contemporary social life, does not rely upon a fixed assumption of *where* a community will be found. Rather, it develops upon the notion of 'communities of care' – the networks of obligation and respect between the individual and everyone who cares about him or her the most, which are not bounded by geography (Braithwaite and Daly, 1994, p.195). It marks a significant development in the understanding of contemporary communities. These communities of care are supposed to be more relevant to contemporary modern living in urban societies. They encompass an expanded notion of 'community' that, in part, is subjective in that the ascription to community membership or social identity is personal and does not necessarily carry any fixed or external attributes of membership. The fact that communities of care do not carry connotations of coerced or constrained membership is one of the concept's distinctive appeals.

Community, in this sense, begins to look like a set of bilateral relationships of trust, rather than a dense, complex social order with rule-making capacities and the means to induce compliance, and which is set in a larger social matrix that can, and often does, affect and invade those internal orders. Insofar as it extends beyond individual feelings of affection and trust, community tends to be seen in symbolic terms as a set of shared or collective attitudes. As such, it lacks what Currie calls 'structural awareness' and therefore fails to see community in 'much more structural, or institutional terms not just as a set of attitudes we can "implant" or mobilize, but as an interlocking set of long-standing institutions which in turn are deeply affected by larger social and economic forces' (1988, pp.282–3). If community is a product of free-floating social identity, internally ascribed and easily escaped (as Braithwaite and other restorative justice commentators imply), then it does not have the significant characteristics around which to induce compliance. If community is inherently volitional, comprising a collection of similar people who have voluntarily chosen to be together on the basis of some shared commonality; then what is its norm-making and norm-affirming capacity? How much compliance can a community command if individuals are free to move from one community to the next? In order to hold some normative sway over their members, to some degree, communities must be able to exact a measure of compliance, by means of regulation, sanction, and/or coercion.

Hence, for restorative agendas, the present weakness of 'community' is often seen simultaneously as the problem (the cause of most contemporary social ills) and as its saving grace, in that people are assumed to be able to move freely between communities if they disagree with their practices or values and/or remain within a community and dissent from the dominant moral voices therein. On the one hand, contemporary 'light' communities are held up as examples of how communities can allow sufficient space for individual or minority dissent, innovation, and difference – and yet they are also seen as insufficient with regard to informal control.

This brings us to pose the following question: What is actually meant by the claim to 'restore' or 'reintegrate' communities, as advanced by proponents of both community and restorative justice (Braithwaite, 1998, p.325; Clear and Karp, 1999; Van Ness and Strong, 1997, pp.120–2)? The very notion of restoring communities suggests a return to some pre-existing state. Is this appeal to community a quest for retrieval or re-imagining of tradition and authority in some historic sense? Is it born of a nostalgic urge to turn back the clock to a mythical golden age of genuine human identity, connectedness, and reciprocity? Or does community constitute a dynamic force for democratic renewal that challenges existing inequalities of power and the differential distribution of life opportunities and pathways to crime?

In order to consider the genuine potential of restorative and community justice, we need to shed the rose-tinted glasses worn by many advocates and confront the empirical realities of most communities. The ideal of unrestricted entry to, and exit from, communities needs to be reconciled with the existence of relations of dominance, exclusion, and differential power. The reality is that many stable communities tend to resist innovation, creativity and experimentation, as well as shun diversity. These communities may already be able to come together for informal social control, and the way these processes play out lacks inclusive qualities and offender-sensitive styles. These communities can be, and often are, pockets of intolerance and prejudice. They can be coercive and tolerant of bigotry and discriminatory behavior. Weaker parties within such communities often experience them not as a home of connectedness and mutuality but as a mainspring of inequalities that sustain and reinforce relations of dependence (for example, with regard to gender roles and the tolerance of domestic violence or child abuse). They are often hostile to minorities, dissenters, and outsiders.

Communities are hierarchical formations, structured upon lines of power, dominance, and authority. They are intrinsically exclusive – as social inclusion presupposes processes of exclusion – and many solidify and define themselves around notions of 'otherness' that are potentially infused with racialized overtones. Challenging and disrupting established community order, its assumptions and power relations may be a more fundamental aspect of a progressive restorative justice program. *Transforming* communities may be more appropriate than *restoring* communities.

However, the related question begged by this assertion is whether transforming communities is either a feasible or appropriate task of restorative justice.

The feasibility of restoration and the transformation of communities

Restorative justice holds out the promise that communities can give redress to victims for what has been taken from them and can reintegrate offenders within the community. Yet, not all communities share the same access to resources, nor can they feasibly restore victims or reintegrate offenders in the same ways or to the same extent. Communities are marked by different capacities to mobilize internally on the basis of mutual trust and a willingness to intervene on behalf of the common good – what Sampson and colleagues refer to as 'collective efficacy' (1997) – as well as differential relations that connect local institutions to sources of power and resources in the wider civil society in which it is located – what Hope refers to as 'vertical power relations' (1995, p.24). This reminds us that restorative justice, in its appeals to community involvement, must not disconnect a concern for community approval or disapproval from a concern with political and economic inequality.

Neither restorative justice nor community justice should be allowed to become a byword for geographic (in)justice, Rather, they need to be based in an understanding of social justice and a concern for political economy that link notions of restoration with wider social and economic relations. A concern for intra-community attributes must be connected with attention to the context of a community.

The allied questions are: 'Who restores what, to whom and why?' and 'whose quality of life improves?' These questions raise issues directly concerning obligation and legitimacy. The legitimacy of justice and restoration must rest on the legitimacy of the community itself. Why would someone want to be restored to, or reintegrated within, a moral community that has abused them, marginalized them, or merely not valued them? Many offenders live peripatetic lives on the margins of communities. They may experience community not in its benign form but as one of alienation and sometimes hostility. For them, the community may suffer from significant and important empathy deficits. If we accept the empirical reality that thin and frayed lines exist between offending and victimization, offenders may themselves have been the victims of crimes against which the community has failed to act or respond (particularly given the high levels of nonreporting and nonrecording revealed by victim surveys). This has particular implications for legitimacy in restorative and community justice, which calls out for a mutuality of respect. Similarly, young people who have been the victims of powerful adult abuse may have good reasons not to accept as legitimate the dominant moral voice of a community that neither recognizes their suffering as worthy of attention nor addresses their marginalization. Communities have obligations and responsibilities to offenders and victims if they are to be seen as legitimate moral communities. This raises questions about the feasibility of community integration and, hence, the feasibility of reintegrative shaming.

To what degree is a more or less socialized youth required for reintegrative shaming to be possible? People commonly misunderstand what shame means. Shame is the emotion a person feels when confronted with the fact that one's behavior has been different to what one believes is morally required. Shame is moral self-reproach. Shame is thus personal; it is not produced by the actions of another. A person may humiliate or embarrass someone by a public act of rebuke, but that does not guarantee that such a public act will produce the emotion of shame. The exposure by another will produce shame only when the exposed person holds an aspiration to a different standard than has been exhibited by that past behavior. A community's shaming response may generate a person's humiliation, but humiliation may not lead to reintegration. Rather, it may lead to what Sherman (1997) has described as 'counter deterrence' if the person being humiliated does not feel ashamed. Therefore, we need to differentiate the personal emotion of shame from processes of shaming that may be inscribed into community and restorative justice practices without necessarily producing their desired result. Community and restorative justice should seek to encourage the former – which may be better described as 'remorse' (Morris and Maxwell, 2000, pp.215–17) – and avoid the latter. How we inculcate in others a moral self-view that makes productive shame possible is then a major challenge for restorative and community justice enthusiasts.

This raises questions about the feasibility of timescale – the extent to which restorative justice interventions are both *timely* (appropriate in time for parties) and *time enough* (sufficiently durable over time to effect change) – and of community integration. Can a limited intervention (such as that envisaged by a family group and community conferences) really turn around people's lives (Levrant *et al.*, 1999)? This is particularly problematic if these interventions are unable to address the structural problems or the causes of their criminality in a long-term and sustained manner. Questions of cost and the availability of adequate resources often hamstring restorative justice practices and community justice initiatives.

From the perspective of the victim, there are also concerns regarding the feasibility of restoration. Victims need to recompense for their harm. Although this is a goal to which restorative justice appeals, most young people who have offended will not necessarily be able to make sufficient reparation. In this context, the public interest lies in public restoration to victims of crime (through schemes of compensation, for example). Under the benevolent veil of restorative justice, the state should not be allowed to abandon its responsibility to compensate. Public forms of restoration and redress should not be substituted merely with private restoration.

The appropriateness of community transformation through restorative justice

Making amends and restoring troubled relations in an unequal society may mean restoring unequal relations and, hence, reaffirming inequality. Moreover, restoring the preexisting equilibrium may mean reinstating and reaffirming relations of dominance. As such, Braithwaite is right to note these limitations of restorative justice, which

> cannot resolve deep structural injustices that cause problems ... Restorative justice does not resolve the age-old questions of what should count as unjust outcomes. It is a more modest philosophy than that.
>
> (1998, p.329)

He goes on to identify two demands for restorative justice in this light. The first is that restorative justice should not make structural injustice worse. The second is that the deliberative processes of restorative justice should require that the outcome be grounded in a dialogue that takes account of underlying injustices (1998, p.329). All too often, however, in practice, negotiation avoids such dialogue regarding structural conflicts (Crawford, 1997). Consequently, Braithwaite's two demands constitute important bounding mechanisms to which practitioners would do well to accord. Importantly, they place a crucial responsibility for the public interest upon third-party facilitators. There is no reason why the restoration agenda cannot have as an objective the development of socially just improvements in those communities hardest hit by crime.

This also raises the question of the role of the state. The modern welfare state, with its claim to a 'solidarity project,' has striven to mediate and mitigate such differences in power and relations of dominance. Despite some commentators' arguments that neo-liberal discourses of government have been dispensed with the aim of 'governing through society,' resulting in what Rose (1996) has called the 'death of the social,' the nation state remains the fundamental 'power-container.' Nevertheless, appeals to community as embodied in restorative and community justice developments clearly problematize the notion of the social. Not only does community represent the territorialization of political thought and how conduct is collectivized, but the 'social' and 'community' aspects are no longer necessarily complementary and of the same broad rationality of rule. They constitute different and potentially 'competing problematics of government' (O'Malley and Palmer, 1996, p.140). There is a danger that community justice developments become 'club' goods that benefit their members, rather than 'public' goods that seek to benefit society at large. How are the particularistic and parochial interests and desires of communities to be accommodated within a wider frame of *social* justice? We need to think about and problematize the nature of the ruptures and disjunctures between social justice and local or parochial justice and determine how these should be regulated and mitigated in the name of the public good.

Moreover, if these new forms of justice seek social control outside of the state, then with what or whom does power-containing rest? The role of community in restorative and community justice raises important questions about the nature, place, and role of third parties in the processes of justice (Walgrave, 2000). If the third party is a representative of the community rather than the state, then the question is: Upon what notion of representativeness does their legitimacy rest? Does it rest on the mere fact that they are not employed by the state? Moreover, there is a further contradiction in that the more attached to the community third parties are, the less likely they are to hold the required 'detached stance' that is a central value in establishing facilitator neutrality and legitimacy. The more that facilitators or mediators represent particular interests or value systems, the greater the danger that the interests of one of the principal parties may become sidelined or lost altogether. Ironically, of course, it is exactly this pressure to provide neutral and detached facilitators that increases the likelihood of professionalization of third parties and the formalization of otherwise fluid and open restorative processes.

Much of the community justice and restorative justice literature is infused with an explicit, and sometimes implicit, antistatism. It is no coincidence that the rise of restorative justice and the ascendancy of neo-liberal ideology have unfolded simultaneously. They both proclaim an end to universality and state monopoly and imply a privatization of disputes and justice by prioritizing private and parochial forms of control. Yet, a more plural and party-centered form of justice needs to recognize the crucial role of the state as power-container and norm-enforcer, and must seek to hold in creative tension the ideals of restorative justice and those of state justice. Tensions that are at the heart of attempts to integrate restorative justice into mainstream justice should be acknowledged and used as the source of productive forces as one strives to check the abuses of the other. As Lode Walgrave noted, 'It is one of the most delicate challenges in the restorative justice undertaking, to conceive the role of the state (or government) in such a way that it does not impede the real restorative process, while playing its norm-enforcing role' (2000, p.261).

If this new justice movement is to be an element of a much wider policy concerned with constructing the conditions under which civility and mutuality breed, then it must be recognized that restorative justice (unlike community justice) is limited by its reactive nature. It requires harms to be inflicted before restorative interventions can begin to be put in place. This reactive essence confines restorative justice's potential as a transformative ideology. Restorative justice needs to be connected to a wider program of crime prevention and community safety for it to be anything other than reactive and led by individual case. Moreover, it will need to move beyond a narrow focus upon crime to wider concerns about safety in communities from criminal and noncriminal sources of harms. Wiles and Pease (2000) have termed this a 'pan-hazard' approach to community safety. There is much to be gained from a vision that moves beyond reactions to crime to proactive interventions that extend far beyond criminality and disorder. Such an approach would see restorative justice as a limited aspect of broader politics concerned with the promotion of social goods. To some degree, it is this larger picture to which some Republican criminologists, such as Braithwaite (1989; 1995), allude. All too often, however, the restorative justice literature fails to make these broader connections and holds up restorative justice as both an end in itself and the primary transformative logic in the reinvigoration of moral communities.

Social and economic policy (including employment, education, health, and housing) rather than criminal justice policy, regardless of whether it is restorative, must be the primary vehicle for the construction of a just and equal social order. The danger is that restorative justice, by itself, accords a centrality to the reaction to crime that would not have been accorded even by Durkheim (1893). Responses to crime are fundamentally social and cultural events that seek to reaffirm a collective consciousness and social cohesion, but they are not the mainstay out of which the collective consciousness springs. In claiming a centrality in the construction of a just social order, restorative justice proponents give the reaction to crime an overriding position that it may not deserve. A potential consequence is that fundamental public issues may become marginalized, except insofar as they are defined in terms of their criminogenic qualities. The danger is that, as a consequence, we may come to view poor housing, unemployment, racism, failed educational facilities, the lack of youth leisure opportunities, and so on, as no longer important public issues in themselves. Rather, their importance may be seen in terms of the belief that they lead to crime and disorder. The fact that they may do so is no reason not to assert their importance in their own right. The fear is that social deficiencies are being redefined as 'crime problems' that need to be controlled and managed rather than addressed in themselves. This would represent the ultimate 'criminalization of social policy'. Hence, there is an anxiety that a high degree of influence given to restorative justice may result in social policy, as well as its direction and funding, being redefined in terms of its implications for crime alone. This is rendered all the more worrysome given the place of inequality within both neo-liberal ideology and the dominant Durkheimian discourse of 'social (dis)integration' that underlies much of liberal thinking (see Levitas, 1996). Inequality, in this context, increasingly is viewed as something that is a problem only because, if extreme enough, it is disruptive of social order – or at least perceived to be potentially disruptive (as in the fear of crime).

Lessons from the past 20 years of research into community crime prevention suggest a certain degree of caution regarding the long-term benefits of restorative and community justice as community empowerment. Almost all studies of local crime-prevention activities identify difficulty in sustaining participants' interest and enthusiasm over time, even in places where initial levels of awareness and participation were high (Palumbo *et al.*, 1997; Rosenbaum, 1988). Communities organized solely or primarily around concerns about crime are often short-lived (Podolefsky and Dubow, 1981). As Skogan notes, 'concern about crime simply does not provide a basis for sustained individual participation' (1988, p.49).

Finally, given crime's capacity to evoke intense emotions and bifurcate through deep-seated fears of 'otherness,' it may be an inappropriate vehicle around which to construct open and tolerant communities, as opposed to those that solidify around 'defensive exclusivity' (Crawford, 1998).

Some concluding thoughts

Implicit in restorative justice is a re-evaluation of the responsibilities of government, communities, and individuals for responding to victimization and the harms of crime. Where traditional notions of justice treated the public as the recipient of an expert service provided by criminal justice professionals, restorative justice calls upon public participation and active citizenry.[2] Individuals and groups become reconfigured as partners in the process and coproducers of the outcome. The pluralization of responsibility acknowledges the limits of the sovereign state with respect to crime control and security. It begins a recognition that the causes of crime lie far from the traditional reach of the criminal justice system and, as such, it acknowledges the need for social responses to crime that reflect the nature of the phenomenon itself and its multiple etiology, as well as the importance of mechanisms of informal social control in the prevention of crime.

This allows for a more participatory civil society that fractures the state's monopolistic and paternalistic hold. However, it also presents a danger of a conflation of the responsibilities of the state and those of individuals – victims, offenders, and 'significant others' – as well as communities and other networks of care. Strategies of responsibilization should seek to clarify the distribution of responsibilities and to ensure the appropriate conditions under which the exercise of those responsibilities can be fulfilled and maximized. Unfortunately, much of the restorative and community justice literature and current policy tends to obfuscate the role of the state and third parties, replacing these with a particularly ambiguous appeal to community ordering and individual choice.

The aim of this chapter has been to raise some critical questions for consideration in a period of significant policy activity and thought regarding the potential of an alternative justice paradigm. The manner of this chapter has been deliberately skeptical. It has sought to connect these developments to wider sociopolitical change and to highlight their possible ambiguous implications. As the modern state appears to be coming to terms with its own inability to guarantee order, albeit in a hesitant and ambivalent manner, we need to ask whether the developments reflect a growing civilianization, humanization, or privatization of criminal justice. The latter option raises the concern that governments should not be allowed to use restorative or community justice as a means of unduly shifting the burden of justice onto individuals and communities. These reforms should not result in the state 'washing its hands' through the privatization of disputes. Moreover, there is a danger of confusion of aims within restorative justice that is in part driven and reaffirmed by the diverse support that restorative justice has received across the political spectrum. Are all the aims of restorative justice feasible or desirable? Or should proponents prioritize realizable objectives for practice? The danger is that restorative justice initiatives can end up falling short on a number of fronts.

There is a need for restorative and community justice advocates not only to recognize limitations but also to develop an acute understanding of intra- and inter-community relations. With regard to intra-community relations, restorative aims need to acknowledge differences within (as well as between) communities and not encourage the perpetuation of an 'ideology of unity' (Crawford, 1997, pp.137–9), in which a moral order or consensus is taken as given, rather than constructed through nuanced and complex negotiations. Instead, the ground rules of communication need to have etched within them processes that bind the contending parties together while simultaneously rendering the existing differences sharper and more explicit, even while the parties may arrive at a negotiated outcome. Here, community is not idealized as a cohesive unity but presupposes that differences are acknowledged within it. Such strong bonds require an engagement, over time, with intra-communal differences.

We can imagine, however, a notion of restorative justice that may offer a more fertile soil from which a progressive criminal justice policy can begin to establish itself and flourish, one that turns away from the 'punitive populism' of recent years. Moreover, it affords the potential to challenge many of the modernist assumptions about professional expertise, specialization, state paternalism, and monopoly, which have become established aspects of traditional criminal justice. It would empower victims and offenders and enable them to be treated more humanely and with respect to their interests and needs. Until the economics of criminal justice become a part of the community and restorative justice picture, though, there is always the question of how to resource the initiatives that result in greater justice across communities.

In essence, the current system in the United States involves a massive, officially managed, economic transaction of the following sort: residents of affluent communities transfer their wealth in the form of tax revenues to rural communities (where the prisons are) to pay the salaries and living expenses of people who 'watch' the residents of poor communities for a couple of years, then send them home. The scope of the investment is striking. One study (Rose and Clear, 1998) estimated that about $4.5 million was spent incarcerating a one-year sample of offenders in a 10-by-15 block neighborhood in Tallahassee, Florida. Another study (CASES, 1998) found that $50 million was spent incarcerating the offenders from the Brownsville section of Brooklyn, NY, in 1996–$3 million on residents of a *single* block. These dollar figures reflect the investment of public funds in response to public safety problems in poorer communities from the tax base in wealthy and middle-class neighborhoods to the economies of prison communities. The irony is that almost nothing from this investment goes into the economic infrastructure of the offenders' communities. The justice system investment in these communities is solely 'addition by subtraction': removing certain citizens in the hope that it will be easier for those who remain to improve their circumstances. The economics of community justice must come to see these investments as opportunity cost centers. If some portion of the investment in prison community economies can be refocused toward high-crime communities, then the resources for community justice and restorative justice to address structural and other criminogenic problems in communities can be substantial.

A shorthand way of thinking about the economics of restoration goes along the following lines: traditional criminal justice systems route public funds from tax-paying communities to communities providing prison services, leaving crime-affected communities out of the direct economic loop. Community justice (and, to a lesser extent, restorative justice) seeks to capture some of those funds (both human and financial capital) for direct investment in high-crime locations, in the form of improved physical plant, social support, and even contributed offender labor – the kinds of resources that may contribute more broadly to an improved quality of life and, thus, public safety. One of the best examples of this in the United States is the way in which the Deschutes County (Oregon) Department of Community Justice recaptures dollars intended for juvenile training schools and uses them for community crime prevention (Maloney and Bryant, 1998).

Finally, the realization that community justice can be conciliatory and socially constructive, but also punitive and intolerant, requires the construction of more rigorous criteria for the evaluation of both the malignant and benign elements and attributes of community justice. As such, it necessitates standards against which developments and practices can be assessed or, in a different discourse, it requires a basic conception of human rights.

Moreover, a limited notion of restorative justice may offer a fertile soil from which a more progressive criminal justice policy can be established, one that turns away from the 'punitive populism' of recent years. Moreover, it affords the potential to challenge many of the modernist assumptions about professional expertise, specialization, state paternalism, and monopoly that have become established aspects of traditional criminal justice. Consequently, restorative justice may empower victims and offenders as well as enable them to be treated more humanely and with due respect to their interests and needs.

It is our contention that neither restorative justice nor community justice can be held out as the primary means through which civil society is to be (re)constructed. Although crime may be a 'regressive tax on the poor', it does not follow that reactions to crime should be (or even can be) the appropriate site of redistributive justice. Criminal justice is intrinsically reactive, bound up with state coercion, and limited in its scope. As such, it is not the cradle of a society's civility. It should, however, reflect and express this civility, particularly with regard to the treatment of all those who turn to, or are caught up in, its machinations. In this respect, a qualified understanding of restorative justice that begins to address some of the questions posed in this chapter – while holding in creative tension the notion of the public interest and that of parochial relations – will enable the ideals of restorative justice and those of state justice to act as fundamental social correctives to each other. With an appropriate concern for the real problems affecting life in high-crime communities, restorative justice paradigms can offer some foundation for more just communities.

Notes

1 For example, restorative justice ideas inform recent legislative changes to juvenile justice enacted by the Government in England and Wales through the Crime and Disorder Act 1998 and the Youth Justice and Criminal Evidence Act 1999. Together, these pieces of legislation and allied policy initiatives have advanced what policy documents have referred to as, 'the 3 Rs of restorative justice: Restoration, Reintegration and Responsibility' (Home Office, 1997). This has led at least one British commentator to suggest that these changes should ensure that restorative justice is 'no longer a marginal, irregular and highly localised activity' (Dignan, 1999, p.53).

2 This is explicit in Braithwaite's 'republican theory' which sees restorative justice as a part of wider changes in participatory democracy (1995). See also Pettit (1997).

References

Abel, R. (1995) 'Contested communities', *Journal of Law and Society*, vol.22, pp.113–26.

Braithwaite, J. (1989) *Crime, Shame and Reintegration*, Cambridge, Cambridge University Press.

Braithwaite, J. (1995) 'Inequality and republican criminology', in Hagan, J. and Peterson, R.D. (eds) *Crime and Inequality*, Stanford, Stanford University Press, pp.277–305.

Braithwaite, J. (1998) 'Restorative justice', in Tonry, M. (ed.)*Handbook of Crime and Punishment*, New York, Oxford University Press, pp.323–44.

Braithwaite, J. and Daly, K. (1994) 'Masculinities, violence and communitarian control', in Newburn, T. and Stanko, E.A. (eds) *Just Boys Doing Business? Men, Masculinities and Crime*, London, Routledge, pp.189–213.

Braithwaite, J. and Mugford, S. (1994) 'Conditions of successful reintegration ceremonies: Dealing with juvenile offenders', *British Journal of Criminology*, vol.34, pp.139–47.

Bursik, R. and Grasmick, H.G. (1992) *Neighborhoods and Crime: The Dimensions of Effective Community Control*, New York, Lexington Books.

CASES (1998) 'The community justice project', Center for Alternative Sentencing and Employment Services, New York, September.

Christie, N. (1977) 'Conflicts as property', *British Journal of Criminology*, vol.17, no.1, pp.1–15.

Clear, T.R. and Karp, D.R. (1999) *The Community Justice Ideal: Preventing Crime and Achieving Justice*, Boulder, CO, Westview.

Crawford, A. (1994) 'The partnership approach: Corporatism at local level?', *Social and Legal Studies*, vol.3, no.4, pp.497–519.

Crawford, A. (1997) *The Local Governance of Crime: Appeals to Community and Partnerships*, Oxford, Clarendon Press.

Crawford, A. (1998) *Crime Prevention and Community Safety: Politics, Policies and Practices*, Harlow, Longman.

Currie, E. (1988) 'Two visions of community crime prevention', in Hope, T. and Shaw, M. (eds) *Communities and Crime Reduction*, London, Her Majesty's Stationery Office, pp.280–6.

Dignan, J. (1999) 'The Crime and Disorder Act and the prospects for restorative justice', *Criminal Law Review*, pp.48–60.

Durkheim, E. (1893) *The Division of Labor in Society*, New York, The Free Press.

Home Office (1997) *No More Excuses*, White Paper, London, Home Office.

Hope, T. (1995) 'Community crime prevention', in Tonry, M. and Farington, D. (eds) *Building a Safer Society: Crime and Justice a Review of Research*, Chicago, IL, University of Chicago Press, vol.19, pp.21–89.

Hudson, J., Morris, A., Maxwell, G. and Galaway, B. (eds) (1996) *Family Group Conferences: Perspectives on Policy and Practice*, Annandale, Australia, Federation Press.

LaPrairie, C. (1995) 'Altering course: New directions in criminal justice, sentencing circles and family group conferencing', *Australian and New Zealand Journal of Criminology*, vol.28, pp.78–99.

Levitas, R. (1996) 'The concept of social exclusion and the new Durkheimian hegemony,' *Critical Social Policy*, vol.16, pp.5–20.

Levrant, S., Cullen, F.T., Fulton, B. and Wozniak, J.F. (1999) 'Reconsidering restorative justice: The corruption of benevolence revisited?', *Crime and Delinquency*, vol.45, no.1, pp.3–27.

Maloney, D. and Bryant, K. (1998) *Deschutes County Community Justice*, Bend, OR, Deschutes County Community Justice Department.

Merry, S.E. and Milner, N. (eds) (1993) *The Possibility of Popular Justice: A Case Study of Community Mediation in the United States*, Ann Arbor, University of Michigan Press.

Morris, A. and Maxwell, G. (2000) 'The practice of family group conferences in New Zealand: Assessing the place, potential and pitfalls of restorative justice', in Crawford, A. and Goodey, J.S. (eds) *Integrating a Victim Perspective within Criminal Justice*, Aldershot, Ashgate, pp.207–25.

O'Malley, P. and Palmer, D. (1996) 'Post-Keynesian policing,' *Economy and Society*, vol.25, no.2, pp.137–55.

Palumbo, D., Ferguson, J.L. and Stein, J. (1997) 'The conditions needed for successful community crime prevention,' in Lab, S.P. (ed.) *Crime Prevention at a Crossroads*, Cincinnati, OH, Anderson Publishing, pp.79–98.

Pettit, P. (1997) *Republicanism: A Theory of Freedom and Government*, Oxford, Clarendon.

Podolefsky, A. and Dubow, F. (1981) *Strategies for Community Crime Prevention*, Springfield, IL, Charles C. Thomas.

Rose, D.R. and Clear, T.R. (1998) 'Who doesn't know someone in prison or jail? The impact of incarceration on attitudes toward formal and informal social control', Presentation to the National Institute of Justice Research in Progress Series, March, Washington, DC.

Rose, N. (1996) '"The death of the social?"': Refiguring the territory of government', *Economy and Society*, vol.25, no.3, pp.327–56.

Rosenbaum, D.P. (1988) 'Community crime prevention: A review and synthesis of the literature', *Justice Quarterly*, vol.5, no.3, pp.323–93.

Sampson, R.J., Raudenbushs, S.W. and Earls, F. (1997) 'Neighborhood and violent crime: A multi-level study of collective efficacy', *Science*, vol.277, pp.918–23.

Sherman, L. (1997) 'Counter-deterrence', Presentation to the American Society of Criminology, November, San Diego.

Skogan, W. (1988) 'Community organisations and crime', in Morris, N. and Tonry, M. (eds) *Crime and Justice: An Annual Review of Research*, Chicago, IL, Chicago University Press, pp.39–78.

Strang, H. (1995) 'Replacing courts with conferences', *Policing*, vol.11, no.3, pp.212–20.

Stuart, B. (1994) 'Sentencing circles: Purpose and impact', *National Canadian Bar Association*, vol.13.

Stuart, B. (1996) 'Circle sentencing: Turning swords into ploughshares', in Galaway, B. and Hudson, J. Monsey (eds) *Restorative Justice: International Perspectives*, Monsey, NY, Criminal Justice Press.

Van Ness, D. and Strong, K.H. (1997) *Restoring Justice*, Cincinnati, OH, Anderson Publishing.

Walgrave, L. (2000) 'Extending the victim perspective towards a systemic restorative justice alternative', in Crawford, A. and Goodey, J.S. (eds) *Integrating a Victim Perspective within Criminal Justice*, Aldershot, Ashgate, pp.253–84.

Wiles, P. and Pease, K. (2000) 'Crime prevention and community safety: Tweedle-dum and Tweedle-dee?', in Battantyne, S., Pease, K. and McLaren, V. (eds) *Secure Foundations: Key Issues in Crime Prevention, Crime Reduction and Community Safety*, London, Institute for Public Policy Research, pp.21–9.

Wright, M. (1991) *Justice for Victims and Offenders*, Milton Keynes, Open University Press.

Yngvesson, B. (1993) 'Local people, local problems, and neighborhood justice: The discourse of "community" in San Francisco community boards', in Merry, S.E. and Milner, N. (eds) *The Possibility of Popular Justice*, Ann Arbor, The University of Michigan Press, pp.379–400.

Young, R. (2000). 'Integrating a multi-victim perspective into criminal justice through restorative justice conferences', in *Integrating a Victim Perspective Within Criminal Justice*, edited by Crawford, A. and Goodey, J.S., Aldershot, Ashgate, pp.227–51.

Zehr, H. (1990) *Changing Lenses: A New Focus for Crime and Justice*, Scottsdale, PA, Herald Press.

Acknowledgements

Grateful acknowledgement is made to the following sources for permission to reproduce material in this book:

Part One

Chapter 1: Christie, N. (1977) 'Conflicts as property', *British Journal of Criminology*, vol.17, no.1, pp.1–15, by permission of Oxford University Press. **Chapter 2**: Harris, M. Kay (1987) 'Moving into the New Millennium', *The Prison Journal*, pp.83–97, © 1987 Sage Publications, Inc. Reprinted by permission of Sage Publications, Inc. **Chapter 3**: Zehr, H. (1998) 'Fundamental concepts of restorative justice', *Contemporary Justice Review*, vol.1, Taylor and Francis Ltd, 4 Park Square, Milton Park, Abingdon, OX14 4RN. **Chapter 4**: Tauri, J. and Morris, A. (1997) 'Re-forming justice: the potential of Maori processes', *The Australian and New Zealand Journal of Criminology*, Australian Academic Press Pty Ltd. **Chapter 5**: Braithwaite, J. (1997) 'Restorative justice and a better future', *The Dalhousie Review*, vol.76, no.1, Dalhousie University Press Ltd.

Part Two

Chapter 6: Umbreit, M. and Zehr, H. (1996) 'Restorative family group conferences: differing models and guidelines for practice', *Federal Probation: A Journal of Correctional Philosophy & Practice*, vol.60, no.3, Administrative Office of the United States Courts. **Chapter 7**: Bazemore, G. and Taylor Griffiths, C. (1997) 'Conferences, circles, boards and mediations: the "New Wave" of community justice decision-making', *Federal Probation: A Journal of Correctional Philosophy & Practice*, vol.61, no.2, Administrative Office of the United States Courts. **Chapter 8**: Young, R. and Goold, B. (1999) 'Restorative police cautioning in Aylesbury – from degrading to reintegrative shaming ceremonies?', *Criminal Law Review*, Sweet & Maxwell Ltd. **Chapter 9**: Dignan, J. and Marsh, P. (2001) 'Restorative justice and family group conferences in England: Current state and future prospects', in Morris, A. and Maxwell, G. (eds) *Restorative Justice for Juveniles: Conferencing, Mediation and Circles*, Hart Publishing Ltd. **Chapter 10**: Alder, C. (2000) 'Young women offenders and the challenge for restorative justice', in Strang, H. and Braithwaite, J. (eds) *Restorative Justice: Philosophy to Practice*, Dartmouth Publishing Company Ltd, © Heather Strang and John Braithwaite (2000). **Chapter 11**: Morris, A. and Gelsthorpe, L. (2000) 'Re-visioning men's violence against female partners', *The Howard Journal of Criminal Justice*, vol.39, no.4, Blackwell Publishing Ltd. **Chapter 12**: Levi, M. (2002) 'Suite justice or sweet charity?', *Punishment & Society*, vol.4, no.2, © Sage Publications Ltd 2002. Reprinted by permission of Sage Publications Ltd.

Part Three

Chapter 13: Braithwaite, J. (2000) 'Restorative justice and social justice', *Saskatchewan Law Review*, vol.63, no.1, University of Saskatchewan, College of Law. **Chapter 14**: Ashworth, A. (2002) 'Is restorative justice the way forward for criminal justice?', *Current Legal Problems 2001*, vol.54, Freeman, M.D.A. (ed.). Reprinted by permission of Oxford University Press. **Chapter 16**: Daly, K. (2002) 'Restorative justice: the real story', *Punishment & Society*, vol.4, no.1, © 2002 Sage Publications Ltd. Reprinted by permission of Sage Publications Ltd. **Chapter 17**: Crawford, A. and Clear, T.R. (2001) 'Community justice: transforming communities through restorative justice?', in Bazemore, G. and Schiff, M. (eds) *Restorative Community Justice: Repairing Harm and Transforming Communities*, © 2001 Anderson Publishing Co., 2035 Reading Rd, Cincinnati, OH 45202.

Every effort has been made to locate all copyright owners, but if any have been overlooked, the publishers will make the necessary arrangements at the first opportunity.

Index